THE LENIN PLOT

THE UNKNOWN STORY OF
AMERICA'S WAR AGAINST RUSSIA

BARNES CARR

PEGASUS BOOKS
NEW YORK LONDON

THE LENIN PLOT

Pegasus Books, Ltd.
148 W 37th Street, 13th Floor
New York, NY 10018

First Pegasus Books paperback edition September 2021
First Pegasus Books cloth edition October 2020

Interior design by Maria Fernandez

ISBN: 978-1-64313-847-3

10 9 8 7 6 5 4 3 2 1

Printed in the United States of America
Distributed by Simon & Schuster
www.pegasusbooks.com

For Rosemary James and Joseph DeSalvo

CONTENTS

PREFACE

This narrative history tells the strange but true story of how America and the Western Allies invaded Russia, fought a war against the Red Army, and conspired to mount a coup d'état in Moscow and assassinate the first Soviet dictator, Vladimir Ilych Lenin. It's also a study of the espionage careers of DeWitt Clinton Poole and Xenophon de Blumenthal Kalamatiano, two of the most important figures in the history of American intelligence.

The story includes plots, counterplots, secret missions, money laundering, a high-level sting operation, invasions, naval duels, hard-fought battles in the Russian snow, mutinies, murders, victories, and defeats. The characters include patriots, traitors, special agents, double agents, triple agents, executive agents, agents of influence, agents provocateurs, and at least one femme fatale.

The plot was initiated by U.S. Secretary of State Robert Lansing, a bored pacifist who doodled and daydreamed in Cabinet meetings until Lenin seized power in October 1917 and removed Russia from the World War, part of a secret deal the Bolsheviks had struck with Germany.[1] With the Allies facing defeat on the western front, Lansing sprang into action and used his office as a bully pulpit to press for the overthrow of Lenin.

Lansing proposed that the United States install an Allied-friendly dictator in Moscow to get Russia back in the war. Despite President Wilson's public posturing against interfering in the affairs of other nations, he told Lansing the Moscow coup had his "entire approval." Lansing advised Wilson that using American funds to openly finance a foreign coup was probably illegal, so they enlisted the French and British to launder the money as U.S. aid to the Allies.

The U.S. State Department's spymaster in Russia was Consul General Poole, a tennis star nicknamed Poodles. His main field officer was Kalamatiano, a Russian-American businessman in Moscow and former track star at the University of Chicago. Poole and Kalamatiano plotted their coup with the advice and consent of U.S. Ambassador David Francis. Despite his mellow image as a bourbon-sipping old Confederate gentleman, Francis was a determined man who once stood up to a Bolshevik lynch mob armed only with a shotgun.

At first, France was America's premier partner in operations against Lenin. Ambassador Joseph Noulens set the pace by going on a crusade to collect 13 billion francs the Soviet government stole from French investors. Noulens was a grandiose monarchist who traveled like a rajah. He was assisted by General Jean Lavergne, chief of the French military mission to Russia, a hard-driving warrior who feared that each passing day was a lost opportunity to defeat the Bolsheviks.

Lavergne's efforts were aided by Consul General Joseph-Fernand Grenard, an author and former explorer who dispatched agents across Russia to recruit resistance armies to march on Moscow in support of the Allied coup. One of Kalamatiano's closest street associates was Henri de Verthamon, a French saboteur who wore a black trenchcoat and cap and slept with explosives under his bed. Another was the impressively named Charles Adolphe Faux-Pas Bidet, a former Paris cop who had worked the French case against Mata Hari.

In time, the British became equal partners in the Lenin Plot. London's chief conspirators included Bruce Lockhart, a special agent of the Foreign Office. Lockhart was a dedicated footballer, a dyed-in-the-tartan Scot who didn't particularly like the English. He was also a connoisseur of exotic Russian women, one of whom was later identified as a spy for the Soviets and the Germans.

Lockhart teamed up with Sidney Reilly, a Russian adventurer and profiteer hired by the British Secret Service. Reilly saw himself as a Napoléon reincarnated; at other times he thought he was Jesus Christ. One of Reilly's biographers wrote that Ian Fleming told a contemporary at the London *Sunday Times* in 1953 that he had created James Bond after reading about Reilly's exploits in the archives of British intelligence during World War II, a conversation verified by foreign correspondent Leonard Mosley. Lockhart was also mentioned as a possible inspiration for 007.[2]

Besides Reilly, the main Russian plotter was Boris Savinkov, the most infamous international terrorist of the time. He ran an anticommunist underground army that was hired to support the Allied coup. He was known as Bloody Boris and he had been killing tsarist officials for years; now he turned his sights on Reds and monarchist generals. He killed Russian style, with dagger, pistol, and bomb. Savinkov saw himself as a Nietzschean Superman but was more of a revolutionary Hamlet, haunted and conflicted. He was also a superstitious drug addict whose delusions included the belief that silk underwear protected him from bullets.

Savinkov and Reilly advanced the Lenin Plot from a simple kidnapping plan to a murder conspiracy. But the Western powers had not declared war on Russia. Thus, assassinating Lenin could have made America and the Allies party to an act of international terrorism.

Lenin was shot in August 1918, but survived. The Soviets responded by stepping up their Red Terror. Nearly 32,000 people, mostly Russians, were arrested. More than 6,000 of them were shot. Another 21,000 were sent to prisons or labor camps. When the Soviet secret police, the Cheka, started rounding up Western agents, they gunned down a British naval spy, Francis Cromie. Then they arrested Kalamatiano and sentenced him to death.

The military side of the Lenin Plot was an invasion of Russia by a Western force composed mostly of American and French combat troops, under British command. That force intended to seize Moscow to support the coup.[3] They were led by British Brigadier General Edmund Ironside, the model for the spy Richard Hannay in a series of thrillers written by historian John Buchan.

The Lenin Plot is still remembered in Russia, Britain, and France, under various names. But John Cudahy, a U.S. army officer who wrote an account of his combat experience in Russia, said American veterans of the military invasion of Russia were "shunted off to civilian life and the whole embarrassing matter expunged from the record. All inquiry concerning the Expedition has been met by specious pleas in evasive avoidance."[4]

When it came to decorating troops for their service against the Red Army, 73 Americans were cited by the British, 72 by the Russians, 52 by the French, and 14 by the United States. In some cases, entire American companies were cited for bravery, but not by the U.S. War Department.[5] The public knew few details of the war until the 1920s, when veterans such as Cudahy started writing memoirs of their experiences.

That "evasive avoidance" described by John Cudahy would continue for years in Washington. When President Franklin Delano Roosevelt wrote a letter to the Soviets in 1933, proposing that diplomatic relations be restored between the United States and Russia, FDR claimed that a "happy tradition of friendship" had existed between Russia and America "for more than a century."[6] Later, President Ronald Reagan, when trying to establish better relations with the USSR, said on American television: "Tonight I want to speak to the people of the Soviet Union, to tell them it's true that our governments have had serious differences, but our sons and daughters have never fought each other in war."[7]

❖

I first became interested in the Lenin Plot when I was a student at Tulane, living in an inner city brick pile that wasn't air-conditioned. So in the hot months I took afternoon naps at the university library. It was there that I met an amiable, brandy-sipping old gentleman whose guayabera matched the white socks beneath his sandals. He was a native New Orleanian who had graduated from Tulane after the "first war." Then he went to live a few years in Paris.

There he knew some Americans who had fought in America's war against Soviet Russia.

Wait a minute. I'd never heard anything about that.

"Look it up," he said. "You'll see."

So I did. At least I tried. But that was before the internet and keyword searches, and I had to thumb through dozens of trays of index cards to pursue the subject. I quickly found that the topic of "Russia, history of," occupied most of the library's third floor. To narrow my search I went up into the stacks and pulled down old bound copies of the London *Times* and a French news magazine, *l'Illustration*. Then bingo, sort of.

The *Times* called it the "Russian expeditions." *L'Illustration* described it as "*les événements en Russie*." Further investigation, in the pages of the *Literary Digest*, one of the American news magazines of that period, revealed the name by which it's still known today. It wasn't called an invasion of Russia or a war against Russia. Apparently that was not "politically accurate," as old Bolsheviks liked to say. Instead, it was listed as the Allied Intervention in the Russian Civil War.

Armed with this new I-word, I was able to track down some documents in the National Archives in Washington and the Hoover Institution at Stanford. But this was my first serious research project and I quickly found that government records were often vague, misleading, contradictory, and subject to frustrating redactions. The State Department admits on their website that certain documents have been "edited" before being posted to the internet. They say that other documents, or parts thereof, have been omitted in order to "avoid impeding current diplomatic negotiations." It seemed that "official" sources were best used as a starting point, simply as a clue to what really happened.

I didn't want my story to be just a simple recitation of facts and figures, without a cohesive narrative, without a feeling of time, place, and mood. I wanted to peel the artichoke, layer by layer, and find out who the personalities really were. Those things I found in news accounts, interviews, autobiographies, memoirs, reminiscences, testimonies, and letters and papers left by eyewitnesses. My guides were Shelby Foote's narrative study of the American Civil War and Teddy Roosevelt's advice that written history should not only be interesting, but also lively.

But solving the mysteries of Western intrigues in Russia was a major endeavor. Often things didn't make sense, as every researcher finds at various times. Certain details were supposed to fit neatly into the puzzle. But they didn't.

What was I doing wrong?

I finally remembered something I'd been told by a young Russian I used to play pinballs with at a sports bar in Washington when I was a low-echelon editor at the *Evening Star*. He claimed to be an "accredited correspondent" for TASS, the Soviet news agency. It was a standard KGB cover, like "agricultural researcher." It was a joke we shared. I saw him as a potential source for information from inside the Russian embassy. He probably saw me as an avenue for leaking disinformation to the press. Ultimately, we weren't much help to one another in either of those areas.

But he told me something I found useful when writing this book. It was what he called the "riddle of the tea cup." It was part of the Russian playbook for solving problems such as confirming the bona fides of a defector, and I found out later it had become a favorite story among Western spies.

You started with a pile of broken crockery. If you picked up a piece, you might say it came from a tea cup. But you couldn't be certain. It might be a piece of Lenin's chamber pot. Only after you put all the pieces together could you say that you held a tea cup in your hands. That was supposed to be the full picture. But beware of chips, cracks, and missing pieces, my friend warned.

I took his advice and tried to put together the pieces of the Lenin Plot. A few chips are still missing, but I think I've come up with a reasonably convincing example of a Russian tea cup, cracks and all.

If the term Cold War can be defined as an attempt to defeat another country economically, politically, ideologically, or militarily without the niceties of formal declarations of war, then it didn't start after World War II, as the media and some historians would have us believe. It continues today, in electronic spying, by the largest arms race since the Reagan years, and by political meddling. According to Professor Dov H. Levin at the Institute for Politics and Strategy at Carnegie-Mellon University, the United States interfered in foreign elections eighty-one times, and the Soviet Union or Russia thirty-six times, between 1994 and 2000.[8]

The Lenin Plot was the true beginning of it all. More than a hundred years later, we still live in the shadow of 1918.

PART I
THE FIRST ATTEMPT

Most of the people who engaged in this unsavory work had very little interest in the cause which they were paid to promote. They did not take their parts too seriously, and one or the other would occasionally go over to the opposite side, for espionage is an international and artistic profession, in which opinions matter less than the art of perfidy.

—Richard Lewinsohn,
The Man behind the Scenes:
the Career of Sir Basil Zaharoff[1]

1

A FORGOTTEN MAN

The first American spy to ever be sentenced to death in Russia sat in his Moscow cell on a cold November night waiting for his appointment with the firing squad. The roll call for execution started every night at ten o'clock after most of the day's interrogations had been concluded. When the night shift came on, the guards were given the kill list. It was called the hour of terror. There was no ambiguity to it. If your name was called, it meant only one thing.

The cells were hidden away in damp and dark underground passageways. The American agent, Xenophon Kalamatiano, was held in a solitary confinement cell about six by eight feet, with an automobile headlight hanging from the ceiling to keep the chamber lit at all times. A small Judas hole in the door allowed guards to look in at regular intervals. And below that, a hatch allowed a cup of tea and a glop of buckwheat kasha or a bowl of watery fish soup to be passed to him. There was no proper bunk, just a shelf built onto the wall with a blanket on top. The toilet was a bucket on the floor that had to be emptied every morning. The cells smelled of urine, excrement, tobacco smoke, and unwashed bodies. Fleas, lice, roaches, bedbugs, and rats were constant companions.

The hour of terror was preceded by a period of quiet, as if the prisoners might be able to hide in their own silence. Even without watches, they knew the time as it approached. They sensed it collectively, instinctively, like hunted animals. Sometimes the guards wore felt boots so the condemned prisoners wouldn't hear them coming. But within those close walls, the noise of a thrown bolt was amplified out of proportion, sounding like a guillotine blade banging home.

Some nights, nobody was called. But Marguerite Harrison, a U.S. military spy locked up in the same prison as Kalamatiano, said female inmates put on clean clothes every night just in case they were going to be shot.[1] When the names were called, some of the prisoners went quietly, with defeat and resignation echoing in their footsteps. Others cried out, wept, begged for mercy. Prisoners who resisted were beaten into submission. Then there was no sound but the scrape of shoes on the floor as they were dragged out.

Tonight was no different. Kalamatiano, a young American from Illinois, sat in his cell, alert to the slightest sound. For a while, he'd had company as an agent from the Cheka, the secret police, was planted in his cell to pick up information. It wasn't a very original tactic. Kalamatiano ignored the man.[2]

Now he was alone again. If Kalamatiano had possessed a mirror he would have seen a haggard fellow with a shaved head and eyes that held the look of homeless men who slept on sidewalk steam vents in winter.[3] But he could handle that. This was not a resort. The thing that got to him was not knowing when he would get a call from the guards.

It hadn't happened last night. Was it going to be tonight? How much time did he have left? Would his wife and his family back home ever find out what happened to him?

Three interrogators had been working on Kalamatiano. They questioned him two or three times a night, using a Mutt and Jeff routine. One Chekist played the bully, berating Kalamatiano and roughing him up. The second questioner was the logician. He pointed out that Washington had not protested Kalamatiano's arrest. They weren't claiming him. They had forsaken him. He was a forgotten man.

The third interrogator was the smoothie. He offered immunity if Kalamatiano would only give "satisfactory" testimony. Why not be reasonable? Let's make a deal. Let's conclude our business as gentlemen. Just sign this statement and we'll get you out of this place. We'll transfer you to a bright facility with a view of the river. There'll be fresh air, good food, books, and a clinic. Otherwise, you'll die in here.

One of the Cheka's favorite techniques was to deliver this spiel to a sick and half-starved prisoner while the interrogator enjoyed a hot dinner at his desk. It might be accompanied by a pot of coffee, real coffee, not the *sovieteski* (barley substitute) the proletariat had to swallow. Maybe the Chekist finished off his repast with a glass of vintage Burgundy confiscated in a raid on a "subversive" wine shop.[4] Then perhaps the smiling face behind the desk would light up an American cigarette. To a smoker like Kalamatiano, the sweet smell of quality tobacco was a torture in itself.

We are the only ones who can help you, the interrogator would purr. You see that, don't you? It's very simple. We help you and you help us. So, let's ink the deal. This, with a gentle nudge of the pen across the desk.

Kalamatiano's network of agents had been rolled up but he had not confessed to spying. He refused to be tricked into using the words "intelligence" or "espionage." He insisted he was a businessman running an "information service" on Russian affairs for his consulate because newspaper reports were unreliable. To his credit, he also held fast to another cardinal rule of the spy trade: never sign anything.

Once you signed a "statement," it would all be over. They would have what they wanted, so they might as well shoot you.

At first, executions were conducted in the basements of Cheka headquarters and in local prison yards. But municipal authorities complained that blood was flowing out sewers and polluting the Moscow River. So now many prisoners were taken into small nearby streets and shot there. Truck engines were started up to hide the sound of the gunfire.[5] Later, the killings were done at a park where Dynamo, the local soccer team sponsored by the Cheka, played its games. Rival teams called Dynamo *Musor* (Garbage), which was slang for the police.

Finally, Kalamatiano's interrogations stopped. A good sign? Had they believed his story? He waited in his cell.

Footsteps came down the corridor and stopped. His door was unlocked and pulled open.

The guards ordered him to get up and come with them.

This time his destination was not the office where he was usually questioned. Now he was stood up before a firing squad. His interrogators seemed to have run out of patience.

When you faced the rifles, you had a last chance to think it over. If you did sign the confession, maybe they really would commute your death sentence to a prison term, just to show the world what compassionate people they were. And later a pardon could be arranged, or a swap for a Russian held by the other side. There were stories circulating about prisoners who had cut deals like that. Yes, they were moved to more humane facilities. But then later *Pravda* (Truth), the official Communist Party newspaper, announced they had committed suicide by jumping out a window.

A prison window with no bars?

No thanks.

Kalamatiano took a last look of the world he never expected to see again.

"Lock and load," the commander of the firing squad told his men.

The silence was broken as the rifles were cocked.

"Take your aim."

Still no confession came forth.

"Fire."

2

THE CHICAGO GROUP

Xenophon Kalamatiano's wartime journey from Russia to America and then back to Moscow for a reservation on death row probably began with a letter he wrote on May 11, 1915, to Samuel N. Harper, 5728 Woodlawn Avenue, Chicago. Harper had been a classmate of Kalamatiano's at the University of Chicago. They were the same age. They had graduated together.

"Referring to our past conversations on the subject," Kalamatiano wrote, the United States had a great lack of men "trained for foreign fields." Young German men went to different countries to complete their education, he noted, and in that way became "specially trained" for foreign work.

"I would propose that some American young men, interested and otherwise fitted for such a course, go directly to Russia with the purpose of staying there one to three years merely to become acquainted with the language and commercial customs of the country, with a view of using this knowledge as an asset in later life," he continued.

If Harper approved of that idea and picked some suitable candidates, Kalamatiano wrote, "I would take up the matter further with our association" and possibly "be in a position to help them on the other side."[1] The reference was to the Russian Association of Commerce and Industry in Moscow. Kalamatiano was the American representative for the group.

Harper was almost certainly a recruiter for American intelligence, though he never admitted that in his letters and papers. Kalamatiano's letter ostensibly doesn't offer evidence of anything except Kalamatiano's desire to offer the services of his Moscow company and possibly drum up some business in the process. The world war had just started, and America was neutral. Lenin was in exile, and the Bolsheviks posed no immediate threat to the West. The main concern of the Allies, including Russia, was Germany.

On the other hand, perhaps Kalamatiano foresaw coming problems and was making an early pitch to serve his country. His Moscow trade association would be in a good position to acquire confidential information from business associates. A letter he later wrote to Harper regarding U.S. army spy Marguerite Harrison shows that Kal was very savvy about Western operations in Russia.[2]

The biggest business deal America had ever cut with Russia was the purchase of Alaska, for two cents an acre. But that was in another century. Russia in 1915 was well known for ballet, Cossacks, Peter the Great, vodka, caviar, and some of the world's best writers. But other than that, many Americans saw it as a backward place of fairy-tale uniforms, illiterate peasants, dirt roads, pogroms, and terrorists. In effect, a glorified Mexico. Why was Russia suddenly important again?

The answer to that, and to the mystery of Kalamatiano's activities in Russia, begins with an examination of a certain "Chicago group" of Russophiles and information gatherers—businessman Charles Richard Crane, University of Chicago president William Rainey Harper, and his son Samuel N. Harper.

❖

William Harper, PhD, an American Baptist from Ohio, was hired in 1891 as the first president of the one-year-old University of Chicago. He was thirty-five years old, a big man built like a wrestler, but with a kind face behind his scholarly spectacles. Dr. Harper was a visionary, a hard-driving manager, an impatient "dynamo in trousers."[3] He was a popular president. Students called him "the old man of the C."[4]

But in 1900, after completing nine years of teaching classes, campaigning for donations, hiring instructors, and carrying out the other work required for fast construction of a major university from scratch, Dr. Harper was tired. He admitted this over tea one afternoon with Charles Crane, a younger gentleman he had known since first coming to Chicago. Crane was a wealthy philanthropist and world traveler who liked to be called simply Charlie.[5] He offered to take Dr. Harper along on his next visit to Russia. President Harper snapped up the invitation and they set sail.

America did not have a Central Intelligence Agency or a National Security Agency at that time. Washington's overseas spies were in the State Department, the Office of Naval Intelligence, and army military intelligence. But their effectiveness was hampered by politics and budgets. Incoming information was so scarce that reports by "casual" agents were solicited.[6]

Casuals were civilians such as businessmen, teachers, clergy, students, and vacationing families returning to the United States from foreign travels who could offer information on what they had seen abroad. But they were not trained in the finer points of intelligence gathering. Their reports were often vague, sloppy, confused, or contradictory. What Washington needed was a quiet army of patriotic men and women volunteers who could move about freely in foreign lands, who knew what to look for and whom to talk to, and who could pay their own expenses. Kalamatiano would later start out as a U.S. casual in Russia.

Charlie Crane had already created his own private club of casuals, and after that 1900 trip, President Harper persuaded his son Sam to come aboard.[7] Crane and Sam Harper would become two of America's most valuable intelligence sources during that chaotic time when Old Russia was changing as dramatically as America had changed after 1865. The team of Crane and Harper would provide mortised joints that held together the frame of America's intelligence gathering in Russia until paid spies such as Xenophon Kalamatiano took over to recruit systemized, compartmentalized networks.

❖

There weren't many American experts on Russia at that time. Russian studies were a wide-open field. Dr. Harper convinced Sam to start spending six months every year in Russia and devoting his life to becoming an interpreter of that exotic land.

Sam was an honor student at U of C and a member of Alpha Delta Phi (the members called it the anti-fraternity fraternity). He was also a member of the mandolin club, the banjo club, and the glee club.[8] But President Harper realized that a background like his own, in ancient languages, wouldn't do his son much good in Russia if he wasn't a linguist. He sent Sam to Paris for a year of studying modern languages.

Sam worked as a guard at the 1900 world's fair, the Exposition Universelle, and roomed with a French family. He studied the language with his hosts while enjoying the fair and Paris nightlife. When Sam returned to Chicago two years later he admitted he hadn't learned much French or Russian but had gained a valuable education in how to get around in a foreign country (and have a good time).

Back at the university, Sam took a Russian language course that Kalamatiano was teaching. "All Russians are proverbially bad teachers of Russian and I am afraid that Kalamatiano was no exception—at least, I did not learn much about the language," Sam recalled.[9]

Charles Crane began taking Sam into his confidence on Russian matters, discussing that country with his young protégé and inviting him to sit in on conferences. Sam returned to Paris after graduation in 1903 to study Russian at the l'École des Langues Orientales Vivantes.

Sam moved in with a group of Russian students his second year in Paris. They turned out to be radicals. But they were nice boys, he thought, and he helped them address revolutionary literature to be mailed to Russia. Then Sam expressed what they considered some politically incorrect views. They turned on him. Their hostility got so vicious that he moved out. He was glad to, anyway. He said the place was "unhygienic."[10]

Harper finally said goodbye to Paris. His next stop was that fabled country he had heard so much about: Old Russia.

3
AGENTS OF INFLUENCE

Frozen sparkles of Russian winter skated past the window of Samuel Harper's compartment as his train pulled into Moscow in February 1904. He arrived on the day the Japanese launched a surprise attack on the Russian naval base at Port Arthur, a tactic that foreshadowed Pearl Harbor. The attack set off a nineteen-month war that resulted in defeat for Russia and an end to her expansionist ambitions in Asia. It was a humiliation for Tsar Nicholas II and contributed to the coming Russian Revolution of 1905.

Armed with an introduction from Charlie Crane and his own engaging American smile, along with an astrakhan on his head and an enormous pair of snow boots, Sam Harper tramped across Russia to talk with bureaucrats, journalists, workers, and peasants. He was welcomed with dependable Russian hospitality. But he would soon find a bitter taste beneath that pleasant flow of tea from the samovar.

On Sam's second trip to Russia, in October 1904, he went to work full-time on Ambassador Robert Sanderson McCormick's staff at the embassy in St. Petersburg. The job was arranged by Charles Crane. Charlie considered himself a "natural Democrat" and had already been a Russian adviser to President Grover Cleveland. But getting this appointment for Harper showed that Crane also had influence in the Republican administration of Theodore Roosevelt. Charlie Crane and Sam Harper moved freely in Russian government circles, making them "agents of influence" who used their positions not only to gain information but also to put in a word for American interests.

They didn't use the word "spies." They were "observers" collecting "information" and "advising" Washington. But what's the difference between a political observer and a spy? It's as slim as the blade of a dagger. Both gather information. They beg, borrow, buy, and steal it. The information is then used by their government in formulating foreign policy, including war. Even in peacetime the information can be used against certain industries, banks, or individuals in either enemy or friendly nations.

The main difference is how the collectors are treated by the host country. A political observer might be wined and dined and hit up for foreign aid. A spy working the same corridors could get hanged. The work that Crane and Harper did in Russia was precariously balanced between those definitions. "Political operatives" is probably a more accurate term for them.

Sam Harper's cover was a press card from the *Chicago Daily Tribune*. A foreign correspondent's credentials demanded a measure of respect, even if the paper was thin and the ink a bit blurred. Sam assured the real news correspondents in Russia that he wasn't filing stories and had no intention of trying to scoop them. He shared his information with most of them, except for the *Associated Press* correspondent, whom he dismissed as "biased" against Russia. Sam was closest to German journalists. He thought they knew Russia better than the American reporters.[1]

Sam enrolled as a student at Moscow University (now Moscow State), a sanctuary for non-conformists and free thinkers. Campus radicals demanded a republican form of government for Russia. They marched to protest the war and they fought the police in the streets. But when the smoke cleared they sadly put on their student uniforms again and went back to class.

Sam was not a revolutionary. Like Crane, he was a true liberal, a man interested in all points of view. But his curiosity turned dangerous. One afternoon he and the American consul in Moscow stood outside a café watching a street demonstration. Cossacks and mounted police armed with whips, carbines, swords, and pistols attacked the students and killed nine of them. Afterward, Sam hid one of his Russian tutors for several days in his hotel room. Then, on January 22, 1905, in St. Petersburg, he witnessed one of Russia's most notorious historical moments.

Russian workers singing hymns marched to the Winter Palace in the capital to air their grievances before the tsar, who liked to be called *Batyushka* (Little Father). But Nicholas wasn't in town to give orders regarding the march, so soldiers, police, and Cossacks made their own decision to attack the crowd. Five hundred were killed; hundreds more were wounded. The massacre led to industrial strikes, peasant revolts, and military mutinies. Sam Harper was at the palace when the first shots were fired at the crowd. A Cossack chased him away and he didn't stop running until he reached the American embassy. There, over tea, he treated the ambassador and his guests to a breathless account of the attack. Bloody Sunday, it was called. It set off the 1905 revolution.

Politicians in Western Europe feared the Russian Revolution would infect their own fiefdoms, so they intervened. According to Lenin's first biographer, an emissary of the Crédit Lyonnais slipped into St. Petersburg on a ship with a barrel of gold for Nicholas, 2.250 million francs' worth, to be precise (845,750,000 rubles). That loan, at 10 percent interest, was backed verbally by German and Austrian bankers. Their conditions: Nicholas had to restore order in the country and establish a parliament, a Russian Duma.[2]

Batyushka complied with the conditions, though in his own imperial fashion. He did set up the Duma, though it didn't have much real power, and he later dissolved it several times when he didn't like what they were doing. At the same time, he used mass terror to quash the revolution, first in the cities, then in the provinces with punitive expeditions. Pyotr Stolypin, the tsar's German-born interior minister, was a reformist who gave religious freedom to Jews and set up insurance plans for workers, but when it came time to deal with radicals, his courts served up swift and harsh punishment. The hangman's noose came to be known as "Stolypin's necktie."

Sam Harper expanded his investigations of the Russian situation. He began covering Duma sessions and reporting back to Ambassador McCormick, a Republican from the Chicago family that had founded International Harvester. Sam was most at home talking to the liberal or radical representatives rather than the conservatives. But he had his doubts about the extreme left.

"Often see the revolutionists, people whose last name one never asks," he wrote in a letter to Crane. "But I recognize their emptiness and irresponsibility more clearly every day and dread to think what will happen if they succeed in their mad plan of setting up a genuine bloody revolution."[3]

Sam almost got arrested several more times. Once it was while he was explaining to a crowd outside the Duma what was going on inside. Police dispersed the crowd and ran him off. He pushed his luck further by attending secret meetings of Social Democrats. There were raids, but his luck held and he got away.

Sam Harper returned to the University of Chicago in 1906 to teach Russian under a grant set up for him by Crane. It would pay Harper's salary for several years to come. Sam began touring America when he had a chance, delivering lectures on Russia and setting up study centers where publishers, educators, and businessmen could get together and discuss events happening over there. Those conferences undoubtedly allowed Harper to act as a recruiter for Crane's band of private intelligence agents.

Sam Harper was a close friend of Richard T. Crane II, Charlie's son and another Chicagoan. Richard was working for the State Department, and after the war would become the first U.S. diplomat to the new nation of Czechoslovakia. Richard Crane was close to Joseph Patrick Tumulty, Wilson's personal secretary. Through Tumulty and Richard Crane, Sam Harper was able to get Wilson's ear on Russian affairs.[4]

One of Sam's recruits might have been his old schoolmate, Xenophon Kalamatiano, though it's not known when or where the approach took place, if one took place at all. Kalamatiano might have decided on his own to volunteer his services to the consulate in Moscow.

Harper's information gathering expanded briefly to the United States when he accepted a political science fellowship at Columbia University in 1909. There in New York he got a taste of American radical chic. Anarchist Emma Goldman invited him to a dance thrown by her *Mother Earth* magazine. Sam was condescendingly introduced as a "bourgeois friend" of the group—leading him to reply that he smoked a cheaper brand of cigarette than *they* did. He was offended by their "disturbing" elitism and declared there was a "certain element of slumming" in such expeditions.[5]

Sam taught at the University of Liverpool from 1911 to 1913 and was editor of the *Russian Review* there. After his last year in England he was hired by the U.S. Department of Labor to tour Russia and expose spies of the Kaiser who were working in German steamship companies. That made him still another kind of agent, a paid operative for Washington.[6]

❖

Charles Crane became an adviser on Russian affairs for Thomas Woodrow Wilson when the president first took office in 1913. Earlier, Crane had been appointed U.S. minister "designate" to China by President William Howard Taft. But Philander Chase Knox, Taft's secretary of state, didn't follow through and confirm the appointment, so Charlie resigned his appointment. Crane later wrote that his support of Russia in their war against Japan had offended certain Wall Street interests who feared he would not tolerate their "financial designs" in the Far East. Some companies, he said, notably United States

Steel, had been burning up the phone lines to pressure "Sleepy Phil" Knox to nix his appointment.[7]

After that, Crane decided he'd had enough of the establishment Republicans and became a progressive. The term had a different meaning back then. These days, *progressive* is a substitute word for *liberal*. In Crane's time a progressive was anyone who believed in honesty and efficiency in government. Teddy Roosevelt, a Republican, was a progressive. So was Wilson, a Democrat.

Charles Crane first met Wilson after he took over as president of Princeton University in 1902. Wilson was the son of a Presbyterian minister from Augusta, Georgia, and had witnessed first hand the Civil War and the devastating Reconstruction of the South engineered by Radical Republicans in Congress. It was an experience that left him convinced that war was a brutal and unchristian way of solving disagreements. After graduation from the College of New Jersey (now Princeton) and the University of Virginia Law School, Wilson earned a doctorate at Johns Hopkins University and began teaching political science. At that time he had a reputation as a conservative.

The Democratic machine in New Jersey, run by conservative party bosses, persuaded Wilson to run for governor in 1910. They intended to install him as their boy in Trenton. But he turned around and bit them. He campaigned on a reform ticket, won the governorship, then ran for president in 1912. As a progressive coming out of New Jersey's reactionary Democratic party, Wilson was something of a "political freak," in the words of Rudolph Forster, White House executive secretary.[8]

Wilson called his presidential platform the New Freedom, which stressed both individualism and states' right. His opponents in the 1912 election were Teddy Roosevelt of the Progressive Party, Howard Taft for the Republicans, and Eugene Debs from the Socialist Party. Wilson received only 42 percent of the popular vote but won overwhelmingly in the electoral college. He would be only the second Democrat to be elected president in a seventy-two-year span, 1860–1932.

Wilson didn't smoke, and drank only occasionally. He prayed and read his Bible daily, and wept over letters from old acquaintances. He was a trim man who dressed fashionably in tailored white suits and white patent leather shoes, giving him an image of both glamor and sanctimony seen in revivalists who worked Madison Square Garden. The press liked that. They saw him as an East Coast executive and a Southern gentleman, with Hollywood and the

Bible thrown in for good measure. But French President Georges Clemenceau wasn't so kind.

"He thinks he is another Jesus Christ come upon the Earth to reform men," Clemenceau remarked.[9]

Wilson didn't like his picture taken. When a camera was set up in his office he never smiled, giving the impression he was a stern old schoolmaster. Actually he was a charming and courtly man who liked to sing and dance, and was convinced he could have made it in Vaudeville. He often gave his Secret Service protection detail the slip so he could sneak out of the White House to take in a show at one of his favorite theatres. He liked ribald limericks and when riled up he could curse with the best of them. His idea of a good time, though, was an evening with family and friends in the White House parlor where he performed hilarious imitations of political hacks he'd known over the years.

But Wilson's health was not good. He had high blood pressure and got headaches, nausea, and nervous exhaustion. His physician, Rear Admiral Cary T. Grayson, was always nearby. Wilson's health apparently didn't affect his reasoning during the war, but often forced him to stop work and go to bed for a while, losing valuable time demanded by affairs of state.

Some Wilson critics accused him of being an intellectual snob. One of those was Clinton Wallace Gilbert, an editor at the *New York Tribune*, a Republican newspaper that had beat the editorial drums for Southern Reconstruction. Gilbert compared Wilson to a "small boy who, when his companions refuse to play with him, says to himself that he is smarter than they are, gets higher marks in school, that he has a better gun than they have or that he, when he grows up, will be a great general while they are nobody."[10] Wilson, in turn, didn't like New York. He dreaded making appearances there.

Charles Crane had been a big contributor to Wilson's presidential bid and campaigned for him in Chicago. He saw Wilson as a progressive "prophet" ushering in a "new political era" of honesty.[11] After the election, Crane sold most of his family business holdings to his brother, leaving him the time and money to pursue a life of travel, philanthropy, and reporting to Wilson on world affairs.

Crane's reports on Russia helped prepare Wilson for the president's coming role as one of the instigators of the Lenin Plot.

4

GO SEE THE ELEPHANT

The World War of 1914–1918 was probably the last era when spies—if not all officers and gentlemen—were at least products of the better schools and tailor shops. The same went for women spies, a good example being Marguerite Harrison, who came from a moneyed family in Maryland, attended private schools, and enjoyed a social whirlwind as a debutante before marrying.

Spies were not police officers. They were multilingual cosmopolitans, international in outlook and comfortable in casinos and embassy receptions where they enjoyed Champagne and caviar as they shook hands and sized up the crowd for potential recruits as agents. Later on, spying became a working-class trade, as evidenced by Morris and Lona Cohen and Julius and Ethel Rosenberg.[1] But in the first two decades of the twentieth century, spies traveled in the highest social, diplomatic, and military circles and were dressed to kill (sometimes literally).

Xenophon Kalamatiano, with his spats and cane and his noble background in Russia, fit the required image. His glasses and his mop of thick brown hair lent him a look that was scholarly but not stuffy; he was a neat dresser but not a fop, favoring conservative three-piece suits that complimented his cover as a businessman. He was a physically fit athlete, a broad-shouldered man with a pleasant, slightly Mediterranean face. He was bright and affable, and fluent in several languages. His old-world charm put him at home in different countries and cultures. By 1915 he had been an established businessman in Russia for several years but also was as American as hot dogs and Jack Daniel's Old No. 7. He spoke Russian without an English accent, and English without a Russian accent. His bona fides were solid.

Records show he was born July 13, 1882, in Paris, son of Verra Xeno-
phontovna Kalamatiano. (Later in America she spelled it Vera.) The birth
was registered at the Russian embassy and the Russian Church in Paris. Vera
said she was single and did not list the father's name, suggesting the child was
illegitimate. According to Vera's granddaughter, the father ranked somewhere
in the Russian nobility and possibly was married. Vera named the baby after
her father, Ksenofont (Xenophon) Dmitrevich Kalamatiano, an admiral in
Russia's Black Sea fleet. The family reportedly had emigrated to Russia from
Greece in the 1700s.[2]

Vera later said she had lived in France for years.[3] When she wrote a book,
an American reviewer described her as a "countess." In time, she would elevate
her media status to "princess."[4] She had a friend who knew Leo Tolstoy, and
in time Vera would go into business with the count.[5]

Vera married Constantine Paul (C.P.) de Blumenthal around 1895, when
Xenophon was thirteen years old. The Blumenthal name was German but C.P.
said his family had lived in Russia for generations. Indeed there were many
Germanic Russians in the country. Nicholas II was a cousin of Germany's
Kaiser Wilhelm, and Tsarina Alexandra was originally known as Alix of Hesse
and by Rhine. Vera took de Blumenthal as her married name. In college,
Xenophon would hyphenate his surname as de Blumenthal-Kalamatiano.

❖

C.P. de Blumenthal was a graduate of St. Petersburg Imperial University, with
degrees in modern languages and law. He was practicing law in St. Petersburg
when he married Vera. He was around thirty years old, she was about thirty-two.
In a newspaper interview later, C.P. said he had held liberal political views in
Russia and was connected to a secret group working for a constitutional form
of government. In 1896, the year after C.P. married Vera, members of that
organization were arrested in Moscow by the tsarist secret police, the Okhrana,
predecessor to the Cheka. C.P. heard about this through friends, and with the
temperature of Old Russia heating up, he decided to redeploy to a cooler clime.[6]

Vera and Xenophon were vacationing in Switzerland that summer. C.P.
had a passport allowing him to leave Russia without difficulty and he expected
to join them in the mountains for a while. But something happened. Perhaps
the police closed in on him. He suddenly sold all his property that he could,
and through friends he put mortgages on some real estate he owned in Ufa

Province. (Encumbered property could not be seized by the government until the encumbrance was paid off.) He sent money to his wife and stepson in Switzerland, then went to Hamburg and sailed for the United States. He landed in New York with twenty-five dollars in his pocket.

C.P. settled in Bloomington, Illinois, a quiet green college town. He worked at a grocery store until he was fluent in English. Then in 1897 he got a job teaching third-year German at Illinois Wesleyan University, a small Methodist school in town.[7] He also enrolled with advanced standing as a junior in the Wesleyan law school. He was described as a "courteous, polished gentleman."[8] Vera and Xenophon followed C.P. to Bloomington. They lived at 601 Locust Street on the East Side, a neighborhood of wide lawns and modest homes five blocks south of the Wesleyan campus.

C.P. became a naturalized American citizen. Through her marriage to C.P., Vera became a U.S. citizen, too. But there is some question as to whether Xenophon became a citizen through C.P., since Vera's family in Russia blocked adoption attempts by de Blumenthal.[9] Nevertheless, Xenophon claimed American citizenship and was later issued a U.S. passport.

❖

At first, Xenophon attended public school in Bloomington. Then C.P. got a job teaching French, German, and Spanish at Culver Military Academy, a new but respected boarding school in Indiana.[10] C.P. brought Xenophon to Culver and enrolled him, taking advantage of a tuition discount offered to children of faculty members. Vera stayed in Bloomington and taught French at Wesleyan.

Xenophon graduated with honors on June 8, 1899, and won a scholarship to the University of Chicago, which was already building an academic reputation. After Xenophon went to Chicago, Vera and C.P. moved there, too. C.P. got a job teaching at a boys school while Vera began importing lace from Russia with the assistance of Professor Pavel Milyukov, a historian in Russia. Vera sold the lace in America, returned the profits to the peasant weavers, and set up a fund in Russia to train new lace workers.[11] She also published a volume of folk tales translated from Russian and began work on a children's history of Peter the Great and a collection of Swiss legends. A reviewer of her folk tales described Vera as an "unselfish lover of humanity" and said that profits from the book would be turned over to her "poor compatriots" in Chicago and the American West.[12]

C.P. left Chicago after a while, probably to look for higher-paying positions. He taught at a state teachers' college in Oklahoma and, in 1905, at a military academy in Los Angeles. Then he and Vera moved to Pasadena, California. C.P. introduced himself around town as "Captain" de Blumenthal, a courtesy title given faculty at military schools. They lived in the rear apartment of a bungalow at 35 North Euclid Avenue owned by the Hotel La Casa Grande.

C.P. and a Russian partner formed a business, the Realty Trust Company, to bring over thousands of Russian families who belonged to a persecuted Protestant brotherhood in Transcaucasia. The idea was to settle them on a farm, called Little Russia, across the border in Mexico.[13] C.P. was the front man and business manager for the deal. The first hundred or so families that settled on the farm brought in the first year's harvest at a profit of $35,000 ($870,000 today).

Then the scheme collapsed. Some of the farmers challenged the terms of their employment. They went on strike. C.P. disappeared. Where did he go? Where did the *money* go?

A bannerline across the front page of a Los Angeles newspaper screamed that C.P. might have been murdered on the farm.[14] Then the press suggested suicide. Vera was reported "prostrate." Reporters camped on her doorstep.

But to paraphrase Mark Twain, reports of Cap'n Blumenthal's death were greatly exaggerated. Soon he was reported living in Mexico City as a rich oil man. Later he emerged in Moscow, on his way back to Ufa, ostensibly to visit his sick mother.

"Captain de Blumenthal was a man of a peculiar temperament," Vera later told a reporter. "He was shy and of a shrinking nature, and a man who found it hard to face adversity. He was absolutely honest and generous to a fault." She denied he had done anything dishonest. He was "disheartened and sick" after the mutiny on the farm and that's why he left, she said.[15]

The couple divorced and Vera remained in Pasadena to continue selling Russian lace and returning the profits to workers back in the old country. C.P. would later work as a judge in Russia, and during the civil war he joined Admiral Alexander Vasilyevich Kolchak's forces fighting the Red Army in Siberia.

Xenophon does not seem to have had much patience with his stepfather. While C.P. could not quite come to grips with his destiny, Xenophon was more organized and more focused, more in control of his life.[16]

In that world of the early twentieth century, the United States was mostly a land of small towns and farms. Few young people ventured very far from home. Those who later put on a uniform for the long trip over to the European battlefields would tell their folks that they were "going to see the elephant." It was a joke based on the fact that in rural America the most exciting thing to happen, other than a meteor shower or church on Sunday, was usually the arrival of the circus. Going to see something as big and mysterious as an elephant was a life-changing event. So was going to war. It was also called a boy's "great adventure" in life.

Xenophon Kalamatiano never served in the military. His great adventure was going to be spying in Revolutionary Russia.

5

XENOPHON THE TERRIBLE

X enophon Kalamatiano was an academically average student at the University of Chicago, but his foreign languages courses, his athletic accomplishments, and his fraternity membership would all serve him well later as a spy in Russia.

Xenophon completed the junior college program in the College of Arts after seven quarters and two summer sessions, with courses heavy in Latin, French, German, and Hebrew. His grades weren't particularly impressive, mostly Bs and Cs, with a few Ds here and there. He received his bachelor's degree on August 29, 1902, with a B-minus average.[1]

Chicago developed a reputation as a sports powerhouse early on. The University of Chicago was a founding member of the Western Conference (now the Big Ten) and athletic director Amos Alonzo Stagg coached the Maroons to two national football championships. Kalamatiano's game was track. On January 18, 1902, he set a university indoor record for the two-mile run, coming in at 10 minutes 30 seconds. In the Chicago YMCA meet on February 1, 1902, he scored second in the indoor mile run, assisting in the team's 62–33 win. And at the Amateur Athletic Union championship indoor meet in Milwaukee on March 1, 1902, he was second in the two-mile race, with Chicago winning overall. He was secretary-treasurer of the track team his senior year.[2]

After graduation, Kalamatiano tutored French and Russian at the university and taught at the Princeton–Yale School, an affiliate of U of C. He was also a founding member of the Sigma Alpha Epsilon chapter on campus, forming ties that would help him later when he was in prison in Russia. The SAE national leader, William C. Levere, a former temperance campaigner and reporter for the *Chicago Evening Post*, took an instant liking to Xenophon. Levere predicted he would go far in the world.

"He was distinguished in appearance, with an air of Old World culture" and "exceedingly pleasant and companionable," Levere wrote.[3]

Kalamatiano's brothers in the frat house loved his thirteen-syllable name. At rush parties they sang "Xenophon de Blumenthal Kalamatiano" to the tune of "Maryland, My Maryland."

> *Xenophon de Blumenthal*
> *Kalamatiano*
> *Xenophon de Blumenthal*
> *Kalamatiano*
> *Xenophon de Blumenthal*
> *Xenophon de Blumenthal*
> *Xenophon de Blumenthal*
> *Kalamatiano!*[4]

He admitted it was a great name. Because of his running speed, one of his nicknames was the Terrible Russian. The other was simply Kal. He signed his name as "X/Kal."

❖

After leaving Chicago, Kal taught school in Racine, Wisconsin, an industrial town of 30,000 on Lake Michigan just south of Milwaukee. He married Agnes McAvoy, a stenographer who worked for a lawyer. The McAvoys were a large family and apparently well-off, since they owned a livery company.[5] Xenophon and Agnes had a daughter, Vera.

Kal changed jobs in late 1905, probably to better support his wife and daughter. He went to work as a salesman for the J.I. Case Threshing Machine Company in Racine. It was a peach of a job for a trainee, paying $125.00 a month.[6] That's over $3,000 in today's currency. It wasn't a bank president's salary, but there were no income taxes or sales taxes back then. Above the front door stood a statue of the Case logo, Old Abe, the bald eagle mascot of Company C of the 8th Wisconsin Infantry. Case also made automobiles and entered three cars in the first Indianapolis 500, on May 30, 1911.

Case was the biggest farm machinery company in the United States. They had expanded to South America and Europe, and in 1899 opened their first Russian office. Kal's employment record at Case shows that on

October 1, 1908, he signed a new three-year contract and transferred to the
Odessa office in Ukraine. With his Russian background and his social skills,
he was a natural for the position.

❖

For Kal it must have been an eerie experience returning to his homeland after
so many years, like arriving in a town that was strange to him but where he
nevertheless knew what to expect up every street. Odessa was the fourth
largest city in Russia, a hot and humid collection of traditional Ukrainian
buildings with French and Italian Mediterranean influences, built on hills
overlooking the Black Sea. It was an important port and rail hub and a choice
location for Western imports, especially in winter when North Russian docks
were frozen in.

Kalamatiano got regular pay raises in Odessa. A favorable exchange rate
between the dollar and the ruble allowed him to live well. Russia was primarily
an agricultural nation and supplied more than a third of the world's wheat. It
was also the largest country in the world in land mass and the second biggest
in population. But only two Russian factories could produce farm machinery,
and one of them was tied up making artillery for the army. That left Russian
growers dependent on imported machinery.[7] Russia was a profitable market
for American companies, and Case had sales and distribution offices not only
in Odessa but also in Moscow.

Kalamatiano's biggest competitor was International Harvester, which in
1910 began manufacturing farm machinery in a plant near Moscow. IH had
a big advantage since it operated by royal decree and did not have to pay the
import duties that interfered with Kal's efforts at Case.[8] Later on, the Soviets
would adopt the hammer and sickle as the symbol of Red Russia. The hammer
stood for industry, the sickle for agriculture. But the sickle was an antiquated
tool used by small farmers, and by the time Kal arrived, most of Russia's millions of acres were being harvested by machinery. A more accurate symbol for
Russian farming might have been the IH logo, or Old Abe.

During Kal's first year back in Russia he was at the top of the list of sixteen salesmen in Odessa. In January 1910 he was in second place. Then he
left Case. He became an independent agent and went into a partnership with
Claude M. Nankivel, an import-export broker in New York. They represented
around thirty foreign companies doing business in Russia.[9]

It's not clear how long Kalamatiano worked with Nankivel. But later on he said he was business manager for Case in Russia, 1912–1915, so apparently Kal went back to his old company after a couple of years with Nankivel.[10] And business for Case was booming. The company reported worldwide sales of more than $12 million (almost a third of a billion in today's dollars) and paid 7 percent on its preferred stock.[11]

❖

Kal returned to the United States in 1915 as American representative of the Association of Commerce and Industry in Moscow. That group wanted to drop Germany as Russia's top trading partner and move America into first place. Before war broke out, 50 to 60 percent of Russia's total import/export trade was with Germany. But Allied blockades had shut that down.

"There is in Russia a strong movement on foot to interest the manufacturers of the United States in trading direct with Russia, and to cultivate closer commercial relations," Kal told reporters in New York. The purpose of his trip back to America was not to "buy or to sell" but to explain to U.S. businessmen "what and how the Germans sold to Russia and why other countries have hitherto not done more business directly." American goods "have been very successful" in Russia, he continued. He cited as an example the fact that Case had recently sold a hundred automobiles in Russia, "all we had in stock."[12]

Kal gave his new American business address as the office of A.S. Postnikoff, formerly of International Harvester in Russia, at 1133–1135 Rookery Building, Chicago.[13] Kal and Postnikoff organized a meeting of U.S. manufacturers on August 30, 1915, in the Hotel La Salle in Chicago. Postnikoff outlined his plan to establish an International Manufacturers' Sales Company of America, headquartered in Chicago, with branch offices in New York and Moscow. He wanted to create a consortium of fifty manufacturers to cooperate in sales in Russia. Kal would run the Moscow end of things.

Sam Harper addressed the Chicago meeting as a longtime observer of Russia. He said the country contained "untold resources" but that Americans had not won their proper share of Russian trade because they lacked direct representation over there.[14]

William Chapin Huntington was also at the meeting. The thirty-one-year-old Huntington was an Iowan who held a doctorate in engineering from the Royal Technical College at Aix la Chappelle, Prussia, and a mechanical engineering degree from Columbia University. His specialty was metallurgy and he was fluent in French, German, and Russian. In Chicago he was a commercial agent for the U.S. Bureau of Foreign and Domestic Commerce. He would soon go to work for the U.S. ambassador to Russia and assist in the Lenin Plot.

The Chicago meeting came a few months after Kal wrote that letter to Sam Harper offering his services in Russia. Then Kal returned to Moscow to continue his work for his trade group. Before he left, though, he finished up a bit of legal business: a divorce from his wife. Agnes got custody of their daughter Vera, leaving Kal a man on his own again.

6

WASHINGTON NAPPING

The Russia that Xenophon Kalamatiano found on his final trip over was not the country he had left just a few months before. The old Russia of empires and tsars was dying. What replaced it put him on death row.

As Kal resumed his business interests in Moscow, the new war was only in its second year. The press at first referred to it simply as "the European war." It had begun the way major events often do—in a place that many people had never heard of. In this case it was the quiet and picturesque old Alpine industrial town of Sarajevo, down close to the Adriatic Sea.

Sarajevo was capital of the Balkan provinces of Bosnia and Herzegovina, which Austria-Hungary had taken from the Ottoman Empire. Sarajevo's streets were lined with both old Turkish and new European buildings, including Roman Catholic and Orthodox churches, synagogues, and mosques. Ancient ox carts shared the cobblestones with Europe's first electric tram lines. With its dozens of nationalities and political points of view, Sarajevo was a place where East truly met West. And with such a clash of religions and cultures came dangerous politics.

Many Bosnians saw Austria-Hungary as an occupying power. So seven Bosnian teenagers armed with bombs and pistols gathered in Sarajevo on June 28, 1914, with murder on their minds. They had been trained by the Black Hand, a nationalist Serbian secret society. Their mission was to assassinate the Austrian heir apparent, Archduke Franz Ferdinand. Two of the plotters were sixteen years old. One was a Muslim.

The fifty-one-year-old Franz Ferdinand, looking very Germanic with his square jaw, crew cut, and handlebar mustache, was in Bosnia-Herzegovina to observe Austrian military summer exercises in the country. Actually, he was a mild-mannered pacifist who wanted to peacefully unify the Slavic peoples of the Balkans. But his visit to the country proved hot from the very start as the radiator of his car boiled over.

"Our journey starts with an extremely promising omen," he noted sarcastically. "Here our car burns, and down there they will throw bombs at us."[1] Little did he know how true his prophesy would be.

The armed Bosnian boys waiting for the archduke did not consider themselves terrorists, but "patriots" who wanted their country to become part of a "greater Serbian empire." Their idea of an assassination, though, seemed to be simply to stand on a sidewalk and throw a bomb. But how about an escape plan? A professional knows that's the third important element. First the planning, then the killing, and finally the escape.

Franz Ferdinand and his wife Sophie rode up in their open car. She was a Czech and had been deemed unfit to join the House of Habsburg, meaning her children could never inherit the Austrian throne. But she and her husband were very much in love and they accepted what they could not change. She accompanied him everywhere. On this trip she had gone shopping in Sarajevo and had visited an orphanage.

One of the assassins tossed a grenade as the royals approached. Franz Ferdinand batted it down. It blew up in the street and injured about a dozen spectators, including one of the archduke's men in a car behind. Franz Ferdinand rushed to city hall and marched up the steps, his plumed hat shaking with indignation. He confronted local officials and lodged an angry complaint about the reception he and his wife had just received.

"It is outrageous!" he said.

Then he and Sophie rode out again, this time to a hospital to visit people wounded in the bombing. One of the assassins, Gavrilo Princip, a nineteen-year-old consumptive, was waiting when the royal couple's car passed in the street. He fired two shots with a Browning semi-automatic pistol.[2] Sophie was hit in the stomach, Franz Ferdinand in the throat.

"Sophie dear, don't die!" Franz Ferdinand cried out. "Stay alive for your children!"

But they both succumbed to their wounds and were dead on arrival at the hospital. Reporters noted that the assassination had occurred on an otherwise warm, pleasant, and quiet Sunday morning.

Eight plotters were arrested, convicted of treason and murder, and sentenced to prison. Princip would soon die of tuberculosis. In Vienna, Austrian

Emperor Franz Joseph used the murders as an excuse to declare war on Serbia, a Slavic Orthodox nation culturally and politically tied to Russia. In response, Russia mobilized for war. That prompted Kaiser Wilhelm, who had wanted a "preventive war" for years, to attack Russia.

Then France, bound by treaty to Russia, went to war against Germany and Austria-Hungary. Britain, tied to France by treaty, jumped in next, and was joined by Japan. After that, the Ottoman Empire (Turkey) sided with Germany and Austria, creating the Triple Alliance. With the addition of Bulgaria, the name was changed to the Quadruple Alliance, then the Central Powers. Russia, France, and England were called the Triple Entente at first, but as other countries such as Italy joined their side they became known as the Allies.

On and on it went until thirty-two nations were banging away at one another in Europe, Asia, Africa, and the Middle East, with acts of political terror and sabotage extending to North and South America. Later on, the American press began to call it the World War. To England it was the Great War.

This was the big one that people had said would never come. But the major European powers had been competing in a massive arms race for years. Bigger guns and battleships were built, huge armies trained. Bombers, fighter planes, and submarines were developed, along with the most feared field weapons ever devised—machine guns, tanks, flame throwers, and poison gas.

American intelligence was not prepared for the war. United States military attachés had been assigned to consulates in Europe for years but mostly they acquired "open intelligence" from newspapers, academic journals, and government reports. Producing hard intelligence on war threats was beyond their realm.

Overall responsibility for U.S. Army intelligence sat with the Military Information Committee of the Department of War's General Staff. But they were concerned mainly with keeping an eye on Mexico. When American forces landed in Veracruz in 1914, Captain Douglas MacArthur reported that army intelligence down there was "practically useless."[3] The U.S. Office of Naval Intelligence also had attachés to Europe, but again they were not concerned with political intrigues. They sent Washington reports on topics such as the light bulbs used in Italian warships.

That left the State Department as America's chief source of foreign intelligence. They sent in information from legations and executive agents, but had no reliable system for indexing and storing the reports. In 1914 the memory banks of Washington headquarters were in the head of the oldest man in the office, seventy-two-year-old Alvey Augustus Adee, second assistant secretary of state. He had joined the diplomatic service in 1869, before the office had electric lights or telephones. But his memory was said to be prodigious. He read all incoming and outgoing paperwork, and in a few minutes could pull a report from a file twenty or thirty years old.

Unfortunately, when war broke out in 1914, Adee was on a three-month biking vacation. Others in the office were also on holiday to get away from Washington's summer heat. Frank Mallett, vice-consul in Belgrade, wrote a dispatch on July 13 forecasting war between Austria-Hungary and Serbia, but because of State Department stinginess, he had to mail it instead of sending it by cable. It didn't reach Washington until July 27, the day before Austria-Hungary started bombarding Belgrade to start the war. State was caught napping.[4]

❖

At the start of hostilities, Russia boasted the biggest army in the world. Alfred Knox, a British military adviser sent to Russia, estimated that St. Petersburg could draw on a manpower pool of 15 million. More than 5 million were immediately mobilized, and 3 million sent to the front lines. The "Russian Steamroller," they were called.[5]

A revealing look at what happened to the Russian Imperial Army in the war and how those events brought on the revolution and the rise of the Bolsheviks was recorded by a soldier, Maria Leontievna Botchkareva. Her eyewitness accounts are found in her autobiography, *Yashka*.[6]

Later on, during World War II, women combat soldiers would be fairly common in Russia. But Botchkareva was one of the first. She was an illiterate *moujitchka* (peasant woman) who had grown up barefoot and in rags on a farm near Tomsk, Siberia. Her father was a freed serf and a drunkard who beat his wife, leading Maria to marry at age sixteen just to get away from home. Her first husband was Afanasi Botchkarev; in the Russian style, her married name became Botchkareva. But he, too, was a drunkard, and once he tied Maria to a post and flogged her. After a failed suicide attempt, she left him and married Yakov Buk, aka Yasha.

Yasha was drafted for the war and taken prisoner by the Germans. Maria never heard from him again. But she was passionately patriotic and kept up with the fighting through the newspapers. There was "something holy" about the way Russia responded to the call to arms, she wrote. "It was an elevating, glorious, unforgettable moment." She saw a new world coming, "a purged world, a happier and godlier one." A voice told her to go to war herself and help save her country.[7]

Maria Botchkareva walked into the headquarters of the 25th Reserve Battalion and asked to see the commander.

For what? the clerk asked her.

"I want to enlist," she announced.

The clerk looked her over, a stocky woman with long brown hair, a heavy face, and a determined expression. "Here is a *baba* who wants to enlist!" He and the other men in the office had a good laugh.

Botchkareva stood her ground. Seeing that she wasn't going away, the clerk showed her in to see the adjutant. The adjutant repeated that a *baba* (woman) could not enlist. It was against the law. Again she demanded to see the commander. She got her interview, but the commander was just as resistant.

"I have no authority to enlist a woman even if I wanted to," he told her.

Join the Red Cross, he suggested. That didn't interest her. Then he thought of a way this matter could be settled. Send a telegram to the tsar asking for permission to enlist, he told her.

She did just that. But she had to borrow eight rubles from her mother to pay for the wire. Fine, Nicholas replied. Join up. When Maria's mother heard that, she tore up her picture of the tsar. She would never pray for him again. "No, never!"

Botchkareva got her wish and enlisted, probably in 1915. She had to sleep in the barracks with the men, and for a while her nights in bed were interrupted by hands (hers) slapping other hands (theirs). Then she had to take showers with them. Men and women bathing together naked in rivers was not an uncommon sight in Russia, but still she kept to a corner by herself.

Fighting a war was men's work. Women should be sweeping streets and cleaning out sewers. That's what they told her. But she continued to stand her ground. After she didn't report them for harassing her, and after she qualified on the firing range as a marksman, the boys figured she wasn't so bad after all. They gave her the nickname Yashka, by which she would always be known. She became one of the gang. They even took her with them to a brothel. When the house got raided, the men scrambled out the windows, leaving her to get arrested.

She was taken to the military prison. The commander looked her over. What's this, a *baba* in a uniform? What had she *done*?

Botchkareva assured him she was not in the practice of hanging around whorehouses. She had gone there with her comrades simply to "investigate" the place. Right. He ordered her to stand at attention for two hours, then get out.

A week later, Yashka's regiment was deployed to the front. The local town turned out to cheer them as they marched to their train.

"I have never seen such a body of men in such high spirits as we were that February morning," she said. "Woe to the Germans."[8]

❖

As it turned out, the Russian Imperial Army was not the monster machine it had first appeared to be. An Austrian military writer at the time described the Steamroller as a "heavyweight muscle-bound prizefighter who, because of his enormous bulk, lacked activity and quickness and would therefore be at the mercy of a lighter but more wiry and intelligent opponent."[9]

General Aleksey Alekseyevich Brusilov, commander of the Russian Eighth Army, went further than that. He said the imperial army was doomed from the start. Stavka, Russia headquarters, had no competent mobilization plan or war strategy in 1914, he wrote. The army possessed few machine guns, and the ones they had were hauled around in horse carts. Railroads were single track, too slow for fast deployments. No trench mortars or hand grenades were available, and the army's airplanes were outdated. Officers were insulated from their men. Code books were missing. Sometimes messages had to be sent in the clear.

Rifles were in short supply and many troops had to charge enemy machine guns without weapons of their own. They were told to pick up rifles from the dead. If they tried to turn back, they were shot down by their own combat police. The lack of weapons was due in part to incompetent and crooked government bureaucrats. Also, Russia was buying weapons from U.S. manufacturers who were not turning out massive amounts of arms the way European factories were doing. A Russian arms purchaser complained that U.S. factories were so slow in keeping up that shortages struck when guns were needed most.[10]

Massive infantry attacks sending thousands of troops charging wildly across open fields into concentrated enemy gunfire were an antiquated tactic from the days of the American Civil War. When that tactic collided against twentieth-century technology, the result was what President Wilson called the greatest disaster in history.

Another problem for Russia was that many peasant soldiers had no real understanding of the war, no enthusiasm for it. They enlisted simply because they were patriots like Botchkareva. It was expected of them. They trusted God and Little Father. They did not question what they were told to do.

"The result was that the men were led like sheep to the slaughter without knowing why—that is, at the whim of the tsar," Brusilov said. [11]

Because of that, an alert observer even in 1915 could have heard the first rumblings of a coming upheaval in Russia.

A LAST HURRAH

The affection that Xenophon Kalamatiano felt for Russia was based on pleasant memories of a posh childhood, leavened with adult hopes and ambitions. But war had brought a measure of uncertainty and suspicion. Being an educated, cultured, well-dressed man of the world, though, Kal moved about easily as he pursued his business interests, undoubtedly taking advantage of his family's social contacts.

Nicholas II had changed the name of St. Petersburg to the patriotic Russian form, Petrograd, for the war. Peter the Great had used slave labor to build the city out of swamps in the early 1700s, at almost the exact time that New Orleans was built, also out of swampland. He intended *Piter* to be his modern, sophisticated window on the West. Indeed, it was a dramatic change from the old capital of Moscow, which by comparison was a medieval country town of log cabins and dirt roads. The insignia of the Russian empire fit in well with Peter's ideas—a two-headed eagle facing both east and west.

Nicholas had ordered a national prohibition on alcohol for the war but Kal and others who could afford it found that vodka and Champagne still flowed in the restaurants, cafés, and hotels. By 1916 the capital was booming with jobs, and Petrograd's population had burst past two million. Factories operated full speed, turning out uniforms, boots, guns, wagons, and horse furniture. So many people had moved in from the country that only a third of the wartime population of Petrograd was local.

Apartments became scarce. The government tried to cope by building monolithic poured-concrete housing blocks. Many foreigners were trapped in the city by the blockades but their currency converted to rubles at a favorable exchange rate, allowing them to rent an entire house in Petrograd for what an apartment might cost in Paris.

But Kalamatiano had an increasingly difficult time financially. He couldn't import any new tractors, threshers, or cars. He probably had to rely on service contracts for existing machinery. He got married again. His second wife was a thirty-year-old Muscovite, Ekaterina (Katherine) Kulikova (née Suslova). They were wed in November 1916. Katherine had been married before and had a nine-year-old son, Vladimir Sergeevich Kulikov, whom Kal adopted. But Kat and Kal had no children of their own.[1]

The Allied war plan called for France, Italy, and Britain to invade Germany and Austria-Hungary from the west while Russia attacked from the east. The Russian Steamroller had swept through Poland into East Prussia in 1914 and 1915, and from there Berlin was only 180 miles away. In a few weeks Cossacks would parade triumphantly down the Unter den Linden, Russian newspapers crowed.

But then Russia was defeated in six battles. The Russian march on the land of the "Huns" became a macabre dance of retreat and defeat. Two Russian armies got wiped out. Thousands were killed, hundreds of thousands wounded or taken prisoner. A general committed suicide. The Steamroller became a piece of junk lying rusted on the side of the road.

Botchkareva saved fifty wounded men after an attack on German trenches went bad. In the process, she was shot in a leg. When she returned to duty four months later, she got frostbite and had to go back to the hospital. Then she was shot in her other leg. After that third recovery, she was given a medal, promoted to corporal, and put in charge of eleven men. The men liked her. They trusted her. But the winter was severe. Life in the trenches was cruel.

"Death was a welcome visitor," she said.[2]

Some ice-covered corpses were found in the sitting position, as if the men had simply been eating a meal or watching the front lines when caught in a hard wind. Supplies started to run out. Boots and coats were salvaged from the dead. When the snow thawed, the true extent of the Russian losses was revealed.

"Like mushrooms after a rain, the corpses lay thick everywhere and there was no count to the wounded," Yashka wrote of that spring. "One could not make a step in No Man's Land without striking a Russian or German body. Bloody feet, hands, sometimes heads, lay scattered in the mud."[3]

The war had turned the new century old before its time. Russia was breaking down.

The tsar attempted to stem the losses. He sacked his brother, Grand Duke Michael, and took over the army himself. That was done at the urging of the tsarina and their personal peasant guru and faith healer, Grigori Yefimovich Rasputin. Trouble was, Nicholas was a "mere child" in military matters, General Brusilov wrote, a dilettante at the mercy of bootlickers who flattered him to cover up their own inadequacies.

"We had no real supreme commander-in-chief," Brusilov said. "War is not a pastime or a joke. It demands from its leaders a depth of knowledge which comes not only from the study of the profession of arms but also from the possession of natural talents which practice alone can bring to full stature . . . His lack of knowledge and ability, his weakness of character and his vacillating made him totally unfit for any such post."[4]

Foreshadowing the later Western plots against Lenin, some Russian army officers conspired to turn out Nicholas in a coup. A fighter pilot offered to crash his plane into the imperial railcar in a suicide attack. Even Grand Duke Michael considered taking his command back by force. Some politicians in Petrograd decided to stage a putsch, replace Nicholas with his twelve-year-old son Alexis, and name Michael as regent. But Alexander Fyodorovich Kerensky, the Duma delegate who would later head the Russian Provisional Government, said those plots were "completely infantile" and never got off the ground.[5]

The Russians pinned their hopes for victory on the Brusilov Offensive of June 1916, fought in Austrian Galicia (now in Southwestern Ukraine). It began with a massive artillery attack. In two days Brusilov fired more shells than the United States had in her entire arsenal.[6]

After the softening-up barrage, three armies of Cossacks and Russian cavalry charged across the border. Behind them, infantrymen shouted "Hurrah!" while climbing out of their trenches for yet another charge through cannon fire and gas into enemy machine guns. Botchkareva was wounded again, this time by artillery shell fragments. One lodged in her spine and paralyzed her.

The Russians captured vast stretches of enemy territory in the Brusilov Offensive. But Turk reinforcements were rushed in to assist the Austrians and Germans, leaving Brusilov facing a pumped-up enemy force of 2.2 million. The arrival of cold weather mercifully halted operations in November.

The 1916 offensive was technically a success because Brusilov had broken the Austro-Hungarian army. But Russian casualties were staggering: 1.1 million dead, 1.9 million wounded or otherwise excused from service, 2 million missing or captured, 1 million deserted.[7] Mother Russia in that one offensive had lost more of her sons than there were troops in the entire U.S. army, navy, marines, and national guard combined.

The war was a long hard struggle for Russia. A total of more than 14.5 million troops had been mobilized, and the fighting was costing 50 million rubles a day.[8] Government bureaucrats remained faithful to the war because many were following tradition and getting fat by skimming money from military contracts. But Ivan Ivanov, the proverbial Russian man in the street, was tired of it. The long lines of wounded returning to Russia from the Brusilov Offensive and the trainloads of coffins portended the coming upheaval.

When Botchkareva returned to the front from the hospital that last time, she didn't recognize the war she had left a few months before. Most of her comrades were dead or disabled. The catastrophic defeatism that would soon destroy the army had not yet set in, but Yashka noticed that young draftees didn't trust their officers. They had no patience with the war. They wanted it to end.

"The spirit of 1914 was no more," she said.[9]

The 1916 Brusilov offensive was the tsar's last hurrah in the war. After New Year's, the régime began to break down.

On January 9, 1917, 140,000 workers went on strike in Petrograd, 30,000 in Moscow. Additional strikes broke out in Baku, Nizhniy Novgorod, Novocherkassk, Voronezh, Kharkov, Rostov-on-Don, the Donbass, and other cities.[10] The strikes were accompanied by street demonstrations. Ostensibly, people marched to commemorate the twelfth anniversary of the 1905 revolution. But the demonstrations were also a protest against the war and the dwindling food supplies. People had to stand in line for hours to get a potato or a chunk of meat while the rich lived in isolated splendor. The authorities responded by forbidding people to queue up before 6 A.M.

At the same time, mutinies broke out among the 330,000 soldiers stationed in Petrograd and the suburbs. The mutinies quickly spread to sailors in the Baltic Fleet. Some of the troops were anti-war. Others were incensed at the incompetence of the government and the tsar. Nicholas and his crooked bureaucrats were seen as the main impediments to victory in the war. Rumors spread about treason in the tsar's court, and officers with Germanic names were singled out for suspicion.

The January demonstrations were twice as large as those the year before. Regiments of soldiers cheered the protestors as they marched past. Police were called out to disperse the crowds, and the strikes lasted only one day. But they showed a widespread dissatisfaction with the status quo that had been building since the Brusilov Offensive the year before.

Later on, some would call the Russian Revolution of 1917 the February Revolution. But the January disturbances were the true beginning of it all.

8

WHO'S IN CHARGE?

Xenophon Kalamatiano, Chapin Huntington, and Charles Crane were all in Russia during the winter of 1916–1917, watching storm clouds gather for what Maria Botchkareva called an "immense tragedy." Huntington had arrived in Russia in June 1916 and spent that summer touring and exploring the country. Now in 1917 he was assigned to the embassy in Petrograd as a commercial attaché.

Crane continued talking to people in the government and in the Duma, acting as an agent of influence for Washington. His reports went to Ambassador David R. Francis in Petrograd for relay to Washington. Kalamatiano was trying to keep his import business afloat. He wasn't officially working for the State Department yet but undoubtedly was sharing information as a casual agent.

That winter was one of the coldest on record. On February 23, 1917, the temperature in Petrograd dropped to 45 below freezing (°F). Ice and snow shut down 57,000 trucks and 1,200 locomotives. Homes lost telephone and electrical service. Trolleys and ambulances operated only after streets were cleared. Supplies of coal and paraffin for heating ran out. Food could not be brought in. Meat, sugar, buckwheat, and potatoes disappeared from the tables of workers. The government set the bread ration to a quarter pound a day. Then bakeries ran out of flour.

It was difficult to work all day on a miserable chunk of bread, so some of the factory workers walked off their jobs after what passed for the lunch hour. Next day, women got tired of standing in line on frozen sidewalks in front of bakeries and began shouting "Give us bread!" Mounted police and Cossacks rode in to disperse them.

The following day, a general strike shut down the factories. Crowds of women marched to the Kazan Cathedral in Petrograd crying "Give us bread and we will go to work!" Workers and students streamed into the city center shouting "Down with the government! Down with the Romanovs! Down with the war!"

Mounted police charged the crowds and used whips to try and disperse them. It didn't work. They had to fall back. The army was called in. But many of the soldiers sympathized with the crowds and began fraternizing with them. At six o'clock the police started shooting into the crowds. That set off street battles. Many were killed, especially on the Nevsky Prospekt, Petrograd's main street. Then Cossacks and soldiers turned on the police and attacked them.

General E.A. Vertsinsky, the new commander of the 18th Army Corps, found that a reserve battalion of the Volyn regiment had rebelled and taken to the streets during the disorders in Petrograd. The district court building and the Transfiguration Cathedral were set on fire and the arsenal was seized, while a General Zabudsky was killed.[1]

Huntington and Crane made daily reports to the embassy. The reports were coded, ciphered, and wired by Ambassador Francis to London for relay to Washington. But the British had a monopoly on transatlantic cable service, and London censors delayed the traffic before sending it along. That caused backlogs. The British said they did this to block information that might be useful to the Central Powers. But Americans suspected the English were being deliberately uncooperative because the United States had not yet taken sides in the war. London also held up cablegrams sent by U.S. businesses. That allowed the British to conduct industrial espionage against America by stealing trade secrets and the details of contracts.[2]

Thus, reports were increasingly sent to Washington by diplomatic couriers. They were U.S. Marines wearing civilian clothes. They took trains across the border into Finland, Norway, or Sweden, and then either boarded ships for America or transmitted their reports in code by wireless. Some couriers went the other direction, on the Trans-Siberian Railway to Vladivostok, and handed their reports over to new couriers who then sailed for San Francisco.

American agents in Russia used the State Department's Green Cipher. It replaced the old Blue Cipher after a blue book was stolen from the Petrograd embassy. Code books were similar to dictionaries. They listed words and phrases alphabetically. But instead of definitions, the book assigned groups of numbers to the selected words. Then, as added security, the coded numbers were added to groups of ciphered numbers before being sent. Code books could run over 1,000 pages.[3]

The speed of events in Russia picked up quickly. The tsar dissolved the Duma. The delegates defied him and stayed in session around the clock. Kerensky, a lifelong populist lawyer and leader of the radical left in the Duma, shouted "Down with the government!" British agent Bruce Lockhart blamed the tsar's shutdown on German *agents provocateurs* operating in palace circles. Lockhart said they wanted to provoke a revolution and force Russia into a separate peace with Berlin.[4] Kerensky, too, charged that the palace was infiltrated by German agents.[5]

The Duma formed an executive committee and set up the Russian Provisional Government. An opposition group, the Soviet of Workmen's and Soldiers' Deputies, aka the Petrograd Soviet, was created to compete with the provisional government. Soviets (workers' councils) were first formed in factories during the 1905 revolution for the purpose of making demands against the government. Lev (Leon) Davidovitch Trotsky was one of the early organizers. His 1905 soviet included a motley crew of radicals including Mensheviks, Bolsheviks, anarchists, and Socialist Revolutionaries (SRs). The SRs were formed in 1902 as a terrorist alternative to the Social Democrats (SDs). The SRs believed that peasants, not urban workers, were the revolutionary class, and that Russia could leap from feudalism to socialism without capitalism.

Many in the Petrograd Soviet of 1917 refused to recognize the new revolution. They hadn't started it; therefore, it was not legitimate. Kerensky wrote that the Petrograd Soviet "from the very beginning tried to thwart the normal development and sound force of the revolution."[6]

The throne was next to fall. Nicholas II had lost the support of his soldiers, his people, and his parliament. Now some of his top officers staged a quiet coup. It happened on a bitterly cold night as Nicholas was returning from Stavka to Tsarskoye Selo, his beloved country home. His train was diverted to Pskov, a small station southeast of Petrograd, near the Estonian border. There, rebellious soldiers surrounded the train in the deep snow. A group of the tsar's generals entered his car for a talk. They advised him that Petrograd was in a state of anarchy. It would do no good to send in more troops, for they would just go over to the revolutionaries.

"Then what is to be done now?" he asked.

Alexander Ivanovich Guchkov, a former chairman of the Third Duma (1907–1912), replied, "You must abdicate the throne." Guchkov was not exactly a close adviser to the tsar. He was a monarchist, all right, but he was also an Orthodox Old Believer who had been plotting a coup against Nicholas since 1915.

Suddenly Nicholas was a dead man whose friends had followed him to the grave, but not into it with him. He was all alone, with no more sycophants to assure him that he possessed the greatest military mind since Caesar. He took a walk outside on the station platform, then returned to his car and signed two documents of abdication. The first turned the crown over to his son, Alexis. Then he changed the abdication in favor of his brother, Grand Duke Michael. But Michael refused the throne.[7] With that, 305 years of rule by the Romanovs ended. Guchkov was arrested that night by workers who thought he was part of the tsar's inner circle.

The existing Fourth Duma proclaimed the country was now the Russian Revolutionary Republic. The new Russian Provisional Government scheduled elections for a constituent (constitutional) assembly to meet and decide what kind of political system the country would have in the future. Within two weeks, U.S. Ambassador Francis gave official diplomatic recognition to the fledgling new nation. France, Italy, and Britain soon followed.

❖

Maria Botchkareva was at the front when news of the revolution arrived. The provisional government sent a manifesto urging the soldiers to hold the line against Germany and defend Russia's new freedoms.

"Yes, we will!" the soldiers shouted.

But then they received the infamous Order No. 1 from the Petrograd Soviet. It abolished all army titles. Officers were to be disarmed and their epaulets torn from their tunics. Soldiers would elect committees to run the army and follow orders from the Petrograd Soviet, not the provisional government. Kerensky called it a "hothouse" creation by some people in the soviet who thought they had military minds.[8]

Those competing orders posed the big question of 1917: Who exactly was running the revolution—the Duma, or the Petrograd Soviet?

There were meetings, meetings, meetings, speeches, speeches, speeches. As a result of Order No. 1, duty was abandoned in the army. Orders were ignored. Everybody was his own commander.

"The front became a veritable insane asylum," Botchkareva said.

German and Austrian forces on the other side of No Man's Land greeted all this with smiles. Fraternization began. "Come over here for a drink of vodka!" enemy soldiers shouted to Russian troops made pliant by Bolshevik propaganda. By one estimate, 165 of Russia's 220 front-line divisions fraternized with the enemy.[9]

Germans, Austrians, and Russians met in the middle of the field. Vodka flowed, courtesy of the Germans. Many Russian soldiers decided that the Germans and Austrians were true revolutionary, peace-loving comrades. They invited them back to their trenches for tea.

The Russians' new "friends" thoroughly enjoyed themselves by using the occasion to scout out Russian artillery positions. Some Russian officers saw what was going on and tried to stop the fraternization. Their own troops threatened to kill them. The Germans and Austrians finally waved goodbye and carried the information they had gathered back to their own commanders. Then the enemy artillery started shooting again, this time zeroing in on the Russian guns.

It was a brilliant double-cross by the Germans and Austrians. They had made fools of the Bolshevik soldiers and it had cost only some bottles of vodka.

❖

Some of Botchkareva's troops refused to obey her orders. They insisted they were going to elect their own *natchalnik* (commander). She threatened to resign her commission and go home. Mikhail Vladimirovich Rodzianko, head of the Duma's provisional committee, went to her aid. Rodzianko had been the chairman of the last Duma before the revolution. He favored a constitutional monarchy for Russia and was an enemy of the tsar's wife, Empress Alexandra. Rodzianko had urged soldiers to ignore Order No. 1. He called Yashka a *heroitchik*, bought her a dress uniform, and paid her way to Petrograd to meet with Kerensky. That was in May 1917.

Botchkareva was a lieutenant now. She asked permission to form a First Russian Women's Battalion of Death. Her idea was for women soldiers to go into battle as an example to wavering male comrades. Yashka vowed to restore discipline. No committees would be allowed. General Brusilov approved the idea. So did Kerensky.

Two thousand women volunteered for her battalion. But many couldn't pass the physical. Others acted silly and childish, and she sent them home. Then Bolsheviks infiltrated the group. They persuaded some of the girls to form a committee and run the battalion themselves. Botchkareva refused to go along with that. She pared her group down to a trusted 300. They represented all levels of Russian society, from peasant to princess.

But then General Pietr Alexandrovich Polovtsev, second in command of the Petrograd military district, called her in and ordered her to form a committee.

"I won't," she said.

"Then there is nothing left but to disband your battalion."

"If you wish."

Polovtsev reported her to Kerensky, who at that time was the provisional government's minister of war. He turned on Botchkareva in a rage. He banged his desk.

"I demand that your form a committee tomorrow!" he screamed. "Otherwise, I will reduce you to dust!"

"No!"

She stormed out, slamming the door behind her.

Her faithful survivors marched on Polovtsev's office. The general, suddenly surrounded by 300 menacing women, agreed not to disband them. But he again demanded that Botchkareva allow a committee. Again she refused.

"I am a general!" he shouted. "I will kill you!"

Yashka tore her tunic open. "All right, you can kill me! Kill me!"

Polovtsev threw his hands up. "What the devil," he said. "This is a demon, not a woman."

The battalion was not disbanded. But the Bolshevik committee was.[10]

Yashka's First Russian Women's Battalion of Death faced its first trial by fire in the summer of 1917 in Petrograd when the Bolsheviks organized a protest march against the war. Botchkareva's battalion was assigned to march in a counter demonstration. The battalion's instructors were armed with revolvers, just in case.

When the women reached the Field of Mars, the capital's big parade ground, they were attacked by a Bolshevik mob. Botchkareva's instructors opened fire and two of them were killed in the ensuing gun battle. Another two were wounded, as were ten of the women. Botchkareva was knocked out by a blow to her head.

The Bolshevik mob was suppressed. But rumors went out that Yashka had died in the hospital. Rodzianko and a repentant Kerensky rushed to her bedside.

Finding Yashka alive, Kerensky complimented her on her hard head.

9

LENIN'S GERMAN KEY

History waits for no man. This was evidenced by the fact that the target of the Lenin Plot was not in Russia when the revolutions of 1905 and 1917 broke out. Lenin had been in Geneva as a political exile when he heard about the 1905 revolution. He was a refugee in Zurich when news of the 1917 uprising reached him.

He had sunk into himself during his exile years. Through his prodigious output at the typewriter writing about revolution, he had become a paper statue of his own ambitions. But after the failure of the 1905 revolution he was convinced that a second one might not come for many years, maybe not in his lifetime. Hence, he was stunned at the news in February 1917. He ran from comrade to comrade in Zurich seeking more information. When confirmation came, he decided to return to Russia and try to take over the revolution in the name of his Bolshevik Party.

One of the ironies of the 1917 revolution was that two of its major players, and bitter enemies, Lenin and Kerensky, came from the same hometown, Simbirsk, a sleepy Volga River community of 40,000 or so, east of Moscow. Lenin and Kerensky had attended the same high school in Simbirsk. Kerensky's father was a teacher there and their families were friends. Simbirsk is now called Ulyanovsk, after Lenin's birth name, Vladimir Ilyich Ulyanov. It has grown into a large and prosperous administrative center but is still noted for being the hometown of two of Russia's most memorable political figures.

Lenin's parents were conservative monarchists, and Ilyich was baptized in the Russian Orthodox Church, though he grew up to become a confirmed atheist. He never used his first name; to friends and family he was simply Ilych. His law degree from the St. Petersburg Imperial University got him work briefly as an attorney, but beyond that he spent his early adult life mainly as a propagandist for the Russian Social Democratic Labor Party. That was a

Marxist group that wanted to unite all Russian revolutionary parties under their umbrella. Their efforts failed, as evidenced by Lenin's walking away from the SDs with his breakaway Bolsheviks (from the Russian, meaning majority). Because his family owned a farm, Lenin claimed to be a member of "the nobility." But in Russia that simply meant he was not a peasant or worker.[1]

Lenin was forty-six years old at the time of the 1917 revolution. Despite his success in forming his Bolshevik Party, he was still basically what he always had been, a provincial bourgeois from a country town. He had grown up short and stocky like the peasants he so ardently hated, and as a young man he had red hair and liked rural pastimes such as hiking, skating, swimming, taking naps under trees, and hunting rabbits. When he ran out of shotgun shells he clubbed the rabbits to death. He was a neat dresser with reserved and correct manners, Victorian in thought and sedate in social behavior. He hated the clichéd revolutionary style of dressing in boots, army tunics, and leather caps, and preferred to wear a business suit, not expensive, but presentable.

As Ilyich aged he lost his hair and grew a beard. Lenin biographer Valeriu Marcu wrote that Ilych looked "mongol, with a strong jaw and the bright and humorous eyes of a smart tradesman." He lectured with "the cut and dried finality of a dervish."[2]

Lenin's mind was quick and he was able to play two games of chess at once. But he possessed the arrogance and intolerance of a political elitist. Aside from peasants he also hated royalty and middle-class liberals. In his mind, liberalism led to tolerance and moderation, a surrender of revolutionary principles.

Lenin's paternal grandfather had been a serf, the Russian equivalent of a slave. Lenin's mother was the daughter of a Jewish doctor who converted to the Orthodox faith. Russian historian Dmitri Volkogonov wrote that Ilyich's sister Anna in her later years contacted Stalin to explain that Ilyich came from a poor Jewish family, but that the anti-Semitic "Uncle Joe" fiercely covered up the information.

"Absolutely not word about this letter!" Stalin demanded.[3]

Lenin also had German, Swedish, Kalmyk, and Russian ancestors. He might have inherited his flat face from the Kalmyk side.

Lenin was at the top of his class in school and the favorite son in the family. That resulted in his developing a puffed-up superiority and a rude disdain for the views of others. Contrary to what some Soviet biographers later claimed, Lenin showed little interest in revolution when he was growing up. But when he was eighteen, a traumatic event turned him into a hateful, spiteful radical.

His older brother, Alexander, whom he looked up to, was arrested for plotting to assassinate Tsar Alexander III (1845–1894).

Alexander III became tsar in 1881 after revolutionaries with Narodnaya Volya (People's Freedom, or People's Will) assassinated his father, Alexander II, the "liberator tsar" who freed the serfs. Alexander III started out as a serene ruler. He kept Russia out of war and was called "the peacemaker." But as revolution threatened his rule he became cruelly autocratic. Many of his opponents were arrested and executed.

The Ulyanov family couldn't believe that Alexander, known as Sasha, had been involved in an assassination plot. The boy was studying zoology at St. Petersburg Imperial University. He was one of the brightest students there and had seemed indifferent toward politics. But friends introduced him to the writings of Karl Marx, Friedrich Engels, and Georgi Valentinovich Plekhanov. Sasha's comrades convinced him that only violence could stop the tsar's oppression of the people. Alexander III had to be removed.

This little group was a self-organized terrorist squad modeled after Narodnaya Volya, which was suppressed after they killed Alexander II with a bomb. In March 1887, on the sixth anniversary of that assassination, Sasha's group set out to bomb Alexander III in his royal carriage as he rode to St. Isaac's Cathedral in St. Petersburg. But the police intercepted a letter written by a member of the group and rounded up the squad before they could strike. All were tried and sentenced to death.

Because of their youth, the judge offered to reduce their sentences to hard labor if they would ask for clemency. Sasha and four of his comrades refused.

"I cannot do it after everything I said in court," Sasha told his mother. "It would be insincere."[4]

The five were hanged at the notorious Shlisselburg political prison on the Neva River east of the capital. Throughout this whole affair the Ulyanov family was snubbed by friends and neighbors. Some refused to ride in the same carriage with them. Such humiliations hardened Lenin as he picked up the mantle of the revolutionary cause. Some say he named himself after the Lena River. Marcu said Lenin had been Sasha's nom de guerre.

After joining the Social Democrats, Lenin was arrested several times for radical activities. He was exiled to Siberia for three years, and when he returned he tried to reorganize the SDs into a more militant group. That failed, and he walked out with his Bolshevik faction in 1903, leaving the SDs in the hands of the tamer Mensheviks. One of the issues that caused the split was whether banks should be robbed to raise party funds. Lenin was all for such "expropriations." In his view, they were just stealing what had already been stolen by the tsars. But in one spectacular fiasco, the Bolsheviks killed three guards as they stole 340,000 rubles, which they found were in such large denominations that they couldn't be spent.

In the years between the 1905 and 1917 revolutions, Lenin and his wife Nadezhda (Nadia) Krupskaya lived in political exile in several cities in central Europe. Their rent was usually around twenty dollars a month. In Zurich their apartment was next door to a sausage factory so smelly they couldn't open the windows. After 1905, Lenin spent his days studying for the next revolution, often pacing the floor and talking to himself passionately in public libraries. He never hobnobbed with workers or peasants but read in books the things that got them riled up. Lenin lived off his mother and off donations to his little Bolshevik Party. He ate in greasy cafés and eked out an existence that allowed him a new suit only every three or four years. He was also trapped in a barren marriage.

Nadia was an intelligent, dedicated revolutionary who had been loyal to Lenin since the days when they were young Marxists together in St. Petersburg in the nineties. But she apparently lacked the drive to establish independence from Lenin. Some said she was a better writer than Lenin but that he did not allow her works to be published under her own name because her talent would show him up. It seemed that the best Nadia could do in life was to hitch a ride on Lenin's shooting star. Lenin admitted that she served him well as typist, editor, and personal assistant. That seemed to be all he expected of her.

As Nadia got older she developed Graves' disease, a glandular condition that left her with a bloated body and disfigured face. Her eyes bulged and seemed to leer at people. Some called her Fish. A story went around that Nadia was living proof that Lenin didn't like women.

"In none of the mass of writing about Lenin is there any mention of an affair of the heart in his youth," Volkogonov said of Lenin. "It appears that his preoccupation with books and revolutionary dreams left no room for the normal feelings that usually occupy the mind of any young man."[5]

❖

But in fact there had been an affair of the heart for Ilyich, directed toward Inessa Armand, a French radical he met at a café in Paris in 1909. She was born Elizabeth d'Herbenville in Paris to a French father and Scottish mother, both music hall performers. She was four, five, or nine years younger than Lenin, depending on the birthdate she gave to various police agencies that arrested her. Growing up, her nickname was Inés. After her father died, her mother could not support three children, so Inés went to live with an aunt and a grandmother in Russia who were tutoring the children of a wealthy French industrialist named Armand.

Inés grew up in Russia with the Armand children and married one of the sons. But a teacher had introduced her to advanced political ideas and she rejected the life of a sheltered wife and mother. She left her husband, then ran off to live with his brother. He, too, steered her toward radical ideas. She got involved with the Bolsheviks and adopted the cover name of Inessa. Later she was jailed several times, and finally exiled to Archangel province, almost inside the Arctic Circle.

Political exiles like Lenin and Inessa Armand were not considered dangerous and usually weren't closely monitored. They were simply dumped in remote villages hundreds of versts from the nearest train station and told to stay out of trouble.[6] There was no electricity or telephone, no rail line. They were given an allowance to cover their rent and food, and they spent their years reading, writing, teaching, playing chess, and arguing over the politics that had got them there in the first place. They also took hikes, chopped firewood, slept, and had parties. The days, months, and years fell aside like clothes dropped to the floor. But with such a lack of stress, many exiles returned home after a few years looking remarkably young and rested. It was as if those years had never happened.

Inessa, though, had no plans to sit around communing with reindeer. After ten months in her village, she walked out. On the road, she and a fellow escapee slept in the woods in daytime and walked at night to avoid detection. They trudged more than 200 miles to Archangel city. There she caught a train for Moscow, where she resumed her radical activities.

Polina Vinogradskaia, one of Inessa's friends, described her as tall and slender, with a thin face, an "aquiline" nose, large "greenish expressive" eyes, and "long luxuriant" hair.[7] She was cultured and carried herself in a reserved, aloof manner. Like Lenin, there was nothing Bohemian about her.

Inessa was as smart and as devoted to revolution as Nadia was. Beyond that, the two women had little in common. Inessa was fashionable, elegant, charming. Nadia was not. Marcu described Nadia as "homely" and "dumpy."[8]

Lenin was also smitten with Inessa's linguistic and musical talents. He normally had no ear for music but he loved the way she played Beethoven's "Sonata Pathétique" on the piano. After all he had gone through—the years of exile, of waiting and plotting, of living in cheap boarding houses, of being rejected by publishers—he felt he had found his soul mate.

Inessa latched onto Ilyich the way Nadia had. Inessa became his translator and girl Friday. She moved next door to the Lenins and conducted an affair with Ilyich openly in front of Nadia. Nadia was a patient sort and seemingly took it all in stride as an eternal good sport. But it must have been humiliating to her. She offered to leave. Lenin insisted she stay.

Historian R.C. Elwood wrote that Ilych and Inessa's affair was "never a secret" to their old comrades.[9] Bertram Wolfe, a founder of the Communist Party of America, said that when he interviewed Angelica Balabanoff, secretary of the Communist International in 1919, she claimed that Lenin and Inessa had a child.

"What happened to Lenin's daughter then, I do not know," Balabanoff said.[10]

Inessa eventually found there were limits to the mutual admiration society she shared with Ilyich. She was a determined feminist. Lenin was not. Like his inspiration, Karl Marx, Lenin had no patience with such diversions. Lenin saw women as politically naïve. Their place was in the kitchen, cooking kasha and ironing shirts. As far as he was concerned, feminism was a phony issue, not a class struggle but a war of the sexes, a pastime of handwringing liberals.

When Inessa wrote a pamphlet endorsing free love, Lenin dismissed it as "bourgeois." He acted more and more condescendingly toward her opinions, translating them into his own terms and then turning them against her. He ridiculed her to the point that she finally left him. She then went to work organizing women factory workers. But when she attempted to break down traditional family forms through communal laundries, dining halls, and nurseries in the factories, the workers stonewalled her.[11]

Before all that happened, though, Inessa joined Lenin's entourage when he finally returned to Russia in 1917. Although Lenin had missed the outbreak of both the 1905 and 1917 revolutions, he made up for lost time getting back to Russia, thanks to a lucrative deal the Bolsheviks had cut with Berlin.

❖

The German high command wanted to get Russia out of the war so they could devote their efforts to winning in France, the main battleground. Their earlier efforts using German agents inside the tsar's palace had failed to do that. Lenin was their Plan B. He in turn wanted Russia to be defeated because he was convinced that a military catastrophe would set off another revolution, or civil war. Then in the midst of that chaos, he would seize power.

Lenin had no particular loyalty toward his own country. He saw no morality in politics, only pragmatism. Lenin considered himself an international revolutionary. Russia was simply a laboratory where he could grow revolutionary bacillus to spread across the world.

Germany gave him assistance through a Russian revolutionary from Minsk named Alexander Lazarevich Helphand, aka Parvus. Like Trotsky, Parvus had been a major player in the 1905 revolution, while Lenin was mostly an extra, scampering over walls to escape the police. Parvus was exiled to Siberia, and escaped. He emerged in Germany, where he became Maxim Gorky's literary agent. He was run out of Germany after he cheated Gorky of 100,000 marks. Parvus then landed in Constantinople and began setting up business deals between Turkey and Germany. By the time the war started he was a millionaire. But he was still a Marxist and wanted to set off a second revolution in Russia.

In May 1915, Parvus went up to Bern to make Lenin a proposition. Despite the war, Germany was still selling humanitarian goods like medical supplies and clothes to Russia through neutral countries in Scandinavia. Parvus proposed setting up a front organization in Stockholm through Yakov Stanislavovich Ganetsky (aka Jakub Fürstenberg), one of Lenin's most trusted agents. Berlin would ship allowed goods to this firm for sale to Russia. The profits would then be funneled to the Bolsheviks and Lenin could use the money to pursue his revolutionary agenda.

Bolshevik operatives deposited the laundered German money into Russian banks with ties to the party. A million here, a million there, it was hard to keep up with it all. The biggest item on the Bolshevik budget was propaganda. They published forty-one newspapers, with a combined circulation of 320,000. That included 90,000 copies of *Pravda* published every day. The German money was also used to pay Bolshevik salaries and to finance anti-war agitation on the Russian fronts. (The "Russian Front" actually consisted of three fronts, Northern, Western, and Southwestern, stretching about 1,000 miles from the Baltic to the Black Sea.)

Russian counterintelligence investigators collected twenty-one volumes of evidence against Lenin, known collectively as the German Key. They accused him of being a German agent. But Lenin wasn't an agent in the sense of an intelligence officer reporting back to Berlin. He was an agent in the financial sense, acting to represent the interests of another.

For his part, Lenin alternately admitted and denied the accusations. Once when he was in a confessing mood he wrote to a comrade that he indeed had shared an "understanding" with Germany. "There was a coincidence of interests," he said. "We would have been idiots not to have taken advantage of it." [12]

❖

The logistics of returning Lenin to Russia were a problem. The new provisional government was releasing political prisoners, welcoming exiles back home, and relaxing border security, so actually getting Ilych across the frontier could be done legally. But for safety reasons, where could Lenin cross?

Not through Poland or Austria, since they were in the middle of hot combat zones. Not through the Ukraine, since Odessa and other Black Sea ports were blockaded by the Allies. What about Vladivostok, the Far Eastern terminus of the Trans-Siberian Railway? No, with the war on, it might take months to ship Lenin halfway around the world just to put him on a train. And British warships were patrolling the Baltic. Still, Lenin put out a feeler to London. Could they slip him through a blockade somewhere? No, they knew what he was up to. They turned him down.

General Erich Friedrich Wilhelm Ludendorff, director of German army operations, and Baron Friedrich Gisbert von Romberg, the Reich's foreign minister, came up with a plan. They would haul Lenin through Germany on a train and deliver him to Petrograd through an area in Scandinavia that was under German U-boat protection.

But Germany, like Russia, was war-weary and facing starvation. They didn't want Ilyich making speeches at every station and stirring up revolution. So the idea of a "sealed" train was born, as in a sealed diplomatic pouch. Lenin would have no contact with Germans, and vice-versa. As it turned out, the train really wasn't sealed. Lenin and his group were simply restricted to one car behind a chalk line drawn on the floor. They gave money to German officers who bought food for them on the way. [13]

But before Lenin's journey started, he tried to make a last-minute appeal of some kind to the United States. Allen Dulles, a young consular officer at the U.S. legation in Bern, answered the phone in the office on a Friday afternoon. Western diplomatic stations were closed in Berlin and Vienna for the war, and Bern was the new diplomatic and spy capital of Central Europe. Dulles had contacts with exiled revolutionaries in Switzerland, so the caller at the other end of the line was no stranger.

Lenin spoke in an agitated voice. He demanded to talk to somebody in charge. That wasn't Dulles. He was at the bottom of the legation's totem pole. And he was trying to close the office.

Dulles told Lenin to ring again the next day. Lenin was adamant. He wanted to talk to somebody now. Allen was equally insistent. He had a tennis date with a girlfriend. Whatever Lenin wanted, it would have to keep until Saturday. Then he hung up the phone.

Who can say what Lenin wanted at that last moment? Could history have been changed if Dulles had taken the time to listen? Later, when he was director of the CIA, Dulles warned his students to never refuse to talk to anybody.[14]

❖

Lenin's trip back to Russia began on a Swiss train that left Zurich on April 9, 1917, with thirty-two people in his party, including Nadia and Inessa. At the German border town of Gottmadingen they got on the special train that Berlin had provided. Then for three days the entire group slept in their seats. Lenin spent his time reading newspapers and talking to himself. Inessa kept a log of the trip and tried to get Lenin to wear pajamas at night. Cooped up together like that, especially with children, tempers were short. Ilyich ordered one woman banished to a distant compartment because of her irritating laugh.

The train passed through Frankfurt and Berlin, and at the German port of Sassnitz the travelers took a ferry across a narrow neck of the Baltic to Malmö in neutral Sweden. At Malmö they boarded a train for Stockholm, where Lenin bought new shoes and trousers. Then they set off on another train trip, this one through Finland, a former Russian grand duchy, into Petrograd.

After sitting on the sidelines for so many years, Lenin had lucked out through the actions of other people—those who had actually been in Russia to start the 1917 revolution. Now he intended to take the wheel himself, to fulfill his ambition to become the new dictator of Russia. In his eyes he deserved what he could get. He called himself "tsar of the Reds."[15]

At this point, Lenin was not yet a threat to the Allied war effort. He was simply another noisy Russian rabble-rouser. There had been plenty of those over the years, and none seemed to have gotten very far. But Lenin had a major military power behind him. His secret deal with Berlin would turn out to be the first of several steps he would take to threaten Western interests in the war.

That deal, in turn, would lead to formulation of the Allied plot to assassinate him.

10

THE YANKS ARE COMING

B ecause of the war, Petrograd had turned into a warehouse of anger and loss. But now, in revolution, many dreamed of hope and reconciliation through the coming constituent assembly. Lenin arrived with a different message. He stepped off the train at the Finland Station in the capital on the night of April 16, 1917, almost two months after the revolution had begun. The street was enameled with ice, and a spotlight illuminated the platform under a light snow as Lenin made a rousing speech to warm up a crowd of supporters who had turned out to greet him. Soviet reports later put the number at thousands. News reports at the time described a few hundred.

He told them he stood for peace, free bread, free rent, and free land. But as always, his message quickly turned dark. He returned to his signature messages of hatred, paranoia, and vengeance. The provisional government's extension of amnesty to political prisoners had resulted in his own return, but that meant his old enemies were also on the street again. They had to be exterminated. He encouraged his followers to fight to the end for a complete victory of the proletariat. They should do that through the kind of mass violence endorsed by Marxists of the previous century, including Engels, the German son of a rich capitalist who co-authored *Das Kapital* (Capital) with Marx and called for the proletariat to seize the state and the state's means of production to produce a classless society.[1]

"Long live the worldwide social revolution!" Lenin shouted.

That was the mantra Lenin would repeat over and over again for the next six months as he struggled to overthrow the provisional government and seize control of the revolution. Lenin had few original political thoughts; aside from Marx and Engels, he took ideas from Georg Hegel and the French Revolution, then cooked them until they came out to his particular taste. But historian Peter Eltsov gives him credit for originality in several spheres such as "the theory of the state as the machine of oppression, the nationality issue and self-determination, subjective versus objective factors in history, and the theory of the revolutionary situation."[2]

An important thing Lenin had learned was that blind political faith was based on simple issues such as death and terror and enemies and settling old scores. Vengeance was the beginning, not the end.

"Hatred was the flame that warmed him in his days of cold despair, when friends stumbled and fell, when hopes and aspirations perished," Marcu wrote.[3]

One of the faces in the crowd that April night in Petrograd was that of Boris Viktorovich Savinkov, who had arrived at the station at the same time as Lenin. Savinkov was a professional terrorist who used to belong to the Socialist Revolutionary Party, aka the SRs.[4] Now he was an independent SR with his own agenda aimed at both monarchists and Bolsheviks. Lenin did not later mention having seen Savinkov at the station. But Boris, a vain man, was reportedly offended because the crowd was not there to greet *his* return from exile.

The SRs—not the monarchists, the Mensheviks, or the anarchists—were the Bolsheviks' main enemy in Russia. (Cossacks came in a close second.) So, it was no secret that Savinkov was gunning for Lenin. Boris saw it as a duel to the death. Boris carried a Browning pistol, so why didn't he shoot Lenin that night? That would have been a quick way of preventing a Bolshevik coup.

The answer probably lay in Savinkov's style of assassination. He was a meticulous assassin. He spent weeks researching his target's movements in advance, and carefully planned the hit at just the right time. Lenin's unexpected arrival that night caught him off guard. Also, Savinkov preferred to use a bomb in a killing, but apparently didn't have one on hand that night. Nor did he have a team in place. He had to let it go, for the time being. He would find other chances later.

❖

Despite his cozying up to the proletariat, Lenin had no intention of bunking with bedbugs and roaches in a working-class tenement in Petrograd. He was driven to the former home of Mathilde Kschessinska, a Polish ballerina who had been Nicholas II's mistress before he married. Mathilde owned a two-story stone and brick villa located across the river from the Winter Palace, next to the

Peter and Paul Fortress, and surrounded by a tall iron fence. A small balcony on the second floor faced the street where Lenin's disciples could gather and listen to him harangue them nightly with his call to arms.

In early June 1917, Lenin planned an uprising against the provisional government. But the government caught wind of it and it fizzled out. Then news of the casualties of Brusilov's new summer offensive reached Petrograd in July. That set off widespread anger. The Bolshevik central committee decided to exploit the situation by staging a big street demonstration aimed at forcing the provisional government to resign. Thousands of workers and soldiers were called out. Lenin pumped them up with tirades as they streamed past his balcony. There were shootings. Wine cellars were looted. Pogroms were reported. The government responded in force and the attempted putsch was defeated. Many Bolsheviks were arrested. The July Days, as they were called, were probably the first shots fired in the Russian Civil War.

The prosecutor in Petrograd charged Lenin with treason for his links to Germany and for his interference with the conduct of the war. Lenin went on the run. He was not a brave man like his brother. He seldom took risks. He was used to writing about revolution, not actually getting shot at. Counterintelligence agents went door to door looking for him. He took on false identities and fled from one safe house to another.

When the knocks on the doors got too close, he shaved off his beard, put on a woman's wig, and fled the capital with a false factory pass. He hid in a fisherman's shack in Razliv, northwest of Petrograd, then went to Helsinki. It would take him two months to get back to Petrograd, and even then he continued his disguises.

As the summer heated up, Lenin's troubles deepened, as did those of the provisional government. A major conflict between Kerensky's government and the Bolsheviks was shaping up. During all that, the United States stepped into the middle of Russia's affairs.

❖

Since George Washington's time the United States had kept a distance from European wars. What business were they of America's? President Wilson agreed with that when he first took office. He felt that a nation should spend its resources on the development of jobs, schools, and hospitals. Wars were low-class, unchristian ways of settling disputes. He stuck to his guns, so to speak, after the war started in 1914. America should remain neutral in thought as well as deed, he said. And many Americans backed him up. The song "I Didn't Raise My Boy to Be a Soldier" was popular on Vaudeville stages:

> What million soldiers to the war have gone,
> Who may never return again.
> Ten million mothers' hearts must break
> For the ones who died in vain.
> I didn't raise my boy to be a soldier.[5]

But American opinion changed after the sinking of the British liner *Lusitania* by a German U-boat in May 1915. The attack killed 1,198 men, women, and children, including 128 Americans. It set off a wave of indignation. Wilson sent three notes of stiff protest to Berlin but maintained his position of neutrality.

Some newspapers that supported Wilson's neutrality drew violent responses. One editor faced down a lynch mob in his front yard after writing an editorial urging the country to stay out of the war. He dispersed the mob by going out on his porch with a revolver and announcing that if they tried to hang him, he would take the first six of them with him.[6]

Wilson was re-elected in 1916 by a narrower margin than four years before—277 to 254 votes in the electoral college. "He kept us out of war" was one of his 1916 campaign slogans. But opposition to neutrality was growing more intense. Threats were made against him. Wilson was sworn in privately on March 4, 1917, and when he rode to the Capitol the next day he was escorted by mounted cavalry. As he appeared outside the Capitol to take the oath publicly he was shielded from the public by a line of soldiers. Hundreds more troops stood by in nearby streets. Library of Congress photos show a machine gun set up on the Capitol steps, aimed at the crowd below.

Demands for war increased with the sinking of five Americans ships, the *Vigilancia*, the *City of Memphis,* the *Illinois*, the *Healdton*, and the *Algonquin*, by German submarines. Twenty-one Americans died when the *Healdton* went down.[7] But the straw that broke the camel's back was the infamous "Z Note."

The Z Note was a telegram from German Foreign Minister Arthur Zimmermann to Johann-Heinrich count von Bernstorff, the amiable and heretofore popular German ambassador to the United States. Wilson had tried to end the Mexican civil war by invading the country to topple the dictator

Victoriano Huerta, who had taken power in a 1913 coup and had murdered the previous president. Wilson imposed a naval embargo on European guns to Mexico, and Huerta fled the country. His successor, Venustiano Carranza, secretly proposed to Berlin an economic and military deal that included building a German submarine base in Mexico, close to the U.S. border.

Zimmerman vetoed that idea but sent a telegram to Bernstorff instructing him to get Mexico to enter the war against the United States. In case of victory, Germany would return to Mexico her "lost territory" of Texas, New Mexico, and Arizona. The galling thing to the Wilson administration was that the ciphered Z Note was sent through the offices of the U.S. State Department in an arrangement supposedly reserved for peace negotiations.[8] The Monroe Doctrine was made for days like that.

Wilson had been shown the Z Note on February 24, 1917, but didn't say anything about it publicly. The note hit the front page of newspapers on March 1, three days before he took his second oath of office. With that, the genie was out of the bottle. Wilson had to do something. On April 2 he asked Congress for a declaration of war against Germany. Wilson cited the Zimmerman telegram as "eloquent evidence" that Berlin intended to "stir up enemies against us at our very doors."

But Wilson insisted that America was not entering the war as an Allied power. Instead, the United States would be an "associate" of the Allies. That was because he didn't trust the Allies any more than he trusted the Central Powers. He feared that after the war they would all continue their long tradition of carving up Europe, Africa, and the Middle East for their own purposes, despite what the conquered countries had to say about it. Most of the rest of the world, though, considered the United States an Allied power. The French, Italians, and British certainly did. So did the Russian provisional government. The Allies had suffered enormous casualties. They were almost broke and nearly whipped. They desperately needed America and were in no mood to argue semantics.

At first, America's marching song for the war was going to be "Dixie," the national anthem of the Confederacy. Then a drinking song popular in both North and South, "When Johnny Comes Marching Home," was considered. "The Battle Hymn of the Republic" was also a top contender. But the army's corps of music critics said no. As stirring as those songs were, they just didn't seem right. Apparently it had something to do with cadence. That's when songwriter George M. Cohan stepped in. He wrote a ditty called "Over There," especially for the war:

Johnnie get your gun,
Get your gun, get your gun,
Take it on the run.
Hear them calling, you and me,
Every son of liberty.
Over there, over there,
Send the word, send the word over there
That the Yanks are coming,
The Yanks are coming.[9]

❖

Now that America was in the war, Wilson recognized the need to keep Russia in it, too. First, there was a strategic need to keep the Russian fronts intact. That would force the Central Powers to continue fighting in two theatres. Second, he had economic reasons for turning his attention to Russia.

When war broke out, America was a debtor nation still reeling from the recession of 1913–1914. But a big recovery took off as the United States started selling goods to the European belligerents. Then, in 1917, after war was declared, Washington began awarding its own military contracts. Factories that once manufactured automobiles and stoves now made guns and trucks. Millions of women joined production lines as men went off to fight. Some 3 million jobs were added to the military, and 500,000 in the federal bureaucracy. The national jobless rate dropped to 1.4 percent. Most of the war's financing was met not by running up huge deficits but by selling war bonds (for 58 percent of the cost) and by raising taxes (22 percent).[10]

The streets of Washington, formerly a sleepy Southern town run by the horsey set, filled with cars, buses, army convoys, and battalions of people talking in different accents as they hurried to get somewhere. Overhead, warplanes circled the city enforcing a no-fly zone. Washington became a truly national city, and with its contradictory feel of both discipline and disorder, Pierre Charles L'Enfant's gift to Foggy Bottom acquired the trappings of a citadel under siege. And while they were at it, Americans changed the name of German chocolate cake to "victory chocolate."

Russia was a huge factor in all this because Wilson figured the United States, with a population of 103.2 million, would be packed with surplus goods after the war.[11] To prevent America from sliding back into recession, he wanted to sell those surplus products overseas. Russia would be a prime market for American cars, locomotives, blue jeans, sneakers, jazz records, Western movies, and cigarettes.

Officially, Wilson's closest adviser in his developing Russian policy was Secretary of State Lansing. The unofficial voices were those of Charles Crane and Wilson's old friend Edward Mandell House. But there was another influence who was closer to him than all of those. That was his second wife.

❖

Wilson's first wife, Ellen Louise Axson, daughter of a Georgia pastor, had been an artist who won a medal at the Paris International Exposition. She was Wilson's first true love and they were married twenty-nine years. Ellen died of Bright's Disease after seventeen months in the White House. The president was devastated. For a horrifyingly long time he wouldn't allow her body to be removed from their bedroom. He then suffered months of depression and loneliness before meeting Edith Bolling Galt, wealthy owner of one of Washington's premier jewelry stores and a descendent of Princess Pocahontas.[12]

"Our boss was in love," Edmund Starling, chief of Wilson's Secret Service detail, later wrote. "She's a looker" and "He's a goner," two White House employees told Starling.[13]

They were married in December 1915. He called her Miss Edith. To her, he was Tommy. The press loved her. Wire service reports noted her black hair and blue eyes and described her as "charming, tactful and intelligent . . . still retaining the good looks for which she was famous in her youth."[14]

Edith Wilson was an important figure in the Lenin Plot. She was the president's companion day and night, and his closest political adviser. She was the only person in the White House who held Wilson's special presidential code, which he used outside of official channels for top secret messages to embassies, consulates, and military missions. She ciphered and deciphered his signals, and advised him on his wartime decisions. The press called her the "secret president."

Telephone and telegraph equipment was installed across the hall from the Oval Office in the West Wing and became Wilson's war room, staffed by around seventy clerks. Members of Wilson's administration dropped in at all hours to read the latest reports from the fronts. Edward House, Wilson's chief foreign affairs adviser, became increasingly unwelcome. The first lady didn't like House, evidently because of his closeness to Wilson. She began to cut off House's access to the president.

That left Wilson and Lansing as the primary American architects of the Lenin Plot, with advice from Miss Edith.

11

SEND IN THE SPIES

S ummer had opened the eyes of Russia. The countryside lay lush and green as President Wilson's first official crew of advisers crossed the country on the Trans-Siberian Railway. This group was called the Root Commission. Before they left, in May 1917, Congress appropriated $3 billion in loans to the Allies ($58.437 billion today), including $100 million for Russia ($1.947 billion).[1] The Root Commission was assigned to find out what Russia needed to stay in the war.

The commission was a bipartisan group of political and military figures headed by seventy-two-year-old Elihu Root, a Republican. He had been secretary of war under Roosevelt and William McKinley, and was one of those credited with modernizing the U.S. military. The commission included a Socialist Party member, Charles Edward Russell. Charles Crane was also a delegate. Sam Harper was their unofficial guide.

The first thing the Root Commission found upon arriving in Vladivostok on June 2 were 700,000 tons of American freight, including 8,000 automobiles still in their original crates, piled up in the rail yard. Those supplies could be used in the war. But the hundreds of locomotives that could transport them were sitting there with no one to service them. The commission then boarded a special train to Petrograd. The 6,100-mile ride took seven days.

Kerensky was minister of war by that time. He ordered a new Russian offensive to show the visiting Americans that the provisional government was committed to staying in the war. General Hugh Scott, U.S. army chief of staff and a sixty-four-year-old veteran of the Indian wars in the American West, toured the Russian front lines. Scott was a strong, heavy man with white hair and mustache, bow-legged after a lifetime in the saddle. As a young recruit, he had slept on the floor of Custer's house after the colonel was killed.[2]

Scott found that the soldiers of the new Russian Revolutionary Army were "brave, patriotic and enduring." But the Cossacks, he added, were "more loyal and intelligent" than the draftees. All the troops were forced to endure bad food and shabby clothing, which didn't seem to concern their officers, Scott noted. At the Southwestern front in Galicia, Scott slept on a cot under a blanket saturated with formaldehyde.

"Death was all about one here," he wrote in his memoirs.[3]

Because of the anti-war agitation the Bolsheviks were conducting down there, the southwestern was called the "Lenin front." And because Kerensky was campaigning to keep Russia fighting, this new attack was called the "Kerensky offensive."

Kerensky was thirty-six-years years old in 1917, though his soft clear face made him look younger, almost like a college student. He wore an infantry uniform, but in keeping with the spirit of Order No. 1, it held no epaulets or rank designation. With the Root Commission as witness, Kerensky toured the front to rally the troops. He stood in his open convertible and made wonderful speeches. He wept, he implored, he kissed the sacred soil of Mother Russia. And the boys cheered as he rode off to another camp.

Trouble was, Russians loved wonderful speeches. They cheered everybody who made them, including Bolsheviks. But what was this provisional government? To attack and die, that wasn't provisional, the Bolsheviks said. Many Russian soldiers remained faithful to the war, but German and Bolshevik defeatist propaganda was taking its toll in the ranks.

The Root Commission didn't accomplish much in Russia except to fly the flag and spend money. General Scott at times seemed an anachronism. He wore his sword everywhere he went and thought a modern army should keep its horse cavalry and continue to charge with sabers drawn. He seemed unaware of those newfangled battle tanks that had entered the war. But Scott supported U.S. aid to the provisional government. Without American help, Russia would go bankrupt that winter and starve before the next spring, he told Washington.[4]

An American military mission was opened in Petrograd to advise the provisional government on battle tactics. Other missions had been opened earlier by the French and British. Chief of the U.S. mission was Brigadier General William Voorhees Judson, a fifty-two-year-old graduate of West Point and the army's engineer school. Judson had worked on river, harbor, and canal projects in Illinois, New York, and Texas, and was a consultant on the Panama Canal. He had also been a military attaché to the Russian Imperial Army during the Russo-Japanese War. Judson would later prove a controversial figure in the Lenin Plot.

The Root Commission members individually supported the 1917 revolution, as did President Wilson and Secretary of State Lansing. But General Scott wondered why Kerensky didn't do something about the Bolsheviks. They were threatening the revolution and the continuance of the war. British adviser General Knox had a simple solution: just shoot them, shoot all the Bolsheviks.[5] Kerensky, though, seemed to feel that the revolution was threatened more from the right (monarchists) than from the left (Bolsheviks).

Scott didn't trust Kerensky. Despite his mild manner (most of the time), Kerensky's behavior could turn erratic without warning. Worst of all were his fits of rage. He was in ill health, and his violent behavior might have been due to his drinking and to his morphine addiction. (German intelligence gave him the code name "Speedy.")

In addition, Scott thought Kerensky was too radical. Technically, Kerensky represented the Trudovik (peasants') Party in the Duma. But he was actually a longtime Socialist Revolutionary. Sir George William Buchanan, British ambassador to Russia, described Kerensky as the "leader" of the SRs in the Duma.[6] George V. Lomonosov, a railroad manager for the Duma, confirmed that.[7] Kerensky was a member of the Duma at the same time he was a delegate to the Petrograd Soviet, which had issued the infamous Order No. 1.

So where, exactly, did his loyalties lie?

A clue might be found in an old attempt by Kerensky to join an SR terrorist squad. It was during the 1905 revolution. Kerensky later wrote that he was given instructions for a sidewalk meeting with a terrorist recruiter, a clean-shaven man wearing an overcoat and an astrakhan. This agent would ask Kerensky for a light. That would be the recognition signal.

"Take a box of matches with you," Kerensky was told. "He will take a cigarette out of a silver case and while he is lighting it, tell him briefly what you want. He will give you his answer and walk away briskly."

Young Alexander showed up for the meet and went through the routine as instructed. But after he made his pitch he was rejected as an amateur, just another dreamer.

"Nothing doing," the recruiter said as he walked off.[8]

❖

While the Root Commission was in Russia, the provisional government asked for an additional loan of $75 million ($1.460 billion today) to pay army salaries. The money was approved in Washington.[9] It would also be used to buy rifles and ammunition, artillery and shells. Even before then, Westinghouse had signed a contract to manufacture 1.8 million Russian rifles at a cost of $48 million ($935 million today).[10] Humanitarian assistance was coming from the American National Red Cross, the commander of which would turn out to be one of the top spies in the Lenin Plot.

But the loans came with a condition. In Elihu Root's words to Kerensky: "No war, no loans."

Kerensky complied. At 4:40 A.M. on June 29, 1917, Brusilov's guns resumed the war in the southwest (the Lenin front). Austrian and Hungarian soldiers down there were nearly starved and were suffering from the same leadership problems as the Russians, and they retreated early. At first the Russians captured much ground and took many prisoners. But then the Germans rushed in three army corps as reinforcements. They broke through Russian lines and Brusilov's offensive fell apart.

Up to 1917, total Russian army casualties in the war had exceeded 7 million. Desertions had been running about 6,300 per month. But now the desertions hit almost 38,000 a month. Because of that, the casualty rate for the 1917 Brusilov Offensive was only 150,000, mercifully lower than it had been the year before.[11]

One of the first big desertions was reported at 10 A.M. on July 20, when detachments of the 607th Mlynoff Regiment abandoned their trenches.[12] They had received radio messages from Petrograd that the Bolsheviks had taken power and the war was over. Some later attributed those reports to Bolshevik and German agents working in the Petrograd telegraph office.

Soldiers were promised free land back home if they would throw their arms down. Thousands complied. They started walking back to Russia on the dusty roads. They climbed onto the roofs of trains. Photos show British advisers drawing weapons and trying in vain to stop them. A Russian general was shot in the back. The retreat became massive. Fleeing Russian soldiers looted and burned villages as they drunkenly fled for home.

❖

On October 10, 1917, Lenin met with the Bolshevik central committee in Petrograd and again insisted on a coup. Hearing about this, Kerensky left the capital to find more troops to defend the city. An aide said that if Kerensky could raise enough loyal troops, the "whole affair" of the Bolsheviks would be "liquidated in five days."[13] Kerensky brought back a group of Cossacks, but they were disarmed by Bolshevik Red Guards. Kerensky saw that he had lost control of the government, the army, and the Duma, the way the tsar had. He fled the capital.

On the night of October 24, a Bolshevik mob surrounded the Winter Palace. Provisional government ministers were holed up inside, waiting for Kerensky to ride in with the cavalry. The Reds cut off electricity to the building, but the outside lights remained on, so the junkers (military cadets) and women soldiers inside the palace enjoyed a firing advantage over the Reds. The Bolsheviks fell back.

According to Trotsky, capturing the palace was intended from the beginning to be a bloodless operation. In the harbor, the cruiser *Aurora* was positioned to fire some blank shells at the palace from its smaller guns. The noise and flash of a blank was more intimidating than the sound of an actual shell, but if that didn't scare the ministers into surrendering, then the *Aurora* would fire a live round. At the same time, a cannon at the Peter and Paul Fortress would join in. But the fortress canon was rusty and not good for much. That left the weight of the assault on the *Aurora*.

A blank shell was fired. The ministers didn't give up, but terrified onlookers along the quay scurried for cover. Then the *Aurora* started firing live rounds. But the shots went off the mark. The ship was within sight of the palace, so either the gunners weren't very good or they intentionally missed.

"Out of thirty-five shots fired in the course of an hour and a half or two hours, only two hit the mark, and they only injure[d] the plaster," Trotsky wrote. The other shells went high, "fortunately not doing any damage in the city."[14]

Trotsky noted that the firing didn't attract much attention from Petrograd citizens. Theatres and restaurants remained open, and people went about their business. After a while the lack of progress got a bit embarrassing. Lenin sent angry notes from his headquarters at the Smolny Institute, a former girls' finishing school. He didn't want this thing to go on all night. Wrap it up.

Trotsky sent word to the *Aurora*: Fire more shells. And try to hit something this time. But the commanders were nervous about the possibility of injuring people. They evaded the orders.

Finally a Bolshevik mob stormed the palace. The palace commandant surrendered and the defenders were disarmed. Nikolai Sukanov of the Petrograd

Soviet found the provisional government ministers in a meeting room, calmly sitting around a table in candlelight waiting to capitulate.

"It's no use," one of them said. "We give up. No bloodshed!"[15]

The mob looted the palace, leaving feces in bathtubs as their calling card. Vladimir Antonov-Ovseyenko ("the Bayonet"), commander of the Bolshevik military revolutionary committee, arrived at 2 A.M. to restore order.

Maria Botchkareva wasn't among the women defending the palace. Yashka and her battalion were at the front. But other women's battalions had been raised. DeWitt Clinton Poole, a U.S. consul in Moscow, said 400 women soldiers were killed in Petrograd while fighting the Bolsheviks, but he admitted he wasn't there, that he heard this in Moscow from a courier.[16] Bessie Beatty, an *Amerikanka korrespondent* for the *San Francisco Bulletin*, said no women soldiers were harmed. They were taken to the headquarters of the Pavlovsky Regiment and held there while relatives were called, she wrote. Then they were told to take off their uniforms, change into dresses, and go home. Beatty also admitted she hadn't been there, that she, too, heard her report from others.[17] The Bolsheviks didn't report anyone killed at the palace, so her story might be more believable than the rumor Poole received.

❖

For the rest of the night the Bolsheviks seized strategic facilities in Petrograd. "But no resistance was shown," Nikolai Sukanov recalled. "Beginning at 2 in the morning the stations, bridges, lighting installations, telegraphs, and telegraphic agencies were gradually occupied by small forces brought from the barracks . . . in general, the military operations in the politically important centres of the city rather resembled a changing of the guard."

Soviet propagandists and radical American correspondents later wrote that the Bolshevik attack that night was a heroic struggle. But Sukanov's eyewitness account disputes that.

"From evening on, there were rumors of shootings and of armed cars racing round the city attacking government pickets. But these were manifest fancies. In any case, the decisive operations that had begun were quite bloodless; not one casualty was recorded. The city was absolutely calm. Both the centre and the suburbs were sunk in a deep sleep, not suspecting what was going on in the cold autumn night."[18]

Actually there were reports that two or three Bolsheviks were killed, apparently accidentally by their own people. But Sukanov's main point was that the Reds mostly argued their opposition out of business. With that, the provisional government fell. Kerensky had dropped the ball and Lenin picked it up.

The Soviets would call it the October Revolution or the Bolshevik Revolution or the Great October Socialist Revolution. But it wasn't a true revolution as a general uprising of the people. That had already happened, in February. The tiny Bolshevik Party staged a coup, and a mostly quiet one.

The real violence started the next day. Government bureaucrats, telephone operators, and railroad engineers refused to cooperate with the Bolsheviks, and Lenin ordered the head of the Nicholas Railway arrested. Lenin nationalized factories and coal mines, and took land from the peasants. He seized churches, symbol of everything he hated about Russia, and turned them into Bolshevik meeting halls. Newspapers ran stories of Red Guards hunting down cadets from the Petrograd military school and killing them. In street fighting between Reds and their opponents in Petrograd, 300 were reported killed on both sides in one day.[19]

A German spy in Petrograd reported that Bolshevik mobs broke into banks and stole cash boxes, and robbed and murdered people in their homes. He described how a man was tortured to death before his family.

"After chopping off his fingers one by one and putting out his eyes, they dragged him half-conscious down the stairs and clubbed and bayoneted him to death. The seventeen-year-old daughter sat in a corner of the room weeping steadily . . . the little sister, three years old, sat under the table and played with her doll."[20]

It got worse in Moscow, where a fierce battle was fought for the Kremlin. First a small group of cadets from the Alexander Military School tried to defend the citadel. They were run out by Red Guards. The cadets came back with a larger force and took the Kremlin again. Then the Reds bombarded the gates and stormed in. The cadets were thirteen to fifteen years old, privileged children of the hated nobility. Reports said "great numbers" of the boys were slaughtered. Things calmed down after a week, but by that time the death toll for Moscow alone was anywhere from 2,000 to 4,000.[21]

❖

The Russian Civil War had begun tentatively with Lenin's failed coup attempt in July. Now in October it exploded in all its fury. In war rooms in Washington, Paris, Rome, and London, telegraph tickers tapped out news of the fast-moving developments. The Western capitals were stunned by the reports coming in. The Russian Revolutionary Republic had fallen. The Bolsheviks had seized power and stopped the revolution. They were taking the country back to old tsarist days of mass terror. And Lenin was proceeding with plans to open peace talks with Germany and deliver his end of his bargain to take Russia out of the war.

In President Wilson's government the most ardent opponent of the Bolsheviks was Secretary of State Robert Lansing. The Lenin Plot would be his idea originally.

Lansing made speeches. He gave interviews. He sent notes to Wilson and fired off telegrams to consuls and ambassadors. Lansing occupied what Teddy Roosevelt used to call the "bully pulpit."

"This government has found it impossible to recognize Lenine [sic], Trotsky and their associates as the de facto government of Russia since there is inadequate evidence that they are the real agents of the sovereignty of the Russian people," Lansing said. The Bolsheviks had seized the legitimate Russian revolutionary government "by force" and set up a régime of "arbitrary and irresponsible authority," he added.[22]

Lansing came from Watertown, New York, a small factory town north of Syracuse. He graduated from Amherst and worked for the family law firm in Watertown, specializing in international law and representing the U.S. government in international hearings. Lansing was active in the Democratic Party machine in that part of the state and was the uncle of two men who went on to take high positions in the American government—John Foster Dulles, who would serve as secretary of state under President Eisenhower, and Allen Welsh Dulles, who joined the U.S. foreign service in 1916 and later became CIA director and architect of the Bay of Pigs invasion in Ike's last months in office.

Wilson's first secretary of state had been William Jennings Bryan. While Bryan was in office, Lansing applied for the position of assistant secretary of state, but was turned down. A better job opened up a year later, and in April 1914 Lansing became State Department counselor. That was the No. 2 job in the department, equivalent to today's under secretary of state. Bryan was a lawyer from Illinois and a former Omaha newspaper editor and presidential candidate. He got appointed secretary of state as payment for helping Wilson secure the Democratic nomination in 1912.

But Bryan was a dyed-in-the-wool pacifist, even more so than Wilson. He clashed with Wilson over the president's vigorous protest of the *Lusitania* affair. The way White House executive secretary Rudolph Forster saw it, Bryan wanted Wilson to be a "doormat for the kaiser."[23] Bryan resigned and Lansing moved up to secretary of state in June 1915 at the age of fifty-one. Like Wilson, he dressed well and preferred music and books to the more visceral attractions of saloons and ball parks. There the similarities ended.

Wilson had always intended to be his own state secretary. All he wanted Lansing to do was put diplomatic notes in proper form. That was supposed to be their agreement and it seemed absolutely logical to Wilson. But Lansing got bored. He became withdrawn in meetings. He sat doodling and daydreaming. The Bolshevik coup finally got him out of his chair. He became the administration's chief crusader against the Bolsheviks and his influence in the White House grew.

In the past, Russian history had been recorded patiently, with a new book written every few years or so. Now every day in Russia was an emergency. A new chapter was penned every week. Lansing recognized that if the Allies wanted Russia to support the war effort, they would have to do something besides the usual routine of viewing events with concern. In his new position as secretary of state, Lansing was in position to do something daring, something radical.

Washington and London had been planning a joint intelligence operation in Russia since June 1917, when Edward House discussed the subject with Lieutenant Colonel William George Eden Wiseman, head of the British Secret Service in America. That was before the Bolshevik coup, when the main focus was on countering German designs in Russia. After that meeting with Wiseman, House talked to Lansing, and Lansing talked to Wilson. The president okayed the new cooperation project.[24] Wiseman would soon recruit a top British spy to work against the Bolsheviks for Wilson.

The French at this time were operating independently against the Bolsheviks and the Germans in Russia, but would soon team up with the Americans and British.

Meanwhile, Washington and London moved quickly to send in spies—this time, professionals.

12

INDOOR MINDS

F acts, like beliefs, are subtle and delicate concepts, susceptible to creative interpretation and not always to be trusted. When it came to Russia, whom could President Wilson trust? Information gatherers such as Charles Crane and Samuel Harper were important sources of intelligence. But they had been in Russia a long time. Perhaps their views had been colored by old friendships, old animosities, old points of view. The same went for French, Italian, and British diplomats in Russia. Wilson needed new eyes in Russia. So did the other Allied powers.

Washington and London decided to dispatch an experienced spy who was better known for writing books. This was William Somerset Maugham, one of the most popular authors of the time in both Europe and America. Maugham was British, and Colonel Wiseman chose him to go in. Maugham's mission would be a strange one, considering the fact that Washington would not allow the British to decipher his Russian reports.

❖

Somerset Maugham had been born in Paris, son of a lawyer who handled legal matters for the British embassy. Maugham's parents died when he was young and he ignored the family's legal tradition and became a physician. Willie stammered and had bouts of depression, but seemed quite good at setting bones and stitching wounds in the emergency room. Then he wrote his first novel, *Liza Lambeth*, a slum melodrama with characters based on patients he was treating at the charity hospital where he worked. It turned out to be a huge success. He left medicine for the literary life.

Along with other writers, Maugham volunteered as an ambulance driver for the British Red Cross in France during the war. He might have been the only one of the "literary" drivers who was a bona fide doctor. His *Of Human Bondage*, an autobiographical novel about a young man consumed by a self-destructive love for a cold-hearted waitress, was published during the war and was praised as his *pièce maîtresse*.

As Maugham got older he found less and less patience with women. He saw them as neurotic, manipulative, and sexually insatiable. He felt his wife Sylvie had trapped him into marriage. He considered her an emotional and financial burden, and needed a drink before facing her.[1] He looked for another adventure, far away from her, and found it during a trip to New York in 1917, where he ran into Colonel Wiseman, an old family friend.

Wiseman had served in the Duke of Cornwall's light infantry in the war and was gassed. After recovering, he went to New York as head of the British purchasing mission, ostensibly to buy war supplies. That was his cover as British spy chief in the States.

Wiseman hired Maugham in July 1917 on behalf of both the British and American governments. His assignment: go to Petrograd, gather intelligence, and financially assist the Mensheviks, the surviving faction of the old Social Democratic Party, in defeating German propaganda and keeping Russia in the war.

Maugham had worked as a spy for the British Secret Intelligence Service in 1915. The SIS stationed him in Geneva and assigned him to relay information to British field agents. Maugham was a good people watcher and liked taking an occasional trip as a cutout, an operative delivering messages and documents between control officers and field agents. The rest of the time he found intelligence work tedious and often useless. In Switzerland he played bridge, dined out, enjoyed mountain sunsets, and wrote long reports. Mostly he spent his time working on a series of autobiographical spy stories featuring a fictional agent named Ashenden.[2] That was his cover in Switzerland—writing. That's what he told the Swiss police he was doing when they showed up in his hotel room to have a chat. His mission lasted about a year and he returned to London.

But after spending some more time with his wife, Willie had to get away again. That's when he told Wiseman he would go to Russia. It not only appealed to his patriotism but would also give him a chance to immerse himself in that mysterious land that had produced novelists such as Tolstoy and Dostoyevsky, whom he thought were superior to European writers. He went over armed with $21,000 ($400,000 today) to cover his expenses and to help finance the Mensheviks.[3] The trip was hard on Maugham. One of his biographers said Maugham was suffering from health problems that couldn't be masked by his "rather conceited" and "very precise" manner.[4]

Maugham was forty-three years old when he arrived in Petrograd in August 1917. He sent his reports by diplomatic pouch to the British consul general in New York. The consul general handed them over to Frank Polk, State Department counselor and the man in charge of coordinating non-military intelligence for the government. Polk in turn passed the reports to Lansing and Wilson. Continuing Wilson's practice of not trusting any of the belligerents in the war, the president had issued Maugham a special private cipher that could be read only by the White House. Maugham signed his reports "S" (for his code name, Somerville).

Maugham himself might have had something to do with this arrangement to shut out the British from his reports. One of his homosexual lovers, an American, had been arrested in London earlier, and perhaps he was bitter about that.[5] At any rate, his orders were to start an intelligence and propaganda service in Russia for America and the Allies; writing for U.S. magazines was his cover. Once he went to see a play in Petrograd. He didn't understand the Russian dialogue but the play looked awfully familiar. After the first act, he realized it was his own *Jack Straw*, a popular English farce.

"He was ruthless, wise, prudent, and absolutely indifferent to the means by which he reached his ends," Maugham wrote of his secret agent Ashenden, who was based on himself and some of the spies he dealt with in Russia. "There was in the end something terrifying about him . . . He took an artist's delight in the tortuous ways of his service . . . he would not have hesitated to sacrifice his friend or his son."[6]

Maugham made contact with Kerensky through a Russian woman who'd been Willie's lover in London. She acted as interpreter when Maugham took Kerensky out to dinner every week for political discussions. In "Mr. Harrington's Washing," one of Maugham's Russian stories, Ashenden says he would not be able to do anything in Petrograd unless the provisional government survived for another three months, but that looked unlikely, since winter was coming on, food was scarce, and the Bolsheviks were up in arms.

"Plans were drawn up," Maugham wrote. "Measures were taken. Ashenden argued, persuaded, promised. He had to overcome the vacillation of one and wrestle with the fatalism of another. He had to judge who was resolute and who was self-sufficient, who was honest and who was infirm of purpose. He had to curb his impatience with the Russian verbosity . . . He had to be aware of treachery. He had to humor the vanity of fools and elude the greed of the ambitious. Time was pressing . . . Kerensky ran hither and thither like a frightened hen."[7]

Maugham's mission died in an odor of frustration. He was not able to counter German propaganda in Russia. He couldn't save the Mensheviks or the provisional government. Nor could he recruit any resistance armies to fight the Bolsheviks. Mostly he dined with people, and talked. Russians loved to talk. And they had such passionate feelings toward the salvation of poor Russia. But something always got in their way. Vodka was one of them.

"Russians take their liquor sadly," Maugham wrote. "They weep when they are drunk. They are often very drunk. The nation suffers from *Katzenjammer*."[8]

Aside from writing spy thrillers and dining out with Russian weepers, the main thing Maugham did was deliver an appeal in person from Kerensky to British Prime Minister David Lloyd George asking for more guns for the war and for the firing of Ambassador Buchanan. Lloyd George said no to both requests. Maugham then proposed that Washington spend half a million dollars a year ($9 million today) on anti-German propaganda in Russia. Again, nothing was done.

When the Bolsheviks seized power in October 1917, Maugham refused to deal with them. Lenin added Maugham to his enemies list and he fled back to London. The SIS offered him more work. He declined and checked into a sanitarium for treatment of his tuberculosis.

Thus ended the short unhappy mission of America's first real spy in Russia who wasn't connected with the State Department or military intelligence. Next to arrive was Raymond Robins, who wasn't a soldier, a diplomat, or a professional spook. He was a preacher, and a radical one at that.

❖

Raymond Robins had led an unhappy childhood in his hometown of Staten Island, New York. His father left the family, his mother went into an insane asylum, and Raymond was raised by relatives. He worked in Tennessee and Colorado coal mines in the early 1890s, then took a law degree from Columbian University (now George Washington University). He joined the Klondike gold rush in 1897 when he was twenty-four, and made a pile. Then he moved to Chicago, became a social worker, and joined the National Christian Social Evangelistic Campaign.

Although Robins described himself as a radical, he was also a firm advocate of Christianity, patriotism, and capitalism. Like President Wilson, he believed that a strong economy meant better jobs and living conditions for the masses. Robins joined Teddy Roosevelt's Progressive Party and was chairman of their 1916 convention. He was considered for the vice presidential nomination but withdrew his name.

Robins worked for the YMCA and the American Red Cross in France early in the war and was sent to Russia in July 1917, with the rank of major. Red Cross personnel serving overseas in the war wore U.S. army uniforms and used army ranks. The ranks were recognized by the American military and were used to determine benefits such as housing and access to officials.[9]

Robins was forty-five years old when he arrived in Petrograd. He conducted himself in a confident and determined manner, leading Bruce Lockhart to compare him to an Indian chief with a Bible for a tomahawk. Raymond's commanding officer was Colonel William Boyce Thompson.

When Thompson heard that a Raymond Robins had reported in, he stood up from his desk. "Major Robins? Raymond Robins, that uplifter, that Roosevelt shouter? What is he doing on this mission?"

As Robins explained it later in testimony before Congress, "You could not get two persons more absolutely alien in all past associations and habits of thought than Colonel William B. Thompson and myself. He was a stand-patter. He was the friend of those whom I had fought in American politics. He was in association with the large financial interests of the country."

Major Robins was referring to the impression by some that the American Red Cross mission to Russia was a front for Wall Street. In those days, armies did not have big medical services. The Red Cross in each country sent its own doctors, nurses, and ambulances to the front lines. They picked up wounded from the battlefields and performed surgery on them at dressing stations and in Red Cross hospitals. Then they helped them in their rehabilitation. But the American Red Cross was low on funds. They needed subsidies. Those were provided by big corporations including Chase National Bank, International Harvester, National City Bank, Liggett & Myers, and Swift & Company. Some said those Wall Street companies used the Red Cross mission as an "operational vehicle" in Russia to plot future financial influence in the country.[10]

But despite their differences, Major Robins recognized that Colonel Thompson had "that thing that is common in America among successful businessmen . . . an outdoor mind, a mind that does not take chatter, that constantly reaches out for facts, that has had to do that to be successful in business."

An example of indoor minds today would be politicians who think from "inside the Beltway" and refuse to listen to their constituents. In Revolutionary Russia, Robins said, the indoor thinkers were the sheltered, privileged Russian bourgeoisie. They were "the richest and most attractive and delightful persons you will meet anywhere, interested in education, in art, in literature, in the ballet, in the opera, in painting, in fine large expensive things, but utterly incompetent."

Raymond's list of incompetents included Kerensky and the Russian Provisional Government. They had little personal contact with workers or peasants, Robins said. Kerensky ran a "paper government" that ruled by decrees issued from the top, similar to today's presidential executive orders and regulations imposed by unelected bureaucrats. Once Robins and Thompson agreed on that, their two outdoor minds began to work together.

Major Robins started recruiting spies in the Russian army to report on the Bolsheviks. Soon he was running agents at the front lines and in barracks back in Petrograd. He reported not only to Thompson but also to Ambassador Francis.[11] In time it was said that he ran the most efficient American spy network in Russia.

The American Red Cross in Russia was subsidized almost entirely by Colonel Thompson, who was director of the Federal Reserve Bank in New York. Robins later told Congress that Thompson contributed 12 million rubles of his own money to the mission.[12] Robins went to work providing food, shelter, and medicine to sick and homeless refugees from the war. Once he delivered 400,000 cans of condensed milk for distribution to Russian children. He went on trips to Siberia, Moscow, Vologda, and Ukraine. But mostly he worked in Petrograd, which in 1917 was still the capital.

One of the most shocking things Robins learned was the extent of German influence in Russia. Their tactics included infiltration of both the palace and the revolutionary groups.

"I had part of the records of the old secret police in my possession while in Moscow," Robins testified later before Congress. "I wanted to know the situation so that I could stand on my feet with some reasonable intelligence, and this is what I found, that German agents and German money had been working in Russia for twenty years vigorously in two groups utterly unconnected in Russia, both taking orders from the German secret service in Berlin—one working with the extreme left, and the other the extreme right. One favored revolution and the other favored the autocracy."

Under this dual strategy, German agents in the palace during the war tried to influence Rasputin and the tsarina to persuade Nicholas to sign a separate peace with Berlin. At the same time, German agents spread the class-warfare line among radicals who wanted to overthrow the tsar and take the country out of the war themselves. Robins cited a general strike that had been called in Petrograd and Moscow early in the war. It was suppressed by Cossacks but not before Berlin paid the revolutionaries a million marks, he said. [13]

Robins also revealed how German agents exploited society women in Petrograd and Moscow who had fallen on hard times and needed money. How could they pay the servants? How could they buy Champagne for their dinner parties? Berlin came to the rescue and cash was exchanged for a service. It worked this way: a lady would invite some radicals into her palace for a secret meeting. They would all talk about the horrors perpetrated by the cruel tsar.

"What can I do?" the society dame would cry as she broke into crocodile tears.

The reply from the revolutionaries was simple: Give us money.

So she did. But it wasn't her money. It was supplied by Berlin, and she took her cut off the top. It was just one way that "very skillful, competent" German agents ran revolutionaries in Russia, Robins said. [14]

❖

After the Bolsheviks took over, Robins found himself in the position of having to ask the Soviet government for help in getting Red Cross supplies moved over the rails. Such movements required phone calls, orders, and passes. So Robins dusted off his tunic and his boots and had his chauffeur drive him over to the Smolny for a conference with Trotsky. Signed orders from Trotsky could start a train, stop a train, get a train loaded and unloaded, with everything protected by Bolshevik soldiers.

But as soon as Robins walked into Trotsky's office, a Bolshevik captain recognized him. Raymond's appearance was about as welcome as it had been when he first met Colonel Thompson. This captain remembered hearing

Robins make a speech in an army barracks supporting the provisional government and denouncing the Bolsheviks. And all good Reds knew that Raymond's boss, Colonel Thompson, was a lackey of Wall Street, the ultimate enemy of Bolshevism. This captain began vilifying Robins in front of Trotsky.

Finally, Robins cut him off. Raymond was a solidly built man, looking more like a footballer than a preacher. He stood his ground. Yes, he admitted, he had supported the provisional government. But that was then, this was now.

"I know a corpse when I see one and I regard the provisional government as dead," Robins said.

Trotsky looked him over. Colonel Thompson had recently left Russia because his Wall Street connections had put him in a compromising position with the Soviet government. Robins had been promoted to colonel and was now running the American Red Cross in Russia. Trotsky saw that this was a man he could work with. Robins sat down and they talked. The conversation concluded with Trotsky giving Robins the signed orders he needed.

Robins later told Lockhart that Trotsky was a "poor kind of son-of-a-bitch but the greatest Jew since Christ." [15]

Robins worked closely with Ambassador Francis and General Judson, chief of the American military mission in Russia. That meant Raymond's information was shared with both the State Department and U.S. army intelligence. It also placed Robins in the position of operating as a spy against the Bolsheviks at the same time he was one of the ambassador's unofficial negotiators with them.

But so far as working on the ground to organize a coup against Lenin, DeWitt Clinton Poole was going to be Washington's man in Russia.

13

WANTED: ONE DICTATOR

D eWitt Clinton Poole Jr., the man who would become America's spymaster in the Lenin Plot, reflected the best of his country—young, optimistic, confident, patriotic, religious. Shake a lot of hands, hide that big stick behind your back, and flash that All-American smile. Righteousness had arrived. But as least Poole was aware of those things. He knew who he was and what he represented.

Poole was born near Vancouver Barracks, Washington, where his father, Lieutenant Colonel DeWitt Clinton Poole, was stationed. Vancouver Barracks was a famous old army fort, the first in the Northwest, built in 1848 to protect settlers in the new Oregon Territory. Seventy officers who attained the rank of general were stationed there at various times, including Ulysses S. Grant, Philip H. Sheridan, George B. McClellan, and George Pickett.[1]

Colonel Poole's family had moved from Amsterdam, New York, to Madison, Wisconsin, in 1854 and opened a crockery story on the town square. Madison was the state capital. It's the second largest city in Wisconsin now, but back then it was a frontier prairie town built in the midst of swamps and forests, surrounded by several lakes, and plagued by snakes and mosquitoes. Less than 2,000 souls lived there when the Pooles arrived. But Madison grew quickly as the railroad came in and the state bureaucracy grew. In 1861, when the American Civil War began, it was the state's main recruiting center for Union soldiers.

The senior Poole was thirty-three years old when he joined up in '61. His unit was the Governor's Guard (National Guard) of the 1st Wisconsin Infantry. He was quickly promoted to lieutenant colonel and appointed commander of the new 12th Wisconsin Volunteer Infantry Regiment. He saw action in several battles during the war, including Sherman's march through Georgia. In Tennessee, Colonel Poole told his men they were not fighting to free the slaves but to put down an illegal insurrection. He recruited slaves to his regiment to fight those slaves enlisted as troops for the Confederacy. The *Chicago Times* was banned from the regiment because the newspaper had appealed for peace talks with the South.[2] At the siege of Vicksburg, Poole's men captured a steer, tried the beast for spying, executed it, and roasted it for dinner.[3]

In 1864, Poole was assigned to head up President Lincoln's army security detail, which failed to prevent his assassination. After that disaster, Poole was sent off to serve as provost marshal (head of military police) at Utica, New York, a minor peacetime job in "the city that God forgot."[4] He returned to the field in 1870 and was assigned to an infantry column protecting surveyors laying out the Northern Pacific Railroad from Minnesota to Montana. Lieutenant Colonel George Armstrong Custer also went along. In 1871, Poole married a Missouri girl, Maria Pettus, whose family had formed the famous Pettus Law Firm in St. Louis. Poole then helped round up the Sioux who slaughtered Custer and his men at the Battle of Little Big Horn in 1876.

Poole retired in 1892 and returned to Madison, where his son grew up. Poole and his wife toured the world before he died in Madison in 1917 at the age of eighty-nine.[5] His colonel's grade seems to have been a brevet rank, since he retired as a major. The family lived at 122 West Washington Avenue, a rooming house next door to the rectory of Grace Episcopal Church. It's now an office building in the central business district.[6]

Despite his birth in the West, DeWitt Jr. considered Madison his home. It was still a small town of around 20,000 souls when he started high school, but it was rapidly growing. It boasted of twelve schools, dozens of factories, two hospitals, telephone and telegraph service, a municipal gas and electric company, and seven pool halls. This was before the days of supermarkets, so you shopped at one of Madison's twenty butcher shops, sixty-eight green grocers, and eleven bakeries.

Most homes had indoor plumbing, but not everybody had water heaters, so ten establishments offered hot baths. And, Madison being the state capital, there were many visitors to the city when the legislature was in session. To service their needs, Madison offered twenty-five hotels, sixty-one cigar stores, three breweries, and eighty saloons, including one at the Board of Trade, which offered a convenient business cover for afternoon drinkers.[7]

Residents of Madison (the old-timers, at least) considered themselves to be of hearty stock. They had to be, considering the length of the winters. There were lots of Germans (Millers), Swedes and Norwegians (Olsons), and Irish (a seemingly endless list of names beginning with O'). Poole's antecedents hailed from England.

❖

In 1898, DeWitt Jr. entered the original Madison High School. During his senior year he served on the arrangement committee for the "senior informal ball" and played a servant onstage in Shakespeare's *Henry IV*. When he translated Virgil, he inserted the name of a girlfriend, Anna. He seems to have had a crush on one of his teachers, a Miss Oakley, and was kidded for spending too much time in her classroom. In his senior yearbook he's quoted as saying his goal in life was to be "tall, dark and dissipated."[8]

Poole graduated from high school in 1902 and entered the University of Wisconsin in Madison that autumn. Wisconsin was a land-grant college dedicated to engineering and agriculture. Over time, the university would add a liberal arts curriculum, a law school, and a medical school. By the time DeWitt Jr. enrolled at Wisconsin, it was one of the largest universities in America, but with less than 4,000 students. America was segregated in those days, and UW faculty and students were all white. But Wisconsin stood firmly for academic freedom.

"Whatever may be the limitations which trammel inquiry elsewhere, we believe that the great State University of Wisconsin shall ever encourage that continual and fearless sifting and winnowing by which alone the truth may be found," the regents wrote in 1894.[9]

Poole moved into the Chi Psi fraternity house at 627 Lake Street, on campus. Immediately behind the house is University Bay, a popular destination for boating in summer and ice skating and hockey in winter. Poole's freshman class cheer was:

> *Woo-ha, Woo-ha,*
> *Woo-ha, Wive!*
> *U Wisconsin,*
> *(Add anticipated year of graduation)!*

Poole was still the athletic sun-tanned young man he had been in high school. His nickname at Wisconsin was "Poodles." He took mostly language courses—English, Greek, Latin, French, and German—with a few classes in history and political science. Most of his grades were in the 90s. He scored lowest (70) in military training, a required course.[10]

Poole was a manager of the tennis team his freshman and sophomore years. A yearbook entry said that when he dressed out in whites and swung a racket, he looked like he had just come in from an afternoon of game, set, and match at the country club. DeWitt submitted some stories to the *Madison Democrat* while he was a student, and was elected president of the Press Club. His senior thesis was titled "Tai's Method as Applied to Macaulay." It was an impressive subject, considering DeWitt had not taken any math courses. He wrote in his senior yearbook that he wanted to be a missionary.[11]

DeWitt once attended a sobriety lecture at the First Methodist Church, given by evangelist Edward W. Stearns, who told of being "rescued from a life of drunkenness and brought to one of temperance and righteousness" by a passing Salvation Army band. At the close of the sermon a local lady sang a prohibition wailer called "Oh Where Is My Wandering Boy Tonight?" Then a collection was taken and DeWitt marched down the aisle to sign a pledge of abstinence.[12]

Poole's father took him on a trip to Germany in 1904. They gave their address as the American embassy in Berlin, providing young Poole with an early look at the diplomatic life he would later pursue.[13] DeWitt graduated from Wisconsin in 1906. He pursued a journalism career for a while, as an editor at an East Moline, Illinois, newspaper.

Poole went on to graduate school in the new College of Political Sciences at George Washington University, a private institution named by Congress to honor America's first president. The university had shut down during the Civil War after students left to serve in the Confederate army, but Poole doesn't seem to have had any objection to going to school with young men and women whose families had been on the "other side" in the war. Now diversity had brought in students from all over the United States, along with some from China, Serbia, Cuba, and Java. The university was supposed to be white-only, but students from Howard University in Washington, one of America's historically black schools, could take courses at GW, though they weren't officially enrolled.

The School of Political Sciences was founded by Dr. Richard D. Harlan, son of Justice John M. Harlan. The school was set up specifically as the nation's main training ground for consular service. The curriculum included courses in international law and diplomacy, duties of consuls, economics, finance, banking, tariffs and treaties, modern history, and modern languages. Poole received a Master of Diplomacy degree in 1910.[14] He entered the consular service that fall and married Rachel Simmons.[15]

Poole first worked as a researcher for the State Department's Office of Trade Agreements in Washington. He was an ambitious young man who did his work well and was rewarded a year later with his first foreign assignment, as vice consul in Berlin. After war broke out in 1914 he was transferred to Paris, and two years later was promoted to American consul there. It was a challenging and thrilling job in the thick of diplomatic and intelligence intrigue. He probably learned more in a month in wartime Paris than he would have learned in a year in peacetime.

DeWitt Clinton was thirty-one years old when he was dispatched to Russia in 1917. Lansing had ordered more consuls sent to Russia to investigate alternatives to both Kerensky and Lenin, and that's how Poole came to be a passenger on a long hot train ride from Vladivostok to Moscow on the Trans-Siberian. His traveling companion was Somerset Maugham, who might have given him a briefing on the world of espionage.

When Poole arrived in Moscow he found himself in the midst of the Bolsheviks' campaign of riots, robberies, looting, and murder that preceded their coup. He reported for duty at the consulate on September 1. His chief was Consul General Maddin Summers, who had married a Russian and steadfastly supported anybody opposed to the Bolsheviks. Summers was the one who had requested additional consuls for Russia.[16]

❖

As the new man in the office, Poole drew his share of routine consular duties. Ranking diplomats like Summers and Francis met with movers and shakers in business and government circles and they tried to keep American–Russian relations on a steady course. A consul like Poole lived in a more workaday world. He saw visitors and fielded questions. An American had found his car stolen. How could he get it back? Another countryman had lost his money when a bank failed. Who could he sue? Poole also answered mail and arranged for documents to be translated. He tended to passport and visa problems. He tried to help Americans get back home when they were down and out. He tried to get them out of jail when he could.

Three months after Poole arrived, his work got dangerous. Cossack generals in the Don region of South Russia were mobilizing to turn out the Bolsheviks, restore order, and get Russia back in the war. They called themselves the Southeastern League. On December 4, 1917, Lenin declared war on the league and sent a Bolshevik army to confront them.

The next day, General Brusilov, who had been shot and wounded by the Bolsheviks, called Summers to his hospital bed in Moscow. He said that Cossack General Mikhail Vasilyevich Alekseyev was raising a force of 50,000 cavalrymen and infantry. In case the Bolsheviks dissolved the coming constitutional assembly, Alekseyev intended to proclaim Cossack country as the seat of the Russian government and send forces to Moscow and Petrograd to overthrow the Bolsheviks. Brusilov said the British had already promised money for Alekseyev.[17]

Alekseyev's Volunteer Army and the other Cossack military forces in South Russia are often called "White" armies. There are several theories about the origin of the term. One says that the designation came from the French Revolution, when those supporting the monarchy adopted the flag of the Bourbon dynasty, gold fleurs-de-lis on a field of white, as opposed to the red banner of the revolutionaries. But the term Whites should be used with caution. Not all opponents of the Bolsheviks were monarchists. That amounts to saying socialists were all Communists, or vice versa.

Few of the former imperial army commanders opposed to the Bolsheviks wanted to restore the old régime. They'd had enough of the tsar's bungling, his wife's interference, and their German friends prowling the palace corridors. Some of the commanders in South Russia wanted a British-style constitutional monarchy with a parliament and one of the grand dukes as head of state. Russians, after all, were addicted to the idea of a tsar-like figure running the country. Other commanders favored a pure parliamentary republic like France, with no inherited offices. The Southeastern League's federal republic idea envisioned individual Russian states in the American style.[18] The league has also been called the Southeastern Federation and the Southeastern Confederation.

The main problem was that the exiled generals often had bitter clashes over strategy. They tended to be jealous of one another and didn't cooperate well. In time, they would be shown to be incapable of carrying out a major coordinated offensive against the Bolsheviks.

Nevertheless, on December 10, 1917, Secretary of State Lansing told President Wilson that the only hope for Russia lay in setting up a "military dictatorship."[19] Lansing's idea was to choose one man and make him boss of Russia on the side of America and the Allies.

But Lansing and Wilson faced problems in trying to set up a dictator in Russia. First, their man would need an army large enough to deliver a coup. The Cossacks, though, were a good start there. Cossacks were not the regular army. They were the traditional ancient Russian national army, a fast-moving strike force of mounted shock troops that could completely mobilize and move out within forty-eight hours.

Christian Cossacks wore the same uniforms as regular army cavalry, except for a different color of trouser stripe. Muslim Cossacks dressed out in traditional costumes with fur hat, leather arm bands, long body vest, flowing breeches, and a *kindjal* (dagger) on a chain. But the profession of all Cossacks was warrior. Their place was in the saddle with their sword. They refused to do manual labor. That was women's work.

The Bolsheviks considered the Cossacks to be their mortal enemies. The feeling was mutual. Hence, whatever Cossack the White House chose for a coup would probably summarily execute Lenin. Since the Western nations had not declared war on Russia, such a killing could not be considered an act of war. It would place the United States and her allies as party to an assassination of a foreign head of state. That could fit the description of international terrorism.

A second problem would be supplies. But that could be solved if the French and British lifted their blockades of Russian ports and imported war matériel that way. And, as General Scott had noted, thousands of tons of supplies, including locomotives, were sitting rusting at Vladivostok. Additional Allied supplies were stored in Archangel.

Then there was the money question. Who exactly was going to pay for all this? Britain and France supposedly had promised money to the Cossacks, but England was almost broke and Paris was busy trying to deal with mutinies in her army.

Would secret funds need to be used? If so, and the scheme backfired, it could spell real trouble for Wilson and the Democrats in the coming mid-term congressional elections, and for Lloyd George and the Liberals in the next parliamentary vote. The same went for seventy-six-year-old Georges Clemenceau, who was trying to maintain power in war-weary France.

And finally, what would the Allies do with their dictator once the Bolsheviks were thrown out and the war against Germany was won? Would he step down voluntarily after the constituent assembly decided on a new government?

This puppet ruler might decide that he liked power and he was going to stay, thank you. Then the Allies would have to raise still another army to get rid of *him*. The Allies had spent four years in the most destructive war in history. Did they want yet another?

But first things first. The new Caesar had to be chosen.

❖

"Kaledin is a man of ponderous determination who is unaffected alike by victory or defeat," Lansing told Wilson in that note proposing a dictatorship for Russia. "He is a strong character who carries through his purpose regardless of opposition. As a commander he resembles Grant. He radiates force and mystery." Lansing thought General Aleksey Maximovich Kaledin should be contacted "without delay" and should be assured that the United States was ready to prop him up.[20]

Two days later, Lansing showed Wilson the draft of a telegram he wanted to send to Walter Hines Page, U.S. ambassador to Britain. It said that the armies of Kaledin and Lavr Georgiyevich Kornilov offered the "greatest hope" for a return of stable government to Russia and a resumption of the war on the Russian fronts.

Of those two commanders, Lansing favored Kaledin. But it would be "unwise" for Washington to support Kaledin "openly," Lansing wanted to tell Page. That might complicate matters with the "Petrograd authorities [Bolsheviks]." But at the same time, Kaledin should be shown that the Allies were "most sympathetic" toward his efforts.

"Without actually recognizing his group as a de facto government, which is at present impossible since it has not taken form, this [U.S.] government cannot under the law loan money to him [Kaledin] to carry forward his movement," Lansing continued. "The only practicable course seems to be for the British and French governments to finance the Kaledine enterprise in so far as it is necessary, and for this government to loan them the money to do so."[21]

There it was. Covert American military aid would be laundered by the French and British, then passed along to the Cossacks in a plot to overthrow Lenin and the Bolsheviks. As Lansing suggested, some might say this was illegal. Still, Lansing directed Page to act "expeditiously" and confer with France and Britain on the matter.

"This has my entire approval," Wilson said.[22]

14

MONEY, GUNS, CHAOS

D eWitt Poole left Moscow on December 15, 1917, on his secret mission to hire a Cossack army to overthrow Lenin and set up an Allied dictatorship. His control officer was Maddin Summers. Poole carried two sets of identity papers, one from the American consulate and the other from the Bolsheviks. If Poole got captured by either side, and they found those conflicting papers, he could get shot. His survival would depend on a mix of personal charm, nerve, and a talent for bluffing his way through tight spots.

Poole's destination was Rostov, 665 miles south of Moscow, close to the Ukrainian border. It had been built about fifty years after St. Petersburg, making it one of Russia's "new" cities. Also called Rostov-on-Don, it was the largest city in Cossack country. Poole spent three days in a berth in a sleeping car as he traveled down to Rostov, watching out the window as the train passed scenes of battle between Bolsheviks and Cossacks. Occasionally the train got stopped, and troops boarded to search the passengers for weapons. When they reached Poole, he just looked dumb and rattled on in English.

"Oh, to hell with him," one soldier said in Russian as he walked off.[1]

In case he got questioned, Poole's cover story was that he was there to "investigate the commercial situation" in Rostov and open a consulate. With his Wilsonian three-piece suit, high white collar, and pince-nez glasses, Poole could have easily passed for a commercial attaché. Like Kalamatiano, he carried a cane, the mark of a gentleman. A cane was also useful for self-defense. Some canes came with a sword blade inside; others were hollow so an agent could hide his money and codebook inside, as Kalamatiano would do later.

With his splayed feet and his cane, Poole looked a bit like Charlie Chaplin. But he was a man who spoke with the full power of the United States government behind him.

Alekseyev and Kaledin had captured Rostov the day that Poole left Moscow. But Bolshevik forces were still around. They might counterattack and seize the city at any time, so it remained a dangerous combat zone. When Poole arrived in the city on December 18, he wasn't certain exactly who held the city—the Reds or the Cossacks.

What should he say if he got detained at a checkpoint?

He walked the corridors of his hotel eavesdropping on conversations. He didn't know much Russian at that point but was able to understand a man saying "Bronstein" and "ufa." The man spoke with contempt and almost spit the words out. Bronstein was Trotsky's real name. And "ufa" meant a Jew. He was calling Trotsky a dirty Jew.

"So that was the solution," Poole said, with relief. "We were in anti-Bolshevik country."[2]

Poole immediately set out shopping for a dictator, not hiring anybody right off, not writing any checks, not making any promises, just auditioning the talent. Summers had told him to do whatever his "judgment dictated."[3]

"In the south I was circulating and gathering information," Poole wrote in his reminiscences. "I was simply what we would now call an intelligence officer."[4]

❖

On December 21, Poole visited the headquarters of General Alekseyev and General Kaledin at Novocherkassk, the traditional capital of the Don Cossacks, a modern city laid out with flowered boulevards and serene parks in the Parisian style. Poole found three main military forces in Don country: Alekseyev's Volunteer Army, Kaledin's Cossacks, and the Southeastern League. Those forces controlled the region's valuable coal and grain supplies, which the Bolsheviks were desperate to get their hands on.

Alekseyev's army, made up of war veterans, cadets, and students, was the dominant group, Poole said in a lengthy report on his visit. Kaledin's Cossacks were under Alekseyev's ultimate command.

The Southeastern League was the smallest group, made up of other Cossack tribes and mountain men of the Caucasus. The federation maintained contact with anti-Bolshevik forces in Ukraine, Siberia, Transcaucasia, and Bessarabia.[5]

Alekseyev of the Volunteer Army was a peasant cavalryman, son of an army private and a graduate of the army staff college. He was the senior *hetman* or *ataman* (commander) of the Don Cossacks. The Cossacks had a long history dating back to the mid-16th century. The word "tsar" was the Russian form of "Caesar," meaning emperor. Indeed, Ivan was the first Russian ruler to begin building a Russian empire outside Slavic borders. He was also a reformer who went to war against Russia's old hereditary nobility and used the Cossacks to slaughter thousands of them. For that, he was called Ivan the Terrible. In 1917 the Cossacks were still basically what they had always been, frontier soldiers like Davy Crockett and Daniel Boone, except for their uniforms. Their long coats, riding boots, and fur hats were impressive.

Alekseyev had been named imperial army chief of staff after Nicholas II took over as commander in chief. Alekseyev was a brilliant tactician, a key planner of the Galician campaign that defeated Austria-Hungary. Following the emperor's abdication, Alekseyev was promoted to commander in chief of the provisional government's Russian Revolutionary Army. But he refused to tolerate the committee system and its breakdown of discipline in the ranks. He, too, was fired by Kerensky and he went back to Don country to raise his Volunteer Army.

Alekseyev assured Poole that he wished to restore order in Russia, call free and open elections, and put the country back in the war—in short, overthrow Lenin and the Bolsheviks. That's what Poole, Summers, Lansing, and Wilson wanted to hear.

❖

But Kaledin and his Cossacks seem to have been Washington's favorite. Kaledin had been a protégé of Brusilov's during the war. Kaledin commanded the Russian Eighth Army at the Battle of Lutsk during Brusilov's 1916 offensive, caught the Austro-Hungarian Fourth Army by surprise, and forced them off the field with 130,000 casualties. And that was just in the first two days. But, like Alekseyev, Kaledin refused to have anything to do with the army's committee system and its loss of officers' authority after the revolution. He blamed those breakdowns on Kerensky and the Petrograd Soviet. It was no surprise, then, that Kerensky added Kaledin to his pile of discarded commanders. Kaledin returned to the Don, became Alekseyev's lieutenant governor, and helped raise the Volunteer Army.

The third general that Poole interviewed was Lavr Kornilov, who had been appointed army commander in chief by Kerensky back during the July Days in Petrograd. But in September 1917, Kornilov tried to install himself as dictator through a coup against both the provisional government and the Petrograd Soviet. It failed, and now he was back home again.

Kornilov came from a well-off Siberian peasant family. He commanded what he called his "Wild Division" (aka the "Savage Division"), made up of Siberian and Caucasian troops, many of whom didn't speak Russian. Poole thought Kornilov a great cavalry leader, the Sheridan of the Russians. But at the moment his track record wasn't so good. One of his commanders had surrendered Kornilov's army in that failed coup against Kerensky and then went off to shoot himself.

Kerensky had Kornilov locked up after his failed putsch. But this was Russia, where stubborn jail locks could sometimes be opened by the application of gold. Kornilov's people sprung him and they rode off into the night.

"Kerensky's supreme mistake was in splitting with General Kornilov, who had gathered behind him the only force capable of handling the Bolsheviki," Charles Crane wrote later. After Kornilov's coup failed, Crane had felt there would be no help for Russia for a "long time to come," and he went home to Chicago.[6]

❖

While at Novocherkassk, Poole met Brigadier General Raymond de Candolle, an army railroad engineer from the British military mission in Rumania (now Romania). On Christmas day, 1917, a Colonel Hucher from the French military mission in Rumania arrived. Like Poole, Candolle and Hucher were in the Don to raise armies to defeat the Bolsheviks. The French were concentrating on Ukraine, Crimea, Bessarabia, and Rumania. The English were most active in the Caucasus and the Don.

On December 27, Hucher told Alekseyev that Paris had approved a credit of 100 million rubles to restore order in Russia and get the country back in the war against the Central Powers—that is, to mount a coup against the Bolsheviks.[7]

Alekseyev said he needed the money to raise forty-eight battalions of infantry and artillery (38,400 men) and twenty-one artillery batteries (eighty-four guns) by April 15, 1918. At present he had only 1,500 to 2,000 men. But they were not deserters from the "Lenin front." They were "earnest soldiers, under good discipline and without committees" who were doing well against larger Bolshevik forces in the Don, Poole said in his report.

Kornilov added two regiments of Kalmuck volunteer cavalry and six infantry battalions from the mountain tribes of the Caucasus. He already had on hand the "Kornilov regiment" of 500 to 600 men and two divisions of native troops from Circassian mountain tribes left over from his failed coup back in August.

Kornilov was trying to stimulate recruiting by raising the pay of both officers and men. Alekseyev had been paying enlisted men twenty rubles a month, while the Bolsheviks paid twenty a day. Kornilov also started buying stolen weapons from Bolshevik soldiers in the Caucasus: 1,000 rubles for a field piece, 500 for a machine gun. Kornilov was raising Alekseyev's army with "a vigor unusual in Russia," Poole said in his report.

Poole admired all these exiled generals. In his opinion, they had risen to the top of the army because they were men of great courage and ability. They were fierce fighters, not apple polishers or Bolshevik slackers. But politics began to sully the waters of this early Lenin Plot, both in the Don and in Washington.

❖

Boris Savinkov appeared in the Don and demanded to be included in Alekseyev's command structure. Savinkov had been an army commissar for Kerensky, a fellow SR, on the Russian Southwestern front in 1917 and then deputy minister of war for the provisional government.

"He threatened, by intimidation, to attack Alexiev [*sic*] before the people as a counter-revolutionary and pro-anarchist," Poole said in his report. "Savinkov's threat had some validity, however, because there had naturally rallied about General Alexiev certain elements which have been designated, for purposes of political propaganda, as counter-revolutionaries."

At the same time, another group was forming around Kornilov, causing Poole to worry that the whole movement might "miscarry for want of agreement between these different groups." The French, though, intervened to stop the squabbling and set up a leadership council. Alekseyev would be minister of war. Kornilov would continue organizing the Volunteer Army and command all forces outside the Don. Kaledin would head up the Cossacks and all defensive operations within the Don.

Alekseyev yielded to Savinkov and included Boris in the leadership council. Savinkov then demanded the inclusion of three other members—Agiev, a leader of the left wing of the Don Cossacks and president of the Don Parliament (the Krug); Vinderzgolski, a former commissar of the Eighth Army; and Mazurienko, president of the All-Russian Peasants Union of the Don. Alekseyev agreed to Savinkov's demands. Then others, both conservative and radical, were added, including SDs, SRs, Kadets (Constitutional Democrats), a banker, and a prince.

Alekseyev envisioned his group becoming the new Russian provisional government. He promised to get back in the war on the side of the Allies and call a new constituent assembly. But Savinkov left the Don after six weeks with a "profound distrust" of what he had seen there. At his trial later in Moscow, he said that Alekseyev, Kaledin, and Kornilov were surrounded by cliques "occupied chiefly with intrigues, career-hunting and scandals . . . everybody busy with his own little affairs." He said he was looked upon as an enemy because of his past terrorism against the tsarist government. At one point, a Cossack artillery officer was sent to Savinkov's tent to assassinate him. But the man didn't have the courage to draw his weapon, Savinkov said. The officer asked that the matter be dropped, which Boris agreed to do. [8]

Savinkov's presence suggests that Poole, the French, and the British might have been dealing with Bloody Boris in a coup conspiracy against Lenin long before other high-profile plotters such as Bruce Lockhart and Sidney Reilly came aboard. There's no evidence to suggest that Kalamatiano was involved with Poole's activities in the Don, but Kal was a businessman traveling throughout Russia and undoubtedly volunteered information useful to U.S. interests.

❖

In Washington, high-level dissent against the Lenin Plot came from Edward House, Wilson's executive agent (a man empowered to make confidential deals abroad for the president without congressional approval). House's father had been a mayor of Houston, Texas, a cotton planter, and a Confederate who sent out blockade runners against Union ships during the American Civil War. After his father's death, Edward House sold the plantation and became a rich banker and a political strategist for several Texas governors. One of them gave him the honorary title of "colonel." He was a liberal Democrat who had supported Wilson as reform governor of New Jersey. They became close friends, and the press called him Wilson's "silent partner." Wilson referred to him as "my other self."

At first, House opposed financing a Cossack army. "Personally I consider it dangerous for the reason that it is encouraging internal disturbances without our having any definite program in mind or any force with which to back up a program," he said in a wire to Lansing after conferring with the French, Italian, and British prime ministers in Paris.

Senator Elihu Root, on the other hand, was all for supporting the Cossacks. Wilson, who had approved that plan earlier, also had second thoughts, probably because of House's report.[9]

Poole, in his first report from the Don, urged the "countenance and support" of the American government for the Cossacks. He said the Southeastern League had extended its influence throughout the country and was the "one serious hope of saving at least a part of Russia." In a follow-up report, Poole said there was an "urgent" need for cash "at once," 200 million rubles to last until the end of April 1918.

Poole also reported that "clandestine preparations" were being made for "counter-Bolshevik outbreaks" in Moscow and other cities, confirming that a Lenin Plot was afoot in December 1917.[10]

Then House changed his mind. "On the other hand," he told Wilson, "if they [the Cossacks] are not given money or encouragement they may go to pieces."[11]

Wilson, on December 26, finally agreed to secretly advance the French and British whatever funds might be "necessary" to finance the Cossack coup against Lenin.[12] The Allied PMs in Paris then sent French and British military scouts to the Don to see what the Cossack program looked like. Those were probably the two envoys Poole met down there.

Felix Willoughby Smith, the U.S. consul at Tiflis (now Tbilisi), the capital of Georgia, had already sent three telegrams to Lansing, insisting that financial aid for the southern armies was "essential." He said this money had been requested by the provisional government.

"Anxiously awaiting instructions," Smith said.[13]

There are several estimates of what Alekseyev asked for—400 million rubles, 500 million, and so on. But official documents do not indicate how many, if any, dollars were actually disbursed. It was, after all, supposed to be a secret payoff. Whatever the amount was, the money failed to save the planned Cossack coup.

In January 1918, Kaledin and Alekseyev were forced to face opposition from Donets coal miners sympathetic to the Bolsheviks. And many of the 40,000 young Cossacks returning from the front were infected with Bolshevik defeatism. Kaledin's headquarters at Novocherkassk fell to a superior Soviet force. The Krug felt they had to negotiate for peace with the Bolsheviks, or face obliteration.[14] They also accused Kaledin of causing the Cossack defeats.

The situation was complicated by a message from Alekseyev demanding reinforcements against the Bolsheviks. The Krug refused. That was too much for Kaledin.

"The Don is unable to value its leaders and will pay dearly for its faults," he said.

Kaledin went into a private office and shot himself in the head with his pistol. But the angle of fire was wrong and the bullet was deflected off his skull. He fired again, this time into his heart. That was the shot that killed him.[15]

Lacking desperately needed reinforcements, Alekseyev's outnumbered army was defeated by the Bolsheviks the next month.[16] Kornilov died two months after that. Alekseyev led the remnants of his army back to the Don and joined up with General Anton Ivanovich Denikin. But Alekseyev later died, and that was that.

The attempt by America and the Allies to mount a coup against Lenin and install their own dictator in Russia was quit for 1917. But the Lenin Plot was still alive. It simply segued into 1918. DeWitt Poole was still leading the charge for the United States, and he would soon be joined by new players, new armies, and new infusions of cash.

PART II
VICTORY OR DEATH

15

A REMARKABLE AMERICAN

Xenophon Kalamatiano had grown up in the old Russia of tsars, palaces, and privileges. Russian folk tales were his childhood companions long before he discovered Tom Sawyer and Buffalo Bill. But now he saw life through the eyes of an American of the new century, logical, practical, and democratic in thought, though part of him was still European. He knew about the cruelties, the xenophobias, and the class wars of the ancient régimes, but to his credit they do not seem to have tainted his own soul.

Kal (as he liked to be called) volunteered to work for the U.S. State Department in Moscow "sometime after" the Bolshevik coup in 1917, DeWitt Poole wrote in 1952.[1] One of the pages in Kal's State Department employment record does give his start date as 1917, though with a question mark beside it. But Poole had told Congress in 1920 that Kal went to work for State in "early 1918."[2]

Whatever the date was, Kal's employment file says he was paid $2,400 a year.[3] That's around $39,000 in today's money, a little more than what he made when first starting out at Case thirteen years before. Russia was blockaded and the country had fallen into depression under Bolshevik rule. The value of the Red ruble plummeted to around ten American cents, causing Kalamatiano to lose customers for his Moscow trade association. He had a wife and stepson to support. He needed a dependable American job with a regular paycheck. He signed on with State.

Kalamatiano might have been referred to Poole by his friends Sam Harper or Chapin Huntington. Harper and Huntington both knew Poole, Ambassador Francis, and Consul General Maddin Summers. When Kal went to work for State, Poole was No. 2 in the Moscow consulate. But Summers was a workaholic, and on May 5, 1918, he died of a stroke at the age of forty-one. "We are all tired out here," he had complained earlier.[4] Poole moved up to take his place.

Poole's promotion made him the most important diplomatic officer in Russia below Ambassador Francis. His promotion was recommended by Francis, who called Poole a "fearless, loyal and able representative of his government."[5] Francis intended to use Poole as a special agent, a backchannel for dealing with the Soviets.

On March 3, 1918, Lenin signed the Treaty of Brest-Litovsk, making a "separate peace" with the Central Powers that alarmed the Allies. American consulates in Russia were ordered to step up their delivery of information to the State Department. But in this time of war and civil war, cable service was often unreliable. Poole told Francis that the Alexandrov cable was slow and "fearfully overloaded," with a capacity of only 30,000 words per day. Also, service was often interrupted by electrical storms and by the Soviet government, which could pull the plug on a customer any time they wanted.

Unauthorized copies of ciphered telegraph messages sent by the U.S. consulate in Moscow were secretly delivered to Soviet "code artists" in Room 205 of the Hotel Metropol, the capital's answer to the Ritz in Paris, occupied lately for more proletarian purposes than candlelit dinners.[6] Codebreakers at the Metropol tried to decipher the telegrams and report the findings to the Bolshevik government.

Sending a cable "directly" to Washington sometimes meant pursuing a path of telegraph relay stations around the world, only to see it show up at the State Department a month later, or not at all. That's why wireless became popular. Radio waves moved at the speed of light, most effectively at night. And wireless stations bypassed British censors who controlled underwater cable service to America.

Poole's operatives developed informants throughout Russia and Ukraine. Kalamatiano was his main field officer and recruiter. Kal's agents included around thirty men and women who provided political, military, agricultural, financial, and economic reports.[7] Kal condensed the reports into "bulletins" that he sent to Poole in Moscow. Poole shared them with Consul General Roger Culver Tredwell and commercial attaché Huntington, both in Petrograd, along with Ambassador Francis and French and British officials.

The establishment of Poole's networks leaves no doubt as to his importance to U.S. intelligence in Russia. In just a few months he had moved up from a simple consul to the control officer for dozens of spies. In Russia he was known as America's *chefagent* (German for chief agent, or spymaster).

❖

Poole in 1952 described Xenophon Kalamatiano as a "very remarkable American" who "rejoiced" in his exotic multisyllabic name. "Here he was, his business was in suspense [*sic*], he knew Russian perfectly, and he was an educated man and spoke excellent English," Poole remembered. "He offered his services. His services proved to be of the utmost value. He was a very hard worker."

Kalamatiano translated the Brest treaty into English for the Moscow consulate so it could be sent along to Washington. "It was a whale of a task and called for an unusual degree of intellectual training," Poole said.

Then Kal volunteered to organize that "information service" for Poole. It was "on the lines of a secret service but not for the purpose of gathering secret information," Poole later testified to Congress. "The information we needed was simply the ordinary flow of news such as one would read in the newspapers in a normal situation, but in view of the Bolshevik totalitarian methods of government and their strict control of information, it was necessary to organize this on the well-known secret service system of cut-outs—that is, only two or three men were to know and have any contact with Kalamatiano."

Each agent that Kal recruited ran cells of two or three other agents known only to one another. It continued that way on down the line.[8] Although Poole in 1952 said he personally had been an "intelligence officer" in Russia, he had refused to use that term in his congressional testimony in 1920.

Even after leaving Russia in 1919, Poole stuck to his "information service" cover. So did Kalamatiano. As far as Congress and the press were concerned, they weren't spies. They were just supplying their government with simple updates on developments in the brave new Soviet millennium. This, despite Poole's use of classic espionage terms like "secret service" and "cut-outs." And using a rule of three (or any other number) to compartmentalize cells was standard spy practice.

George Alexander Hill, a British War Office spy, confirmed Kal's espionage bona fides. He described Kal as "the head of the American secret service" in Russia.[9] And Sidney Reilly, the British spy who would emerge as one of the prime operatives in the Lenin Plot in 1918, listed Kal as one of the "Allied agents" operating in Russia.[10]

Hill, it should be noted, was using the term secret service in the British sense, as in His Majesty's Secret Service, or the Secret Intelligence Service. The British Secret Service was an international spy agency. The U.S. Secret Service was a police agency protecting the president and tracking down counterfeiters. It had no agents in Russia. British SIS was also called MI1(c), later MI6.

❖

The Brest-Litovsk treaty that Kalamatiano translated into English was a key factor in the Allies' continued efforts to get rid of Lenin and the Bolsheviks. Those peace negotiations had begun in December 1917 as Trotsky traveled to the big Russian fortress of Brest-Litovsk in Belarus, which had fallen to the Germans in 1915. News photos show the Russians getting off the train bundled up in fur coats and hats, looking small before huge German officers who came out to meet them.

The Germans were looking for a quick peace with Russia so they could concentrate on winning the war in the west. Berlin felt this separate peace would be a just payback for their financing the Bolsheviks before their coup. But Trotsky bogged the proceedings down with windy speeches predicting a coming Bolshevik world revolution. He demanded peace without Russia losing any territory or paying any reparations. The German delegates tentatively agreed. They added a few terms of their own, but otherwise just wanted to get on with it.

Trotsky, though, continued making speeches. The world press covered them. German newspapers printed them. That alarmed Berlin. The last thing Germany's political and financial establishment wanted was a revolution in their own back yard. Trotsky's faithful echo, Karl Bernardovich Radek, a small Bolshevik central committee member with a thin beard, thick glasses, and a "monkey-like" face, blew pipe smoke in the face of General Max Hoffman, who had defeated the Russians at Tannenberg.[11] That was it. The Germans declared a fourteen-day armistice and walked out. Trotsky, for once, was left speechless.

When the negotiators returned in January 1918, Trotsky continued to rail against the Germans and threaten a world revolution. Raymond Robins, who knew Trotsky personally, said Lev Davidovich was an intelligent, educated man who also carried the weakness of his gifts—acting like a prima donna.

"In hours of success he is unreasonable, heady, high-handed; and in moment of failure he is moody, gloomy, irascible, and lacking in steadfast patience and steady nerve," Robins told Congress after he left Russia. "I personally have always had a question mark over Trotsky, a question as to what he will do, a question as to where he will be found at certain times and places, because of his extreme ego, and the arrogance." Robins said he knew Trotsky would prolong the conference and continue it as long as possible because "it was the fullest expression of his ego that he had ever had. He was the center of the world, he thought . . ."[12]

American military spy Marguerite Harrison was a bit more charmed by Lev Davidovitch. When she caught up with "citizen commissar" on a Moscow street and called his name, Trotsky turned around and looked astonished at being halted in such a manner by an unknown foreign woman. But he didn't look forbidding, she remembered later.

"He was dressed in Red Army uniform and looked very smart in his well-fitting tunic, Sam Browne belt and high leather boots. He was of middle height, broad-shouldered, slightly inclined to stoutness at the waistline but erect and military in his bearing. A mass of curly chestnut hair protruded from under his cap. He had gray-green eyes, a prominent chin brought into short relief by a small goatee, and a close-clipped mustache. The lines of his mouth were thin and hard and rather cynical, but as he looked at me they relaxed into a whimsical smile and suddenly I realized that this grim-visaged man could be very charming."

They chatted in French, and Trotsky asked about conditions in America and her impressions of Soviet Russia. Then Trotsky had to go. He kissed Marguerite's hand the way a gentleman of the old régime would have done, gave her a military salute, and turned on his heels to march briskly away. *"Au revoir,"* he said.[13]

The Germans figured that Trotsky was stalling for time until the Allies came to Russia's rescue. But the Western powers did not appreciate the Bolsheviks surrendering the Russian fronts. Even more appalling was how the Bolsheviks had forcefully dissolved the Russian constituent assembly in January 1918.

❖

In countrywide voting for the constituent assembly, the Russian and Ukrainian SRs together got 17,134,161 votes. The Bolsheviks drew 9,844,637. That was a bad start for Lenin. It got worse for him on New Year's Day, four days before the assembly was to meet. Lenin spoke to a mass meeting at the

Mikhailovsky riding school in Petrograd, then walked out to his car. With him were his sister, Maria, and Fritz Platten, a Swiss socialist who had come to Russia with Lenin from exile in Switzerland. They got in the car. As it pulled off, an assassin walked up and fired into the back seat.

Platten, a big man, shoved Lenin down on the seat and shielded him with his own body. They drove away fast. Platten was hit in an arm. But it wasn't a serious wound. The attack foreshadowed the shooting of Lenin later in the year. He had previously refused bodyguards, but after this attack he gave in to his advisers and traveled with a detail of hand-picked gunmen. Then, after a while, he went back to his old ways of refusing close protection.

When the constituent assembly met on January 5, 1918, at the Tauride Palace in Petrograd, Lenin showed up with a force of sailors armed with rifles and bayonets. They stood along the walls while the SRs were awarded 370 seats, with 175 for the Bolsheviks. Yakov (Jacob) Mikhailovich Sverdlov, chairman of the central committee of the Petrograd Soviet, read a "Declaration of the Rights of the Toiling and Exploited People" that asked for "all power to the Soviets." He was voted down, 237–136. Lenin had lost again. He walked out.[14]

The vote count wasn't a surprising result. European Russia (west of Siberia) had a population of about 120 million in 1918.[15] Around 100 million were peasant farmers, and most of them supported the Socialist Revolutionaries. The SRs stood for revolution not just against the monarchy but also against the agrarian system itself. They wanted to give the land to the peasants. The other 20 million people in the country were made up of royalty, the bourgeoisie (middle-class capitalists who employed workers) and the urban proletariat (working class). The proletariat numbered about 2 million, or one-fiftieth of the population.[16]

That meant that the Bolsheviks controlled only a small slice of Russia's demographic pie. According to a report that Kalamatiano filed, 600–700 thousand Russians belonged to the Communist Party. That meant the country was ruled by about 1 percent of the population.[17] The party's strength lay mainly among workers in two cities, Petrograd and Moscow, and among disgruntled soldiers and sailors. All of them were waiting for Lenin to fulfill his promise of free food, free coal, free rent, and free land.[18]

The main reason the Bolsheviks had not been able to effectively extend their control beyond Petrograd and Moscow was because they were tied up fighting a war against anarchists in those two cities and against SRs, Cossacks, and peasants in the countryside. So, while the Bolsheviks did hold

Petrograd and Moscow, it was basically a case of *holding on*. In Moscow, they felt safe only in the Kremlin, the Lubyanka, and the Metropol Hotel, which was heavily guarded for central committee meetings.

Lenin's defeats in the constituent assembly at the hands of the SRs were humiliating to him. He could not let them stand. Writing earlier in *Pravda*, he had called for "ruthless military suppression of opposition" and said decisive class battles should be "settled by bullets."[19] Lenin's sailors dispersed the delegates at gunpoint. Street fighting broke out in support of the assembly and several people were reported killed.[20]

More violence came the following Sunday in Moscow when the Bolsheviks organized a street demonstration of about 30,000 followers. As the marchers neared the opera theatre, two shots were fired from a hotel. Panic broke out and the crowd ran for cover. Apparently the shots had come from an anti-Bolshevik provocateur. But the Bolsheviks responded by using rifles and machine guns to open up on their own crowd of men, women, and children. Forty were killed and more than 200 wounded.[21] But that didn't seem to make any difference to at least one top Red commander.

"We must not stop short in our terror until we have completely exterminated all our enemies," Nikolai Vasilyevich Krylenko, the Bolshevik military chief, said the next day.[22] This might have been the true beginning of the Red Terror, in the political sense, though the Bolsheviks had been killing their various military enemies since the day after the October coup.

The constituent assembly would be Russia's last free and open election until 1991. The suppression of the assembly ended Western hopes for a democratic Russia emerging under the Soviets. It set the agenda for the next seventy-three years—wars, sometimes hot, sometimes cold, pitting democracy against totalitarianism.

❖

Before Lenin signed the Brest-Litovsk treaty, Trotsky had refused to have anything to do with it. He insisted that Russia would simply stop fighting, and he expected the Germans to do the same. Then he got up and walked out. General Hoffman responded by ordering a new offensive. German troops advanced all along the Russian fronts and seized thousands of square miles of territory. In some sectors the depleted Russian army tried to hold the line. In other areas they turned and ran.

As Germans marched on Petrograd, Lenin hurriedly moved the capital down to Moscow. Then he called a conference to ratify the Brest-Litovsk treaty over fierce opposition from some other top Bolsheviks. Russia lost Finland, Poland, Lithuania, Estonia, and Livonia. The most stunning loss was Ukraine, also known as Ukrainia and Little Russia.[23] Ukraine had signed the treaty on February 9, gone independent, and aligned with the Central Powers.

The loss of Ukraine was another major defeat for Lenin. Ukraine was considered Russia's breadbasket. The loss drastically worsened Russia's desperate search for food. At the same time, Turkey got Russia's Caucasian border provinces. The Germans also demanded reparations from Russia. In the months to come, newspaper photos would show wagon loads of gold and silver "expropriated" by the Bolsheviks for delivery to Berlin, further crippling the Soviet economy.

Trotsky wasn't present when Lenin signed the treaty. "He was sulking in Petrograd," Raymond Robins said.[24] President Wilson denounced the settlement. Germany had scored a "cheap triumph in which no brave or gallant nation can long take pride," he said. "A great people, helpless by their own act, lies for the time at their mercy."[25]

Yes, it was a shameful peace, Lenin admitted. But it had stopped the German advance, for the moment. Now Lenin had a brief *peredishka*, a breathing spell, for getting his house in order. The Allies intended to take advantage of that pause as they plotted to depose Comrade Chairman.

16

A CONFEDERATE AT COURT

The first thing the Soviets needed to do after Brest-Litovsk was raise a new Russian army to block further advances by Germans and Cossacks. The Council of People's Commissars had already created a voluntary Workers' and Peasants' Red Army on January 15, 1918, and Lenin named Trotsky commissar for war on March 13.

To Trotsky, raising a new army was "a question of life and death."[1] He reinstated the draft and modeled his new force after Western armies and the old Russian imperial army. He abolished committees and returned the discipline that had been abandoned after the Petrograd Soviet's Order No. 1 the year before.

"We need to take from the old institutions everything that was viable and valuable in them, in order to harness it to the new work," Trotsky said.[2]

No slackers were allowed in the new Red Army, no refusing to obey orders, no running away, no fraternizing with the enemy. The men had to stand and fight, or get shot by Trotsky's battle police. He recruited former imperial army officers. Each one was hired as a *spets* (special adviser). Some signed up voluntarily because they wanted to continue their military careers. Others went along after their families were threatened.

On March 8, the Bolsheviks' Seventh Congress bowed to Lenin's wish and changed the name of the party. It now carried the more "scientifically correct" name of Communist Party. That paid homage to the Paris Commune of the Franco-Prussian War. "The Internationale" became Soviet Russia's national anthem, originally written in French by Eugène Pottier, a member of the defeated Paris Commune.

Communists adopted the color red: red star, Red Russia, Red rubles, Red Guards, Red Army, Red Terror, and Lenin as "tsar of the Reds." Bolshevik use of the red flag as a symbol of revolution, insurrection, and martyrs' blood dated back to the raising of a red banner over the Paris Commune. But John Turnbull's painting, *The Death of General Warren at the Battle of Bunker Hill, June 17, 1775*, shows an earlier revolutionary red flag for the American army. And the Confederate States of America flew a red flag, 1861–1865.

The new Russia was first called the Union of Socialist Soviet Republics (USSR). Later the words Socialist and Soviet were transposed to the present form. Most people used the abbreviated form, Soviet Russia.

❖

Russia's losses at Brest-Litovsk confirmed what President Wilson feared would happen: Europe was getting chopped up by the belligerents, and the fighting wasn't even over. Borders were moved, nationalities shifted around like cattle. People in one country suddenly found themselves belonging to another country where they didn't even speak the language.

But a more immediate problem was that Germany was still camped out on Russia's doorstep, even though they had temporarily stopped advancing. Aside from the military threat, Germany's presence challenged the Western powers that had an eye on Russia's economic resources. Post-war Russia could turn out to be one of the world's biggest markets for consumer goods. Germany wanted control of those Russian shoppers just as the Western nations did. Even if Germany lost the war in the west, look what the Fatherland could have in the east.

Meanwhile, Ambassador Francis reported that the Brest-Litovsk treaty was welcomed in Petrograd with a peace parade. "Germans arriving daily and making no effort to conceal their identity," he reported.[3] Most Russians were tired of the criminal chaos in their country. Some wanted the Germans to restore the throne. Others welcomed them because of the reputation of the German army. In war zones under German occupation, troops patrolled neighborhoods and enforced a curfew. Loud noise, public drunkenness, riots, robberies, and pogroms were not tolerated. Lights out at ten o'clock, all streets clean and quiet. Looters were shot and the crime rate disappeared.

"All the bourgeoisie in Russia is jubilant at the approach of the Germans," Lenin complained.[4]

The Western powers, though, were still at war with the Central Powers, and most of their embassies fled Petrograd at the approach of German forces. Ambassador Francis said the German army was so close they could occupy Petrograd within forty-eight hours.[5]

Francis and the other Allied ambassadors settled in Vologda, an ancient town to the east. British diplomatic and military officials remained in Petrograd. Their ambassador, George Buchanan, had been recalled; with him safe from kidnapping, there was little reason for the remaining officials to evacuate. British consular officials remaining in Petrograd could also continue to collect intelligence there for the Allies.

Despite its remote location, Vologda was about to become one of the coordinating centers for the American invasion of Russia and the plot to remove Lenin.

❖

For over 700 years Vologda had been an important highway hub. In 1918 it offered direct rail passenger service for couriers traveling to Petrograd, Archangel, and Moscow. Vologda was noted for its little kremlin (fortress) and its impressive white stone cathedral. The local soviet (not affiliated with the Bolsheviks) welcomed the ambassadors with speeches and dinners. The town counted only about 30,000 residents but now it boasted of being Russia's new diplomatic capital.

The U.S. embassy in Petrograd had been located in the fashionable Singer Company Building at 28 Nevsky Prospekt, the main business thoroughfare in the city. It was an ornate Art Nouveau edifice, seven stories tall, with blue glass windows and a red and gray granite façade adorned with bronze sculptures of Industry and Navigation.[6] And then there was the Vologda embassy—a peeling, wood-frame clubhouse with a leaky roof, drafty windows, and a porch that seemed determined to wander off from the main house.

The Brazilian chargé d'affaires and the Siamese minister moved in with Francis and his staff. Once settled in, Francis and fifty-four-year-old French Ambassador Joseph Noulens emerged as the grand old men of the diplomatic scene in newly important Vologda. As the year progressed, Francis welcomed his Moscow and Petrograd operatives into the Vologda embassy. Like President Wilson, he liked to be called "Governor." Despite his lack of experience in diplomatic intrigues, Francis was a man who valued horse sense. He saw what was going on in Russia and he stepped up to become a major figure in the Lenin Plot.

❖

When David Rowland Francis was born in Richmond, Kentucky, in 1850, Nathaniel Hawthorne had just published *The Scarlet Letter* and Mark Twain had taken his first job, as a printer's devil. Most homes back then were lit by candles or oil lamps, and heated by fireplaces and wood stoves. There were few railroads, almost no good roads. Major cities were built along rivers and on the coasts. When you went to visit somebody in a distant town, you usually took a boat.

As a boy, David wanted to be a stagecoach driver. But his horizons widened as he grew up. He graduated from Washington University in St. Louis in 1870, and six years later he and his brother opened a grain merchants' office. He served as mayor of St. Louis, governor of Missouri, and briefly as interior secretary under President Cleveland. He was president of the Louisiana Purchase Exposition (the St. Louis World's Fair) in 1904. In 1910 he was among several millionaires arrested on tax charges, and released on a $200 bail.[7]

Francis was a progressive Democrat who had supported Wilson for president. Wilson reciprocated by appointing Francis ambassador to Russia on March 9, 1916. Francis had no illusions. He knew he was no diplomat. He was a businessman. His mission was to negotiate a new trade treaty with Russia. And because America was still neutral at the time, Francis was assigned to look after 1.5 million German/Austrian prisoners of war and 270,000 civilians interned in Russia.[8]

Francis was sixty-six years old when he went to Russia, a heavy graying man with a courtly manner. He was accompanied by Philip Jordan, his "loyal colored valet." But Phil Jordan was more than that. He was a St. Louis businessman and had been on Francis's executive staff since his days in the governor's mansion. Jordan was more of a personal assistant and bodyguard. In Vologda he laid out a small golf course to give Francis some exercise. Then he surprised a few people in the embassy by quickly picking up the Russian language.

There was no way Vologda could be rationalized as an exciting diplomatic post. But Francis opened a commissary in the clubhouse for his staff and let them use the embassy's Ford, though acquiring gasoline seemed to require a major act of the local soviet. Francis and his guests played poker and bridge at night and drank bourbon while swapping stories about the good old days in Russia before the bloody Reds took over. For eighty days or so, beginning late in May, the quiet countryside was bathed in the gauzy glow of a sun that never completely set. White Nights, they were called. This twenty-four-hour sunlight heated up the far northern lands like the tropics. People slept outside. They talked all night. They swatted mosquitos. They amused themselves by getting drunk at a *traktir* (tavern) and getting in fights.

Francis was active in efforts to turn out the Bolsheviks. Sam Harper came to talk. So did Raymond Robins. DeWitt Poole and U.S. military attaché General Judson stayed in touch by telephone and telegraph. Charlie Crane was also a regular visitor. He had earlier given Francis the nickname of "a Missouri Confederate at Tsar Nicholas's Court." Francis liked that. He also liked to chew tobacco. He carried a spittoon with him from room to room and amazed the French ambassador with his ability to ring the pot from several feet away.

"He was a kind old gentleman who was susceptible to flattery and swallowed any amount of it," Bruce Lockhart wrote. Lockhart noted the ambassador's *dégagé* attitude toward being posted to a dangerous country. "He was as simple and as fearless as a child," Lockhart said.[9]

Lockhart's criticism might have been influenced by long-smoldering British resentment toward the United States. France was America's oldest ally. The French had sent 10,800 soldiers and twenty-eight warships, along with guns, ammunition, and uniforms, to help the colonial army defeat the British in the American Revolution. Schoolchildren in the nineteenth century on both sides of the Atlantic had been taught that the most contact America and Britain had experienced over the years was a series of wars they fought against one another. During this current war, the U.S. ambassador to Britain, Walter Hines Page, reported that Americans were still more unpopular in England than the French.

"Why is it?" he asked British Foreign Secretary Arthur Balfour. "Is it because of old textbooks?"[10]

That was part of it. Another part was America's ignoring British efforts to enforce naval blockades during this war. The United States sold goods to European nations other than the Central Powers, but some of those ostensibly nonaligned customers turned around and sent the supplies to enemies of the Allies. That prompted Britain to begin seizing and searching U.S. ships, in violation of international law. Some people began to wonder if America was going to have to fight Britain once again.

But to be fair to Lockhart, it should be noted that he didn't like the English, either. He was a Scot and bragged that he didn't have one drop of English blood in his veins.[11] Lockhart's comment about Francis being fearless did ring true, though. The year before, a Bolshevik lynch mob had marched on the

American embassy in Petrograd. This, out of rage over a rumor that a Russian radical was about to be executed in the United States. It was propaganda that some suspected had been put out by radical American writer John Reed, an employee of the Bolshevik government.[12]

Somebody in the government phoned Francis and warned him the mob was coming. He was advised to get out of town. Francis refused. First he sent his dinner guests home. Then he loaded his shotgun. He and Philip Jordon braced themselves in the foyer as the mob beat on the door. Finally Francis opened the door and told them the embassy was American soil and that he would shoot the first man who violated that diplomatic sanctity. Facing a pistol was one thing. A shotgun loaded with buckshot was quite another matter. On the western front, American troops called shotguns "trench dusters" for their ability to kill several people with one shot. The lynch mob withdrew.[13]

❖

Ambassador Francis sent reports, some of them very long, to Lansing in Washington, but often didn't get a reply for weeks on end. That could be blamed on the slow pace of cable service. Also, Washington was occupied at the time by events on the western front, and Russia seemed to be on the back burner.

But Francis, Poole, Kalamatiano, and other American operatives in Russia knew that Lansing and Wilson wanted Lenin and the Bolsheviks gone, and they acted accordingly. Most of the time, Washington didn't know what their people in Russia were doing. They did sit up and take notice, though, when Francis, Robins, and Judson proposed giving de facto recognition to the Bolsheviks. Robins figured that would help the United States gain control over Russian raw materials. That control could also influence Russian economic development and open the country to American trade.[14]

"Conferences are now being held with Bolshevik authorities who have expressed willingness to deal on this basis with the United States and desire American assistance and cooperation in railway reorganization," Robins said in a message sent through Francis to Red Cross Colonel Thompson back in the States. "Commercial attaché at embassy [Huntington] is conducting negotiations and ambassador [Francis] will strongly urge action by government."

Robins asked that Huntington be given funds immediately to make contracts with the Soviets to "assure [American] control of Russia's surplus products most needed by Germany."[15]

Huntington controlled a lot of U.S. funds in Russia. During 1917–1918, he spent more than $47 million ($747 million today), mostly to buy oil, flax, and textiles to keep them out of the hands of the Germans. But also included was $2.46 million ($40.8 million) paid to the American Red Cross, which indicates that the organization was not entirely dependent on Wall Street for support.[16]

This commercial activity by Huntington allowed him to gather intelligence from brokers and traders for relay to Poole and Francis.

Though it wasn't mentioned in Robins's note, establishing ties with the new Soviet government might also persuade the Reds to get back in the war against Germany. But Washington, Paris, Rome, and London turned down the idea. Both Lenin's government and the Central Powers continued to be the enemy. The Western nations, though, didn't mind giving Lenin the impression that they were dealing with the Soviet government as the de facto government in Russia, at least unofficially, through back channels. That would work to the advantage of the Lenin plotters.

17

HEADHUNTERS AND MOLES

The main American operatives in Russia working on the 1918 Lenin Plot were in place—Francis, Poole, and Kalamatiano, and their Russian agents, along with Huntington, Judson, and some consuls and former YMCA officers. But that summer brought hard times for the Allied plotters, and for the Soviets, too.

Lenin's main problem was the incompetence of his government. Most factory managers in Russia before the war had been Germans. After war broke out, they left the country and the tsarist government replaced them with skilled Russian managers. But the Bolsheviks removed those managers because they were members of the bourgeoisie. In their place, Bolshevik workers were installed as managers. Many were illiterate and abusive; their only qualification was that they had been picked by the party. When equipment broke down, they didn't know how to get new parts. When a worker complained, they threatened to have him shot. And to complicate matters, everybody was paid with increasingly worthless Red rubles. Employees were accustomed to being managed by efficient managers and getting paid with real money. It was no surprise then that many workers walked off their jobs in 1918 just as they had in February the year before.[1]

Many factories got shuttered. The strikers had no money and little food beyond a daily ration of a chunk of bread or a couple of potatoes, if available. The Reds had confiscated all automobiles and trucks except those under diplomatic protection, so there were no motor taxis for the public, just horse cabs and overloaded streetcars, when the drivers weren't on strike. Sometimes the riders were terrorized by Red Guards drunk on *samogon*, moonshine vodka. In Petrograd, cholera broke out. The government responded by putting out barrels of boiled water for drinking. But people contaminated the supplies by dipping dirty cups and hands into the water.[2]

In abandoned factory districts, waste water mixed with horse manure clogged the gutters. Caustic smoke from fires coated windows with soot and left the atmosphere poisoned. People looked thin and sickly, coughing as they plodded along in dulled nothingness. They averted their eyes when someone approached, but made no attempt to walk away quickly. There was a saying: Someone in a hurry had business. Someone with business was under suspicion.

For Allied spies, their main problem was the Cheka, the Emergency All-Russian Commission for Combating Counterrevolution and Sabotage. It was created in late 1917 by Lenin to liquidate his political enemies. (The latter words of the title were changed in 1918 to Profiting and Corruption.) The name was commonly abbreviated to VCheka, or simply Cheka. But some people liked to say that *che'ka* was the sound made when a Chekist cocked his Mauser pistol.

The Cheka had two branches—political, and criminal. The criminal branch was made of former municipal police detectives, who in tsarist days had been known as *agenturi,* or *fileri.* They wore suits and handled routine police work and answered the calls that came even in time of civil war—arson, robberies, murders, kidnappings. Uniformed officers had formerly been called gendarmes, though some people used the traditional term, blue archangels, or simply, blues. The Bolsheviks changed the name of the police to "militia."

The political branch was the dreaded secret police. They tracked down enemies of the party, a category that included everybody from nosy newspaper reporters to foreign spies. Some of them were experienced holdovers from the Okhrana. Some were Germans, who had a reputation for efficiency and discipline. The old hands wore suits and were more quietly efficient than the younger recruits who strutted about in leather caps and jackets, khaki trousers, and brogans, with pistols tucked into their waistbands. Those were called headhunters.

A favorite time for a Cheka raid was in the dark just before dawn. Sometimes suspects taken in for questioning were released after their stories were checked out. Others were tortured until they confessed to whatever crimes the political branch had decided they were guilty of. (Under the Soviet legal system, the accused were considered guilty until proven innocent.) If convicted by a revolutionary tribunal, they could be executed, or sent to a labor camp, where they might survive for a few more years.

The Cheka had a license to kill. They didn't need the inconvenience of a trial. If a Chekist did not kill a subject suspected of being an enemy, then he risked execution himself. But officially, the Cheka didn't murder people. It would not be "politically accurate" to say that. The killings were listed in the office simply as "entered under outgoing."

The Soviet government claimed they had outlawed the death sentence. But that didn't bother Cheka chief Felix Edmundovich Dzerzhinsky. His organization operated as a secret government inside the paper government of speeches and decrees that entertained visiting Western radicals who pressed their ears to the ground in search of great truths from what Bolsheviks called the Bright New Russia.

❖

Dzerzhinsky came from poor Polish gentry near the Russian Polish city of Minsk (now in Belarus). His Soviet biography describes him as a sensitive child who loved nature and liked reading history and poetry. "Love is the source of all that is good, noble, strong, warm and bright," he once wrote to a sister. His family brought him up to be a devout Catholic but he began reading Marx in the sixth grade and turned to atheism. When Dzerzhinsky was eighteen years old he joined the SDs and secretly printed revolutionary pamphlets in a cathedral basement. A year later at boarding school he attacked a "reactionary" tutor. He was allowed to leave the school without criminal charge, and became a fulltime revolutionary.

Dzerzhinsky was exiled several times by the tsarist government and was finally transferred to the Butyrka prison in Moscow, where Kalamatiano would later serve time. Dzerzhinsky was released in 1917, just before the Bolshevik coup. He was forty years old when Lenin appointed him head of the Cheka in December that year. Photos show him healthy looking as a boy, but he battled tuberculosis and a heart condition all his life, and was in ill health when he took the job.

At first Dzerzhinsky ordered his Cheka officers to "never overstep the boundaries of law," and added that those arrested "should be treated with courtesy."[3] But as the Russian Civil War between the Bolsheviks and their enemies increased in violence after the October coup, Dzerzhinsky carried out Lenin's vendettas against royalty, the middle class, Cossacks, peasants, foreign spies, the clergy, bankers, and everyone else on Comrade Chairman's ever-growing enemies list. The provisional government's policy of extending amnesty to its political opponents was buried with no regrets.

Dzerzhinsky was described as a quiet man of correct manners, but without a breath of humor. Like Lenin, he had few friends. Both men were respected and feared, but not liked or trusted. Felix was particularly reviled by Bolsheviks because he was a Pole. Dzerzhinsky almost never appeared at social or political functions. He had a wife and child but his main personal interest apparently was focused on a young singer in a comic opera at the Moscow Arts Theatre.

American army spy Marguerite Harrison described Dzerzhinsky as the "Robespierre of the Russian Revolution." Felix reminded her of Maximilien Robespierre, a champion of guillotine justice during the French Terror, because she thought both men were absolutely honest and inspired by a vision of a new world order.

"Like Robespierre, he was ruthless in sweeping aside all obstacles to the realization of his ideals for humanity," she recalled.

When Harrison, posing as a news correspondent, went to interview Dzerzhinsky at the Cheka's Moscow headquarters in the Lubyanka, she was led up a narrow staircase to a small gloomy-looking room. File cabinets and bookcases reached to the ceiling along two walls. The other walls had windows that looked out on a courtyard where some of the executions were held. The room was furnished with a desk and some chairs. The only door seemed to be the one that had just closed behind her.

An ordinary looking clerk sat behind the desk. He politely told Marguerite and her translator that the director would see them in a few minutes. They sat down.

After a while, the desk phone rang. The clerk got up and went over to a bookcase. Harrison was startled to see him open a secret door hidden behind the bookcase. He told Marguerite and her translator to follow him.

He led them up a narrow passage to a dark "tiny cabinet" with one window facing an outside wall. A small blonde man sat behind the desk. At first, Harrison thought he was another clerk.

No, it was Dzerzhinsky.

The only doorway out of the room was through the secret passage. If Dzerzhinsky got cornered in there by a gunman, it would be all over unless he jumped out the window.

"There was nothing of the proletarian about the man before me," Harrison wrote later. "He was slender, slightly under the middle height, with fair hair rather thin around the temples, a small pointed beard, clean-cut aristocratic features, china-blue eyes rather wide open, a skin as soft as a child's, cheeks touched with hectic color, and long well-kept hands. The sleeves of his Russian blouse were rolled back from his thin wrists, and on them I could see, even in the dim light, the ugly scars that he bore as the souvenir of chains worn in czarist prisons."

The interview turned out to be a monologue by Dzerzhinsky, a justification of the Red Terror. He said that killing thousands during the Terror meant nothing compared to the future happiness of unborn millions.

"Dzerzhinsky did not shirk responsibility or mince matters," Harrison said.

Marguerite had heard stories that Dzerzhinsky wept as he signed death warrants. She doubted that.

"He seemed to me like a man who had a supreme contempt for life and death alike," she said. "Marxism was the *summum bonum* [ultimate goal] for all humanity—it was to be forced upon an unwilling Russia and later a reluctant world. Djerzinsky [*sic*] regarded himself as merely an instrument to that end."[4]

❖

Many political branch Chekists were hardened criminals not adverse to continuing their felonious habits of rape, robbery, and murder. At one point, most headhunters were reported to be Jews, picked because of their traditional hatred of tsarists. But in time, Jews would be purged from the organization and background checks run on new applicants to be sure they were "pure" Russian.[5] By 1922, the Cheka would have 200,000 enforcers in a division called Troops for the Internal Defense of the Republic. At the KGB's peak in the 1980s, the number hit 480,000.[6]

After the Russian Civil War, Soviet intelligence and counterintelligence officers would pride themselves on being nondescript. They wore suits and ties. They shaved. They got haircuts. They were no more tough-looking than anybody else you saw on the street. Under Dzerzhinsky, though, a menacing appearance was *de rigueur* for a headhunter. That included a heavy beard stubble. All Bolsheviks who weren't at a top level were supposed to look shoddy, DeWitt Poole later wrote.

"I suppose they had to shave occasionally. I don't know what they did after shaving—probably laid up at home for a day so that they could grow a stubble."[7]

The Cheka relied heavily on informants. That might be the waiter serving you tea in a café, the schoolteacher living next door to you, the woman driving your streetcar. Informants wore jackets, dresses, municipal uniforms, work clothes, or student attire, all looking invisibly Russian. In return for their services, their internal passports announced they were Cheka "collaborators." That allowed them to pass through checkpoints and to break up in lines. This widespread use of citizen informants would serve as the model for Hitler's Gestapo, Mussolini's OVRA, and the East German Stasi.

Xenophon Kalamatiano and other Allied operatives in Russia had to watch for such informants as they made their rounds collecting information. They had to be suspicious of everyone, including people they thought they knew. Agents got turned all the time. And double agents, today known as moles, were sent in to infiltrate the networks. That's why the cells were compartmentalized.

Kal recruited agents by using his social and business connections. He undoubtedly picked up additional prospects from the consulate. But he had to be especially cautious of volunteers. A walk-in offering information might turn out to be an agent provocateur sent by the Cheka. Another source of danger were journalists skilled at eavesdropping on conversations that were supposed to be secret. One of those listeners would soon contribute to a catastrophe for the Allied plotters.

❖

Kalamatiano's most valuable military informant seems to have been Colonel Alexander Vladimirovich Friede, head of Red Army communications in Moscow. Friede was a Latvian who was secretly anti-Communist. He made copies of incoming military traffic and sent them by courier to Kalamatiano and British agent Sidney Reilly.

On a higher level, French colleagues working with Poole and ambassador Francis included General Jean Lavergne, chief of the French military mission to Russia; Joseph-Fernand Grenard, consul general in Moscow; and Ambassador Joseph Noulens. At one point, Poole told Francis that he and Lavergne were working "along the line of action that you [the ambassador] have recommended." Poole said that Lavergne and a General Romé "were deeply impressed with the need for immediate action, counting each day lost as a threat to the process of any military operations we may eventually undertake."[8]

Consul General Joseph Grenard was a fifty-two-year-old Parisian author, photographer, diplomat, and explorer. He had graduated from the elite School of Political Sciences and the School of Oriental Languages, both in Paris, and traveled with geographer Jules-Leon Dutreuil de Rhins in 1891 in an expedition through Russian and Chinese Turkestan.

In 1899, Grenard joined the French consular service. He served as vice-consul at Siwa (Egypt) and Erzurum (Turkey) and as consul in Riga, Odessa, and Liverpool. In 1916 he worked as commercial attaché in the Eastern Mediterranean area called the Levant (mainly modern Syria). The following year he was posted to Moscow as consul general.[9] Like Lockhart, Grenard liked to play soccer.

Ambassador Joseph Noulens was one of the main plotters in the Allied conspiracy against Lenin, especially in the late 1918 phase of the operation. Unlike Wilson and Lansing, Noulens had been hostile toward the revolution of February 1917 from the very start. But he sided with Wilson and Lansing in their passionate opposition to the Bolshevik coup.

Jacques Sadoul, a member of the French military mission, described Noulens as a pompous old monarchist with an office staff that looked like fixtures at a palace reception. Paul Cambon, former French ambassador to England, was even more colorful in his assessment. He said Noulens traveled like a rajah.

"I am astonished that he does not want to make his entry into Petrograd on an elephant."[10]

Paris was particularly keen to overthrow the Soviets because French investors lost 13 billion francs when Lenin repudiated tsarist debts in February 1918.[11] The money had been invested in bonds purchased by French citizens to finance the war and maintain a Franco-Russian alliance against Germany. Now France wanted her money back. Deposing the Soviets and seizing control of the Russian economy would go a long way toward paying that debt.

Kalamatiano's closest French street associate was Martial-Marie-Henri de Verthamon. Russian historian Yuliya Mikhailovna Galkina researched his career in French Ministry of Defense and Ministry of Foreign Affairs files and found that he was born in 1871, scion of French nobility. He graduated from the École Navale in 1888 and served as a mine officer and artillery officer on a battleship in the French Mediterranean Fleet. He rose to command a destroyer group and in 1914 was transferred to the reserves in anticipation of retirement. He was reactivated two years later and sent to Greece to head up secret naval operations in that area. He was said to have an "energetic military

mind . . . firm but flexible." In 1918 he was named a Chevalier (Knight) of
the French Legion of Honor.

De Verthamon was sent to Russia in early 1918 as a saboteur to work
against both the Soviets and the Central Powers. Galkina wrote that he was a
small man, a cigar smoker whose black hair and moustache matched his black
trenchcoat and cap. He chose "Monsieur Henri" as his code name, which left
Noulens in despair.

The ambassador was also irked that de Verthamon insisted on operating
independently of the French military mission in Russia. But that was Henri's
style. He didn't trust anybody's headquarters; they would be under surveillance
by the opposition. He preferred a portable office. He could move it from his
apartment to a park or a quiet café down a side street somewhere. He sent in
his reports and stayed away from missions, embassies, and consulates.

De Verthamon was thirty-seven when he arrived in Kiev on March 22,
1918. He spoke no Russian and had to rely on the two French naval lieuten-
ants who worked with him. He was fluent in Spanish, though, and carried
a Spanish passport. He and his co-conspirators claimed they were Spanish
refugees fleeing the war. Once they got to Ukraine they set about poisoning
grain supplies the Bolsheviks had promised to Germany after Brest-Litovsk.
Henri then went to Moscow in May and used "the military tact of old France"
to recruit former tsarist officers for his spy network. He's credited with blowing
up a Soviet power plant, three railroad bridges, and some ammunition dumps
and oil wells.[12]

Monsieur Henri also worked with military attaché Pierre Laurent, who
used to be the liaison between the French mission and the provisional government's Russian Revolutionary Army and who was now spying against the
Soviets. Laurent possibly supplied de Verthamon with the explosives he used.
Poole said he later gave false passports to some French and British spies to
smuggle them out of Russia. He said they had been poisoning food supplies
in the Ukraine, so they might have included de Verthamon's team.[13]

Another French spy available to Kalamatiano was the splendidly named
Charles Adolphe Faux-Pas Bidet. Bidet joined the French navy as a boy, and
as he sailed the seven seas he learned seven languages, including Russian.
He left the navy at the age of twenty-nine and joined the Paris Prefecture
of Police in Paris in 1909. In 1914 he was assigned as a detective with the
Sûreté Nationale, the highly efficient French counterintelligence service that
had served as a model for Scotland Yard. Bidet worked the case against Mata

Hari, an exotic dancer hired to spy for the French but who was exposed as a double agent for Berlin.

Bidet also kept an eye on Trotsky in Paris before the war, when Lev Davidovitch was editor of an internationalist newspaper, *Nashe Slovo* (Our Word).[14] Trotsky later complained that Bidet watched him with a "hateful" look.

"He was distinguished from his colleagues by an unusual roughness and brutality," Trotsky wrote. "Our interviews always ended in splinters."[15]

Still, there seems to have been some other kind of relationship between the two men. To keep Trotsky from getting arrested by the tsarist secret police, Bidet deported Lev Davidovitch to the safety of Spain. Perhaps it was an act of mercy. Perhaps Bidet was trying to groom Trotsky as a future mole for the French. Whatever the motivation, it would later save Bidet's life in Moscow. Bidet was sent to Russia in 1917 as one of France's top spies after receiving the Legion of Honor.[16]

❖

Ambassador Noulens was a man as ideologically opposed to Bolshevism as Wilson, Lansing, and Poole were. Noulens and his Western partners saw quickly that Lenin's Bolshevik junta intended to maintain power through a return to tsarist terror, using the Red Guards and the Cheka to eliminate their opposition. The methods of the Cheka drove people to paranoia, or at least to developing useful street smarts. After the Soviets started stealing every automobile they could get their hands on, Western spies learned to never enter a building where a car was parked outside. That indicated Chekists were inside conducting a raid.

Meanwhile, the war continued against the Central Powers, even if Lenin had surrendered Russia. French Marshal Ferdinand Foch, supreme Allied commander, at first advocated cooperating with the Bolsheviks if they would stand up to the German army. Foch's general staff concurred. Getting into bed with the Reds that way was simply a matter of ignoring soiled sheets in the name of expediency.

Noulens, too, showed a patient wait-and-see attitude toward the Reds, at first. So did Louis de Robien, a twenty-six-year-old attaché at the French embassy in Petrograd. De Robien said that if France broke with Russia, Paris would be playing into the hands of the Germans. Then Berlin would have a clear field to make Russia their "most rewarding of colonies."[17]

❖

After Brest-Litovsk, Lansing instructed American diplomats in Russia to withhold contact with the Bolsheviks. But the consuls went ahead and tried to deal with them anyway, discreetly, for a while.

"One has to," Poole said at the time. They were the de facto government.[18]

Then Poole began to press Washington for intervention against the Soviets. But he warned that a purely military operation would fail. It had to be accompanied by economic relief, technical assistance with railroads, and probably some administrative help.

"The bulk of the Russians are generally ignorant and moved only by immediate and material considerations," Poole wrote in a report to Lansing. "The educated political leaders are [Communist] party men lacking in the Western conception of patriotism. No class has developed self reliance, and all dislike hard work." Even with the good will of the Russian people, "we can count on very little serious practical help from them." Poole further wanted to reopen the Russian fronts to keep the Germans tied down in the east.[19]

Trotsky did ask for Allied help in training his new Red Army, and General Lavergne was open to the idea. But diplomats at the Ministry of Foreign Affairs in the Quai d'Orsay, the mother church of old-line French diplomacy, didn't like the idea of helping raise an army that might turn on them. The Quai d'Orsay overruled Lavergne. The idea of Franco-Soviet cooperation turned out to be only a brief flicker of a candle.

After that, the French tried to hedge their bets. Like the Americans, they decided to keep in touch with the Soviets through back channels while at the same time conspiring with anti-Bolshevik resistance groups. Noulens was instructed to tell the Soviets that if they would resist the Germans, France would lend them both money and military supplies. The British held out the same offer. But Lenin didn't trust the Allies. He thought the war served Western capitalism.

Back and forth it went. Finally, Noulens was given authority to act on his own in Russia. He decided it was time for the Allies to invade Russia.

Noulens joined the other Allied ambassadors in Vologda, and by the end of April 1918 he was the most vocal of the envoys urging the removal of Lenin. General Lavergne and the Quai d'Orsay backed him up. Washington and London, though, were still reluctant. Nevertheless, Consul General Grenard got authorization to send out agents to contact underground anti-Soviet groups capable of conducting a coup.

So far, American, French, and British diplomats in Russia had been sharing information with one another. America and France had spies in Russia, but the British Secret Service had not contributed any high-level agents other than Somerset Maugham, who was now gone.

That changed when two important British operatives arrived in 1918. Later, the Lenin Plot would be mistakenly named for one of them.

18

THE INVASION OF RUSSIA

I t must have seemed like the end of a long and winding road for Robert Hamilton Bruce Lockhart when London recalled him from Russia the first time, in 1917. He had no inkling he would ever see that old country again.

Lockhart's odyssey had begun after he finished his college studies in Edinburgh, Berlin, and Paris, then signed on as a rubber plantation manager in Singapore, British Malaya. He tried his hand at journalism with a newspaper in Singapore but his exposé of local prostitution met with little enthusiasm. A weekly shipment of books helped him keep his sanity and "escape from the clutches of the Eastern Trinity of opium, drink and women." A case of malaria caused him to leave the country.

After recuperating, Bruce turned to government service, but not because of any loyalty to England. In the Englishman, he wrote, patriotism manifested itself in a "dumb contempt for everything that is not English." The Scot, he said, had a more practical patriotism—the "glorification and self-satisfaction" of Scotland wherever he happened to be in the world. Nevertheless, Bruce took the British foreign service exam in 1911, when he was twenty-four years old, and the Foreign Office sent him to Moscow in 1912 as vice consul.

St. Petersburg was the shining, sophisticated, Westernized "new" capital while Moscow was an exotic but primitive post, a big country town stuck in Russia's Eastern past, laid out like a poorly planned museum. Admittedly, Lockhart didn't have much diplomatic experience. But as soon as he settled into the Moscow consulate he impressed the staff with his bright amiable manner and his linguistic skills. The British consulate, he wrote later, was in a shabby side street and consisted of one room on the ground floor of the consul general's apartment. The maid answered the bell. If she wasn't there, then Bruce did it. Photos of the office show a couple of desks with electrical wires hanging from the ceiling. They had a typewriter, stacks of newspapers, a map of Russia, and a stuffed fished mounted above a bookcase.

In those days, French was the international language. Diplomats, military officers, professors, and government nabobs were fluent in it. Thus, many foreign service officers didn't bother to learn the language of the country to which they were posted. They hired translators who often turned out to be police agents. Lockhart immediately went against expectations. He rented a room with an educated Russian family and set about learning the language. He became so adept that he was appointed translator at the consulate.

Bruce loved Russia from the start. He delved into Chekov, played soccer with a factory team, and fell into a decadent lifestyle that existed next to the primitiveness of Moscow, including cocktail parties and moonlit sleigh rides with girlfriends to Gypsy clubs where iced vodka flowed like the Neva.

"Had I taken stock of myself at that time, I should have seen a young man of twenty-five, broad-shouldered and broken-nosed with a squat, stumpy figure and a ridiculous gait," Bruce wrote later. "The young man's character was a curious mixture of Lockhart caution and asceticism and Macgregor recklessness and self-indulgence . . . Such accomplishments as he had—a good memory, a facility for languages, and a capacity for sudden bursts of hard work—were largely nullified by a lazy tolerance which always sought the easiest way out of any difficulty, and by a fatal disposition to sacrifice the future for the cheap applause of the moment. In short, a still unformed and unattractive young man, whose self-consciousness at moments amounted almost to a disease."[1]

He gave up the nightlife, though, after he took leave in 1913 and went back to England to marry Jean Haslewood Turner, an Australian. Then Jean almost died giving birth. They lost their baby and both were devastated. But Bruce had his work in Russia to return to. After February 1917 the Moscow consulate was given more money. They hired more staff and moved to larger quarters. Suddenly Bruce had to conform to a more conventional life of inten-sified work and the drudgery of official receptions.

Lockhart spent the summer of 1917 running back and forth between Moscow and Petrograd on official assignments. When representatives of the British trade unions and the Labour Party showed up in Moscow, he acted as their translator and guide. During this time he met a beautiful young "Jewess" he identified as a "Madame Vermelle," and began an affair with her.[2] Then Lockhart was summoned to Petrograd for a heart-to-heart with Ambassador

Buchanan. Buchanan told him that news of his indiscretion had reached his wife in Britain, Lockhart later wrote. It was time he went home for a while. Bruce obeyed without argument.

But was there more to it than that? Did London recall Lockhart simply because he was two-timing his wife back home? Did they really care who he was sleeping with?

According to historian Richard Spence, a check of the 1917 Moscow city directory showed two physicians surnamed Vermelle (Вермель). They were Matvei Borisovich, a bacteriologist-radiologist, and his brother Samuil Borisovich, an orthopedist-physiotherapist. Matvei's office was at No. 2B Lubyanka, headquarters of the Cheka. Samuil was a Communist Party member in charge of the Moscow Scientific Center for Restorative Medicine. He had a younger wife named Alisa (or Elise) Maksimovna.[3]

If Alisa Vermelle was Lockhart's lover, he might have been pulled out of Russia because of the possibility she had ties to the Bolsheviks. That would have made her a threat to British security through her affair with the naïve young Bruce.

❖

Lockhart received a severe wigging in the Foreign Office for his activities in Moscow. Even his grandmother got on his case. But things settled down after a while, until news arrived that the Russian Provisional Government had fallen. The Bolsheviks had seized power in a coup. Lenin was going to sign a separate peace with Germany and take Russia out of the war. The Allies were stunned.

Lockhart conferred with Foreign Office officials and the British War Cabinet. Then after American Red Cross Colonel Thompson stopped in London on his way back to America, Lockhart was summoned to No. 10 Downing Street. Prime Minister Lloyd George informed Bruce that he had been chosen by King George and Alfred Milner, an ardent imperialist in the cabinet, for a special mission.

"I have just had a most surprising talk with an American Red Cross colonel named Thompson, who tells me of the Russian situation," Lloyd George was quoted as telling Lockhart. "I do not know whether he is right, but I know that our people are wrong. They have missed the situation. You are being sent as special commissioner to Russia, with power . . . I want you to find a man there named Robins, who was put in command by this man Thompson. Find out what he is doing with this Soviet government. Look it over carefully. If you think what he is doing is sound, do for Britain what he is trying to do for America. That seems, on the whole, the best lookout on this complex situation . . . Go to it."[4]

Lloyd George's attitude toward British indoor thinkers undoubtedly was influenced by Ambassador Buchanan's earlier hands-off attitude toward the Bolsheviks. In a cable Sir George sent to the Foreign Office, he had insisted that Russia was "worn out" by the war and should be left to decide, on her own, whether to "purchase peace on Germany's terms or fight on with the Allies." Buchanan argued that "for us to hold our pound of flesh and to insist on Russia fulfilling her obligations under the 1914 agreement, is to play Germany's game . . . I am not advocating any transaction with the Bolshevik Government."[5]

Yes, Russia was worn out by the war. But so were Britain, Belgium, France, and Italy. Millions had died. Millions more would die if the fighting continued. This was no time to go weak-kneed with a major German offensive threatening Russia. Buchanan had been ambassador to Russia for eight years. Maybe he had been cozy with the Romanovs for too long. But they were gone. So was Kerensky. It was a Bolshevik show now. They needed to be contacted and persuaded to stay in the war.

The British High Commissioner recalled Buchanan in January 1918. With no one named to replace Buchanan as ambassador, Lockhart was left as the top British diplomatic official in Russia. General Knox, chief of the British military mission to Russia, was also recalled. Knox was an able, patriotic, and sincere general, Robins said, but his solution to the Russian problem was a bit simplistic: kill Lenin, Trotsky, and all the other Bolsheviks.[6]

Another Russia hand who was recalled was General Judson, chief of the American military mission. He considered Trotsky to be the "vital power" in the country and had talked with him about ways of keeping Russian raw materials out of the hands of the Central Powers. He did this without Washington's permission, and was brought home.[7]

Lockhart did not return to Russia as a spy for the British Secret Intelligence Service. They were under the War Office. Bruce was Foreign Office. He was an "unofficial agent" assigned to pursue "unofficial relations" with the new Soviet government.[8] He had cipher privileges through the Moscow consulate and was supposed to be protected by diplomatic immunity. In time, that immunity would be severely tested.

❖

When Lockhart arrived in Petrograd in late January 1918 he sent Raymond Robins an invitation for dinner. Robins refused. Then Raymond acquiesced and went to see Bruce for a brief talk. Bruce convinced him of his sincerity. They had another meeting the next day, and then they met for breakfast every morning.

Robins took Lockhart over to the Smolny Institute, Bolshevik headquarters, to meet Lenin. Ilyich always had time to see Raymond. Lenin thought (incorrectly) that Robins was a friend of the Bolsheviks, and allowed him to use a private telegraph circuit for sending messages every night to Ambassador Francis. Since copies of the messages were also sent to the Metropol for deciphering, that privilege was a cheap way for Lenin to keep up with what the Allies were doing. Robins later said that Lockhart and Lenin were in absolute agreement about cooperating against the Germans at that time.

Next, Lockhart approached Trotsky, who by that time was people's commissar for foreign affairs. Trotsky was the one Lockhart really needed to see about getting Russia back into the war. At first, Lockhart was detained by the Smolny guards. Not recognizing this tall man wearing a khaki British uniform, they took Bruce to the office of the Smolny commandant, Pavel Dmitrevich Malkov. He was a thirty-year-old former sailor and veteran of the 1905 revolution and the capture of the Winter Palace in 1917. Photos show Malkov as a handsome young peasant with a pleasant open face. He was also a dedicated member of Lenin's iron battalions, and looked Lockhart over closely.

"His unconcerned attitude, military appearance, grim, energetic face, the brushed-back head of thick auburn hair indicated a man of experience, though at a glance one might have said he was only in his thirties," Malkov wrote of Lockhart. "He spoke fluent Russian with no trace of an accent."[9]

Lockhart announced he was there to see "Mister Trotsky" and had a pass issued by him. Malkov checked his story and sent him along with two guards.

Trotsky's office had a red carpet, a fine wood desk, and a trash can (apparently a luxury in Bolshevik offices). His real name was Bronstein, son of a Russified Ukrainian farmer and an educated middle-class mother. He was converted to Marxism while in school, and at first was a Menshevik. He served four and a half years in prison and exile before the 1905 revolution, and was exiled a second time in 1907. He was thirty-nine years old in 1918. Lockhart found in Trotsky a man with a quick mind and a deep voice. Bruce also saw Lev Davidovitch as a cartoonish character.

"With his broad chest, his huge forehead, surmounted by great masses of black waving hair, his strong fierce eyes, and his heavy protruding lips, he is the very incarnation of the revolutionary of the bourgeois caricatures," Lockhart wrote.

Trotsky impressed Lockhart as being sincerely angry at the Germans. If the Germans had bought Trotsky, they bought a lemon, Bruce thought. Then, perhaps with a dig at Trotsky's taste for fancy operatic uniforms, Bruce added:

"He strikes me as a man who would willingly die fighting for Russia provided there was a big enough audience to see him do it." [10]

Trotsky was bitter not just toward the Germans, but also the British. He had been in New York City for a while in 1917, editing a Russian newspaper and giving lectures on revolutionary socialism. When he was granted amnesty by the provisional government he booked passage on a liner for Russia. But before leaving New York he made some fiery speeches, including one calling for his followers to "overthrow the damned, rotten capitalistic government of this country." [11]

When the ship carrying Trotsky reached Halifax, Nova Scotia, it was delayed for a week while British authorities questioned the revolutionaries on board. They arrested Trotsky and locked him up with German POWs at Amherst Internment Camp, in an old iron foundry. Trotsky was there for a month while his wife and children stayed in a local hotel. Charles Crane was on the ship when they grabbed Lev Davidovitch. Crane said he was in the smoking lounge and heard a commotion. He looked outside. Trotsky was being hauled away kicking and shouting by British soldiers holding his arms and legs. [12]

In March of 1918, Malkov would encounter Lockhart again, on Trotsky's train. The government was fleeing to Moscow from Petrograd to get away from the German army and Trotsky had given Lockhart and his staff two carriages on the train. Malkov remembered that Bruce was accompanied by his assistant, Hicks, "a lean and lanky, unimpressive Englishman with a narrow face and iron-gray hair," and Lockhart's secretary, "a scraggy, spiteful-looking woman." [13]

Between long conversations with Trotsky, Lockhart plopped down (uninvited) in Malkov's compartment. Pavel found Bruce to be a good raconteur, spinning tales about his travels and about Russia before the revolution, but otherwise thought he was a pest.

"I listened to him readily enough, but gave only monosyllabic replies to his questions."[14]

Lockhart's relations with Trotsky began to sour after the Allies refused to back the Bolsheviks in their signing of the Brest-Litovsk treaty. Trotsky increasingly accused the British and French of plotting against the Bolsheviks, which was true. Trotsky was also fuming over the occupation of Vladivostok by two Japanese battleships and a British cruiser in January 1918. After the loss of Port Arthur in the Russo-Japanese War, Vladivostok had been Russia's main Pacific seaport. It was also the eastern terminus of the Trans-Siberian Railway, the country's only transcontinental rail line. Trotsky saw the capture of Vladivostok as a threat to the Soviet state, which also was true.

To add to Lockhart's problems, he received a telegram from his wife informing him that his efforts at cooperating with the Bolsheviks were not being welcomed by hard-liners in London.

"I was to be careful or my career would be ruined," Lockhart recalled.[15]

Despite the Bolsheviks' separate peace with Germany, Allied diplomats and military attachés did offer to help train the new Red Army. That was their official face shown to the Soviets. At the same time, Western agents continued their secret plans to recruit resistance armies and overthrow Lenin.[16]

❖

Allied efforts against Lenin and the Bolsheviks were intensified after the Germans launched their *Kaiserschlacht* (Kaiser's Battle) on the western front on March 21, 1918. Just as the Allies had feared, the Germans had shifted combat divisions off the Russian fronts after Brest-Litovsk and over to France and Belgium. Kaiser's Battle was a massive offensive intended to defeat the Allies before the American Expeditionary Force arrived in large numbers. It was followed by three more offensives, Georgette, Gneisenau, and Blücher-Yorck. Britain had to raid high schools and insane asylums to recruit reinforcements. The Germans advanced forty miles before finally being stopped by the French, who brought up large reserves.

The spring of 1918 was also the time that the United States joined France and Britain in joint combat operations in Russia. The location was the town of Murmansk, in northwest Russia, just inside the Arctic Circle. Murmansk faced Kola Bay, an inlet of the Barents Sea. The town had long cold winters but the port was relatively ice free because of the Gulf Stream. The Russian imperial government had built a dock there in 1915 so Allied ships could unload war supplies onto a single-track railroad running south to Petrograd. [17]

Murmansk was just a bleak smattering of houses hanging onto muddy banks beneath hordes of flies and mosquitoes. But the Allies wanted to fortify the town before the Germans could invade from neighboring Finland and seize the Murmansk-Petrograd railroad for an invasion of the Russian interior.

On March 6, Royal Navy Admiral Thomas W. Kemp on the British warship *HMS Glory* with four 12-inch guns dropped anchor off Murmansk and sent ashore a landing party of 200 royal marines. They were welcomed by American Red Cross majors Allen Wardwell and Thomas D. Thacher, who had been sent there by Colonel Robins. Major Wardwell had been on the scene since January 7, Major Thacher since March 4, making them the first Americans to arrive in Murmansk.

Next the *HMS Cochrane* with her ten big guns came in, on March 7. On the 19th, the French heavy cruiser *Amiral Aube* arrived with her thirty-four guns. A few British and French military personnel had been in Murmansk since the year before to keep an eye on Allied arms stored there, and some more French were stationed in Kola, not far away. [18]

It was a quiet occupation. No shots were fired, and the Murmansk soviet welcomed their new protectors. With few barracks available, the men had to bunk in railroad freight cars. At first, Lenin and Trotsky were too occupied with Brest-Litovsk to pay much attention to what was going on in Murmansk. So was the world press. But they took note when President Wilson, under French and British pressure, sent the cruiser USS *Olympia*, Admiral Dewey's flagship from the Battle of Manila in the Spanish-American war, to Murmansk.

The sleek white *Olympia* was a fast steel warship longer than a football field. She had twenty-eight officers and 400 men commanded by Captain Bion B. Bierer. The ship was equipped with machine guns, torpedoes, ten 5-inch guns, and a knife-shaped bow for ramming enemy vessels of iron or wood. [19] She arrived on May 24 from Charleston, South Carolina. Eight officers and 100 men went ashore on June 8 to join the French, Italian, and British troops already in Murmansk. [20] That was the first time American combat troops had ever invaded Russia. (Marines landed later in Vladivostok on June 29.) Some of the Italian troops in Murmansk entertained the locals by singing opera every day. They were said to be very good.

More British sailors arrived at Murmansk on June 23 to bring the total ground force to around 600. Trotsky initially telegraphed the Murmansk regional council to cooperate with the Allies in defending the port against the

Germans. In return, the French and British recognized the local soviet as the supreme local authority. But when German forces in Finland were increased to 50,000, the Supreme War Council at Versailles ordered Allied reinforcements to North Russia under the command of British Major General Frederick C. Poole. He was given a lift to Murmansk aboard the *Olympia*.

The occupation of Murmansk was the first act in the military phase of the Lenin Plot. Trotsky didn't offer any more cooperation. He sent Red Guards north, ostensibly to help defend Murmansk against the Germans, but in reality to bolster his forces there against the Allies.[21] Newspapers on June 27 carried a story that the Soviets had declared war on the Western powers. Moscow quickly denied that. But it was too late. The sound of marching boots was in the air. The invasion had begun.

American and Allied commanders addressed a mass meeting in Murmansk to pledge support for the Russian people. Captain Bierer from the *Olympia* said the Western forces intended to preserve the Murmansk region "for the great undivided Russia."

But the Murmansk Soviet wanted something in writing. So on July 6, Bierer, General Poole, and French Captain Louis Jules Petit, commander of the *Amiral Aube*, signed an agreement pledging protection, military supplies, food, and money to Murmansk. Admiral William Sowden Sims, commander of U.S. naval forces in the Atlantic, gave interim approval of the pact a few weeks later, on August 3. Ambassador Francis would be informed of it in September, just in time for the larger American invasion at Archangel.[22]

There it was, an international agreement with a Russian soviet—signed, sealed, and delivered. In the absence of anything else, the United States, France, and Britain saw this document as giving legal sanction to their invasion of Russia.

Trotsky hit the roof when he heard about it. He had posters hung in railway stations warning that "anyone who sells himself to the foreign imperialists in order to take part in revolts or in the occupation of Russian territory will be punished with death."

Western agents in Russia initially planned to simply arrest Lenin, Trotsky, and other members of the Soviet government and transport them to London on Royal Navy ships. There they would be put on trial for treason against Russia. The case would be based on evidence gathered by the provisional government's counterintelligence office.

But as new agents and new armies joined the Allied operation, the Lenin Plot quickly got complicated, and deadly.

19

FIRST SHOTS FIRED

X enophon Kalamatiano's agents traveled across Russia in the spring and summer of 1918, gathering information and reporting back to him. Their information was divided into three categories: business, political, and military. On the business side, they tried to determine which factories had closed and which were still open. Had there been strikes? Had the Soviets brought back any German managers? How were the railroads holding up?

Politically, the agents looked for expansions or losses of power by the Soviets in different areas of the country. Had there been protests against them? Any violence on either side? What about food supplies? What did local citizens think about the future of the country? How did they feel about the Germans? The SRs? The Allies?

Military intelligence was of paramount interest. Kal tried to find out what parts of the country were in the hands of the Soviets, the Germans, the Cossacks, and the SRs. Any big battles lately? What was the troop strength on each side, the tactics and weapons used? Were the soldiers competent? Motivated? How about troop movements? What condition were the forts in? Which underground armies were recruiting troops?

Kalamatiano's agents, both men and women, were briefed on what to look for and how to avoid attention. Their identification papers and travel passes had to be authentic and valid. Carrying false documents was extremely dangerous.

The agents had to act calm if they got stopped for questioning. Their cover stories had to be convincing. What are you doing around here? Visiting relatives? Who are they? Where do they live? Where are you from? What's that in your pocket? Letters? What kind of letters?

They had to be especially careful when taking photographs. A target of interest should not be photographed directly. A friend could pose for you, with your target off to the side or in the background of the picture. And most of all, never carry a gun. People got shot by the Cheka for that.

Some of Kal's agents reported to him verbally, maybe while walking down the street with him or having tea with him in a café. Others wrote their reports. After Kal delivered the information as "bulletins" to DeWitt Poole and their French and British colleagues, the reports were transmitted in code and cipher to Ambassador Francis in Vologda and then on to State Department counselor Frank Polk in Washington. Polk ran America's first non-governmental overseas spy agency.

❖

Frank Lyon Polk was a Yale and Columbia graduate and former civil service commissioner and corporate counsel to the New York City mayor. After those jobs, he rose fast to become special adviser to Secretary of State Lansing on foreign policy.[1] Ambassador Walter Page described Polk as an "intelligent gentleman."[2] Once when Lansing went on vacation, Polk sat in for him for a month and ran State. The press praised his "frankness, tact and skill" in press conferences. He was a grandson of Lieutenant General Leonidas Polk, the famous "fighting bishop" of the Confederate Army.[3]

Polk had been appointed to the counselor's job at State on September 16, 1915, when he was forty-four years old. Photos show a handsome graying man in early middle age, fashionably dressed. Lansing left the day-to-day management of State to Polk, meaning he was the No. 2 man in the department. In bureaucratic jargon, Polk "provided guidance" to offices affected by his advice to Lansing. Those offices included the Bureau of Secret Intelligence, an outfit that would prove very useful in America's war against both the Central Powers and Soviet Russia.

❖

"Self-governed nations do not fill their neighbor states with spies or set the course of intrigue to bring about some critical posture of affairs which will give them an opportunity to strike and make conquest," President Wilson had said in April 1917 when he asked Congress to declare war against Germany. "Such designs can be successfully worked out only under cover and where no one has the right to ask questions."[4]

But the Wilson administration had indeed been involved in spying. On May 14, 1915, Wilson issued an executive order authorizing the U.S. Secret Service to conduct surveillance of the German embassy in Washington and the German consulate in New York. The Secret Service sent a detail of agents over to State for the assignment. Technically that was not a wartime measure, since America was still neutral at the time.

Then on November 20 of that year, Lansing sent a memo to Wilson lamenting the lack of coordination between government agencies investigating enemy agents operating in the United States. Lansing wanted to create a "central office" to coordinate the investigations, with the State Department counselor in charge of the operation.[5] Thus was born the idea for a central intelligence agency. Secretary of the Treasury William Gibbs McAdoo thought it a grand idea. Postmaster Albert Burleson and Attorney General Thomas Gregory were opposed. With that kind of interdepartmental warfare, Lansing and Wilson gave up on the idea.

But Lansing was still determined. On April 4, 1916, he created the Bureau of Secret Intelligence.

❖

Most people would never hear of the BSI. Officially, it did not exist. It was not a regular government agency. It had no federal budget, no congressional oversight, no listing in the phone book. It operated off the grid, financed by private donations and staffed partially by dollar-a-year "cowboys" (volunteers).

Lansing pulled Leland Harrison from State's Latin American Division to run the BSI. Harrison was thirty-three years old, a heavy-set man with a quiet and pleasant manner, and very competent. Harrison, like Polk, was a native New Yorker. He had studied at Eton College, England, and graduated from Harvard. Since 1907 he had worked at embassies and legations at Peking, London, and Bogotá. Once he crossed Russia on the Trans-Siberian while traveling from Peking to London.[6] Harrison was assigned the "collection and examination of all information of a secret nature."

Lansing admitted that the BSI was an extralegal agency. But it would have access to information from the War Department, the Office of Naval Intelligence, the Secret Service, and whatever other domestic or foreign agencies that were in a mood to help out.[7] The BSI's home staff was made up heavily of Treasury agents and postal inspectors. They were among the most highly trained federal agents in America.

The Bureau of Secret Intelligence, code-named U-1, was a clearing house for intelligence reports coming in from overseas. The bureau was headquartered in the State, War, and Navy building (now the Eisenhower Executive Office Building), a block-long stone structure constructed in a French Second Empire style next door to the White House West Wing. Government salaries weren't much to write home about in those days, but working in palatial offices with tile floors, granite staircases, bronze balusters, and stained-glass windows offered at least some compensation.

Aside from analyzing reports from embassies and consulates abroad, the BSI also ran an office for the study of captured codes and ciphers. If the signals were in a known code or cipher, it was easy to crack them.

"If they were not, experts in the various countries were set to work to discover the code system used," Lansing later explained. "Sometimes months passed before a message was fully decoded, and in some cases the message could not be deciphered, or only partially deciphered."[8]

That was before the age of computers. But an experienced codebreaker could often sit down with pen and paper and decipher a message in a matter of hours. His memory banks were in his mind.

At 8 A.M. every morning a memo was put on Lansing's desk summarizing intelligence developed by the BSI and other agencies during the previous twenty-four hours. The memo included information from Russia, which Lansing sent along to Wilson. That morning update has survived through the years and is now called the President's Daily Brief.

Although Poole and Kalamatiano were not Bureau of Secret Intelligence agents directly, they did work for the State Department, and their reports went through Polk and the BSI to Lansing and Wilson. So did reports turned in by other State Department operatives and their Russian agents. That made them all important intelligence sources for the BSI.

❖

As reports of an impending American invasion swept through offices and cafés in Petrograd and Moscow in the spring of 1918, Henri de Verthamon stepped up his sabotage work and blew up bridges, Soviet airfields, and ammunition dumps. Kal continued collecting information through his Russian and Latvian agents, and all the Western spies looked for anti-Soviet forces to support the planned Allied coup. A good prospect popped up—the deadly effective Czech Legion.

Czechs and Slovaks had lived in Russia a long time. After war broke out, a Czech unit, *Družina* (Companions), was set up in the Russian army. The enlisted men were mostly Czechs, with a few Slovaks. The officers were Czechs under Russian command. The Companions fought on the Russian fronts and were known for their contribution to the last Brusilov Offensive. Their numbers were bolstered by Czech and Slovak deserters from the Austro-Hungarian army.

After the fall of the tsarist government, the provisional government expanded the Companions into two full divisions, a formidable force of around 40,000 experienced combat veterans loyal to the Allied cause. They were called the Czech Corps, the Czechoslovak Legion, or simply the Czech Legion.

Tomáš (Thomas) Garrique Masaryk, head of the new Czech National Council, went to Russia in 1917 to push for deployment of the Czech Legion to the western front in France. The sixty-seven-year-old Masaryk was son of a coachman and a maid in Moravia (now part of the Czech Republic) who had been a professor of philosophy at Prague and a member of the Reichstag in Vienna. Being an experienced politician, he offered a deal to the Allies. They could show their appreciation for the Czech Legion's service in the war by creating a new nation. It would come from the traditional Czech lands of Moravia and Bohemia, and from Slovak territory held by the Austrians. The name would be Czechoslovakia.

But before then, the Czech Legion had to get out of Russia. Once the German army entered Ukraine after Brest-Litovsk, the Czechs started moving east on the Trans-Siberian from their base in Kiev. They were bound for Vladivostok. There they were supposed to board ships for San Francisco, travel across America by rail to the East Coast, then ship out for France. The Supreme War Council at Versailles gave them official recognition as an Allied force in Russia and placed them under French command.

The Soviets permitted the evacuation because the Czechs had helped the Bolsheviks fight the Germans in Ukraine. One of the Soviet conditions of the Czech evacuation was that they partially disarm themselves. Ambassadors Francis and Noulens opposed this.[9] Trotsky as war minister tried to impose even tougher conditions. But the Czechs didn't trust the Soviets. They kept their weapons.

Trotsky suspected the Czechs were going to join Japanese and British forces in Vladivostok, despite the fact the stated purpose of that occupation was only to restore order, protect Allied subjects, and guard war supplies stored there.[10]

Trotsky's suspicions were correct. British military representatives at Versailles wanted the Czech Legion to occupy Siberia or Archangel, or advance with Japanese troops into the Volga area. Wilson was cool to that idea. Then London got another idea—assign half the Czech force to Siberia and move the others to Archangel and Murmansk.

French Premier Georges Clemenceau opposed that notion. Versailles, however, decided to go ahead and divide the legion. The result was that by the beginning of May 1918, the Czechs were strung out from Penza, south of Moscow, to Vladivostok, 3,800 miles away. Then the fireworks began.

On May 14 one of the Czech trains was sitting in the station at Chelyabinsk, an industrial town of 70,000 south of Yekaterinburg, just east of the Ural Mountains. A train carrying Hungarian prisoners being evacuated from Siberia for repatriation to the west steamed in and stopped next to the Czech train. Hungarians and Czechs didn't get along. Soldiers in both trains started shouting insults at one another. Something was thrown from the Hungarian train, a stone or a piece of metal. A Czech soldier was killed.

The Czechs emptied their train, attacked the Hungarian cars, pulled the thrower out, and lynched him. A local Soviet force intervened and arrested some Czechs as "witnesses." Other Czechs confronted the Reds and demanded the release of their comrades. Those Czechs were arrested, too. Then the rest of the Czechs, still fully armed with rifles, machine guns, and mortars, stormed the local arsenal and freed their comrades.

Eventually the matter was settled at the scene and peace was restored. But in Moscow an enraged Trotsky ordered the Chelyabinsk Soviets to kick the Czechs off their train. He wanted to disarm them and either put them to work in labor battalions or draft them into the Red Army. The Czechs were having none of that. On May 26 they started fighting the Reds for the length of the Trans-Siberian. Trotsky responded by ordering them all shot, which did not happen.

With that, the Soviets could not deny they were at war, declared or not, against the Allies. Murmansk and Vladivostok had fallen. Archangel would be next. Trotsky saw it all as conspiracies hatched by the French, Japanese, and British. Later he would add America to his enemies list, though there's no available evidence that the United States had any advance knowledge of the Czech uprising, or aided it. Russian officers assigned to the Czech Legion had a reputation for being anti-Bolshevik and they might have egged the Czechs on. The SRs could have had a hand in it. They were everywhere.

The Czech uprising was good news to Western agents in Moscow and Petrograd. It was the break they had been waiting for. With the Czech Legion they had an efficient disciplined Allied army fighting the Soviets in the interior of the country. They would be useful in supporting the planned Moscow coup.

The Allies recruited a second anti-Soviet force at about this time. It was a private army run by the infamous terrorist Boris Savinkov. He was an independent Socialist Revolutionary and a sworn enemy of tsarists, Reds, and Germans. Savinkov had worn many hats: revolutionary, patriot, provisional government commissar, deputy war minister, Parisian boulevardier, war correspondent cool under fire, best-selling novelist. He had supported the 1905 and 1917 revolutions, but not the Bolshevik coup. The Soviets had a price on his head.

He was about to become one of the key Allied plotters who advocated advancing the Lenin Plot from a simple kidnapping operation to an assassination mission. Savinkov wanted to kill Lenin, Trotsky, and as many members of the Soviet government as he could get his hands on.

20

THE SAVINKOV METHOD

B oris Viktorovich Savinkov was son of a judge in Warsaw (then in Russian Poland) who lost his job on the bench because of his liberal views. That was a key factor in turning Boris against the monarchy. He was expelled from St. Petersburg Imperial University for engaging in a student riot. In 1902, when he was twenty-three years old, he was exiled to Vologda after getting involved with Social Democrats.

Savinkov was converted to the Socialist Revolutionaries by Ekaterina Breshkovsky, who came from a rich family, looked like a peasant, and pursued decidedly anarchist views. She was an old-line revolutionary, one of the elites of the struggle. She would later be called *Babushka*, the "dear little grandmother of the revolution." When Breshkovsky first met Savinkov, she had left the Social Democrats to become one of the founders of the SRs. She believed that in tsarist Russia there was no possibility of obtaining justice under law, even for the most monstrous crimes. The only solution was assassination of government officials.[1] Savinkov agreed. He became an SR and pursued that strategy as a terrorist working against tsarism and later Communism.

Savinkov admired the style of Narodnaya Volya, Babushka's terrorist party of the seventies and eighties. That was the group that had lured Lenin's brother to his death. Their tactics fit Savinkov like an old shoulder holster. At first, Boris worked in an SR assassination squad (aka battle organization or terrorist brigade) commanded by Yevno Azef, a Belarusian and former journalist, traveling salesman, and embezzler. Later Savinkov left the party and became an independent SR.

Savinkov learned to kill with daggers and pistols. But like many Russian revolutionaries, he preferred bombs, which made a more spectacular statement than a simple shot in the dark. Boris liked to say that an SR without a bomb was not an SR.

Savinkov was an egotist. He had a romantic view of terrorism and saw himself as a Nietzschean Superman. One of his more dramatic practices was to enter a party through a window at midnight, wearing a black hat and cape, with a dagger under his belt. He also believed in signs and omens. He always wore something red or white, he believed silk underwear could ward off bullets, and he would not go outside if it was raining and the sun was shining at the same time. Some described him as a revolutionary Hamlet—insecure, fearful, and at times indecisive. But people who would never get involved in something as déclassé as revolution were fascinated by him.

Savinkov killed many people and produced "collateral" casualties such as innocent bystanders, including women and children. He liked to say that his target had a right to live, as did a chicken, but that did not prevent it from being eaten if necessary. He became known as the General of Terror, and Bloody Boris. An examination of his modus operandi offers a look at the tools in his bag as he began taking money from the Allies as part of the Lenin Plot.

❖

The assassination for which Bloody Boris was most infamous, his signature act of terror, was the killing of Vyacheslav Konstantinovich von Plehve, the tsar's minister of the interior and chief of the Special Corps of Gendarmes, the blue-uniformed government security police.[2]

Plehve supported workers' movements and even encouraged the creation of workers' organizations, though he had no intention of letting them make political demands against the government. As the SRs conducted terror against politicians and rich landowners, Plehve cracked down on revolutionaries. It was said that during an interrogation he preferred to use logic and persuasion rather than torture. Under his guidance, though, thousands of revolutionaries were exiled or imprisoned.

Plehve received so many death threats that he lived in an apartment inside police headquarters at No. 16 Fontanka in St. Petersburg, with guards stationed in the hallway. Unprotected, his life expectancy, like that of a fish out of water, could be counted in minutes.

The SRs targeted Plehve following a savage pogrom conducted in Kishinev, the capital of Bessarabia Governorate, in April 1903. Tensions were running high there after the deaths of a local boy and girl. A Kishinev newspaper published articles claiming Jews were committing "ritual murders." A front-page headline screamed: Kill the Jews! In the ensuing rampage, forty-seven Jews were murdered and ninety-two severely injured. Over 700 houses were destroyed and 2,000 families left homeless. The SRs blamed Plehve for not ordering the gendarmes to intervene; riot control was supposed to be one of their duties. There were also 5,000 soldiers in the city who were not called out.[3]

The SRs believed that the assassination of certain key individuals at a given moment could affect the course of history. They felt that individual assassinations would spark change in a more humane manner than a mass revolution where thousands would get killed. A Russian historian has estimated that between 1902 and 1911, the SRs conducted 263 acts of terror. They included the murders of two ministers, thirty-three governors, sixteen local officials, seven generals or admirals, fifteen colonels, eight lawyers, and twenty-six spies. The SRs' ranks were diversified and included workers, peasants, students, and intellectuals.[4]

❖

Savinkov's assassination technique always started with outside surveillance of the target. That tactic exploited a flaw in the police mind—the cops never watched for assassins on the street. They just couldn't believe that killers would be clever enough to disguise themselves as cab drivers or peddlers. But that's exactly what Savinkov's squad did.

Every time Plehve left his office, Savinkov's squad followed him to see where he went, what he did, and when he returned. The watchers constantly left and returned to St. Petersburg in order to avoid attracting too much daily attention. When in the capital they changed hotels regularly and got their mail at general delivery. Boris rented a local apartment and gave his occupation as a bicycle salesman.

After weeks of study, the date for the assassination was set: July 15, 1904. Early that morning Savinkov went to two railroad stations to pick up four of his men returning to the capital. The assassins were disguised in workers' clothes, except for Boris, who always wore a suit. He admired things American—clothes, cars, airplanes. Because of that, the police had given him the code name *Amerikanets*.

He had eight conspirators in his squad. Four were lookouts and bomb makers. The other four were the actual bombers. They were relaxed and optimistic that morning while they waited to strike. Savinkov drilled one bomber to be sure he was ready. Finally it was time. Savinkov sent them walking up Izmailovsky Prospect, a wide thoroughfare of pink and yellow buildings with the blue domes of Trinity Cathedral shining in the near distance. The air was still cool but the sun had burned off the morning haze and a moist warmth rose from the cobblestones. Streetcars passed, and carriages, and pedestrians. A breeze brought the aroma of coffee from a café. Boris remembered that sunlight glinted off the brass buttons of one bomber's coat.

Each bomber carried a twelve-pound load of dynamite sticks wrapped in newspaper and tied with a string. When Plehve's carriage approached, the first bomber allowed the minister to pass unhindered. The second assassin was the primary thrower. The third and fourth bombers would strike if the first attempt failed. One of Savinkov's agents had volunteered to throw himself and his bomb under the carriage. Savinkov said no. The SRs might have a death wish, but Boris did not run a suicide squad.

Savinkov was the orchestra leader. He followed his team up the sidewalk and directed the operation from a distance. Suddenly he heard a current of excitement sweep through the crowd behind him. A policeman snapped to attention. Two familiar black horses passed Savinkov, pulling Plehve's carriage. The coachman sat up front with a secret service officer riding a bicycle at a rear wheel while two more detectives followed in an automobile.

Boris gave his primary bomber a nod. The young man stepped down into the street. He had his dynamite inside a tin box loaded with pieces of scrap metal to serve as shrapnel. As Plehve's carriage drew abreast, the bomber lit the fuse and gently tossed the bomb into a window of the cab and into Plehve's lap.

"Long live freedom!" he shouted.

The bomb exploded with a white flash. Savinkov remembered what a strange sound it made—not the earth-trembling explosion of an artillery shell, but a strange, heavy thud, "as if someone had struck an iron plate with a heavy hammer."

Fragments of the carriage were blown up and down the street. Some paving stones were pulverized by the blast. The horses' traces were torn loose and the two animals ran bleeding up the street. Plehve's body was torn apart. His coachman and a detective were killed, too. The bomber was injured, along with eighteen other people.

Police came at a run, blowing their whistles. A police captain who knew Savinkov drew his pistol but didn't arrest Boris. He just ordered him to go away. Savinkov and two of his team members escaped while others in his squad were arrested in a police dragnet that pulled in over 1,000 revolutionaries.

The "Savinkov method" was a finely honed style of assassination that the General of Terror had perfected over the years. Careful planning and lengthy advance surveillance, the use of disguises and discreet living arrangements, the training, the last-minute checks, the element of surprise—all were marks of a professional, not an amateur who might stumble in, miss his target, and get killed or arrested in the process. Those elements of the Savinkov method would later be employed in the shooting of Lenin.

❖

Savinkov was arrested in Sevastopol in 1906 and sentenced to death. But with the help of accomplices he escaped by walking out of prison disguised as a guard. He escaped to Switzerland, then to Paris, his favorite sanctuary. In 1908, Yevno Azef, Savinkov's squad chief, was exposed as a police agent and fled to Germany. Boris took over the battle organization and reorganized it into smaller, faster, compartmentalized teams.[5]

Savinkov was wanted dead or alive by the Okhrana, and they sent twelve agents to find him in Paris. He gave them the slip by switching taxis and trains, ducking in and out of buildings, and taking long rides in his car so he could check for tails. He changed apartments frequently. He always rented top-floor rooms with a view of the street below and quick access to the roof. He set booby traps in his apartment in case it got raided while he was out. He later remarked that he became quite adept at fleeing over rooftops and sliding down drain pipes in the middle of the night.

Boris hung out at cafés and race tracks. He enjoyed strolling down the Champs Élysées wearing kid gloves, yellow spats, and straw boater, with cane in hand and his trademark white gardenia in his boutonnière. Chez Duval was his favorite restaurant, Closerie des Lilas his most loved bar. He met spies and revolutionaries at La Rotonde and entertained them with stories of his salad days when he was blowing away tsarist bureaucrats with the regularity of a mail train.

Savinkov published a novel, *Pale Horse*, under the pen name Ropshin. It's a literary account of his assassination of the Grand Duke Sergei. But it's also autobiographical and shows a curious change in the General of Terror's thinking. The main character, George (Savinkov), is a sociopathic playboy to whom terror and revolution are little more than amusing pastimes. George shows a morbid fascination with death, but the book suggests that killing, even for a just cause, is morally corrosive and ultimately unjustifiable.[6]

In his second novel, *What Never Happened: A Novel of the Revolution*, Boris continues to explore his disillusionment with terrorism. The main character, Bolotov (Savinkov), wakes up in his shabby room one morning and realizes that terrorism is a "cold, indifferent and hypocritical" business based on "childish arguments" expressed in words that are "false and meaningless and futile."[7] That book signaled Savinkov's turn to the right. At the same time, other writers wrote about *him*. The terrorist Dudkin in Andrei Bely's novel *Petersburg* is based on Savinkov.[8]

Savinkov was warmed by the literary spotlight in Paris. He was invited to French and Russian soirées and salons. He entertained his admiring public with stories about the life of a glamorous terrorist. He told them he was writing books to open an inner dialogue with himself. As always, ambitious young writers and aspiring revolutionaries hung onto his every word.

Then the Russian police stopped hunting Savinkov. How strange. Boris investigated and found that they no longer wished to kill him because that might turn him into a martyr. The agenturi were instructed to simply contain him, keep him quarantined in Paris. They watched him. They followed him. They wore overcoats and hats with wide brims and tall pointed crowns like spies in a William Le Queux novel. They sat in the cafés where Boris had tea. They attended his literary lectures. It certainly beat running across rooftops.

When war came in 1914, Savinkov underwent a reincarnation. He became a patriot. He saw the war as a struggle for the survival of Russia. He signed on as a combat correspondent in France for a Petrograd newspaper and acquired a reputation for staying calm in the midst of battle. In 1916 he met Alexander Dikhof-Derenthal, a Russian officer serving with the Russian Legion in France. Boris began an affair with Alexander's wife, Lioubov (Aimée), a romance that would continue for the rest of his life, despite the fact that some later felt that the Derenthals set him up for arrest.

❖

When Savinkov returned to Russia in April 1917, he was thirty-eight years old. The Allies allowed him to go back on the theory that he would drum up support for the war. And he did. Provisional government war minister

Alexander Kerensky, a fellow SR, rehabilitated Savinkov and appointed him deputy minister of war. Then he sent Boris to the Russian Southwestern front as chief commissar.[9]

Savinkov took his job to heart and began vigorously executing Bolshevik slackers and deserters. He was said to have maintained an almost 100 percent conviction rate. He also liked to put on a dress and makeup, slip across German lines, and go to a rathskeller. There he would pose as a prostitute and pick up German officers. But when they got to Savinkov's hotel room the officers discovered things were not as they had seemed. Interrogation and torture followed.

After Kerensky became prime minister he promoted Savinkov to acting war minister. Boris took an office in the Winter Palace. His entourage included a cook, valet, personal tailor, and a dozen adjutants and orderlies. He dressed in British uniforms and rode around in a chauffeured convertible. He cut himself off from old revolutionary friends and imposed press censorship while making himself available for interviews.

Savinkov left the government in August 1917. Kerensky wanted him to fire a general connected to Kornilov's putsch attempt but Boris refused. Some say Kerensky fired him. Others say he resigned.[10] Then the SRs expelled him from their party. That was fine with him. He saw nothing in them but "utter confusion, total lack of will power, absence of courage."[11]

Savinkov became an independent SR, and after the Bolshevik coup he went to South Russia for those talks with Poole and the Cossacks. He left the Don in January 1918 (hurriedly) and organized his private army, the Union for Defense of Fatherland and Freedom (*Soyuz zashchity rodiny i svobody*). He was through with meek parliaments and fumbling provisional governments. He felt Russia's salvation lay in installing himself as military dictator until a new constituent assembly could meet. After that, well, the terms of Savinkov's dictatorship would be up to further negotiations.

The Allies definitely wanted their own dictator in the big house. That was part of their war against the Soviets. Savinkov's sister and her husband had been murdered by the Bolsheviks, so he would make a passionate Allied partner. As far as Boris was concerned, the fight between himself and Lenin was a duel to the end. Victory or death.[12]

21

MURDER THEM ALL

B oris Savinkov might have received money from the United States. In May or June 1918, Xenophon Kalamatiano reportedly met with a Russian agent linked to the SRs. On June 27, Kal reported to DeWitt Poole that this man's group planned to mount an uprising two weeks later to turn out the Soviet government. That would coincide with the July revolts that Savinkov planned.[1]

Savinkov could have received payments from Washington through an American official in Europe such as Oliver T. Crosby. He was a U.S. Treasury special representative in Paris who had been assigned to pay Kaledin with U.S. funds laundered by Paris and London. Czech intelligence reportedly contacted Crosby on April 27, 1918, to inquire about the "promised funds" that Kal should have raised for them through British agent Sidney Reilly.[2] If Kalamatiano could get funds for the Czechs, he likely could have obtained cash for Savinkov.

But Boris testified at his 1924 trial in Moscow that his attacks on the Soviets were financed by French Ambassador Joseph Noulens and the Czechs.[3] No available evidence, though, indicates whether that money had originally come from Washington. Savinkov also testified that French Consul General Grenard and military attaché General Jean Lavergne, acting in the name of Ambassador Noulens, told him that an Allied invasion force of "considerable strength" was going to land at Archangel in the summer of 1918.

"It was proposed that this landing force should be supported by armed outbreaks within the country," Boris testified. He was to occupy the upper Volga as an Allied invasion force moved south from Archangel to support him. "In this manner the upper Volga was to be made the base of an advance on Moscow."[4]

The plan called for Savinkov's army to seize Yaroslavl, Rybinsk, Kostroma, and Murman. French forces would advance the short distance from Archangel to take Vologda themselves. Vologda was important because it was the largest town south of Archangel on the rail line down to Moscow. Vologda was designated the link-up point for American, French, British, and Czech forces that would then join Savinkov's army and march on the capital.

Yaroslavl was the oldest town on the Volga River, an industrial center and port 160 miles northeast of Moscow. The city had less than 100,000 residents but it was a major trading post and railroad crossing. Yaroslavl's fortifications controlled river access to Rybinsk, to the northeast. Rybinsk was the inland terminus of the Mariinsk Waterway, a link-up of rivers and canals that flowed through Petrograd to the Baltic Sea. If the Allies controlled that waterway they could ship troops and war supplies deep into the heart of the country.

Kostroma was another old port city in this Golden Ring of ancient settlements that had historic convents, monasteries, churches, and kremlins in the heartland of eastern European Russia (Old Rus'). Murman was about 200 miles south of Kostroma, a quiet merchant town east of Moscow at the confluence of the Volga and Kostroma rivers.

Those towns were important strategically because all of them except Murman could be used to control access to the Volga, the Mississippi River of central Russia. And all were connected to Moscow by trains. Russia had few good roads, and most travel was done by rail or river. Savinkov could move his soldiers and guns to Moscow from those eastern points while the Allied invasion force proceeded south from Archangel and Vologda.

Savinkov testified that he met with Grenard and Lavergne several times. His other negotiations with the French were conducted by his secretary, Alexander Derenthal. Boris said he received money from three sources. First were donations. They didn't amount to much. But the Czechs gave him 200,000 rubles. Then the French added 2.5 million rubles.[5]

Those were probably provisional government rubles, *Kerenskis*, which like the previous Romanov rubles and Duma rubles, were worth much more than Red rubles, or *Leninskis*. The Soviets were printing up to 85 million rubles' worth of paper currency a month but it wasn't backed up by gold the way it had been before. That prevented Lenin rubles from having much value on the international exchange. It was a situation that would endure for years to come.[6]

"From the very outset, our organization was in close contact with the French," Savinkov said at his trial. "They watched its growth very attentively and supported it." His French contacts "incited" war against the Soviets, he added.[7]

The French knew Savinkov would include terrorism in his fight against the Reds, he testified. They simply "presumed" Lenin would be assassinated. "I have always adhered to the standpoint that if I am carrying on a war I conduct it with all means and by all methods . . . all possible methods of struggle, including terror."[8]

At first he hesitated about taking the towns the French listed. He thought his force was too small; better to wait a while and merge it with the Czech Legion. But then he received a wire from Noulens in Vologda, through Grenard.

"It was emphatically reaffirmed that the (Archangel) landing would take place between the 5th and 10th, or 3rd and 8th, of July," Boris said. Savinkov was supposed to start his uprisings on the Volga "precisely" in those time periods.[9] He said the French had advance knowledge that left-wing Socialist Revolutionaries were planning their own Moscow uprising, and Savinkov's attacks in the Upper Volga should coincide with that, though he would not be cooperating with the Left SRs.

❖

Savinkov estimated that his army numbered around 5,000 troops, including infantry, cavalry, and artillery sections. They were seasoned combat veterans from the old imperial army and had not deserted with the Bolsheviks the year before. Yaroslavl was Savinkov's most important target. But Rybinsk was the gateway to Yaroslavl and had to be captured first.

Soviet documents say that Savinkov's Volga operations were blown after one of his agents was overheard talking about the plans while in a hospital. But historian Alexander Orlov wrote that Boris was betrayed by one of his young staff officers, the son of a colonel from imperial army days. This officer's sister had found out that their father had been arrested and sentenced to death for supplying forged IDs to former tsarist officers who wanted to travel to the Don and join the Cossacks.

Orlov's account says the sister went to see Jacob Peters, deputy chairman of the Cheka in Moscow. She promised to expose a conspiracy that was planned against the Soviets if her father's life would be spared. Peters agreed, and they rushed up to Rybinsk in a special Cheka train. There the brother surrendered to Peters. He confessed to the entire plot and a trap was set for Boris.[10]

Savinkov opened his attack on Rybinsk by attempting to take the arsenal. But Cheka agents with machine guns were waiting. They repulsed Savinkov's attack and inflicted heavy casualties. Then government troops came up to reinforce the Cheka and drove Savinkov's force out.

Savinkov moved on to Yaroslavl. It was intended to be his command center. His forces had already taken the city and now they proceeded to execute local Reds, including the chairman of the city soviet and the chief commissar of the military district. Savinkov enlisted local anti-Soviet fighters into a Volunteer National Army. He declared martial law and abolished Soviet decrees put in place after the Bolsheviks seized the city the year before. Savinkov then conducted what the Soviets called a "White reign of terror" in Yaroslavl. More than 200 Reds were killed in the city. Another 200 were put aboard a "death barge" in the Volga. After the barge was sunk, 109 were said to have survived.[11]

Red Army reinforcements rushed in. Their force was larger than Savinkov's. They surrounded Yaroslavl and shelled the city, laying many neighborhoods to ruin. Enormous fires swept through homes and commercial buildings. Historic monuments were destroyed, along with the local lyceum and its library and archives. A third of the city burned down.[12]

Savinkov's coup attempt was suppressed after fifteen days, and reprisals were swift. More than 400 anti-Communists were executed. Savinkov's attempt on Rybinsk was put down in similar fashion. His Kostroma and Murman coups never got off the ground.

Savinkov and two of his top generals escaped to Kazan, an industrial and shipbuilding city of 200,000 in southwest Russia where the Kazan River meets the Volga, 500 miles from Moscow. It was held by Czechs and SRs and was supposed to have been the rallying point for Savinkov's dispersed forces.

Savinkov was bitter over his defeats on the Volga. He said he was "deceived" by the French. He told Lockhart that the French promised two Allied divisions from Archangel and several Japanese divisions from Siberia as reinforcements.[13] But the reinforcements didn't appear and "we were left dangling in the air . . . fooled by the foreigners."[14]

In his later trial, Boris felt he had been deliberately used by the Allies. He charged that Noulens knew there was not going to be an Allied invasion at that specific time but that he wanted Savinkov to mount uprisings anyway as proof to the other Western powers that something was being done about the Soviets.

Allied support of anti-Soviet forces in Russia was ostensibly based in "very noble" motives, Savinkov said—allies coming to the aid of other allies, that sort of thing. But that was only "official twaddle which no one believed." He said it was all about economics—oil, in particular.[15] Oil ran cars, trucks, buses, and airplanes. Oil ran factories. Oil heated homes, offices, schools, hospitals. Oil ran armies. Russia would produce more than 40 million barrels of oil in 1918, making her the world's third largest producer, behind the United States and Mexico.[16] U.S. crude oil prices peaked at $3.75 a barrel ($63 today).[17] Oil, in Savinkov's opinion, was a thing "greatly desired."

Despite his bitterness over his Volga defeats, Savinkov kept up contacts with Western agents plotting a Moscow coup. Lockhart had earlier sent two wires to London reporting that he had been told by one of Savinkov's agents that Boris proposed to "murder all Bolshevik leaders on night of Allies landing ... and to form a government which will be in reality a military dictatorship."[18] As later events would show, Boris did not change his mind about those goals after Yaroslavl.

The father of the young officer who betrayed Savinkov at Rybinsk was freed by the Cheka without being told what his son and daughter had done to get him off death row. The son then committed suicide with arsenic. But he never told the Cheka where Savinkov could be found, and that allowed Boris to once again escape.[19]

There was a saying about Savinkov: Give him a puff of smoke and two seconds, and he was gone.

22

GENTLEMAN AND HUSTLER

The sky above Russia remained red as Xenophon Kalamatiano and his Allied colleagues continued their operation to turn out Lenin. Now a new figure took a prominent role in the plot—the famous (some said infamous) Sidney Reilly. He had been sent to Russia by the Secret Intelligence Service in London before Savinkov's defeats on the Volga. When he arrived in Moscow he was wearing the uniform of a British air lieutenant. He really had been commissioned in the Royal Flying Corps as a volunteer at Toronto the year before, but was not under RFC command in Russia.[1]

Although the Allies were fighting an undeclared war against the Soviets in the summer of 1918, ordered by the Allied Supreme Command and carried out by Western spies and surrogate armies such as the Czech Legion and Savinkov's underground force, the public face the Allies wore in Russia was different. The Allies claimed that they kept their embassies, consulates, and military missions open in Russia to help the Soviets repel German invaders. That is, if Lenin and Trotsky ever decided to do that. Hence, operating openly in a British uniform and carrying legitimate military credentials offered Reilly a measure of protection.

Reilly's destination on the sweltering afternoon of May 7, 1918, was a fearful one. He was on his way to the Kremlin, the ancient brick fortress in Moscow that was now the seat of the Soviet government. He was going there to demand an audience with Lenin himself. The main thing was to avoid getting arrested or shot on the way by Red Guards who didn't care who he was.

A drawing of Reilly shows him forging ahead in a brisk British military manner, with back straight, chin up, swagger stick tucked under his arm, eyes bright with determination. But he was shocked at what he saw around him. Moscow, he wrote later, was a city damned. The streets were littered with garbage. Some of the houses sat in ruins. No shops were open. His observation was backed up by American correspondent Bessie Beatty. She wrote that an "unhappy affinity" existed in Moscow between the electric light, the elevator, and the water system—they all stopped working at the same time.[2]

Men and women of the bourgeoisie—teachers, merchants, lawyers, and businessmen, well-bred, educated, refined—were sweeping the streets under armed guards. They had lost their jobs and homes under the Soviet régime and were now forced to do manual labor to get a ration card for food. Even then, they were placed at the bottom of the list for an eighth of a pound of bread a day.[3] The black market was active, though. For the right amount of money, one could buy sugar, butter, alcohol, or cocaine, all permitted by Reds on the take.

"Not far from the National Hotel, for instance, the sound of drunken singing and brawling emanated each night from the semi-legal cabaret which bore the name Underground," recalled Kremlin commandant Pavel Markov. "Wine ran in rivers, prostitutes shrieked hysterically, a sultry, thickly powdered fellow sang cabaret songs in a nasal twang. The wreckage of old Moscow, destroyed by October [1917], writhed in the agonies of death in such establishments."[4]

Food had become scarce after a drought, a breakdown in transportation under Soviet management, and an insistence on paying farmers with Red rubles. Many farmers ignored government buyers and took their products to town and sold them from wagons they parked in alleys or behind churches. But they ran the risk of getting arrested for profiteering, a capital offense, so they increasingly stayed home. The government retaliated by sending out soldiers and mobs of workmen to raid the granaries. They were met by peasants who dug trenches around their villages and set up machine guns and mortars they'd brought back from the war.[5]

Bakers in Moscow and Petrograd did occasionally get small supplies of flour and turned out bread, but only if coal or wood was available to fire their ovens. And then they had to leaven the bread with straw, sawdust, and in some cases, horse manure.[6] Lenin Loaves, they were called. Crowds dug through trash piles looking for something to eat. Horses hauling cholera corpses out to the lime pits frequently dropped dead in the street and residents chopped them up for food before the flesh could rot in the sun. An Italian correspondent counted twenty-two dead horses on one street in one day. Dogs disappeared. So did squirrels, pigeons, cats, and anything else edible. Trotsky dismissed any ideas of a famine because "we have not yet seen crowds in a queue before the undertakers' establishments."[7]

Reilly didn't see any automobiles in the streets of Moscow. That was good, he figured. The government had seized most all motor vehicles, so the appearance of a car meant the Cheka was on the prowl and it was best to duck into a doorway. He heard no sound but the bite of his heels on the pavement. Shadows startled him. He felt he had stepped into a necropolis.[8]

When Reilly reached the Kremlin it was so hot that the pigeons in Red Square were doing their begging from the shadows. He knocked on one of the gates and announced to the guards that he was an emissary from none other than British Prime Minister Lloyd George. Sidney demanded to see Lenin at once. To his surprise, he was admitted. They signed him in as "Relli."

Reilly was met by Vladimir Dmitrevich Bonch-Bruyevich, Lenin's personal secretary and close friend. Bonch-Bruyevich already knew Sidney. They had met through a mutual friend, Alexander Ivanovich Grammatikov, a Petro-grad book collector who had once been Reilly's lawyer. He also used to be a Bolshevik but was now secretly an SR.

Bonch-Bruyevich and Reilly had a talk. Just as Lloyd George had sent Lockhart to Russia because he didn't trust Ambassador Buchanan's reports, now Whitehall was dissatisfied with some of the conflicting opinions they'd received from Bruce about what to do about the Soviets. Reilly was London's new flashlight in the dark, at least as far as the British Secret Service was concerned.

"My superiors clung to the opinion that Russia might still be brought to her right mind in the matter of her obligations to the Allies," Reilly wrote later. "Agents from France and the United States were already in Moscow and Petrograd, working to that end."[9]

But Reilly specifically wanted to avoid Kalamatiano, de Verthamon, and other Western agents. He thought he could fulfill his mission best if he worked alone and developed his own agents.[10]

But Reilly couldn't get past Bonch-Bruyevich. After a brief talk, Vladimir Dmitrevich got rid of Sidney. Then shortly after 6 P.M., Lockhart answered the phone in his office. Lev Mikhailovich Karakhan, a deputy in the com-missariat of foreign affairs, was on the line. He wanted Lockhart to come see him. He had an extraordinary story to share.

When they sat down to talk, Karakhan told Lockhart about the auda-cious appearance of this fellow called Relli. Was he really a British officer on a diplomatic mission? Or an imposter?

"I was non-plussed," Lockhart recalled, "and holding it impossible that the man could have any official standing, I nearly blurted out that he must be a

Russian masquerading as an Englishman, or else a madman." (There was an old saying about mad dogs and Englishmen in the noonday sun.)

Bruce told Karakhan he would check on the matter and get back to him. Lockhart then returned to his office and called in Ernest Boyce. Boyce was technically head of the British Secret Service in Russia but would soon find that London's new man in town intended to usurp his authority. "Relli" was Sidney Reilly, Boyce said, and he really was from the SIS. That evening, Lockhart summoned Reilly.[11] When Sidney arrived, he corrected a few details of the story Bruce had heard, but otherwise confirmed it.

"The sheer audacity of the man took my breath away," Lockhart said. "Although he was years older than me, I dressed him down like a schoolmaster and threatened to have him sent home. He took his wigging humbly but calmly and was so ingenious in his excuses that in the end he made me laugh."[12]

Reilly took his reprimand patiently because Lockhart worked for a different ministry and had no authority over him. Nor could Boyce touch Reilly, since Sidney had been sent by the SIS chief himself. As far as Sidney was concerned, he was now the head of British intelligence in Russia, whether Lockhart and Boyce liked it or not. He would work with them as the spring and summer progressed, but right now he had his own operations to pursue. So long, chaps.

Who exactly *was* this audacious character? Truth be told, he wasn't an Englishman, or a full British citizen. It's not even certain what his real name was. Despite all that, or because of it, he had already acquired a reputation as one of history's bravest and most mysterious spies. He was also a hustler of the first degree.

❖

For years historians have tried to determine Sidney Reilly's true identity. At various times he stated he was born in 1874, or 1873. He might have been born in Bendzin or Pruzhany, both in Russian Poland, or in Odessa. Without a birth certificate, one can only guess.

It does appear that his birth name was Schlomo Rosenblum, ostensibly a son of Gersh Rosenblum, a wealthy oil man who used several names himself in his business dealings in Russia and Germany. His real father might have been his uncle Vladimir, or a Ukrainian landowner. The boy's mother was called Beila (Paulina). She came from a rich family in Odessa named Altman, or Berenstein, or Bronstein. After marrying Gersh Rosenblum, she supposedly banned the use of Yiddish at home and insisted on Polish or German.

Growing up in Odessa, Schlomo was known as Saloman, Zalman, Sigmund, or Zymunt. Saloman seems to have been his choice until he was in his twenties. His mother wanted him to be brought up as a gentleman, and she got tutors for him in French and English, and the Greek and Latin classics. She sent him to a secular Russian school where he was exposed to different political views. Paulina saw a bright future for her little Saloman. As a result, he became "extremely bothered by being a Jew" and denied his true heritage.[13]

Rosenblum supposedly studied physics and math at Imperial Novorossiya University in Odessa (now I.I. Mechnikov National University). He left Russia suddenly around 1893. He later said he was a revolutionary at heart, and perhaps he got mixed up in a political plot. He was also in love with a cousin, and might have become estranged from his family. He further claimed he studied at Vienna, or Heidelberg, or Darmstadt, or Bonn, or Leipzig, or Munich, or Stuttgart, or Berlin, or Bern, or Zurich. No paper trail has been found for confirmation.

Saloman Rosenblum settled in Paris in 1895. He might have become involved in an Okhrana spy network set up in France by Ivan Fyodorovich Manasevich-Manuilov, a roving diplomat for St. Petersburg and a dispenser of Russian subsidies to the French press, including *Figaro* and *Echo de Paris*.[14] Rosenblum left Paris late that year, again suddenly. Shortly afterwards, two revolutionary couriers riding on a train through France to deliver money from England to Swiss radicals were robbed. Both couriers were killed, one outright. One story has it that Rosenblum and Manasevich-Manuilov were the robbers and that they split up the money. Years later, one Alexander Matzebovich said he was in on the robbery, too.[15]

Saloman Rosenblum then popped over to London, rented a comfy flat, bought stylish clothes, and posed as a Polish aristocrat in town to brush up on his English. Mother's grooming of her boy had not been in vain. He was the very picture of an elegant Mediterranean gentleman and eligible bachelor. He became an English playboy, though he spoke with an accent described as either Muscovite or Odessan Yiddish.

He dropped Saloman as his first name and began introducing himself as Sigmund Georgievich Rosenblum. He got a job as a chemist, which taught him how to work with different inks, a specialty useful to forgers and spies.

He met Margaret Callahan, wife of a sixty-five-year-old Anglican pastor, Hugh Thomas. Margaret got pregnant, and the reverend made out a new will, leaving everything to her.

Nine days later, Thomas died. Margaret wasn't there. Sigmund wasn't either, at least not using his true identity. A doctor T.W. Andrew signed the death certificate but later inquiries revealed that no such doctor was listed as practicing in England. No autopsy was ordered, and the reverend was hastily buried. Had Sidney been the mysterious Doctor Andrew? With Reilly's background in chemistry, he could have mixed up something creative to add to the reverend's evening toddy.

Whatever happened, Sigmund and Margaret got married. That made Reilly rich. But he lost heavily at gambling. In 1899 he announced he was going abroad. His new British passport was made out in the name of Sidney George Reilly, picked up from Margaret's father, a ship's captain named Edward Reilly Callahan. His previous persona of Sigmund Rosenblum was tossed away like an empty arsenic bottle.

Reilly traveled to Paris, then Odessa, maybe on assignment for the Okhrana, maybe for the British government. As with much of Reilly's life, the pages in that chapter seem to be missing. Margaret started drinking heavily while he was gone. Sidney returned to London in 1901 to fetch her, and they sailed for St. Petersburg and then Port Arthur, Manchuria (today Lushun, China). Reilly began exporting timber for a Danish company and sent Margaret off to Belgium to dry out in a sanitarium. Then he went to Japan in 1902, accompanied by a new lover. His presence in Japan led to later suspicions that he might have worked as an agent for Tokyo.

When the Japanese defeated the Russian battle fleet at Port Arthur in 1904, a surprise attack that foreshadowed Pearl Harbor, Sidney fled to New York. There he got into the oil business, then went back to St. Petersburg to negotiate military contracts for the Russian government. When he returned to London again he had a new wife, Nadezhda (Nadine) Zalessky. (Later several of Reilly's lovers found themselves in jail together in Moscow, and to the amusement of their jailors, each one claimed to be his wife.)

In 1912 he was granted the status of "honorary British subject," but not a full citizen. This was undoubtedly a reward for favors he'd done for the government. When war started in 1914, Reilly worked as a munitions buyer in Europe, Asia, and America, and made money on the commissions. In 1916 he scored a major intelligence coup when he posed as a German agent, infiltrated the Imperial Admiralty in Berlin, stole their naval code, and delivered it to London. But beyond such patriotic acts, Reilly had a reputation for being a spy who served whatever side paid him the most, similar to the fictional SPECTRE freelancers that Ian Fleming would later write about.

❖

Reilly's theft of the stolen German naval code seems to have stood him in good stead when he applied to the War Office in London for an intelligence job early in 1918. He emphasized that he was a linguist experienced in dealing with the Russian government. His request ended up on the desk of Commander Mansfield Smith Cumming, the legendary "C," founder and chief of the nine-year-old Secret Intelligence Service.

The British government was not above a spot of anti-Semitism, and Sidney was placed under SIS surveillance not just because of his interesting past, but also because he was a Jew. The British security service, MI5, didn't have anything on him. But he was denounced by an SIS man in New York as being untrustworthy and unsuitable to work for the service. Nadine, too, was under suspicion for allegedly making money in the war by influencing corrupt members of the Russian purchasing commission.[16]

Nevertheless, Sidney was Russian, he spoke Russian, he had contacts in Russia, and he was willing to go back. Truth was, the SIS had trouble recruiting good people because the pay was so low. That led them to hire fresh university graduates, preferably from Oxford and Cambridge, who had their own sources of income. They wore tailored suits and possessed impeccable table manners, but most of them would have trouble impersonating working-class blokes if they were assigned to infiltrate foreign munitions factories and socialist halls.

All of this caused Cumming to rely on ex-coppers, some of whom sounded a little like Inspector Clouseau. Cumming also dipped into the government's old boy network in his search for information, but that was a source just as unreliable.

The solution was to recruit slippery pros like Reilly, who were not adverse to leaving a trail of intrigue behind them as they beat it back to England with the goods. This being wartime, expediency trumped everything else in the spy game. Sidney, additionally, was good at disguises. He could pose convincingly as a businessman, a soldier, a pipe fitter. He had as many different personas as he had wives. His letterhead said *Mundo Nulla Fides*, which translates loosely as "trust no one."[17]

Reilly was assigned the code name ST1. Cumming gave him 500 pounds sterling in cash and 750 pounds worth of diamonds, then put him on the *Queen Mary* for Archangel. It was a gamble, considering Sidney's rather checkered past. But London needed eyes in Russia more reliable than Lockhart's. Bruce had lost access to Trotsky and Lenin, though that wasn't his fault, and he had fallen back on his old ways of picking up strange women. His latest flame was Maria Ignatievna Zakrevskaya Benckendorff, aka Moura, daughter of a Russian landowner and senator under the tsarist régime.[18]

But another reason why Lockhart might have been distrusted in London was because he had Bolshevik friends. After all, he had been in Russia long enough to have made contacts in all quarters. That was what a consular official or spy was supposed to do—get out and meet people and recruit contacts, regardless of who they were. But that had led some to suspect that footballer and *bon vivant* Lockhart had been turned by Reds. A convenient suspect was Madame Vermelle, who earlier had got him recalled to London.[19]

After Sidney left England, Cumming wired ahead to Moscow and informed the SIS station chief to expect him. Reilly was described as a "Jewish-Jap type" about 5 foot 9, maybe bearded, with protruding brown eyes and a deeply lined, sallow face.

"Carries code message of identification," the wire continued. "On arrival will go to consul and ask for British passport officer. Ask him what his business is and he will answer 'diamond buying.'"[20]

Reilly disobeyed orders and got off the ship at Murmansk. He was promptly arrested by British marines. He claimed to be British but they were suspicious of his papers, which included a Russian passport. And the name on the passport was spelled Reilli, which wasn't British. Furthermore, he didn't really look Irish.

There was an explanation, though. Reilly's Russian passport had been issued to him by Maxim Maximovich Litvinov, who called himself Moscow's diplomatic representative in London, though Britain had not officially recognized Soviet Russia. That passport was intended simply to get the enterprising Sidney into Russia. After that, he would have to rely on his British passport. Reilly was released in Murmansk after showing an SIS officer a coded message on a microdot under the cork of an aspirin bottle.

That wasn't very original. It was an early warning of Reilly's rather casual tradecraft methods in Russia, a situation that would later cause serious problems in the Lenin Plot.

❖

Reilly spent four weeks scouting around for information in Petrograd. Like DeWitt Poole, Xenophon Kalamatiano, Charles Crane, Samuel Harper, and the Western ambassadors, Sidney had friends in high places. He sent Cumming a report saying the Soviets were the only real power in Russia at the moment but that opposition was growing. If supported, that resistance could overthrow the Lenin government. But a lot of people would have to be paid off. He asked for one million in cash. "C" said no.

Over succeeding days, Reilly went back to the Kremlin for more talks with Bonch-Bruyevich, who favored a return to war against Germany. Sidney sent more reports to London as he assumed two new covers. In Moscow he became "Mr. Constantine," a Greek businessman, and moved in with actress Dagmara Karozus, Alexander Grammatikov's niece. One of Dagmara's roommates was Elizaveta Emilyevna Otten, a drama student at the arts theatre. Elizaveta spoke several languages, which made her useful to Sidney's needs. He began an affair with her.

In Petrograd, Sidney posed as "Konstantin Markovich Massimo," a Turkish merchant. He shared a flat with Elena Mikhailovna Boyuzhovskaya, a lover from his pre-war past. He went to see a former judge he knew, Vyacheslav Orlovsky, and obtained papers identifying Reilly as a collaborator for the Cheka's criminal branch. Some historians would use that to claim that Reilly was a Cheka agent. But those papers simply allowed Sidney to move freely through security checkpoints. Red Guards saluted him and showed him every courtesy.

In May, Reilly began meeting with Boris Savinkov, almost two months before the attack on Yaroslavl. Savinkov provided Reilly with updates on the resistance armies in Russia, particularly his own Union for the Defense of Fatherland and Liberty. Also in May, Savinkov talked with Lockhart. Then Lockhart started meeting with Kalamatiano, Poole, de Verthamon, and Consul General Grenard.

Reilly wrote in his memoirs that he used Dagmara and her roommates in Moscow to introduce him to Maria Friede, another arts theatre student and a frequent visitor to the apartment. Maria was the sister of Colonel Alexander Friede, Kalamatiano's highest agent inside the Red Army communications office in Moscow.

Since Maria Friede was close to Dagmara and Elizaveta, Reilly was confident of her bona fides as an anti-Soviet. But could she be persuaded to join an operation against the Reds? It was dangerous work. The Cheka had no qualms about executing women.

"When I was sure of Mlle. Friede, I unfolded my proposition to her, namely that her brother should secure me copies of all documents which passed through his hands," Sidney later said. Maria set up a meeting between Reilly and Colonel Friede. After sizing up Reilly, Alexander Friede agreed to help him. Maria would be their cutout.

After that, Reilly said, "many a copy of a highly confidential document he handled was read in England before the original was in the hands of the (Soviet) officer to whom it was addressed."[21]

The document deliveries worked this way: Colonel Friede took copies of army reports home with him at night and gave them to his sister. Next morning Maria Friede tucked them into her music portfolio and discreetly delivered them to various locations such as the U.S. consulate and the French school where de Verthamon worked as a cover. They then forwarded the reports to their control officers.

But one thing all the Allied spy networks had to watch for were infiltrations by enemy moles. The Cheka had the same problem. That's why networks of agents were compartmentalized.

But soon one infiltrator in particular would prove disastrous to the Western agents.

23

PARIAHS OF THE WORLD

Conspiracies can produce a pleasant aroma when cooked up by absentee chefs thousands of miles away. But there is never any guarantee the dish will turn out well, as evidenced by the Allies' failure to recruit a Cossack army and Boris Savinkov's defeats on the Volga. Now the Western powers lit the oven for their next recipe.

The Allies had deputized the Czech Legion and still had Savinkov's Union for the Defense of Fatherland and Liberty on hand to back up a Moscow coup, but the Red Army was growing. Trotsky's goal was a million recruits. The Czechs and Savinkov together could scare up only 50,000 or so troops. That wasn't enough for a proper coup.

A glimpse of the promised land for the Allies was delivered by a man who visited Captain Francis Newton Allen Cromie, naval attaché at the British embassy in Petrograd. Cromie was a decorated former submarine commander and saboteur who had torpedoed a German cruiser and destroyer in the Baltic and captured or sunk ten enemy steamers. Now he was head of British naval intelligence in Russia and involved in intrigues against the Soviets. Alexander Orlov had access to the Lenin Plot case file while he was a Soviet intelligence officer and he wrote that the following happened:[1]

Commander Cromie's visitor introduced himself as a Latvian army officer named Jan Shmidkhen. (Some other historians have reported that Shmidkhen was accompanied by a second Latvian, named Jan Bredis.[2]) A number of Latvian troops (also called Letts) had been trapped in Russia after their country fell to Germany, and the Soviets hired them as mercenaries to prop up the Lenin régime. This meeting with Cromie took place in "early summer" of 1918. Shmidkhen knew Cromie because the English commander had earlier offered to buy information from him.

Shmidkhen told Cromie that the Latvian troops in Moscow were disgusted with the Reds. The Letts were tired of working as Soviet executioners. Shmidkhen said he had a friend, Colonel Eduard Petrovich Berzin, commander of the Latvian First Heavy Artillery Division in Moscow, who could be persuaded to work for the Allies. Colonel Berzin was twenty-four years old. He had studied art in Berlin, joined the Imperial Russian Army, and got decorated in the war. After the 1917 revolution he found himself stranded in Russia. Like a few thousand of his Latvian comrades, he sold his services to the Soviets when they took over.

(Sidney Reilly again offered his own version of things. He claimed he was the one who was approached by Berzin and that the colonel had already been collaborating with Kalamatiano and de Verthamon.[3])

The official 1918 Cheka report on the case says that Berzin went to Jacob Peters's apartment and told him about the approach by Shmidkhen. Peters told him to "not decline" the offer but to string the Allies along and report back to the Cheka on everything that was said and done. Berzin then instructed Shmidkhen to set up a meeting on August 14 to further discuss those "political matters." The talks would take place at Lockhart's apartment at 10 Khlebny Lane in Moscow.[4]

In the interim, two events occurred that worked to the benefit of the Allied plotters by sending Lenin and the Soviets reeling into a position of political weakness unlike anything they had experienced since signing their separate peace with the Germans.

❖

The first of those events took place on Saturday, July 6, 1918. It was the third day of the Fifth All-Russian Congress of Soviets, meeting at the Bolshoi Theatre in Moscow. Reilly, Lockhart, and other Allied agents sat in the hot auditorium watching angry delegates from the left wing of the Socialist Revolutionaries disrupt the show. The SRs had split into left and right wings after the Bolshevik coup. The Left SRs opposed dealing with Germany but reluctantly aligned with Lenin.

Now, however, in the congress of Soviets, the Left SRs turned on Lenin. They shook their fists and shouted at the German and Soviet delegates. They hated the Brest-Litovsk treaty and demanded a new war against Germany.

While that was going on, two men rang the bell at the German mission, the old Berg mansion, in the nearby swanky Arbat quarter. They told the footman they were from the Cheka, and produced ID cards signed by Dzerzhinsky. They said their names were Blumkin and Andreyev. They insisted on talking to Count Wilhelm von Mirbach, the new ambassador to Russia, regarding a matter of great importance.

The mission's counselor and his aide showed Blumkin and Andreyev into a drawing room. When Mirbach walked in, Blumkin and Andreyev said they had come to warn him of a plot against his life. As proof of the plot, Blumkin pulled his pistol and fired three shots at Mirbach.

The shots missed. The ambassador ran from the room. Andreyev dropped him with one shot to the back of his head. Then the assassins threw two grenades into the hall. The explosions covered them as they leaped out the window and escaped in a getaway car. A blood stain was left on the ballroom floor where Mirbach fell, and a report seventeen years later said that cleaning had not been able to remove it.[5]

Those events of July 6 were a catastrophe for Lenin in several ways:

—Mirbach's killers were Left SRs working in Lenin's own government. Was there a secret Cheka *within* the Cheka? Their ID cards had Dzerzhinsky's signature on them. Was Felix hiring Left SR assassins for his own purposes? Was he going to send them to remove Lenin?

—The assassination could be used as a *casus belli* for Germany to start a new war against Russia. Berlin had reduced German forces on the Russian fronts, but if the Kaiser wanted to, he could still send a massive force marching deep into Russia. Many more Russians would be killed or captured, much more land lost.

—Left SRs took to the streets in Moscow and attempted a coup against Lenin, apparently coordinated with the Mirbach assassination. Fighting was fierce. Heavy casualties were reported. Dzerzhinsky was captured briefly by the SRs and Moscow looked as if it were about to fall. Then Soviet reinforcements rushed in and the revolt was suppressed.

—The All-Russian Congress was supposed to have shown the world how unified the different Russian political factions were under the Soviet umbrella. But the disruption of the congress, the assassination of Mirbach, and the Left SR uprising showed just how shaky and chaotic Lenin's government really was.

The German government blamed the Mirbach assassination and the SR rebellion on Allied agents, namely Boris Savinkov. Dutch and Scandinavian newspapers reported that the German army was only 200 miles from Moscow and rapidly reinforcing its ranks. A march on Moscow was expected and

Lenin hurriedly tried to placate Berlin by appointing a special investigating commission headed by Jacob Peters of the Cheka. Hundreds of Left SRs were arrested.[6]

But the Germans did not occupy Moscow. The affair blew over beneath the winds of still more emergencies that Lenin had to deal with.

❖

A much larger political disaster for Lenin was the murder of the Romanov family. This included Tsar Nicholas II, his wife Tsarina Alexandra, their son and heir Tsarevich Alexi, and the daughters Olga, Tatiana, Maria, and Anastasia. The Soviets had refused to let the family leave Russia for exile in England, and imprisoned them in a house in Yekaterinburg. Shortly after midnight on July 17, 1918, they were awakened and herded into the basement. The family doctor, the maid, the cook, and the footman were crowded in with them.

Chekist Yakov Mikhailovich Yurovsky led the execution squad. It was composed of two local Communist Party members, two other Cheka agents, and eleven Latvian soldiers. They tramped down the steps to the basement. Then they lined up in the lamplight in front of the royal family. The death warrant was read.

"What? What?" Nicholas cried.

The murder squad opened fire with pistols. (Four of the soldiers later claimed they refused to fire.) The daughters had jewelry hidden in their clothes and the stones deflected some of the bullets. One of the girls even held up a pillow as a shield. But as they fell to the floor screaming they were finished off with bayonet stabs and head shots.

At least seventy rounds were fired. The killers had to leave the room afterward to escape the smoke. The bodies were hauled away in a truck, stripped of their clothes, robbed of their jewelry, doused with sulfuric acid, and dumped in a mine shaft and burned. Later the remains were buried in a wooded area. Their faces were smashed in with rifle butts and covered with quicklime so they wouldn't be recognizable.[7]

The first official Soviet news release said that only Nicholas was killed, and that his family was safe at another location. Then the truth leaked out. The murders were denounced by most Russian newspapers that had not been shut down by the Reds. An exception was *Moscow Bjedneta*, which wrote: "By order of the revolutionary council of the people, the bloody tsar has happily died. *Vive* the Red terror." The government also announced on the day of the murders that the Romanov fortune worth $2 billion ($33 billion today) had been seized.[8]

Reacting to the initial report, the London *Times* found the tsar's murder "tragic and undeserved."[9] A Tennessee newspaper added, "He was not even tried."[10] But an irreverent West Coast weekly refused to wring its editorial hands. Noting that the tsar's death had been inaccurately reported in the past, they wrote: "Czar Nicholas has been killed again, which means another resurrection is in order. This dying and coming back must be very expensive if the Russian undertakers charge one-half as much as do ours."[11]

Gallows humor aside, the world was shocked at the slaughter of the Romanovs. This, despite Nicholas having been regarded by many as a tyrant and an incompetent military commander responsible for his own empire's downfall. His wife was hated more, at least in Russia. She was derisively called *Nemka*, a Slovenian word meaning "German woman."

Moscow claimed that the local soviet in Yekaterinburg made the decision to execute the Romanovs because the Czech Legion was approaching. That is, the family had to be killed to keep them from being rescued. But Trotsky later wrote in his diary that Jacob Sverdlov, Lenin's right-hand man, told him the murders were carried out on Comrade Chairman's personal orders. Historian Richard Pipes echoed Trotsky's claim. Pipes wrote that a low-level Soviet official said he carried a kill order from Lenin to the Moscow telegraph office.

"Lenin was exceedingly careful not to associate his name with acts of Communist terror," Pipes said in an interview. "He preferred to attribute them to others, usually either government officials or local soviets, partly to absolve himself from blame, partly to remove the onus for these barbarities from the party. Anyone familiar with the way the Soviet régime functioned during his lifetime realizes that nothing of importance was done in Soviet Russia without Lenin's personal approval."[12] An exception, of course, would have been the murder of Mirbach by Left SRs.

The mass murder of the royal family, coupled with the Red Terror and Soviet mismanagement of the country, resulted in the Soviets being treated by the world as pariahs. It confirmed to the Lenin plotters that they were conducting not just a military and political operation against the Soviets, but also a mission of morality.

Historian Peter Eltsov noted that other European uprisings—for example, the English Civil War and the French Revolution—were also brutal, with tens of thousands killed, but that Bolsheviks were different because they "brought a fundamentally new type of threat, a call for a world revolution that would involve the appropriation of all private property. This was clearly anathema to the very ethos of the American experiment."[13]

❖

In Washington, President Wilson felt increased pressure from the Allies to get on board and do something about Russia. The British and French demanded an American invasion of Russia that would be larger than the small landing earlier at Murmansk. London and Paris added some conditions, though, that Washington considered unpalatable. Wilson's decision was not made easier by disagreements within his own government.

First, a warning about a larger invasion was issued by Vice Consul Felix Cole at Archangel. He feared that it would turn into a quicksand sucking in more and more ships, troops, and money. If North Russia were occupied, he said, up to a million and a half citizens in that region would have to be fed. Millions more in the country were simply tired of war. Furthermore, an invasion in the north would not conquer central and southern Russia, the base of the country's industrial, mining, and agricultural strength.

"Every foreign invasion that has gone deep into Russia has been swallowed up," Cole wrote, referring to Napoléon's march on Moscow in 1812.[14] Bonaparte had occupied the city without resistance only to find it deserted and barren of food. Then Russian agents burned the city around him. Nearly 400,000 troops of the French Grand Armée died in the resulting winter retreat.

Cole's memorandum was sent to David Francis at Vologda. But it went against the ambassador's support of intervention. Francis did send the memo on to Washington, but by courier mail. It arrived too late to influence strategy talks in the White House.

British Foreign Secretary Arthur Balfour appealed personally to Wilson. The Russian situation was extremely dangerous, Balfour said. He begged the president to dispatch a brigade of American troops. That was after Wilson had already acquiesced to Anglo-French pressure and sent the warship *Olympia* to Murmansk. Then after Balfour's entreaties, France and Italy jumped in and asked Wilson to join them in deploying up to six battalions to Russia.

That idea was approved by Tasker H. Bliss, the former commanding general of the U.S. Army who had been called out of retirement to serve as America's representative to the Allied Supreme War Council at Versailles. But Bliss would agree to an invasion only if U.S. forces were used to simply secure Murmansk and Archangel and guard the Allied supplies stored there. Archangel could also serve as a rallying point for Czech forces fighting the Red Army but Bliss did not want American troops conducting combat operations in the interior.

With General Bliss on board, Allied representatives at Versailles submitted a note to the full war council on June 3 asking for a joint invasion of Russia. It was quickly approved.[15] German invaders had just been stopped outside Paris, and while the council voted, the sounds of artillery fire could be heard in the distance.

With that vote, the discussion at Versailles was over. Alfred Milner, a member of Lloyd George's war cabinet and the man who had unified the Allied forces on the western front under supreme commander Marshal Ferdinand Jean Marie Foch, informed Wilson of the council's decision. Lord Milner wanted the United States to bear most of the weight of the invasion with three infantry and machine gun battalions, two field artillery batteries, three companies of engineers, and medical detachments.[16]

But there was more. Milner demanded that U.S. troops in the invasion force serve under British command. That popped some buttons in the U.S. War Department. General John J. Pershing, veteran of the Spanish-American War, the Philippine-American War, and the Mexican-American War, and now commander of U.S. forces in Europe, had already dealt with that problem in France. American and Allied armies had been lending divisions to one another temporarily for certain offensives, but after Milner refused to accept U.S. colored troops, Pershing did not allow any more doughboys to serve under British command. The French, Pershing noted, had been eager for the black troops.[17]

Lansing discussed Milner's demand with Secretary of War Newton D. Baker and army chief of staff General Peyton C. March, who had been a military observer with the Japanese army in the Russo-Japanese War. First, they strongly opposed sending U.S. troops to Russia because it would be a drain on American efforts on the western front. Second, they did not want Americans serving under foreign officers. Baker sent a message to General Bliss telling him to try and get Marshal Foch to override Milner's demand.

But Foch refused. When Bliss got back to Washington he was in a subdued mood. He said supplying the troops would be all right in his view if they were used for defense only. If the Red Army attacked them with a large force, he said, they should blow up the stored Allied supplies and come home.

But in the White House the arguments continued, and Wilson was still undecided on what to do. Jean Jules Jusserand, the French ambassador in Washington, delivered a note from Foch to Wilson. The president responded that Foch had not explicitly said America would be justified in sending a U.S. force. The bickering went on and on.

Then Wilson got a surprise visitor in the White House.

❖

His guest was Maria Botchkareva—Yashka—commander of the First Russian Women's Battalion of Death. The Bolsheviks had disbanded her unit because Botchkareva did not allow Communist committees in her ranks. She then set out for Allied-occupied Vladivostok. She had appointed herself to go on a rescue mission for Russia, to travel to America and England and appeal for help in resisting the Soviets and the Germans. All she had was 200 rubles in her purse and she gave some of that away to some poor people she met during her train trip. One day she got arrested. The Red Guards knew she was a popular anti-Communist and that made her an enemy of the state. But the local soviet released her after she convinced them she was sick and simply going to visit relatives.

When Yashka reached Vladivostok she went to the British consulate for help. A Russian colonel serving as a translator there notified the U.S. consulate of her plans, gave her 300 rubles, and sent her to a hotel. He promised to try and get her a Russian passport so she could leave the country. But the local soviet knew who she was. They refused the passport. She hid in her room while her contact at the consulate got her a British passport. Then the American consulate told her she could ship out on the USS *Sheridan*, a transport sailing that night for San Francisco.

Meanwhile, the Vladivostok Soviet concluded, correctly, that Botchkareva was a resourceful woman and would find some way to slip out of the country. They sent fifty Red Guards to surround her hotel and arrest her. But they found her room empty. The proprietor told them she had just left town on a train. The guards raced to the station. There they found that no such train had just left. Next, they descended on the British consulate. The Russian translator there said he hadn't seen her either. They didn't believe him, but there was nothing they could do about it.

Where *was* the dangerous traitor Botchkareva?

She was hiding in the home of the captain of the *Sheridan*. That night she dressed as an Englishwoman, put on a veil, and pretended not to be able to speak a word of Russian. Then she waved her new British passport and boarded the ship. She was accompanied by Lieutenant Leonid G. Filippov, her young English-speaking adjutant from the imperial army. The British were not enlisting Russians, so Filippov was going to America to volunteer for duty on the western front.

But Botchkareva's adventure was not over yet. The local soviet sent Red Guards to search the ship. The ship's captain locked her in a cabin and posted U.S. soldiers outside the door. They informed the Red Guards that a very important German general was held prisoner in the cabin. The door could not be unlocked for any reason. Sorry, comrades. The guards left, again angry and empty-handed.

"After the anchors of the *Sheridan* were raised and the ship began to move," Botchkareva wrote later, "I came out of the cabin to the liveliest merriment of everybody who expected to see a gruff Teuton general emerge from the door."[18]

It was April 18, 1918. Yashka was on her way to see the president of the United States.

❖

Botchkareva arrived in San Francisco in May 1918 and crossed the continent on a train to New York. There she was introduced to Isaac Don Levine, a reporter who had covered the 1917 Russian Revolution for the *New York Tribune*. Levine was born in Russia and his family emigrated to the United States in 1911. He finished high school in Missouri and worked first for the *Kansas City Star*. Levine was fluent in Russian and wrote Botchkareva's autobiography, *Yashka*, as she told it to him in her room at the Prince George Hotel. It was first serialized in *Metropolitan* magazine, then in newspapers across the country. The following year it was published as a book, and Levine got an assignment to return to Russia and cover the civil war.[19]

"With her army breeches tucked into high boots, a row of distinguished service medals decorating her ample bosom, the visitor created a furor," Levine wrote in his memoirs. "I found myself in the presence of a woman who looked several years older than her age, broad of frame, with strong features. She had no schooling and had learned to read with difficulty and to sign her name laboriously; yet she possessed gifts not uncommon among Russian peasants. Her speech was unusually grammatical, vivid, and at times attained an epic quality."[20]

Botchkareva quickly attracted attention. One afternoon she and Levine took a stroll down Fifth Avenue and picked up a trail of gawkers who couldn't believe they were seeing a woman in an army uniform. Levine also took her out to Oyster Bay to lunch with Teddy Roosevelt.

"I don't believe in women going to war," Roosevelt told Levine beforehand, "but bring her out just the same." As it turned out, TR was impressed. "I never enjoyed an afternoon more," he said the next day. "She's a remarkable woman." Teddy gave her $1,000 ($16,000 today) from the money he received for his Nobel Prize.[21]

Florence Jaffray Harriman (née Hurst) was Yashka's sponsor in America. Mrs. Harriman—Daisy, to her pals at Newport—was a New York City socialite, suffragist, and banker's widow. But there was more to Daisy Harriman than that. She had cared for wounded soldiers, both American and Mexican, during the Mexican Civil War. She had organized the American National Red Cross Women's Motor Corps from the District of Columbia, then directed the unit in France.

Daisy Harriman got Botchkareva an appointment with the president. While in town, Yashka stayed at the elegant Powhatan Hotel, two blocks from the White House. Wilson had suffered through some tiresome encounters with the former tsarist ambassador to Washington and he didn't want to see any more Russians. But Daisy Harriman had been a big donor to Wilson's presidential campaign, so he made an exception. Just this one Russian, just this one time.

On one of those steamy summer afternoons for which Foggy Bottom is notorious, Botchkareva marched into the Oval Office wearing her wool uniform, her medals, her battle scars, and her sword. She was accompanied by Daisy Harriman and Lieutenant Filippov, who served as her translator. Wilson called in his own translator, Jerome Lansfield, a State Department official who had lived in Russia and married a Russian.

Levine described Botchkareva as a "natural actress." Wilson appreciated that since he was a song-and-dance man himself. He was also an old softie who wept at letters from friends. That made him a perfect audience for Botch-kareva's dramatic presentation.

She swung her sword to the side and dropped to her knees before the president.

"Russia was a great and brave country," she said. "When the revolution came, we all rejoiced. Then our enemies [the Bolsheviks] went among the soldiers and deceived them with lying words, telling them that the Germans were their brothers and that they should go home, that there would be peace and bread and land. Now they realize they have been fooled and that Russia has been dragged in the dirt. All they ask is a chance to redeem themselves and they will fight to the last drop of blood for their native land."

According to Lansfield and another witness, Yashka grasped Wilson's knees, and with tears streaming down her face, she implored him:

"If the Allies will come, even with a small force, with the Americans in the lead, they will flock around them by the hundreds of thousands. But they must come quickly."[22]

Filippov and Lansfield were startled. Wilson broke out crying. The interview left everyone in the room shaken. As Botchkareva left, she gave Wilson a Russian ikon, a small image of Saint Anne.[23]

Wilson later told Jusserand about his meeting with Botchkareva, and the ambassador said he was "greatly struck" by what she had said about the need for a Western invasion. Jusserand said "nothing that concerns so important a problem should be neglected."[24]

A few days later, Wilson sent a memorandum to the Allied ambassadors agreeing to a Russian invasion.

Botchkareva was not the only factor in the president's decision. Military, political, economic, and moral considerations carried much more weight. But Yashka was the face of the Russia that Wilson had never seen. And that face had been in his office. This encounter, and its influence on the president, an emotional man, can't be dismissed. It's interesting to imagine what Wilson's most intimate adviser, Miss Edith, told her husband regarding Botchkareva's appeal.

But Wilson and Lansing made it clear that the "clear and fixed judgment" of the United States was that an "organized intervention" anywhere in Russia "would add to the present sad confusion" in that country. Wilson would allow American troops to guard Allied stores and help the Russians raise a defense force but had "no expectation" of allowing U.S. forces to take part in combat.

If he got double-crossed, he would withdraw the doughboys and send them to France.[25]

Lord Reading, the British ambassador to Washington, was offended that Wilson did not seem to trust the British. But the president was simply being consistent in his distrust of *all* the belligerents.

Wilson, though, appears to have swept under the rug the main issue that really got the War Department riled up—Milner's demand that U.S. troops in Russia be commanded by British officers. It would be a serious problem from the very day the American expeditionary force set sail.

24

EVERYTHING ON THE DOT

The invasion force that Wilson ordered to Russia was not a surrogate army. They were American volunteers and draftees who would be assisted by British troops, French *poilus,* Italian and Serbian infantrymen, and Russian volunteers.[1] The American Expeditionary Force to North Russia, as it was formally known, came from the 85th Division of the U.S. Army. Most of the AEFNR soldiers hailed from Michigan and Wisconsin and did their basic training at Camp Custer, near Detroit. For that reason, they were called Detroit's Own.

The camp was named for Lieutenant Colonel George Armstrong Custer, who rode with DeWitt Poole's father in the Indian Wars. Camp Custer was one of thirty-six cantonments (training bases) built nationwide by the War Department in 1917. The 85th was also called the Custer Division.

After Congress declared war, America had three armies. One was the U.S. Army, the "regulars," made up of volunteers. The second was the National Guard, operating under control of the various states, most of the time, but federalized for the war by the National Defense Act of 1916. The third was the National Army, consisting of inductees drawn from the nearly 24 million men who had signed up for the draft. The draftees were "citizen soldiers" and would serve only until the war was over.

Secretary of War Baker said that total American army strength before the war was about 100,000, while each major European army had millions. Assisted by National Guard troops, the regular army had been used mainly to secure the southern border against invasions by Mexican forces. But now a total of 4,734,991 American soldiers were going to serve in the World War.[2] Baker said 13 percent of them were regulars, 10 percent came from the National Guard, and 77 percent were National Army recruits.[3]

Some 787,000 African Americans served in the war, mostly in their own divisions, the 92nd and 93rd. Those units were popular among black soldiers. They saw having their own divisions as a matter of racial pride.[4] In Europe they received combat training from the French and fought side-by-side with them. They were commanded by General "Black Jack" Pershing, so called because he had previously commanded a black regiment, the Buffalo Soldiers.[5]

Some say that the term doughboys referred to how soldiers' uniforms got dusty when they tramped across adobe soil in the Mexican War of 1846–1848. Those men were first called "adobes," then "dobies" and finally "doughboys." Another version traces the word back to the American Revolution, when mud on Continental Army uniforms was called "doughy blobs." Some Europeans claimed the name referred to doughnuts, which all American soldiers seemed to eat. A joke said that Americans were "kneaded" in 1914 but didn't "rise" until 1917.

The president was commander in chief but the man running America's new combat machine was Secretary of War Newton Baker, a lawyer. He had grown up in a West Virginia village, attended a prep school in Virginia, and graduated from Johns Hopkins, where he met Wilson, a visiting lecturer from Princeton.

Baker's first political job had been as secretary to the postmaster general during President McKinley's second term. Then he served as mayor of Cleveland, Ohio, for two terms. He admired Wilsonian politics, and on local issues Baker was known as a "reliable radical and prudent progressive." But on national issues, Baker was something of a conservative and isolationist. He belonged to three pacifist societies when Wilson appointed him war secretary on March 9, 1916. Baker knew nothing about the army. The closest he had ever been to a uniform was when he was rejected as a volunteer for the Spanish-American War.

When General Pershing first met Baker he was surprised to find the secretary much younger and smaller than he had expected.

"He looked actually diminutive as he sat behind his desk, doubled up in a rather large office chair," Pershing wrote in his memoirs. But they got along fine, Pershing added.[6]

Baker was forty-five years old when he arrived in Washington and was not even mentioned in the local newspapers. But when the newshounds discovered a pacifist had been named war secretary, one hack exclaimed: "Hell's broken loose!"

Baker found himself wedged in between extremists on the left, who wanted conscientious objectors excused, and those on the right, who wanted them shot. Baker wasn't popular in the press because wartime censorship didn't allow him to tell reporters very much.

Baker felt conflicted about his pacifism. Why should he take charge of building an army of killers when he could be quietly back in Cleveland tending to traffic problems? But once he settled in, he managed the draft, fought to keep political influence out of the War Department, and led the mobilization. He appointed Emmett Jay Scott, a journalist from the *Houston Post*, as special assistant for Negro affairs, making him the highest-ranking African American in Wilson's administration.

Baker wasn't cowed by the army officers he had to give orders to. He had a firm but quiet way of saying no. And he said it only once. Baker later joined Pershing in France for a tour of the western front, but as far as the secretary was concerned, the idea of invading Russia was nonsense from the start.

"Every man and every ship which is diverted from the western front diminishes the aggregate Allied power there," he said.[7] Baker later claimed this was the only issue over which he and the president ever had a serious disagreement.

❖

At its peak in 1918, Camp Custer was home to more than 36,000 trainees and 3,500 horses and mules. The average doughboy was twenty-three years old, weighed 165 pounds, and had to be strong enough to carry an eighty-pound pack on a twenty-mile march.[8] Those were the days before America's obsession with junk food, and photos of Custer draftees show only a few men overweight. Some draftees were underweight because the country had gone through an economic recession before the war and many of the men had not had three meals a day and regular medical attention for years.

The draftees spoke a multitude of languages besides English, including Spanish, Portuguese, German, Italian, Russian, Czech, Slovak, Polish, French, and Gaelic. Some, though, could not read or write any language. The base newspaper published a study guide with simple instructions such as "attention" and "mess call" in English. It didn't matter if you were an alien. If you served in the war, you got U.S. citizenship.

Nearly 4,000 black draftees trained at Custer and were met with "whites only" signs on latrines. "Many of these soldiers are typical southern darkies right from the big plantations," the base newspaper said. But the writer added that some were university graduates who lent "great assistance" in processing the men. At one point a black sergeant lost his flock in a mess hall. He then called out for all men who remembered "Mississippi Blues" played on the phonograph that morning to follow him.[9] Black troops were given their own barracks, recreation rooms, and latrines, and things settled down. They formed a band that gave popular concerts.

The day at Camp Custer began at 5 A.M. with a bugler blowing "Reveille," a tune that quickly became universally hated. Breakfast was ham and eggs, biscuits, and gallons of coffee. That was followed by marching drill, exercises, conferences, study, and quizzes. Lunch and dinner were heavy on beef and potatoes, with all the milk the men could drink.

The men learned to shoot rifles, pistols, and machine guns, and to kill a man with a bayonet and trench knife. They were taught to thrust the bayonet upward into the abdomen below the sternum so the blade wouldn't get caught in the rib cage. The trench knife was modeled after the French model. It had a long stiletto blade with a metal "knuckle duster" guard. Proper procedure was to hit the enemy in his jaw with the knuckle guard and then follow through with the blade to slash his throat. Trench knives were later outlawed in the war; soldiers used the blade of their shovels as a substitute.

Use of 12-gauge pump shotguns with double aught buckshot was also taught. The guns came with sawed-off barrels for cleaning out enemy trenches. The draftees dug their own trenches, by hand, with shovels. When a mock battle was staged, hundreds of people showed up from Battle Creek to cheer on their favorites.

"It is work, work, work and everything must be right on the dot," wrote Frank Murphy, one of the officers in training. Everybody washed his own clothes, shaved in cold water, and made up his mattress from straw. "It is not a pink tea gang running things."[10]

Custer men received special instruction from French and British officers from the western front. They also got training on how to prevent frostbite, which untreated could lead to loss of fingers or toes. The Custer barracks were simple wood-frame structures built of planks and plywood, with no insulation. At night, the heating stoves were allowed to go out and the windows were opened so the men could get used to sleeping in sub-freezing temperatures. After a storm passed through, they would awake to find snow on their blankets, snow on the floor, and snow on the toilet seats. One morning they had to march through two feet of it for four hours, and scores of men ended up in the hospital with frostbite. That led to a protest meeting which some Detroit newspapers tried to suggest was a mutiny. But anybody can be a good soldier in fair weather, training officer Frank Murphy said.

"Only the stout-hearted like it here."[11]

For recreation on base, there was baseball, football, boxing, and sing-a-longs where the boys belted out such patriotic hymns as "Keep Your Head Down You Dirty Hun." Quarterback Harry Costello, a later historian of the American invasion of Russia, led the Custer football squad in 1918. They played college teams and lost only one game. The team was invited to play in the Rose Bowl but declined on the grounds it would be inappropriate while other soldiers were fighting and dying in the war.

Off base, Battle Creek theatres offered matinees and evening shows for a dime. Favorite movies included Dustin Barnum in *The Spy*. There were also concerts at the Liberty Theatre on base featuring the Masonic Minstrels of Kalamazoo and the House of David Band.

For dining out, the All American Military Café downtown offered a full lunch, everything from soup to nuts, for 50 cents. At night, it was turned into a supper club with dancing to an orchestra. But segregation was enforced by both race and rank. Some places in Battle Creek catered only to white enlisted men, or white officers, or colored only.[12] Alcohol was not sold on base. If you got thirsty you had to hike two miles down the road to the nearest watering hole, then two miles back, risking arrest for going AWOL after lights out.[13]

The Spanish Flu hit Camp Custer as part of the most deadly global pandemic in history. The flu got its name because 8 million died of it in Spain in one month. Estimates of deaths worldwide range from 50 to 100 million. One third of the world's population got the Spanish Flu in 1918–1919 and it killed more people than the war did.[14]

It was called *la Grippe* in Europe. It began like a cold, with chills, fever, and coughing. Then your condition quickly worsened into pneumonia. Your immune system overreacted and attacked your lungs. You coughed up blood and your face turned blue. There was no vaccine. Treatment was aspirin, fruit juice, bed rest, and oxygen. But the flu killed quickly, with most victims under age thirty-four.

When the Spanish Flu hit Camp Custer, 4,000 got sick in three days. Twelve died. The base was sealed off, and military police stopped streetcars half a mile away. Some training was continued but individual barracks were quarantined. One black soldier remarked that this didn't bother him, since his barracks was already quarantined. Over 300 enlisted men were given crash training in medical care so they could relieve the regular nurses at night. A total of 620 soldiers and two nurses died at Custer. Eight officers were court-martialed for neglect of duty, mostly for leaving camp to be treated elsewhere.

American government scientists now say that most Type A influenza which has occurred worldwide since 1918 is a descendant of the Spanish Flu. That means it is still killing people, making it much more virulent than the Black Plague of the Middle Ages.[15] The flu would cause considerable problems for the American and Allied invasion forces in Russia.

❖

The 85th Division left Camp Custer on trains for New York City at 4 P.M. on July 14, 1918. They stopped briefly in Detroit, where the Red Cross served them coffee and, yes, doughnuts. They arrived at Weehawken, New Jersey, the next day at 6 P.M. This being the army, they then had to wait, and wait, and wait. Finally, they were ferried out to Long Island City and reached Camp Mills at one in the morning. Over the next five days the men were given physical exams. One company came down with the German Measles.

On July 22 they boarded two troop ships for the Atlantic crossing. One had been built thirty years before in Glasgow as a British passenger steamer, the *City of Paris*, to carry 1,740 passengers. The U.S. Navy bought her, renamed her the USS *Yale*, and sent her down to the Caribbean for action in the Spanish-American War. In 1918 she was rechristened the USS *Harrisburg*, a low, fast cruiser almost two football fields long and armed with sixteen guns.

Her twin was also built in Scotland, as the *City of New York*. She, too, saw service in the Spanish-American War, as a scout ship, the *Harvard*. Her crew rescued 600 survivors from wrecked enemy warships. She was renamed the USS *Plattsburg* in 1918. Both these troop ships, like Camp Custer, were self-contained cities, with sleeping quarters, kitchens, dining halls, recreation rooms, and surgical suites.

The ships set out in a convoy of sixteen vessels. Sometimes the water was calm, sometimes choppy. The sea air at times was hot, then cold. The men were constantly awakened at night by alarm warnings. Once a German U-boat attacked the convoy but was sunk by depth charges. Then the convoy got lost in a fog. When visibility returned, the mass they sighted dead ahead turned out to be Iceland, not England. Back on course, some of the soldiers fell ill

President Woodrow Wilson authorized the American war against Soviet Russia and approved a secret plot in Moscow to depose Lenin and his government. The first lady, Edith Wilson, was his closest political confidante and ciphered his special presidential codes. *Courtesy of the Library of Congress.*

ABOVE LEFT: Samuel N. Harper, a University of Chicago professor, recruited Americans to go to Russia as operatives for the U.S. State Department. *Courtesy of the University of Chicago.* ABOVE RIGHT: Wealthy Chicago industrialist and philanthropist Charles R. Crane used his own money to finance private networks of American agents in Russia for several U.S. presidents, including Wilson. *Courtesy of the University of Chicago.* BELOW LEFT: U.S. Secretary of State Robert Lansing was the original architect of the Lenin Plot. *Courtesy of the Library of Congress.* BELOW RIGHT: Leland Harrison was director of the State Department's Bureau of Secret Intelligence, predecessor to the CIA and NSA. *Courtesy of the Library of Congress.*

ABOVE: DeWitt Clinton Poole, U.S. consul general in Moscow, was America's spymaster in Revolutionary Russia. He ran dozens of American, Russian, and Latvian agents, both civilian and military. *Courtesy of the National Archives and Records Administration.* BELOW LEFT: David R. Francis was American ambassador to Russia and a key coordinator of the Lenin Plot. He asked Washington for 100,000 troops to take Petrograd and Moscow in support of the coup against Lenin. *Courtesy of Washington University.* BELOW RIGHT: Xenophon de Blumenthal Kalamatiano, a Russian-American graduate of the University of Chicago, served as America's top intelligence field officer in the Lenin Plot. He was captured and sentenced to death by a Soviet revolutionary tribunal. *Courtesy of the Library of Congress.*

ABOVE: The U.S. consulate in Moscow was operational headquarters for American agents in the Lenin Plot. The gate on the right was where Kalamatiano was captured. *Courtesy of Vladimir Freydin/Helen Watson.* BELOW LEFT: British author Somerset Maugham, on loan from the Secret Intelligence Service in London, spied for the United States in Revolutionary Russia. President Wilson did not trust the British and would not let them decipher Maugham's reports. *Courtesy of the Library of Congress.* BELOW RIGHT: Colonel Raymond Robins, head of the American Red Cross in Russia, ran one of the most effective U.S. spy networks in Revolutionary Russia. *Courtesy of the Library of Congress.*

ABOVE LEFT: Leon Trotsky, commissar for war, cooperated with the American Red Cross in distributing war relief supplies in Russia, until he found out Raymond Robins was a U.S. spy. *Courtesy of the Library of Congress.* ABOVE RIGHT: Boris Savinkov, an independent Socialist Revolutionary, used his underground army to assist Western agents in the Lenin Plot. *Image from Alamy.* BELOW LEFT: Freelance Russian adventurer and profiteer Sidney Reilly was hired by the British Secret Service to assist in the Lenin Plot. Reilly was a drug addict who saw himself as Napoléon reincarnated; at other times he thought he was Jesus Christ. *Image from Alamy.* BELOW RIGHT: Colonel Eduard Berzin, commander of a Latvian army division in Moscow, acted as an agent provocateur for the Cheka against the Lenin plotters. *Image from Alamy.*

ABOVE: Felix Dzerzhinsky (right) was head of the Cheka and directed operations against the Lenin plotters. Jacob Peters, his chief assistant (left), interrogated captured Western spies. *Image from Alamy.* BELOW LEFT: Fanny Kaplan, another independent Socialist Revolutionary, shot Lenin, an act that amplified the Red Terror. Allied agent Savinkov claimed he gave her the pistol she used. *Image from Alamy.* BELOW RIGHT: Kremlin commandant Pavel Malkov arrested Bruce Lockhart, his staff, and his mistress, along with some of Kalamatiano's Latvian agents in Moscow. Malkov also executed Fanny Kaplan. *Image from the author's collection.*

U.S. forces land in Russia to fight a war against the Red Army and support the coup against Lenin and the Soviet government. President Wilson put American troops under British command, a move he quickly regretted. *Courtesy of the University of Michigan.*

British troops, assisted by Cossacks and other loyalist Russians, ride into battle against the Reds in an armored train. The railroad front was the scene of some of the heaviest fighting in North Russia. *Courtesy of the University of Michigan.*

French *poilus* arrive in Russia to be paired up with American doughboys in combat. British commanders held back food and medical supplies from French and American troops, leading to mutinies against the conduct of the war. *Courtesy of the University of Michigan.*

Trotsky sent a large Red Army force to fight the Western invaders but the troops were short on food, ammunition, and winter clothing. Their casualty rates were much higher than those of the Allies. *Image from Alamy.*

An Allied convoy moves supplies to the front. Overland travel was difficult in winter. Better progress could be made on frozen rivers. *Courtesy of the University of Michigan.*

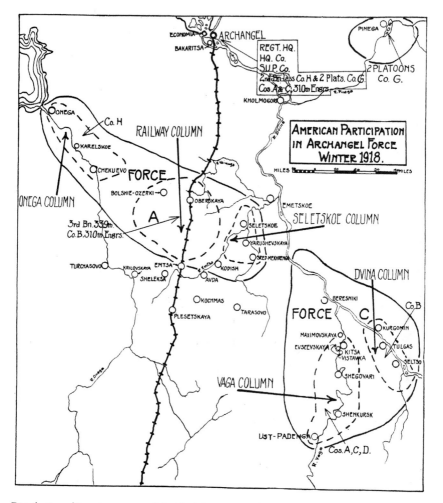

Distribution of American troops of the North Russian expedition during Winter of 1918. *Courtesy of the University of Michigan.*

Smolny Barracks in Archangel was the scene of one of the American mutinies against the war. The officer on the far left is wearing a leather jerkin and fur hat, and carrying an arctic coat, all U.S. army issue. His Shackleton Boots, supplied by the British, were hated by U.S. troops. The officer second from right wears *valenki*, popular Russian felt boots. *Courtesy of the Library of Congress.*

Major Jonas R. Longley was medical officer in charge of the American Red Cross Hospital in Archangel. American troops were denied care at the British army hospital, so they opened their own facility. A Ford ambulance is behind Major Longley. *Courtesy of the Library of Congress.*

A Russian peasant, half-starved under Soviet domination, waits exhausted while American doughboys fetch him a hot meal. *Courtesy of the Library of Congress.*

The New Illustrated

No. 10   VOL. 1.   *A PICTURE-RECORD OF OUR TIMES*   APRIL 19, 1919

British Brigadier General Edmund Ironside took over command of all American and Allied troops in North Russia late in 1918. He replaced an incompetent British general and saved U.S. forces from annihilation. *Image from Alamy.*

Brigadier General Wilds P. Richardson, also a popular commander, brought American troops home in 1919. His arrival in Russia was an affront to the British, signaling that U.S. forces were no longer subservient to foreign command. *Courtesy of the Alaska State Library U.S. Alaska Road Commission Photo Collection.*

Herbert Hoover, here with constant companion King Tut, was director of the American Relief Admin-istration in post-war Europe and brought all American prisoners home from Russia in 1921. Russia was in famine, with millions dying, and the prisoners were swapped for an emergency U.S. food program. *Courtesy of the Hoover Presidential Library.*

from the flu, from seasickness, and from the food. Boat drills at three in the morning didn't help.

"Believe me, after being on that boat with worms in the food and packed like sardines when sleeping, we were glad to see dry land," a medic, DeWitt Millen, wrote in his diary.[16]

The men were told they were going to Britain first, then on to France for frontline duty. But other stories began to spread—nothing definite, just rumors.

❖

After thirteen days at sea, Detroit's Own arrived at the mouth of the Mersey River at 4:46 in the morning. It was August 3, 1918. A river pilot took over and guided the two ships up the river to the Liverpool docks. They tied up there and the men disembarked at 8:45 A.M. on the following day, then marched over wet cobblestoned streets to the train station. The Midland Railway delivered them down to Stoney Castle Camp, near Aldershot Military Town in southeast England. The British had maintained a big training base at Aldershot since the Crimean War. It was called "the home of the British Army." That night the Custer men slept in tents on the heathland and got their first taste of British rations.

"Baa, baa, old sheep," one of them wrote.

The Yanks spent nine days drilling, resting, and exploring London. Then they were split up. One group was sent on to France. The other men were told to give up their American weapons, including Springfield and Enfield rifles and Browning machine guns. They were issued an assortment of French, British, and Russian weapons, and English uniforms. A joke was that the Russian rifles were so "accurate" they could shoot around corners.

Sir Ernest Shackleton, the Antarctic explorer, showed up to give lectures on deep-freeze survival. After that, the men were issued Shackleton Boots he had designed for ice and snow. The men would learn to hate those boots. They turned out to be fine for standing still on guard duty but they slipped like skis when walking. Many men simply threw them away. Nevertheless, the boots confirmed the rumors. They were going to Russia.

❖

The American units deployed to Archangel included the 337th, 338th, 339th, and 340th infantry regiments and the 330th machine gun battalion from the 169th Infantry Brigade. From the 160th Field Artillery Brigade came the 328th, 329th, and 330th field artillery regiments. They were supplemented by divisional troops from the 328th machine gun battalion, 310th engineer regiment, 310th field signal battalion, 310th supply train, 310th engineers, 337th field hospital, and 337th ambulance.[17] (Red Cross ambulance sections operating in the war were being incorporated into the United States Army Ambulance Service.[18]) On September 30 the initial landing force was augmented by the arrival of another twenty-one army officers, and one marine officer, in addition to another 490 doughboys of the 85th Division.[19] Red Cross doctors and nurses accompanied the troops.

The AEFNR troops wore distinctive arm patches on their uniforms. One patch announced "NR" in bold letters. Another showed the profile of a white polar bear on the prowl. Detroit's Own were now called the Polar Bears.

The men took a troop train up to Newcastle-upon-Tyne, a sooty coal town and seaport in northeast England, and boarded three British troop ships, the *Somali*, the *Tydeus*, and the *Nagoya*, for the voyage to Russia. They were called auxiliary ships because they usually served as floating bases at sea for men serving on destroyers and submarines. The AEFNR totaled 143 officers and 4,344 enlisted men, along with Red Cross, Salvation Army, and Knights of Columbus volunteers.

Conflicts with the British arose immediately. First, the British would not allow any U.S. or French officers above the rank of colonel to go to Russia. To enforce that, some British officers on the expedition were given quick promotions to place them above the Americans and French. That kept U.S. and French officers always subordinate to British officers. Second, the British did not load medical supplies on the troop ships as promised. According to three American officers who wrote a history of the expedition, many men on the ships came down with the flu while on the voyage, and 100 died.[20]

❖

Archangel had already been occupied by a small Allied contingent from Murmansk. That force entered Archangel harbor on August 1, 1918, two days before Wilson's invasion force arrived at Liverpool. That first Archangel landing had been accomplished with a British naval flotilla that included an aircraft carrier, light cruiser, two submarine chasers, and six armed trawlers. They were joined by the *Amiral Aube* and the *Olympia* from Murmansk. A force of 1,400 troops of eleven nationalities went ashore, including fifty U.S. sailors commanded by Captain Bierer.[21]

Archangel was a much larger port than Murmansk. Archangel was on the White Sea and connected to Murmansk on land by a lonely snow trail that meandered for 367 miles. The distance was about 50 miles shorter by sea. Archangel was capital of the province that bore its name, and usually around 40,000 people lived in the city. But lately the population had been swollen by Russians fleeing the Reds to the south.

Cheka agents were stealing military supplies from Allied warehouses in Archangel—everything from barbed wire to small arms and ammunition, artillery, trucks, field kitchens, ambulances, telegraph wire, and TNT. Britain alone had delivered 4 million tons of supplies to Archangel, and the Reds were stealing it at the rate of 3,000 tons a week.[22] Trotsky told Raymond Robins that the Soviet government would pay for the stolen Allied supplies, but never did. The Allies weren't worried about the money. They wanted to keep these supplies out of Soviet and German hands.

The Allied naval force that first approached Archangel in August was met by artillery fire from the fortified island of Mudyug, about forty-five miles offshore. A British seaplane bombed the island, knocked out the artillery batteries, and blew up the powder magazine. The Reds then tried to block the channel by sinking two icebreakers. But the Allied ships sailed around them. Next day, the invasion commander, British Major General Frederick C. Poole, went ashore.

Archangel Russians faithful to the Allied cause overthrew the local Bolsheviks and set up a new soviet. These loyalists declared independence for Archangel and welcomed their Western occupiers. The Germans, after all, were in nearby Finland. Cheering crowds and boat whistles greeted the Allied troops as they marched up Archangel's main street. Cheka agents quickly dropped their burglary operations, torched some buildings, and fled on the railroad south to Vologda. Counting Russian soldiers, seamen, and workmen, and Germans, the Soviet force in Archangel had numbered around 8,000.[23]

Just before the August landing, Lenin was reported to have said in Moscow that a "state of war" existed between Russia and the Allies. American, French, Italian, and British diplomats, including DeWitt Poole, confronted Georgy Vasilyevich Chicherin, who had replaced Trotsky as commissar for foreign affairs. They demanded to know if this meant that "de facto" relations between Russia and the Allies had been ruptured.

At first, Chicherin evaded the question. He said Lenin had spoken in a meeting "behind closed doors" and public explanations could not be given about "non-public utterances." Chicherin then said a "state of defense rather than a state of war" existed between Russia and the Allies, and that Moscow wanted to continue relations with the West. He said he would check with the Council of Commissars for further guidance.

But after the Archangel invasion, Chicherin and his assistant Lev Kara-khan met with DeWitt Poole and the consul generals of Sweden and Japan. Lenin, it seemed, had no intention of going public to retract his statement. Chicherin said the Soviet government did not desire a state of war but would take "de facto measures of war" to the extent that such measures were directed against it.

Chicherin argued that "the elementary principle of international law" had been violated by the Allied invasion of Archangel and by the "subsequent execution" of Bolshevik members of the local soviet there. He claimed "no responsibility" for the "future safety" of private citizens the Soviets had taken hostage in retaliation for the Archangel invasion.

"I informed Chicherin that I had no knowledge of events in the north," Poole reported to State on August 5, "but could warn him that the peoples of the Allied nations are not of a character to be intimidated, that the beginning of a system of reprisals by the Soviet government could only result in the individual members of that government being in the end held personally responsible, and in the loss to the Bolshevik cause of whatever respect it may now have in the minds of the civilized world."

Poole complained in his report that he was working "without instructions" from Washington in this situation. This lack of direction from Washington would continue as Poole and his spies plotted their coup against Lenin.

Poole wanted assurances from Chicherin that American and Allied officials would not be molested. Chicherin gave Poole his "solemn assurance" that diplomatic and consular officials "would be respected." But in a report on August 6, Poole said Soviets forcibly entered the French and British consulates after that second meeting with Chicherin and made mass arrests. The prisoners were released at three o'clock the next morning through the "untiring efforts" of the Swedish consul general.

That was it, as far as Poole was concerned. It was time to get out of Russia.

"In these circumstances of manifest bad faith, there was no assurance that the American Consulate General would not be violated at any moment," he added in his August 6 report. "It was necessary to destroy codes and records. The absence of these, together with the continued unlawful conduct of the de facto authorities, now renders it materially impossible, even in the absence of other considerations, to continue the exercise of my functions. I am accordingly asking the Swedish Consul General this afternoon to take over protection of American interests and at the same time request facilities for the immediate departure of the American consular and diplomatic staff. Other Allied consuls doing likewise."

Poole said that Western diplomats would leave via Petrograd and Stockholm. The Swedish consul general asked Berlin to provide them safe passage through the German-occupied areas of the Baltic, though documents do not indicate if any such assistance was rendered.[24]

In Moscow, news of the August landing at Archangel spread quickly. The Soviets at first didn't know exactly how large this landing force was, and plans were made to move the government east of the Urals.[25] Then after a few days the Soviets saw that it was not the big invasion they had feared from President Wilson. Lenin and Trotsky returned to Moscow, and plans to evacuate the government were called off, at least for the time being.

The British and French opened a concentration camp at Mudyug for Reds they captured. The rough wood buildings were built by the first prisoners. The barracks held around 1,000 POWs, of whom about 300 were reported to have died from typhus and scurvy or from torture and execution by prison staff. According to a camp survivor, Russian journalist Pavel Rasskazov, one of the Allied interrogators at Mudyug was a Franco-Russian named Ernest Beaux, a former tsarist perfumer. The elegantly dressed Beaux later emigrated to France and went to work for Coco Chanel. He was said to have been the man who developed Chanel No. 5 to capture the essence of snow melting on black earth in "the land of the midnight sun."[26]

The locals called the camp Death Island. A tall stone obelisk was later built at the site in memory of the victims, and tours of the site are still conducted. The United States does not seem to have been involved in the camp.

25

SECURITY BREAKDOWNS

A s President Wilson's Polar Bears steamed toward Archangel, Latvian commander Eduard Berzin met with Bruce Lockhart in Moscow to talk about the possibility of Lettish troops joining the Allied coup. This was the meeting that had been set up earlier. Jacob Peters in his Cheka report wrote that Berzin went to Lockhart's Moscow apartment on August 14, 1918.

"Lockhart asked about the Latvian units and whether they could be relied upon during a coup," Peters said. "He then indicated that it was necessary to make efforts in this direction so that the Latvian riflemen would rise up against the Soviet state and overthrow it. In pursuing this, Lockhart stressed vigorously more than once that money would be of no cost."[1]

Another meeting was set for the following evening. Lockhart at that time introduced Berzin to French Consul General Grenard and his "agent" Constantine (Sidney Reilly). Peters wrote that Grenard offered "self-determination in the full meaning of the word" to Latvia in exchange for the Letts' help with the Allied coup.[2]

Lockhart asked Berzin how much money he needed for bribing the Latvian officers. Berzin at first waved off such bourgeois considerations. Then he casually mentioned 4 or 5 million rubles. The money was promised—2 million right away and the rest in three weeks. It was agreed that future communications would be made through Shmidkhen, Berzin, and Reilly.

Shmidkhen also suggested at this time that Berzin find someone to deliver a coded message to the Allies in Murmansk regarding the hiring of the Latvians. The Cheka report said the following message was printed on white calico and given to Berzin by Lockhart:

British Mission
Moscow 17 August 1918
  To all British military authorities in Russia
  The bearer of this, Captain of the Lettish rifles, Krish Krankel, has
an important errand for the British General Staff in Russia. I request
that he be granted free passage and assistance in all matters.
                                                            —*R. B. Lockhart*[3]

Reilly became the case officer running the operation. His assistant, George Hill, would step in if anything happened to Sidney.[4]

On August 17, Reilly and Berzin met at the Café Tramble on Tsvetnoy Boulevard, Sidney's favorite Moscow *Treff* (German for secret meeting place). The café was in an ornately decorated three-story domed building on a noisy corner in the middle of town. It was also called the Annenkov House, built in 1776 for the governor-general of Siberia.

In the tradition of Russian cafés of a certain type, the Tramble was a thoroughly democratic place, a favorite hangout for writers, painters, musicians, prostitutes, drug dealers, speculators, spies, and subversives plotting against whomever was in their sights at the time. Tables were positioned discretely behind potted palms while small rooms offered privacy for more covert talks. A couple of violin players serenaded the customers while cocaine was sold under the counter and alcohol was served in violation of the national prohibition. According to German café artist Jeanne Mammen, the bandits who frequented the place did not bother the poets.[5] Berzin, with his trench coat and high-crowned fedora, must have fit in well with the ambience of the Tramble.

During their meeting, Reilly described to Berzin the operation he had in mind. He said it had been suggested by a French general, probably Jean Lavergne. Reilly wanted two Latvian regiments transferred to Vologda. There they would go over to the Allies and prepare the way for the Western invaders to move south from Archangel to Moscow. Reilly wanted the remaining Latvians in Moscow to assassinate Lenin, Trotsky, and other members of the Soviet government. Then former imperial army officers would be called up to establish order in Moscow and transport Bolshevik prisoners to Archangel. Reilly gave Berzin 700,000 rubles and told him to set up a safe house.[6]

The Cheka report continues: Reilly and Berzin met again on August 19, this time at their new safe house, 4 Griboyedovsky Lane. Reilly gave Berzin several assignments, including investigating whether there were wagonloads of gold stored at the Mikino station and guarded by Latvian troops. A third meeting was on August 21. Berzin wanted more money. Reilly returned to the safe house the next day with another 200,000 rubles and promised an additional million. On August 27, Reilly gave Berzin another 300,000 rubles and told him to go to Petrograd and meet with Latvians there. Berzin was given a Petrograd address: 10 Torgovaya Street, Apartment 10. A woman named Elena Mikhailovna lived there. Berzin was to ask for Mr. Massino, Reilly's cover name in Petrograd.

It should be noted that George Hill said Reilly told him on August 22 that he opposed assassination because it would turn the Soviet bosses into martyrs.[7] Reilly wanted to simply arrest Lenin and the others and humiliate them by parading them through the streets of Moscow in their underwear. After that, presumably the British would haul them off to England to stand trial for treason against Russia. But a Cheka agent who infiltrated the Allied spy ring said that Reilly was indeed pushing assassination plans.[8]

The Soviets called the 1918 Allied coup attempt the Lockhart Conspiracy because Bruce was head of British diplomacy in Russia, and if they could blame the Moscow plot on him, they could swap him for Litvinov in London. Others have called it the Reilly Plot because Sidney took it over from Lockhart and paid the Latvians. It could also be the Cromie Conspiracy, since he set the whole thing up. And why not the Poole Plot, since DeWitt had first tried to organize it in 1917? Or maybe the Lansing Plot, since it was his idea originally? Or the Wilson Plot, because he was the head of state who okayed it? Russians have also called it the Conspiracy of the Ambassadors because of the American, French, and British diplomats involved—Francis, Poole, Noulens, Grenard, and Lockhart. With all those competing views, a simpler term is the Lenin Plot.

By getting involved with the Latvians, Reilly was exceeding his instructions. London had told him only to survey the situation and get out of the country. Now he had taken over the role of paymaster in the scheme. Reilly later defended his drifting away from his original instructions by claiming that the planned coup was an opportunity that couldn't be allowed to slip away. Russian draftees were deserting the Red Army in droves, he said. They didn't like fighting before, and the Soviets' new forced conscription hadn't changed their minds. He intended to take advantage of that.

He did have a point. Building the new Red Army was slow going for Trotsky. The provisional government's Russian Revolutionary Army had been lost in a dust cloud after Lenin turned it into a mob of deserters in late 1917, and after that, the ranks of the temporary Bolshevik army had to be propped up with German deserters and Chinese mercenaries. The Red Guards hadn't been much help, either. They tended to be insolent and undisciplined. Many were criminals who continued their activities under color of law. They were being minimized and would soon be disbanded altogether.

The Latvians were the most reliable professional troops the Soviets had in Moscow. But like the Chinese, the Latvians had no patriotic ties to the Reds. They served for money. Whoever paid them controlled the capital. Reilly resolved to be their new commander. He saw himself as a reincarnated Napoléon.

"And why not?" he asked. "A Corsican lieutenant of artillery trod out the embers of the French Revolution. Surely a British espionage agent, with so many factors on his side, could make himself master of Moscow?"[9]

When Berzin got to the apartment in Petrograd, looking for Mr. Massino, the doorman reported that Elena Mikhailovna had left for work and would return around four P.M. He handed Berzin the apartment key and said he could wait for her. The Cheka report on the case said Berzin found an envelope in the apartment while he was waiting. It was addressed to "Citizeness" Elena Mikhailovna Boyuzhavskaya. ("Comrade" was a form of address used only in the Red Army and the Communist Party.)

Inside the envelope, Berzin found a visiting card from Sidney Georgievich Reilly. On the back was written a Moscow address: 3 Sheremetevsky Alley, Apartment 85. Berzin wrote down the address, waited until noon, then left.[10]

Leaving his address on his card was another piece of slack tradecraft on Reilly's part that would come back to burn the Allied plotters.

❖

Reilly's assistant in the Lenin Plot, George Hill, was much better than Sidney in observing operational security. He was born in Estonia, son of an English general merchant, and grew up fluent in several languages, including Russian. That helped him become a successful businessman in St. Petersburg.

Hill was fishing in British Columbia when war broke out in 1914. He joined a Canadian light infantry unit and was sent to France. There he worked as an interpreter and intelligence officer for the Canadian Scottish Brigade. One night he crawled across No Man's Land to listen to Germans talking in their trenches and was wounded by an enemy grenade. When he woke up in a military hospital he found his legs draped with a kilt of the wrong tartan. He said that worried him more than his wounds.

In 1917, after his recovery, he was sent to Bulgaria and Russia as a counterintelligence officer and saboteur. He was twenty-four years old. His code name was IK8. Late one evening a man followed IK8 down a dark street. Hill did not carry a gun. He knew the Cheka could shoot him for that. But he did carry a sword in his walking stick, and he turned around and stabbed his stalker. Then he continued to his hotel. Once he was safe in his room, he examined the blade.

"I had never run a man through before," he wrote later. "It was not a gory sight. There was only a slight film of blood halfway up the blade and a dark stain at the tip . . ."[11]

When the Cheka raided French and British missions and apartments after the August 1918 landing at Archangel, Hill and Reilly managed to escape to one of their dozen or so Moscow safe houses. The raids didn't faze Hill and he ordered his men to continue sabotage operations against the Red Army.[12] So did Henri de Verthamon. Like Savinkov, when de Verthamon's apartment was raided, he escaped by climbing out a window and running across rooftops. But a dozen of his agents weren't so fast and they got arrested.

As Moscow baked in the dog days of August, Berzin assured Reilly that the Latvians in Moscow would be ready for a coup in a few weeks. That should coincide neatly with Wilson's Archangel invasion that was expected in early September. But then another breakdown in security occurred for the Western plotters. This one would prove as devastating to the Allies as the slaughter of the royal family had been to the Bolsheviks.

❖

A group of key Allied conspirators met at the American consulate in Moscow on August 25, 1918. Consul General DeWitt Poole and Xenophon Kalamatiano were there, along with de Verthamon, Reilly, and French Consul General Grenard. The U.S. consulate probably was chosen for the meeting because at that time the Soviets did not consider the Americans as serious a threat as the French and British. But the building was undoubtedly being watched by Chekists. That got the meeting off to a dangerous start.

The U.S. consulate occupied an imposing white stone villa that had belonged to a distinguished Russian bacteriologist named Gabrichevsky, a friend of Auguste Rodin's. A sculpture by Rodin still sits in the garden. "The furniture is beautiful . . . the rooms are large and handsomely finished, and all who have seen it say it is the handsomest consulate in Europe," the late consul general, Maddin Summers, said in a report.[13]

The consulate took up most of the house, with rooms turned into work areas for translators and typists. In anticipation of coming trouble, Madame Gabrichevsky had stored a supply of food in the house for the consular staff. The grounds were patrolled by the butler, a Caucasian dressed in native costume and carrying a dagger, revolver, and cartridge belt.[14]

After the Cheka raids on the Allied missions earlier in August, the Western diplomats had joined Poole in deciding it was time to leave Russia. The purpose of this meeting at the U.S. consulate was to make plans for conducting secret "stay behind" operations against the Soviets after the consuls departed. Those operations were intended to weaken Soviet military and railroad capabilities before a larger Allied invasion force, including the Czech Legion, arrived to liberate Moscow and Petrograd. Kalamatiano and Hill volunteered to stay and collect military intelligence. De Verthamon would keep up his sabotage projects. Reilly was to direct the Latvian uprising in the capital and the murder of Lenin.

But Reilly had experienced a strange premonition about this meeting. It seemed to be a warning of some kind, instinctive and intuitive.

"I had an uneasy feeling (such as one frequently gets in dangerous situations when one's nerves are constantly on the *qui vive*) that I should keep to myself and not go to the meeting," he recalled. "But in the end I allowed myself to be persuaded."[15]

❖

When the conspirators met in Poole's office, Reilly immediately grew suspicious of a visitor who introduced himself as René Marchand, a correspondent for *Le Figaro* and *Le Petit Parisien* in Paris. *Le Figaro* was a conservative royalist paper and the largest national daily in France. *Le Petit Parisien* was one of the biggest newspapers in the world, sensationalist yellow journalism for the masses.

What in the world was a reporter doing there? It was supposed to be a secret meeting of top American and Allied spies. Grenard didn't seem concerned.

He described Marchand as a confidential agent of the French government. Reilly didn't believe it. He told Marchand his name was Rice.

"And here it was that the uneasy feeling which had been haunting me all along became acute," Sidney wrote.[16]

Reilly didn't want to discuss anything around Marchand. He drew de Verthamon into a darkened room for talks. In the middle of their conversation, Reilly looked around. Marchand had crept into the room. He was standing in the shadows by the doorway.

What was he *doing*?

Sidney and Henri quickly ended their talks and got out of there.

The other plotters weren't so cautious. In Marchand's presence they discussed their plan to overthrow the Soviet régime and replace it with an Allied-friendly provisional government under Lieutenant General Nikolai Nikolayevich Yudenich, former chief of staff of the tsar's Caucasian army. Yudenich had been decorated for his victories over the Turks in the war but Kerensky fired him for insubordination after the revolution. Yudenich then supported Kornilov in his attempted coup against Kerensky and Lenin.

Now in August 1918 the fifty-six-year-old Yudenich commanded his own private volunteer army in northwestern Russia. He was standing by to invade Moscow at Reilly's order. After that, he and the Latvians would move into the field and support Savinkov in conquering Petrograd.[17]

Reilly admitted the plan was rather ambitious. Grandiose might be a better word. But the Soviets still held only two major cities, Petrograd and Moscow. Take those away from them and they would be out of business.

After the meeting adjourned, Poole sent Kalamatiano to Samara, an industrial city about 500 miles southeast of Moscow, strategically located at the confluence of the Volga and Samara rivers. Samara was also on the Trans-Siberian Railway, held by the Czech Legion. The Czechs had defeated the Reds near Samara back in June and had set up the Komuch, a committee that planned to govern Russia until a new constituent assembly could meet. It was probably the first real anti-Soviet government formed in European Russia after the Bolshevik coup. The Samara Komuch was made up mostly of SRs, and they set about revoking all decrees ordered by the Bolsheviks. They restored private enterprise, allowed trade unions, and returned farms and factories to their owners.

Ambassador Francis reported to Washington that Poole and Kalamatiano were working on organizing an "all-Russian regeneration movement" in

Samara, through the U.S. consulate there.[18] If they could merge the anti-Soviet forces in southeast Russia, they could support the coming Allied march on Moscow. This was a continuation of Poole's efforts in the first phase of the Lenin Plot, in late 1917.

Kalamatiano was assigned to pick up reports from his agents in Samara and tell the Czechs to hold their position in the area. Poole estimated there were 12,000 Czech troops in Samara.[19] Kal then planned to take the Trans-Siberian to Siberia and meet with additional Czechs and other anti-Soviet forces in the Far East.

But the American and Allied conspiracies in Moscow and South Russia were about to be blown thanks to this mysterious René Marchand. Exactly who *was* he?

26

A TRAITOR EXPOSED

B efore René Marchand was an infiltrator, he probably fit the description of a leech, a netherworld creature who attached himself to first one host, then another, holding onto each while he found a way to exploit it. But he seems to have started life in a conventional way. French historian and journalist Jacques Pierre Bainville, who knew Marchand well, said René came from a "good middle-class family" and that his father was a judge in Cherbourg. After Nicholas II visited France in 1896, young Marchand attached himself to tsarism.

"That day the enthusiastic and brilliant college student René Marchand received the inspiration that changed his life," Bainville said. At Cherbourg he met some officers of the Russian navy, "charming and very foreign." Marchand "mingled with them; he commenced to learn their language. He became enraptured with Russia and dreamed of going there.

"Ten years later, in 1916, I saw René Marchand [as] a complete Russian," Bainville continued. "Heart and soul" he was "more a tsarist than many a Russian reactionary."

Then the revolution came, and the Bolshevik coup. Marchand changed his politics again. He attached himself to Bolshevism.

"He justifies Lenin as he justified even Rasputin and everything else that was not agreeable to see and hear in Russia," Bainville said. "He fights valiantly against the enemies of the Soviet Republic as he fought valiantly against the enemies of the Tsar."[1]

Marchand went to Russia supposedly as an anti-Soviet journalist, which explains why Grenard was deceived. Marchand seems to have been around forty years old when he infiltrated the meeting in Poole's office.

After the meeting broke up, Marchand left and phoned Cheka chief Felix Dzerzhinsky. Marchand said he had some important information for him. But he was afraid of being seen going to Dzerzhinsky's office. Dzerzhinsky sent a Chekist to escort Marchand to Felix's private apartment inside the Lubyanka. There they conferred behind closed doors.

❖

Dzerzhinsky was one of the most feared figures in the Soviet régime. He was noted for being pedantic and secretive, qualities that had drawn Lenin's attention. Because of his ruthlessness toward enemies of the state, Dzerzhinsky was called Iron Felix. Lockhart remembered him as a man of correct manners and quiet speech but without a ray of humor. The eyes were what really bothered Lockhart.

"Deeply sunk, they blazed with a steady fire of fanaticism," Lockhart recalled. "They never twitched. His eyes seemed paralyzed."[2]

Hundreds of suspects were taken to Cheka headquarters every night to be interrogated and tortured, then shot or packed off to labor camps where many of them would die anyway, from work, malnutrition, disease, murder, or suicide. Once during a meeting, Lenin sent Dzerzhinsky a note asking how many anti-Soviet prisoners were locked up in the Lubyanka. Felix wrote 1,500 on the note and returned it to him. Lenin then put a cross beside the figure and sent the note back to Felix. Dzerzhinsky read it, got up, and left. The cross on the note was Lenin's way of confirming that he had understood Dzerzhinsky's information. Felix thought it was an execution order. That night he had the 1,500 prisoners shot.

Estimates of Cheka murders conducted under Dzerzhinsky vary. A Russian historian quoted Cheka official Martin Ivanovich Latsis as saying that the Cheka executed 6,185 people in 1918, and 3,456 in 1919.[3] But the historian said newspapers suggested the figure was over 5,000 just for the last half of 1918. And that applied only to known Cheka murders.

❖

René Marchand told Dzerzhinsky what he had seen and heard at the secret meeting in DeWitt Poole's office. Iron Felix phoned Lenin and informed him. Lenin asked if Marchand would write it down as a report. Marchand refused. He was afraid of being exposed as a Red agent. That would discredit him as a journalist.

Lenin suggested that Marchand write his account in the form of a letter of protest to French President Raymond Nicolas Landry Poincaré. The Cheka could then *discover* the letter in Marchand's room during a routine raid. Marchand agreed. He wrote it and Dzerzhinsky edited it. After that, Marchand went back to his room and put the letter on a table where it would be found by the raiders. Here are the main points Marchand made in his letter:

—He said he was "positively revolted" and "absolutely stupefied" by the plots he heard Reilly and de Verthamon discuss at the Allied meeting. Those plans included blowing up the railway bridge across the River Volkhov near the Zvanka station. Reilly described in the "coolest possible way" how this would cut Petrograd's railway links to the north and east and "immediately result in an absolute famine" for the city. Poole and Grenard were "not for a moment" disturbed by this prospect.

—While Reilly was taking care of that demolition, de Verthamon would destroy the Cherepovets Bridge on the eastern line out of Petrograd, an operation "no less appalling," Marchand said. De Verthamon also offered to destroy Soviet rolling stock carrying war supplies.

—Reilly planned to mount his coup on August 28 during the All-Russian Congress of Soviets in Moscow. Reilly and a combat squad would be hiding behind curtains in the theatre, armed with pistols and hand grenades. At a signal from Reilly, the Latvian soldiers would close all exits and cover the audience with their rifles. Then Reilly and his assassins would jump out and shoot Lenin and Trotsky.

—Marchand said that "official representatives of the United States" were at the meeting in Poole's office and agreed to all of the above. Marchand specifically identified Poole, but not Kalamatiano.

—In conclusion, Marchand said, "Quite a new light was thrown for me upon the real plans of our [Allied] representatives and upon the diplomatic and military measures by means of which they proposed to further the 'speedy success' of intervention. Espionage of the meanest kind; plots and outrages craftily prepared in the dark; appeals to agents with a career before them to discover imaginary documents: to such a pass had come those who had the honour to represent France before the Russian people!"

Marchand claimed he had turned against the Allies because they were run by "gentlemen war profiteers" who served only the "cause of international capitalism."[4] He said every effort was made to represent Bolshevism as the tool of German imperialism because that was necessary to make it hateful in the eyes of the French masses. "This is a low political manoeuvre but a manoeuvre so crude and maladroit as to reveal the straits to which the French bourgeoisie is driven to bolster up its unstable authority." The French government had committed acts to "stifle the cry of revolt" from the country's working class, he added, and their bumbling had led to "disastrous foreign adventures and catastrophes."[5]

Jacques Bainville, though, cut through the revolutionary rhetoric to sum up Marchand this way: "Because I understand René Marchand, this Russianized Frenchman more Russian than the Russians themselves, I understand why Bolshevism survives in that country. It is not a land of level minds, but a country where only unbalanced enthusiasts really thrive."[6]

What did DeWitt Poole have to say about all this?

❖

Poole would appear before the U.S. Congress in 1920 to testify about the Moscow meeting. He was sworn in and promised to tell the truth. But in standard espionage style his answers to questions were vague, evasive, and contradictory.

Under questioning by Senator George H. Moses of New Hampshire, chairman of the subcommittee investigating Bolshevism, Poole admitted there had been a meeting at the consulate but claimed he was not present when any bridge destruction was discussed.

"I deny that I have any recollection of it, or that I had anything to do with it," Poole said.

There had been an "incidental meeting" in his office, Poole said. But he wasn't sure of the date—just August 1918. Then he changed his story a little. It wasn't a "meeting," it was a "conference." Forty or fifty people came in and out of the consulate that day, he said, and four or five people were at this "conference." He named Marchand, Grenard, Kalamatiano, and a "British employee whose name I cannot recall."

Wade Hampton Ellis of Ohio, a former assistant U.S. attorney general, and counsel for the subcommittee, asked if Kalamatiano had been left behind in Moscow to conduct a plot against the Soviets.

"No, in no way whatsoever," Poole replied. "On the contrary, everything of that kind was expressly excluded from his activities. It was our duty to inform our governments of what was going on, and we took such means as were at our disposal to obtain this information. And it was in that connection that Mr. Kalamatiano offered to remain in Russia after my departure, solely for the purpose of obtaining information and transmitting it to this government, which offer was accepted."

Just "obtaining information"? Subcommittee member Thomas William Hardwick, a Washington lawyer and former senator from Georgia, wasn't satisfied with that. He asked Poole directly if Kalamatiano was a spy.

"No. I deny that statement absolutely and entirely . . . His work consisted of going about and being among the people and getting information as to conditions, and reporting to the consul general on them, which of necessity is different from espionage work in the way you use the word. It was a matter purely of information."

Hardwick asked if General Lavergne, the French military attaché, was at the meeting.

"I cannot tell you," Poole answered. "It is very possible that he was."

"It is very possible?" Hardwick asked. "That is as close as you can come to it?"

"Yes. But I cannot recall it."

Was de Verthamon at the meeting?

"It is possible he was there. But I do not recall the name."

Hardwick pressed on. Was Reilly the "British employee" whose name Poole could not recall?

"It is perfectly possible that it was," Poole replied. "But I will tell you very frankly that the employees of my colleagues were certainly something that did not concern me . . . I have heard, after I left Russia, the mention of a so-called British agent Reilly."

Poole then quoted from President Wilson's message regarding the U.S. invasion of Russia: "In taking this action the government of the United States wishes to announce to the people of Russia in the most public and solemn manner that it contemplates no interference with the political sovereignty of Russia—any intervention in her internal affairs—not even in the local affairs of the limited areas which our military forces may be obliged to occupy . . ."

A student of semantics might see Wilson's message as an example of what George Orwell in his book *Nineteen eighty-four* would later call doublespeak. American troops were not going to invade Russia. They were simply going to "occupy" parts of the country. But that wasn't "interference" in Russia's "sovereignty" or "internal affairs."

Poole summed it up this way:

"I want to deny any implication of activity against the Soviet republic."[7]

❖

From now on, the Lenin plotters would find themselves in increasingly dire straits. Much of that came from their own faulty security measures:

—Captain Cromie did not properly vet Jan Shmidkhen before sending him on to recruit Latvian Colonel Berzin for the Allied coup. Berzin reported the approach to the Cheka.

—Reilly wrote the address of his Moscow safe house on that card that Berzin found in Sidney's Petrograd safe house. Berzin gave the address to the Cheka.

—Lockhart wrote and signed a pass for a Latvian courier who was going to meet with Allied forces at Archangel. The message didn't go north. It ended up with the Cheka.

—Reilly gave cash to Berzin, not knowing he was an agent provocateur sent by the Cheka. Berzin turned the money in to the Cheka.

—The Allies failed to check Marchand's bona fides, allowing him to witness the secret meeting in Poole's office and write an account for Dzerzhinsky and Lenin.

With all that evidence in hand, Dzerzhinsky and Jacob Peters began planning a roll-up of Western agents in Russia. The roundup sprang into a full emergency after Comrade Chairman Lenin was struck down by gunfire.

27

"THEY SHOT LENIN!"

Friday, August 30, 1918, was a bloody day for Lenin, for one of his top officials, and for some of his most persistent enemies. The day opened with a shooting, and closed with a shooting. When it was over, a Cheka chief was dead and Lenin lay bleeding on a factory driveway with two bullets in his body. Allied agents seem to have been involved, at least from the shadows.

Moisei Solomonovich Uritsky was the first shot that day. The assassin was Leonid Akimovich Kannengiser, a twenty-two-year-old poet and revolutionary. Leonid's father was a respected and well-to-do Petrograd engineer; people addressed him with traditional courtesy titles such as "your honor." Leonid's mother was a doctor. They had servants and spoke French at home rather than Russian or Yiddish. Leonid, known by the diminutive Lenya, graduated from Gurevich High School in Petrograd in 1913. Two years later he joined something he called the Labor People's Socialist Party.

For a while, Kannengiser was a junker (cadet) at the Mikhailovskoye Artillery School in Petrograd. Later, he claimed to have had connections with an anti-Bolshevik group called the Union of Socialist Junkers of the Petrograd Military District. When the revolution arrived in February 1917 he was a student at Peter the Great Polytechnic Institute. Lenya admired Kerensky and was one of the junkers who tried to defend the Winter Palace during the Bolshevik coup. Then he went on a holy crusade against the Reds. He claimed he was ready to give up his own life in the process.

"My son Leonid was always, from childhood, very impulsive, and he had flashes of extreme excitement, in which he reached insolence," his father, Akim Samuelovich Kannengiser, later told the Cheka. "Therefore, his upbringing was a very difficult, troublesome business."[1]

Kannengiser began writing poetry while he was a teenager. Just before the revolution he recited some of his works at the Halt of Comedians, a basement cabaret at No. 7 Field of Mars, an army training square near the Summer Palace in Petrograd.[2] The word "halt" probably meant an impermanent place. Serge Sudeikin's Expressionist painting, *Halt of Comedians*, shows a dimly lit scene occupied by a court jester, a masked harp player, and a nude woman gazing into a mirror.

Lenya rubbed literary elbows at the cabaret with Anna Akhmatova, Boris Pasternak, and other luminaries from the Silver Age of Russian culture at the turn of the century. He also frequented a club called the Stray Dog. But that was a "malicious, shameful place," the Cheka said, not to be confused with the famous literary café of the same name that had closed at the beginning of the war. The Cheka claimed that Lenya had no real talent as a poet but liked to hang out with those who did. Nevertheless, *Severniye Zapiski* (Northern Notes), a Petrograd literary and political monthly, published some of his poems.

Kannengiser's older brother Sergei committed suicide in 1917. Another brother, a delegate to the Petrograd Soviet, accidentally shot himself to death while unloading a revolver. The young people in the Kannengiser family were "unbalanced," a friend later told the Cheka.

"Once, when talking about God," the friend, Vladimir Ginzburg, said of Lenya, "he told me that God exists and told me to read the gospel, from which he said he found something special."

Kannengiser began to stay away from home in the summer of 1918. He told his father he was involved with a woman. Kannengiser's Cheka file identified her as Pallada Olympovna Bogdanova-Belskaia, a poetess who conducted a literary salon in her home. The Cheka called her a legendary charmer, a Bohemian, and a *charlot* (French for clown).

"A hopeless graphomaniac and a nymphomaniac who loved both men and women," the file said. She "dragged behind her a whole train of suicides of the fans she left . . . She compensated for [her] lack of talent with fertility and exaltation." The file mentioned a rumor, for what it was worth, that Pallada had been a lover of Savinkov's bomber Igor Sazonov just before they murdered Plehve.

Pallada was thirty years old and Lenya was nineteen when she took him as her lover. She used any excuse to keep his attention, including writing the boy long letters (the graphomania). Kannengiser's father became concerned about Lenya's absences from home and his impulsive and romantic nature. Lenya had developed secretive ways but denied he was involved in any anti-Bolshevik activities. His mother, though, was convinced he was playing a dangerous game of some kind.

But why did Kannengiser kill Uritsky?

One story is that the Cheka published a list of twenty-five people they had executed and Lenya found that one of them was a homosexual lover of his. Another story says that the orders to execute the twenty-five had been signed by Uritsky and Alexander Solomonovich Yosilevich, and that Lenya was heartbroken at the idea of Jews murdering Jews.

But the Cheka had another version. They said Uritsky was targeted because he knew that Kannengiser and some of his revolutionary comrades were covertly running an assassination squad and planning a coup in Petrograd.

❖

The man Lenya shot, Moisei Uritsky, was a Ukrainian who originally had been a leftist Menshevik. He went over to the Bolsheviks during the war. He was said to be an ardent revolutionary and a man of inflexible logic, an efficient, ferocious Bolshevik zealot.

"He made fun of all those eloquent speeches full of pathos about the great and beautiful," recalled Anatoly Lunacharsky, minister of education and arts under Lenin. "He was proud of being level-headed and was fond of making play with it, even to the point of apparent cynicism . . . For him, life outside the workers' movement did not exist. His enormous political passion did not seethe or bubble . . . He therefore expressed it only in action—highly effective action."

As Cheka chief in Petrograd, Uritsky used arrests and executions to try and purify the city of anti-Soviet resistance. He was their "most terrible foe," Lunacharsky said. Uritsky was opposed to executions but considered them expedient, Lunacharsky added. He saw Uritsky as a kind and good-hearted man who performed "thankless" work.[3]

Kannengiser went home for a few hours on the morning of August 30th and played chess with his sick father for a while. Lenya seemed tense and worried. When he lost the match, he was upset. He put on a black leather jacket and a cap with his student badge, and went to the Field of Mars at ten o'clock to rent a bicycle. He then rode to Uritsky's office at the Commissariat of Internal Affairs in Palace Square. He carried a Colt revolver he'd had for three months.

Lenya arrived at Uritsky's office at 10:30. He propped his bicycle outside, then calmly walked in and took a seat in the lobby. He smoked a cigarette while watching his bike. Half an hour later, Uritsky came in wearing a suit and tie. Lenya stood up and pulled his pistol from his jacket pocket. He fired once. The bullet entered Uritsky's head through an eye.

The gunshot was deafening in the small lobby. Smoke filled the room and Uritsky fell with blood gushing from his wound. People screamed. Lenya ran out and got on his bike. The elevator operator chased Lenya as he peddled furiously toward Alexandrovsky Square. A group of Chekists jumped into a car and joined the pursuit.

When they all reached the square, the Chekists shouted for Lenya to halt. Some nearby soldiers shot at him. In the confusion, a soldier drew his sword and rushed at another soldier.

"Not me!" the soldier said. "The one on the bike!"

Lenya crossed the square into Moshkov Lane. The Chekists commandeered a second car, belonging to the German consulate. They shot at Lenya. He shot back. He ducked into an alley off Millionaya Street, fell off his bike, and hurt his leg. He ran limping into a backyard and found a door to an apartment building. He ran up the inside stairs, banging on doors.

The Chekists and soldiers arrived outside, still shooting up the neighborhood. Finally a prince of the ancien régime answered the pounding on his door and found the desperate young man standing sweating in the hallway.

"They're following me!" Lenya cried. "Save me!"

"Go away," the prince replied.

He slammed the door. Lenya pounded on another door.

"Save me!" he said.

"I cannot," came the answer.

Finally Lenya barged into an apartment, startled the woman inside, and grabbed an overcoat to pull over his own jacket. He tried to slip down the front stairs of the building but Chekists grabbed him on the steps, took his pistol, and subdued him. Then they threw him into their car and hauled him off to headquarters.

❖

With Uritsky's murder, the Cheka clicked into emergency mode. Grigory Zinoviev, chairman of the Petrograd Soviet, had been the target of an assassination attempt just two nights before, and in June the commissar for the press, agitation, and propaganda, Moisei Markovich Goldstein, aka Volodarsky, was shot down. Now this. Zinoviev phoned Lenin at the Kremlin. Lenin immediately dispatched Dzerzhinsky to Petrograd to take over the case.

At first the Cheka blamed Uritsky's murder on French and British agents. British Consul Arthur Woodhouse and Commander Andrew Le Page, assistant to naval saboteur Francis Cromie, were arrested.[4] The American Red Cross found forty-six more British and twenty French locked up in the Peter and Paul Fortress as a result of the shooting of Uritsky. They were crowded into tiny damp cells with no exercise, no fresh air, no bedding, and almost no food. At the same time, forty-four Czechs were found in other cells, cold and nearly starving.[5] Diplomatic protests got the British and French released. But hundreds of Russians were also arrested, including Lenya's friends and family.

Kannengiser stonewalled Dzerzhinsky. He rambled on about God and hymns and eternal joy. They tortured him until he confessed. He insisted he had acted alone. He was locked up in Kronstadt Prison and executed several weeks later without trial. His family then fled to Poland.

The Allies might have been linked to the Uritsky assassination through Boris Savinkov. The Cheka had previously pinned Volodarsky's murder on Savinkov; they saw him as the backstage director of the assassination. Now they suspected he was involved in Uritsky's murder. A reward was offered for his capture, dead or alive. Later on, Grigory Ivanovich Semyonov (aka Vasiliev), an SR terrorist, was also implicated as one of the plotters.[6]

If Savinkov was tied to the Uritsky assassination, it probably would have been through Maximilian Filonenko, a cousin of Lenya's. During the war, Filonenko had been adjutant to an imperial army commander and was known for cruelty to his soldiers. But after the revolution he had a change of heart and became a defender of soldiers' interests. Savinkov helped him get assigned as a commissar at General Kornilov's headquarters. Following the Bolshevik coup, Savinkov set up his terror headquarters in Moscow. Filonenko ran things for him in Petrograd, where Uritsky was shot.

Vladimir Ivanovich Ignatiev, a member of the executive committee of the socialist junkers party that Kannengiser had belonged to, said Lenya and Filonenko ran their own secret assassination squad. They planned an armed uprising in Petrograd, Ignatiev said, probably assisted by Savinkov. The murder of Uritsky was supposedly their third attempt on his life.[7]

Did Savinkov set up the Uritsky assassination through Lenya and Filonenko? He could have been a good candidate for the job. Assassination was Savinkov's stock in trade. He had been practicing it for years, first against tsarists, then Bolsheviks, and he had been on the Allied payroll all summer. Also, Ignatiev said that Filonenko was taking money from the French, as was Savinkov.

❖

Lenin was the next to be struck down, just a few hours after Uritsky was murdered. Comrade Chairman was scheduled to make a speech that evening at the old Mikhelson Works across the river in south Moscow, but his inner circle was fearful.

"When the news came of Uritsky's death, Lenin's friends and relatives did their utmost to persuade him not to go to the meeting," Kremlin commandant Pavel Malkov recalled. "To calm them, he said over the dinner table that perhaps he would not go; all the same, he himself called up a car and drove off."[8]

Lenin approached these public rallies with a mixture of both pleasure and desperation. The fortunes of the Communist Party were at their lowest. Civil war raged. The still shaky young Red Army was fighting Allied invasion forces at Murmansk, Archangel, and Vladivostok, along with SRs, Czechs, Cossack armies, armed peasants, and roving bands of deserters and professional highwaymen. Another constant pressure on Lenin was the threat of a new invasion by the Germans. To make things worse, Lenin's New Russia was in economic depression, the ruble was still falling, and Moscow and Petrograd lay in the throes of starvation, cholera, and typhus.

The Soviets seemed unable to handle those calamities. After the mass murder of the Romanovs, and Lenin's refusal to pay Russia's foreign debts, the outside world was not rushing in to help the country in any manner, except by military coup. Thus, the Friday rallies by Lenin were necessary to prop up the morale of the proletariat. But he never knew in advance whether he would be welcome or not.

L.S. Sosnovsky, a member of the All-Russian Central Executive Committee, recalled encountering Lenin taking a walk alone outside the Kremlin earlier in the month with his collar turned up against the night's chill. Like President Wilson, Lenin did not want to be pestered by bodyguards. He insisted on no security when he went out for a walk. When traveling, his driver would protect him if necessary. Lenin's refusal to be guarded by a proper security detail would prove to be a bad decision.

Lenin asked Sosnovsky that night what factories he had visited lately and what was the mood of the workers. Sosnovsky told him of "stormy meetings" where he was pulled off the speaker's platform and barely managed to leave the floor.

"The mood of the workers is bad," he told Lenin. "And there are good reasons why. Again, in the last few days, nothing had been distributed on the ration cards. It is terrible to look at the faces of the women workers. They bear the stamp of famine."[9]

There was that word again. Localized starvation in Moscow and Petrograd was one thing. That could be explained away politically by blaming it on peasants hoarding their crops. But like hurricanes in the American South, famines and damaging hot weather had been regular visitors to Russia in the past. In the summer of 1918, Europe was plagued by an "intense" heat wave that was killing people, causing drought, and causing problems for military operations.[10] That led the German command to accuse the Allies of manipulating the weather as some kind of secret weapon.

Lenin knew a nationwide famine was coming. It might last for years. It would mow down millions of Russians like sickles in a wheat field. But was Comrade Chairman truly concerned? Lenin reportedly welcomed the 1892 Volga famine "as a factor in breaking down the peasantry and creating an industrial proletariat."[11]

Now on this Friday evening, August 30, 1918, Lenin's driver Stepan Kazimirovich Gil delivered him to the Mikhelson factory in one of the luxury cars the Soviets had expropriated from tsarist garages. A favorite model for Lenin was described as shaped like a peanut roaster. That would be one of the tsar's French Delaunay-Bellevilles, identified by its barrel-shaped engine compartment.[12]

Despite his health problems of nervousness, insomnia, high blood pressure, headaches, and fatigue, Lenin insisted that all Kremlin officials, including himself, make regular weekly speeches to the workers. He particularly liked the Friday night shows. As long as they were brief they were a good inspirational way to wrap up a hard week of micromanagement at the office. He had already spoken here at the Michelson on August 2, and had received a rousing reception.

But with Sosnovsky's warning in mind, what would tonight bring?

❖

When Lenin arrived at the plant, the sun was low in the distance, glooming across ancient rooftops that lay cooling beneath the marbled sky. The blush of summer had almost faded, and behind it the change of seasons was slipping in. The brick walls of the old factory were still hot from the afternoon, but already a chill was rising with the shadows as Ilych got out of his car.

This old industrial district was still a Medieval neighborhood of peeling tenements, squat log houses, and dirt lanes that wandered past beggars, ragged children, and outdoor stacks of firewood. Abandoned factories backed up to farmland that spread out parched and gray beneath the darkening sky. Drought had killed the crops. Now fires were clearing the debris.

It was around 7:30. A party rally was being held inside, but for safety reasons, Lenin's appearance had not been confirmed in advance. No one knew if he was going to appear, so no welcome committee was waiting for him outside. He walked in alone, leaving Gil at the car. It wasn't far, just a few steps.

The Michelson had been nationalized and was now manufacturing ordinance for the Red Army. When Lenin entered the building he was recognized and escorted to a hand grenade shop. That's where his audience waited.

Earlier, some gunpowder had caught fire and threatened to set off an explosion that would have removed the plant from any Allied agent's list of sabotage targets. But all hands had pitched in to put it out the blaze, resulting in a smudged but admirable victory for the iron battalions of the Michelson proletariat. Now the building had been aired out, the machines wiped down, the floors swept. The crowd waited eagerly.

"*Batyushka! On idet!*"

Little Father! He's coming!

The workers cheered as Lenin strode out onto the shop floor. He had just made a speech at the corn exchange in the Basmanny district downtown, and he was going to talk again on a favorite topic of his: "Two governments, the dictatorship of the proletariat and the dictatorship of the bourgeoisie."

Lenin saw workers everywhere. They stood on the floor, on top of the machines, on the steps to the upper levels, all watching the little man who shunned the clichéd revolutionary red arm band and leather jacket and cap. Lenin wore his customary inexpensive brown suit, color coordinated with his Vandyke beard. He did wear a cap, though it wasn't leather as often depicted in paintings. It was a floppy wool style favored by Belle Époque painters. He especially liked the cap because it irritated some of the stuffed shirts in the Kremlin.

The mob welcomed him with a collective roar.

"L'neen! L'neen!"

He smiled and raised his arms triumphantly.

He was home.

"We Bolsheviks are constantly accused of forsaking the slogans of equality and fraternity," Lenin said as he turned a piercing gaze on the crowd. "So let us now put things straight."[13]

Lenin's friend and biographer Valeriu Marcu said Comrade Chairman always spoke in a cut and dried manner. But Lenin was not a great orator. He was slow to warm up, he had a speech impediment that made him flub the "r" in his words, his speeches were not brilliantly written, and his diatribes were heavy with Bolshevik jargon that the proletariat couldn't understand unless it was patiently explained to them. But his audiences liked to be entertained by a rabblerouser. He played to that, strutting back and forth, puffing and snarling while spouting simplistic warnings of wreck and ruin.

Like Wilson, Lenin was a born showman. But Ilych didn't need a stage. He stayed on the factory floor surrounded by his faithful followers, assuring them he was not only their leader and savior but also their comrade, a man who wasn't too aloof to roll up his sleeves and get down on their level.

"What government replaced the tsar?" he asked. "The Guchkov-Milyukov government, which set about convening a constituent assembly in Russia."

That was the early provisional government, run by a coalition of conservatives and middle-of-the road socialists in the Duma.

They were backed by a "gang of capitalists pursuing their own imperialistic ends," Lenin said.

That would be the Western powers that sent military aid to assist the provisional government in fighting the Germans.

While Kerensky was "in the saddle," the provisional government "was only concerned with the vested interests of their friends, the bourgeoisie," Lenin said. "Power in fact passed into the hands of the *kulaks*, and the working people got nothing."

But if *kulaks* (prosperous peasants) had power in Russia, why didn't any of them belong to Lenin's ruling clique? Nor were there any workers in his inner circle. Lenin was an elitist who surrounded himself with other elitists.

Nevertheless, he was hitting his stride now and the Michelson workers applauded. He hooked his thumbs into his vest. It was one of his favorite gestures, suggesting he was an expert in some way, like a schoolteacher explaining a report card.

"Take America, the freest and most civilized country," he said. "There you have a democratic republic. But what do we really find? The brazen rule of a handful—not even of millionaires, but multimillionaires—while the people are in slavery and servitude. Where is your much vaunted equality and fraternity if the mills, factories, banks and all the country's wealth belong to the capitalists, and side by side with this democratic republic you have feudal servitude for millions of workers and unrelieved destitution? No, wherever democrats are in power, you have real, barefaced robbery. We know the true nature of the so-called democracies."

The United States had abolished slavery and involuntary servitude in the last century, but Lenin was not one to let truth get in the way of his alternative facts. He wiped his face and continued, pumping up the crowd like an evangelist at a tent revival.

"The secret treaties of the French Republic, of Britain and the other democracies have clearly revealed the underlying nature and essence of this whole business. Their aims and interests are as criminal and predatory as Germany's. The war has opened our eyes, and we clearly see the barefaced robber and plunderer in the guise of the defender of the fatherland. This robber raid must be countered by revolutionary action."

"Robber raid" was a phrase poetic in its simplicity and impact, made to swizzle around in the mouth like a drink of vodka. Lenin knew that blind political faith was based on basic issues that even the stupid could understand. His tactic was to pick at longfestering sores, to dig those wounds deeper. Death, terror, enemies, and revenge were his recurring themes.

He told the crowd that "the realities of life have taught the workers to realize that as long as the landowners are snugly installed in their mansions and magic castles, the right of assembly will not exist."

He failed to mention that he himself came from a family of landowners and that he, too, had grown up in a manor house. Nor did he bring up the fact that the Bolsheviks had shut down the constituent assembly last January as the Russian people exerted their right to assembly.

"The British, French, Italian and other workers are making more and more appeals and demands, indicating the approaching triumph of the world revolution," Lenin continued. "And our task today is to carry on our revolutionary work and to scorn the hypocrisy, the insolent outcries and lamentations of the predatory bourgeoisie."

The idea of a worldwide Bolshevik revolution was one of Lenin's recurring visions, like Reilly's ideas of himself as a reincarnated Napoléon. Lenin thought that no matter how bad things got in Russia, inflamed Communists from across the globe would rise up and march in to rescue the Soviet government from its problems.

"We have only one alternative," he said. "Victory or death!"

After that, he added his standard closing line, taken from the last letter his brother wrote before he was hanged: "That is all I had to say to you."

The crowd cheered. Lenin gave them a final wave and headed for the door in his short choppy steps. He didn't believe in encores or signing autographs. His speech had run twenty minutes and now he was hot and tired and wanted to go home.

But then, as he reached the exit, a series of things began to happen in rapid succession like the ticks of a metronome.

❖

According to documents released from the KGB archives and edited by historian Alter Litvin, here's what witnesses said occurred:[14]

First, a man in the crowd wearing a sailor's uniform and following Lenin turned and spread his arms to hold the people back inside the factory. The weight of the crowd pressed on him and he stumbled and fell to the floor. That blocked the doorway and created a bottleneck. Lenin emerged in the driveway almost alone. It was nearly dark. He continued on toward his car, where his driver Gil was waiting.

Three women had approached Gil at the car earlier and asked who was speaking in the factory. Gil, wishing to maintain security, told them he didn't know. The women laughed. "We'll find out," they said. Then they walked off. Now, after the speech, a crowd of men and women intercepted Lenin as he walked across the driveway. One witness estimated this was a crowd of about fifty, but many accounts of the shooting would turn out to be confused or contradictory. Some witnesses changed their stories when interviewed a second time. Others exaggerated their roles in the matter.

One of the women in the crowd was Maria Grigorievna Popova, described by the Cheka as a forty-year-old blonde wearing a gray blouse. She was dissatisfied with the difficulties in finding food. She told Lenin that she had sent her two daughters, Nina and Olga, to buy flour but that they failed because of roadblocks.

Lenin was about three steps from his car. Gil was sitting behind the wheel with the engine running. Popova later told the Cheka that she was to Lenin's right and slightly behind him. He turned to answer her at the same time he reached for the back door of his car.

A man extended his hand from the crowd. He seemed to be clearing a path. Then a woman emerged, wearing a black dress and holding a pistol. She was only a few feet from Lenin. He had his hand on the door handle and was talking to Popova.

Suddenly Lenin's face was lit by the flash of gunshots.

"Beregis!" someone shouted. Watch out!

Lenin was hit twice. He staggered backward, holding his neck. He tried to hook his arm on the car door but fell facedown onto the bricks. Popova spun away, holding her arm. She had been shot once in the left elbow.

Gil turned off the car engine, pulled his pistol from his belt, and ran around the car. He found Lenin lying on the ground. A woman was standing over him, holding a pistol. Gil said he knocked the pistol out of her hand and she ran off.

A man advanced on Lenin. Was he trying to help? Or was it another gunman moving in for the coup de grâce? Gil stepped in front of Lenin as a shield.

"Come no closer or I'll shoot," he said.

The man turned and fled. The crowd rippled out like waves from a stone hitting water. Screams echoed across the courtyard as people stampeded out into Serpukhovka Street.

"They shot Lenin!" a woman screamed.

28

DEATH WATCH

Gunsmoke formed an aura around Lenin as if he were a tragic figure in a Renaissance painting. Time was stopped in a snapshot of a bloody moment in history. One can only imagine the thoughts that raced through his mind. After all that had happened to him, after dancing past death so many times before, was this his destiny? To be shot down in a grimy factory, surrounded by the very working-class stiffs he scorned? Was this really happening to him? Yes, that was his blood on his shirt, his jacket, his hands.

The KGB documents on the case report that a paramedic in the crowd ran to Lenin's side. He and a female medical assistant and an employee of the commissariat of education helped Lenin get up and climb onto the back seat of his car.

"Did you catch him?" Lenin asked. The question suggested that Lenin thought he had been shot by a man.

"Catch Lenin's killer!" a Red Army deputy commissar, S.N. Batulin, shouted as he ran out to the street. He hadn't actually seen the face of the shooter, so he was looking for witnesses who could help identify the assailant. Meanwhile, the paramedic and a factory worker got into the back seat of the car with Lenin. The door was slammed shut. The car bounced as Gil went around and got in behind the wheel.

"There's a clinic nearby," somebody said.

"No," Gil said. "I'm taking him home."

Lenin heard the roar of the engine cranking up. He tried to raise himself up. It was no use. His strength was hemorrhaging with the blood running down his arm.

"Home," he said. "Take me home."

Gil drove down the driveway to the street. He turned and raced for the Kremlin without a police escort. Popova was taken to Pavlovsk Hospital. There she was searched and tied up before her gunshot wound was treated. They thought Popova was the one who had shot Lenin. After investigation, the Cheka dismissed her as an "ordinary philistine" with no dangerous political views, and let her go.

Meanwhile, Commissar Batulin walked up the street, still on the lookout for witnesses. He went a distance, and stopped. He turned around. A woman was standing beneath a tree holding a briefcase and umbrella.

She looked odd, Batulin said later. That's what drew his attention. She looked frightened. She looked like somebody trying to get away from something. Batulin walked up and asked her what she was doing.

"Why do you want to know?" she replied.

That further piqued his suspicions. He searched her pockets and briefcase. Historian Dmitri Volkogonov, who accessed Cheka files, wrote that a Browning pistol was found in the briefcase, but he did not cite a source.[1] The Cheka files released to the public in the 1990s did not mention a pistol in the briefcase.[2] Nor did Vladimir Nikolaevich Soloviev, senior prosecutor assigned to the Investigative Committee of the Russian Federation's General Prosecutor's Office, after he reopened the case in the 1990s.[3]

Batulin decided he had grounds to arrest this woman. He asked her to come with him. She did so, without a struggle. Soviet propagandists would later claim that a mob of incensed Communist children chased the woman down and arrested her.

"Why did you shoot Comrade Lenin?" Batulin asked her as they walked.

"Why do you want to know?" she repeated.

That confirmed Batulin's suspicions.

An angry crowd formed around Batulin and the woman as they went back toward the factory. Batulin feared a lynching. He called over some soldiers to help get the woman into a car. Then they sped off to the Zamoskvoretsky district military commissariat. There they locked her in a room while they called the Cheka.

She was stripped naked and searched by three women, one of them armed, while three soldiers stood at the door watching. They found on her a notebook, a metal brooch, cigarettes, some hairpins, a trade union card, and a railroad ticket to Tomilino, a village sixteen miles southeast of Moscow. Grigory Semyonov, the SR terrorist suspected of having a hand in the Uritsky assassination, had a dacha at Tomilino where he planned his operations.

❖

Lenin's driver pulled up at the entrance to the former Court of Justice, the Kremlin building where Lenin lived. He got out of the back seat with difficulty. The two men who had accompanied him held him up. They wanted to carry him up to his apartment but he insisted on walking so his wife and sister wouldn't be alarmed if they saw him. His helpers supported him on both sides as he made the long climb up the stairs to the third floor.

When he reached his apartment he collapsed on a chair in the vestibule to rest a minute. The apartment contained five small rooms. One room was his office. It held a desk, a rug, a couple of armchairs, and an iron single bed in the corner. There was one window, a portrait of Marx on the wall, and a small black statuette on the desk depicting a chimp holding Darwin's skull and studying it. A telegraph ticker in an adjacent corridor allowed Lenin to carry on conversations by direct wire. Behind his desk was a small escape door leading to the telephone switchboard room.[4]

Four physicians were called. Then a surgeon, Vladimir N. Rozanov, arrived for consultation. Somewhere in the midst of all this, the patient was moved to his bed.

Kremlin commandant Pavel Malkov was in his office when he received a phone call from Lenin's private secretary, Vladimir Bonch-Bruyevich.

"Fetch some pillows, half a dozen ordinary pillows," Bonch-Bruyevich said in a hoarse, shaky voice. "Ilych has been injured, seriously injured." Then he hung up.

Malkov later wrote that he shoved a guard aside and ran over to the Grand Kremlin Palace. He kicked in the door of a wardrobe and grabbed some pillows that used to belong to the tsar. Then he rushed across the street past some Latvian guards and up the steps of Lenin's building. When he got to the third floor he found the hallway outside Ilyich's rooms filled with grave-looking people speaking in low tones. For all they knew, they were on a death watch.

A guard opened Lenin's door and Malkov passed the pillows to Bonch-Bruyevich inside. Then Bonch-Bruyevich's wife, a doctor, went in. Lenin's wife Nadia appeared in the corridor, breathing heavily and walking with difficulty. A commissar held her up as she went into the apartment. She was only in her forties but Malkov thought she looked like an old woman.

The Kremlin had constant electrical problems, and only a few lights burned at night. As darkness gathered in the hallway, more doctors arrived, along with nurses. They all went in without saying a word, and the guard shut the door behind them. The quiet old building spoke with the creak of its floors.

Later, Malkov caught a look at Jacob Sverdlov, chairman of the All-Russian Central Executive Committee, sitting at the desk in Lenin's office. Sverdlov was son of a Novgorod engraver and had been a Bolshevik since Lenin walked out of the Social Democratic Party. Trotsky described Sverdlov as the "organizer-in-chief" of the party and the "president of the Soviet Republic."[5]

Sverdlov was Lenin's top lieutenant, a severe-looking man whose hands and face glowed in the lamplight on the desk as he wrote a manifesto, "To All the Population," calling for a renewed terror against enemies of the state.

The earliest Red Terror can be traced back to the Bolshevik coup and the forcible shutdown of the constituent assembly. It was stepped up in June 1918 after the assassination of Volodarsky. Until now the Terror had consisted mostly of arrests, interrogations, and jailings. As unpleasant as it was, it was a small fire. This new Terror, by comparison, was going to be a major conflagration.

Sverdlov's manifesto prompted Grigory Ivanovich Petrovsky, commissar for internal affairs, to send a telegram to all Cheka units ordering "an immediate end of looseness and tenderness." He ordered large numbers of hostages to be taken from the bourgeoisie and the ranks of former imperial army officers. Any attempt at resistance against Soviet power should be met with "mass shootings" inflicted "without hesitation." Petrovsky warned against "the slightest hesitation or the slightest indecision in using mass terror."[6]

❖

The assassin apparently had aimed at Lenin's head, but missed. Two bullets shattered his left shoulder. One went on to penetrate his lung and lodge there. The other traveled up into his neck. Lenin had lost blood and was weak. His blood pressure dropped. The doctors examined him, then retired to another room to discuss his case. It's curious why a transfusion was not started, since blood typing and cross matching had been developed eleven years earlier.

They decided that the bullets should not be removed because the slug in his neck was close to a main artery, and the round in his lung was near his heart. But the possibility of infection worried them. When they returned to the patient they found him talking and moving around dangerously in his bed, trying to be brave.

"It's nothing," he told them. "*Nichevo* [it doesn't matter]. It can happen to any revolutionist."[7]

They put his arm in traction to keep the broken shoulder in place and to keep him still so his internal bleeding wouldn't get worse. He rallied twice that night but his condition continued to decline. A press agency in Copenhagen reported he had died.

But Lenin survived. The report was corrected the next day with a summary of his vital signs: temperature, 96.8; breathing, 26; pulse 110.

"The patient now feels better," the correction said.[8]

❖

The KGB documents released in the 1990s say that the woman arrested for shooting Lenin was questioned first at the Zamoskvoretsky military commissariat by A.M. Dyakonova, chairman of the Moscow revolutionary council. Commissar Batulin and a Mikhelson worker stood by as witnesses.

The woman identified herself as Fanya Efimovna Kaplan, the name under which she had served in Akatuy prison. Kaplan described herself as a socialist but not a member of any political party. She added that she had supported the constituent assembly and wanted Russia to get back into the war against Germany. She readily confessed to attacking Comrade Chairman.

"Today I shot at Lenin," she told Dyakonova. It was her sole decision and she acted alone, she added. "How many times I shot, I do not remember. What kind of revolver I used, I will not say. I would not want to talk about details. I did not know those women who spoke with Lenin." She added that she had never seen the wounded woman, Maria Popova, before.

But a crime cannot be fully understood unless a motive is established. Exactly *why* did she try to kill Lenin?

"I shot at Lenin because I considered him a traitor to the revolution, and his continued existence undermined faith in socialism," Kaplan said.

That's what the Allies felt—that Lenin had stopped the legitimate 1917 Russian Revolution and returned the country to its reactionary past of autocracy and mass terror. In that sense, Lenin was not a revolutionary, but really a counterrevolutionary. Kerensky and the provisional government had given amnesty to political prisoners and exiles, including Lenin and Kaplan, but the Bolsheviks scorned such a liberal policy. They gave amnesty only to exiled Reds, then set out to exterminate their enemies. Their tool was the Cheka.

Kaplan was transferred to the Kremlin for further interrogation. Jacob Peters, the No. 2 man at Cheka headquarters in Moscow, arrived with Sverdlov and others. The questioning went on into the early hours of the morning. Kaplan told N.A. Skrypkik, head of the Cheka department for counterrevolution, that she shot at Lenin at her "own discretion." She said she fired several times, but didn't remember how many.

"I was not acquainted with the women who were talking to Lenin. The idea of shooting Lenin had matured in my mind a long time ago—"

She then began to obstruct the interrogation.

"I think you have more to say," Peters told her.

"I said everything," she replied.

"You conceal the main thing—accomplices and leaders of the attempt."

Peters argued that planning an assassination was a complicated business. He kept pressuring Kaplan until she started to cry. But Peters could not decide if her tears were those of "repentance, or tired nerves."

After concluding his interrogation, Peters told *Izvestia* that Kaplan belonged to a Socialist Revolutionary group run by Viktor Chernov, leader and chief theoretician of the Right SRs. The Right SRs supported a provisional government, while the Left SRs advocated its overthrow. Peters claimed that a "whole group of people participated in the assassination attempt." He based his opinion on eyewitness reports that Lenin was "detained in the guise of conversations" just before he was shot.

The shooting of Lenin set off panic in the capital. Soldiers built bonfires at major intersections and stopped cars, cabs, streetcars, bicycles, trucks, and wagons to check passengers' papers. Chekists knocked on doors looking for enemies of the government. People locked themselves inside and turned off the lights.

But throughout her late-night interrogation, Kaplan remained frustratingly vague about her background. Who exactly *was* she? What was her connection to Allied agents?

29

A TERRORIST'S STORY

As Fanya Kaplan's interrogation was moved to the Lubyanka, she said her surname was Roydman (Feig in Hebrew). She was born February 10, 1890, in the western Ukrainian province of Volhyn (now called Volhynia). Her father was a teacher. Her four brothers and three sisters were all workers. She was educated at home, and at age fourteen was sent to work as a seamstress.

Ukraine had been plagued with pogroms since the 1700s, but some particularly nasty ones occurred when Kaplan was in her early teens. During Russia's war with Japan, reactionary newspapers and the ultra-nationalist Black Hundreds accused Jews of stirring up protests against the war and the tsar. Government officials looked the other way, hoping that an obsession with Jews would divert public attention away from Russian losses in the war.

In the autumn of 1904, army recruits and local thugs conducted pogroms in several Ukrainian cities, including Rivne, in Fanny's home province. After the 1905 revolution broke out, the attacks intensified. In all, about 700 pogroms were recorded in Ukraine, with hundreds of deaths. They were worsened by the refusal of local police and soldiers to intervene until ordered to do so. But in some cases the troops simply drove the rioters into the suburbs where they continued to rape, burn, and murder. [1]

Kaplan ran away from home and got romantically involved with seventeen-year-old Viktor Garsky, son of a shoemaker from Moldova. Garsky had been an armed robber before joining the Southern Group of Communist Anarchists. Fanny joined the group in 1905, at age fifteen. [2]

Anarchists drew members from the Jewish Pale and conducted a terror campaign to answer the pogroms and the government's attempts to suppress the 1905 revolution. Their terror attacks included a bombing of the Café

Libman in Odessa in December 1905. The Anarchists gave Kaplan the nickname of Dora. She took Fanny Kaplan as her nom de guerre.

On December 18, 1905, Kaplan and Garsky checked into a commercial travelers' hotel in the colorfully decorated Podol section of Kiev. Four days later, at around seven P.M., the hotel was rocked by an explosion in one of the rooms. Somebody had been building a bomb. Kaplan and Garsky ran out of the hotel. It was a time of heightened public fear of terrorism, and a crowd of onlookers grabbed Kaplan.

"I didn't do it," she said. "It wasn't me. Leave me alone."

The crowd turned her over to a policeman. Garsky got away.

When officers searched Kaplan they found on her a Model 1900 Browning 7.65-millimeter (.32 caliber) semi-automatic pistol, popularly known as a Browning Old Style. (Boris Savinkov carried one.) She had a passport in the name of Feiga Chaimovna Kaplan, from Minsk province. A doctor found she had been slightly injured in her right arm, left leg, and right buttock by bomb fragments from the hotel explosion.

Kaplan was charged with manufacturing, storing, acquiring, and carrying explosives for the purpose of violating state security and public tranquility. At her trial she took all the blame and refused to name her co-conspirators, which was the practice among terrorists.

Prosecutor Soloviev in 2010 said Kaplan and Viktor Garsky were planning to assassinate Vladimir Alexandrovich Sukhomlinov, the local governor general. Sukhomlinov would later serve as minister of war, 1909–1915, but was sacked for failing to keep the Russian army sufficiently supplied with weapons. The provisional government convicted him of corruption and treason, and sentenced him to life in prison. The Bolsheviks freed him and he fled to Germany. Sukhomlinov dressed in heavily ornate uniforms with medals, plumes, ribbons, and gold braid. The "Sukhomlinov Effect" is named after him. It contends that armies with the most pretentious uniforms lose wars.

Garsky was later arrested for robbing a bank. He tried to shield Fanny by taking blame for the Kiev hotel explosion, and was sentenced to twelve years at hard labor. Kaplan was convicted by military court on December 30, 1906, and sentenced to hang. But because of her age, the punishment was reduced to indefinite hard labor. That meant she might get out in twenty years on good behavior. Otherwise, she could stay in prison the rest of her life.

❖

Fanny Kaplan was held first in Lukyanivska prison in Kiev, a gloomy pile with dungeon-like cells built during the reign of Catherine the Great. (It's now over 160 years old and holds 2,400 inmates.) In August 1907 she was sent to Maltsev prison, part of the tsarist *katorga* system of Siberian labor camps later replaced by the Stalinist gulags. But despite the wording of Kaplan's sentence, women political prisoners were not forced to do much labor. They cleaned latrines or worked in the kitchens, but beyond that were usually confined to barracks—long wooden buildings with wooden bunks in narrow cells. Desks were made from planks laid across beds. Lunch was potato soup and bread; supper was kasha. The place was short on crockery so cellmates ate out of the same bowl.

The women read and wrote letters. They taught one another languages, mathematics, medicine. In the winter when it was 40 below outside, water that spilled on the floor froze quickly. Mostly they stayed in bed and tried to keep warm.

"The whole world is contained in these four walls," one of the prisoners wrote. "The high stone walls, the endless mountains all around, the 300 versts between us and a railway station saw to it that we did not escape."[3]

Prisoners were not allowed to read political books but that didn't keep them from talking. They discussed the plight of Russia. They dreamed of the future. Fanny met the Socialist Revolutionary terrorist Maria Spiridonova at Maltsev. Spiridonova was serving time for the 1905 assassination of a police chief south of Tambov, Russia. She had almost been beat to death with Cossack whips as she was arrested. Spiridonova convinced Kaplan to abandon the Anarchists, who had a reputation for being bunglers, and join the more professional SRs.

Fanny started having headaches in 1909 and suddenly on a summer evening she lost her sight. Prisoners described her eyes as radiant and clear, but she could not see. Her vision returned after a couple of days, then went out again. Fanny was despondent. She refused to go for exercise. She lay on her bunk all day contemplating suicide. Friends stayed close by to watch her.

Prison doctors examined Fanny and thought she was faking. Nevertheless, they sent her to the hospital at Irkutsk for further tests. Medical records described her as 5 feet 1, with pale complexion, brown hair and eyes, and ordinary chin and nose. A scar above her right eyebrow might have been caused by a bomb fragment in the Kiev explosion, and the wound could have affected her optic nerves. Fanny also had seizures, which suggested that her blindness might be linked to some neurological condition. Nevertheless, they were able to partially restore her vision.

In April 1911, Fanny was transferred to Akatuy prison. In June 1914 she was sent to the Chita prison eye clinic. Doctors there thought she might be suffering from "hysterical" (psychosomatic) blindness. She was given electrical treatments, injected with strychnine, and fed potassium iodide. When she was returned to Akatuy she began to see again. Her family had emigrated to Chicago in 1911 and they sent her a magnifying glass for reading.

In March 1917, at the age of twenty-seven, Kaplan was granted amnesty by the provisional government. She went to Moscow and stayed for a while with Anna Pigit, another freed political prisoner. That summer Fanny went down to Yevpatoria, a Crimean resort on the Black Sea, and was treated at a sanatorium for former political prisoners. A doctor there, Dmitry Ilyich Ulyanov, Lenin's younger brother, suggested Fanny go to an eye clinic in Kharkov, Ukraine. She did so in October and was operated on by a noted ophthalmologist, Leonard Leopoldovich Hirsch. The operation was "very successful," prosecutor Soloviev said.

This medical background on Kaplan is noteworthy because her alleged "blindness" would be used by some theorists who argued that she was incapable of seeing Lenin, much less of shooting him.

While in Kharkov, Fanny was briefly reunited with Viktor Garsky. She sold her favorite shawl, given to her by Maria Spiridonova, to buy scented soap for bathing before meeting him. But he did not want to pursue their old affair, and that was that.

In February 1918, Kaplan returned to Moscow and again stayed with Anna Pigit. Fanny's eyesight was still impaired but she could get around. After being locked up with SR assassins and other criminals for ten years, she emerged from prison the way she had gone in, as a hardened terrorist ready to strike again. She later told Jacob Peters that it was during her second Moscow visit that she began planning to kill Lenin.

❖

Prosecutor Soloviev in his 2010 *Pravda* interview said that before Kaplan shot Lenin, she attended the Eighth Party Council of the SRs at Moscow in May 1918. The party, a supporter of the provisional government, decided on the "immediate elimination of the Bolshevik Party dictatorship," including Lenin, Trotsky, Uritsky, Dzerzhinsky, and Sverdlov.

Kaplan met V.K. Volsky, former deputy of the constituent assembly that had been dissolved by Lenin's troops back in January. She asked Volsky to assign her a "worthwhile affair." In SR code, that meant an act of terrorism. But Volsky did not promise anything immediately.

(Volsky on June 8, 1918, became chairman of the Komuch, the committee in Samara that called itself the legitimate Russian government and which led the struggle against the Reds in the Volga region, the Urals, and Siberia. Volsky was possibly one of Kalamatiano's agents in Samara.)

Kaplan seems to have come a bit unhinged after her contact with Volsky. The Cheka documents released in the 1990s quote a member of the SR central committee as calling her "unquestionably not normal, and with various defects: deaf, half-blind, somehow exalted. Like a holy fool."

But assassinating Lenin would be a huge undertaking. Perhaps a holy fool was what the SRs needed. A central committee member referred Kaplan to the experienced assassin Grigory Ivanovich Semyonov. He ran an terrorist squad he called his central battle unit.

According to Soloviev, Kaplan organized her own terror squad for a while. Members included a former political prisoner, Pavel Pelevin; a lawyer, Vladimir Rudzievsky; and a girl named Marusya. They planned to either poison Lenin or somehow give him an injection that would kill him. At one point Marusya suggested they throw a brick at him.

Semyonov was looking for a suicide killer, someone who could get close enough to Lenin to shoot him or blow him up with a bomb, and who didn't mind dying in the process. That was just the opposite of Savinkov's strategy. Boris wanted his assassins to survive and work again.

Kaplan "had a peaceful, modest and inconspicuous appearance, did not stand out from the crowd, and most importantly she hated Lenin and was ready at any moment to sacrifice herself," Soloviev said in his study of the case.

But it was Dmitry Donskoy, an SR central committee member, who actually pitched the Lenin assassination to Kaplan. She accepted it enthusiastically. She told Donskoy she was devoted to the SRs and was "ready to go to the end," Soloviev said.

Other SRs were added to the plot. One of them was Lydia Konopleva, a former schoolteacher. She and Kaplan began working together as a surveillance team. They watched Lenin go in and out of the Kremlin. They watched

Trotsky at the military commissariat and various army installations. Konopleva and Kaplan discussed which subject to kill first, Lenin or Trotsky. Finally, they agreed to act on the one who first offered them the best chance.

Although Semyonov wanted assassins ready to die for the cause, he didn't want "crazy loners," Soloviev said. Semyonov wanted team players like Charlotte Corday, who belonged to the Girondins, a war party during the French Revolution, and who calmly stabbed Jean-Paul Marat to death in his bathtub as she talked with him. Corday had known she would be arrested immediately, and she was. Then she was sent to the guillotine.

Semyonov wrote a pamphlet and testified against his old SR comrades in a 1922 show trial the Soviets staged in Moscow. Semyonov said it had been decided to shoot Lenin as he left one of his weekly factory speeches. Soloviev consulted Semyonov's pamphlet and testimony when the Kaplan case was reopened in the nineties.

Semyonov was son of an imperial official in what's now Tartu, Estonia. He was a year younger than Kaplan, and like Fanny, poorly educated. He turned revolutionary at age fourteen and drifted from one radical party to another. He was drafted into the army, and after the 1917 revolution served as one of Kerensky's commissars at the front. Following the Bolshevik coup, Semyonov tried to organize military protection for the constituent assembly. Then he went into the SR underground and helped plot the Volodarsky assassination.[4]

❖

The SR central committee gave Semyonov the go-ahead to assassinate Lenin and Trotsky, and he divided Moscow into four surveillance districts. Lookouts were assigned to each district to watch for the two targets. The task was simplified by the fact that notices were published in the press announcing where Communist Party rallies would be held each Friday. The public was welcome. But in the interests of security, those notices didn't indicate where Lenin would speak. Thus, Kaplan and Konopleva, in the Savinkov style, stalked their targets, watching for a chance to strike.

On August 30, 1918, Kaplan arrived at the Mikhelson factory before the party rally started. A witness saw her standing at one of the propaganda tables going through pamphlets, apparently listening for news of whether Lenin was coming.

"The suspicious, painfully ambitious, withering Kaplan craved sensation and glory, which she could achieve by killing Lenin," Semyonov testified at his trial. "I purposely sent Kaplan to the Mikhelson plant."

Once a target was spotted at a location, the watcher was supposed to contact Semyonov's central battle unit. Then additional team members would be sent in for the kill. One of Semyonov's plotters, a worker named V.A. Novikov, was assigned to work with Fanny at the Mikhelson. Novikov hired a taxi and stationed it outside the factory as a getaway car.

Both Kaplan and Novikov were armed with Browning semi-automatic pistols.[5] An "X" was carved into the tip of each bullet. That turned the rounds into dumdums that were supposed to expand upon impact and inflict more damage to the body than ordinary bullets. Dumdums had been banned in international warfare since 1899.

On this Friday, one of Semyonov's gang members, Fedorov-Kozlov, had been sent to the corn exchange to shoot Lenin if he showed up there. Fedorov-Kozlov got close enough for a shot but didn't have the courage to pull the trigger.

After Lenin left the grain exchange, his chauffeur and close protection officer Stepan Gil drove him to the Mikhelson. But not knowing if Comrade Chairman would show up there, no party officials were waiting outside to greet Lenin.

The man in the sailor suit who delayed the crowd coming out of the factory behind Lenin after his speech was Kaplan's accomplice, Novikov. Apparently he was also the man who parted the crowd around Lenin so the mysterious woman in black could shoot. And he might have been the man who charged at Lenin after he was down, only to be chased off by Gil.

After the shooting, Novikov ran out to his waiting taxi. Fanny Kaplan stopped under that tree and apparently waited for him to pick her up. But Novikov fled the scene. Maybe he saw that the crowd in the streets prevented him from picking up Fanny. Maybe he just panicked. At any rate, Kaplan was left standing there with no ride. That's when Batulin arrested her.

Dozens of witnesses were later interviewed by the Cheka but none of them (including Gil) remembered actually seeing the face of the woman in black who was supposed to have shot Lenin. They could not identify Fanny Kaplan. That led to the rise of conspiracy theories.

Who *really* shot Lenin?

Was it Kaplan?

Or did somebody else do it and set up Fanny to take the fall?

Conspiracies have always been popular in certain quarters. But conjecture and rumors are not evidence, or proof. In the case of the Lenin shooting, the anatomy of the crime can begin with identifying the pistol that was used.

❖

A worker, A.V. Kuznetsov, picked up a pistol from the factory driveway and turned it over to the Cheka three days after Lenin was shot. Prosecutor Soloviev identified it as a 7.65-millimeter Old Style Browning, the same model Kaplan was carrying when she was arrested in 1906. Three cartridges in the clip had been fired. Investigators went back to the Mikhelson and examined the crime scene.

Yes, they found Browning shell casings on the ground—but *four* of them.

A surgeon in 1922 removed one of the bullets that had wounded Lenin. The second bullet was removed later, during the autopsy after Lenin's death. Both were identified as 7.65-mm Brownings. Prosecutor Soloviev in 2010 said that on the basis of his investigation it was "absolutely clear" that both bullets came from the Browning found at the scene.

Apparently the slugs had not broken up on impact the way dum dums were supposed to, either because of faulty gunpowder or the pistol's proximity to the target. Or perhaps the bullets were intentionally loaded with less powder. A lower load has more knock-down power at close range.

But if three shots had been fired from the recovered pistol, where did the fourth casing come from?

Some witnesses could not definitely say that three shots were fired. They only said they heard "several" shots. Novikov would seem to have been a logical candidate as a second gunman. So would Lydia Konopleva. Indeed, one witness reported seeing another woman shooting at Lenin from off to the side.

The theory that Kaplan didn't shoot Lenin was pushed by those who claimed she was half blind. But the surgeon who operated on her eyes said the procedure was "successful." The Cheka documents don't explain exactly what that meant, but after her eye surgery Fanny worked for a while in Crimea, training workers. Apparently she could see well enough to function in a workplace. And she was only a few feet from Lenin when he was shot.

Prosecutor Soloviev said that as far as the Cheka was concerned, Kaplan's guilt was "not in doubt." He added that Jacob Peters believed a "whole group of people" were involved with her. That would have been Semyonov and his kill team. Semyonov and Konopleva were arrested in September 1918. They were sentenced to death by a revolutionary tribunal but later pardoned by the All-Russian Central Executive Committee, possibly because they had converted to Communism. They were never charged with organizing an attempt on Lenin, but were shot in 1937 during Stalin's purges.

Another theory: A "Kremlin conspiracy" was behind the shooting of Lenin.

Proponents of that idea point out that Lenin and his government were on the rocks in the summer of 1918. Party membership had dropped to 150,000 for the entire country. Elections of Communists to local councils had dipped drastically. There were peasant revolts, labor strikes, terrorist attacks, starvation, and epidemics. Vladivostok, Archangel, and Murmansk had fallen to Allied invaders, with Japanese and Chinese troops added to the mix in the Far East. In the Russian interior, the Red Army was fighting Cossacks, Czechs, anarchists, and criminal gangs. Furthermore, Lenin had given big chunks of the Russian empire to Germany in the Treaty of Brest-Litovsk, and the Kaiser's armies were only 200 miles from Moscow. Then there was the problem of the Left SRs. They had turned against Lenin because of Brest-Litovsk and staged a coup attempt. And they were operating inside the Cheka. Meanwhile, Allied spies were lining up their own coup plots. It was no surprise that millions of Russians were praying the Germans would invade and take over.

"Actually we are already dead, but there is no one who can bury us," Trotsky had told Mirbach before the ambassador was shot.[6]

In the Kremlin conspiracy scenario, Jacob Sverdlov had decided to remove Lenin and take over the government. He was supposedly backed up by Dzerzhinsky and Trotsky, all three of whom had opposed the signing of the Brest-Litovsk treaty.

"By the summer of 1918 the entire party and Soviet government was concentrated in Sverdlov's hands," Alter Litvin said in his introduction to his collection of Cheka documents. "He was chairman of the All-Russian Central Executive Committee and secretary of the Central Committee of the Russian Communist Party."

Sverdlov "recommended and confirmed the leading party and soviet cadres and was related to those powerful people who always know what they want and are seeking to realize their decisions," Litvin added.

But Sverdlov, Dzerzhinsky, and Trotsky did not take over the government. Lenin survived and retained power.

"Today we can say with complete certainty that the action of the attempt on Lenin was prepared by the terrorist group of the Right SR, Grigory Semyonov, and that the fatal shots were fired by Fanny Kaplan," prosecutor Soloviev said in concluding his investigation. "The conjectures about the organization of the attempt by Sverdlov, Trotsky, Dzerzhinsky, and other Communist leaders have no documentary evidence."

But were Allied agents involved?

The Cheka thought they were, as a roundup of Western spies would soon show. Allied agents Reilly and Savinkov in particular had talked openly of assassinating Lenin.

Savinkov was an experienced assassin. Although he favored spectacular bombings, he also used Old Style Brownings and daggers, for close-in work. And he recruited zealous unbalanced women for his kill squads. Also, Boris had sworn to carry out a duel to the death against Lenin, and he had been financed all summer by Western money. The way Lenin was studied, stalked, and shot certainly fit Savinkov's style, like one of his signature American suits.

So what did Boris himself have to say about this?

When he wrote his memoirs, he told his translator Joseph Shaplen that he gave Kaplan her pistol.[7]

30

BLACK SATURDAY

S trike quick and strike hard."
That's what soldiers and Chekists were told as they searched Moscow and Petrograd for enemies of the state after Lenin was shot. The Communist Party's central executive committee declared Russia a "military camp" and the raiders went street by street, block by block, building by building, room by room.[1] Displaying a thoroughness inherited from the Okhrana, they inspected every apartment house, rooming house, flophouse, priest house, outhouse, dog house, and cathouse. Many of those arrested had nothing to with the Allies but were simply members of the hated middle class. Based on news accounts, a Russian documentarian wrote that 31,489 were arrested by the end of September 1918. Of that number, she said, 6,185 were shot, 14,829 were sent to prisons, and 6,407 were hauled off to labor camps. Another 4,068 were held as hostages.

"This was the answer to the Kaplan shots," she wrote.[2]

In the midst of all this, George Hill delivered some bad news to his Allied co-conspirators. One of Hill's agents inside the Cheka reported that the Lenin Plot had been blown. An informer had betrayed them. Apparently that was Eduard Berzin or René Marchand.[3]

❖

Saturday, August 31: Midnight church bells rang in a new day. Xenophon Kalamatiano was safe, for the moment, on the train to Samara. He was taking his wife and stepson to the U.S. consulate in Samara for refuge from the Cheka. Bruce Lockhart was not so fortunate. He was pulled in about seven hours after the attack on Lenin.

Lockhart and Captain William Hicks, a member of his staff, sat up late that night in Bruce's apartment talking in whispers about what was likely to happen next. Lockhart got his answer at 3:30 A.M. on Saturday. He later wrote that he was awakened by a rough voice ordering him to get out of bed. He said ten armed men had invaded his bedroom and one of them pointed a revolver at him.

"No questions," Lockhart quoted the leader of the raid, Kremlin commandant Pavel Malkov, as saying. "Get dressed at once." Hicks was told the same thing, Lockhart wrote.

Lockhart said the Chekists ransacked the apartment, then put him and Hicks into a car and delivered them to Cheka headquarters in the Lubyanka. It was a grand old building, a former insurance company, in the center of Moscow. Upstairs floors held bright, modern offices. Jail cells, torture rooms, and execution chambers were hidden in the basement.[4]

Malkov told a different story. He wrote that Jacob Peters, deputy chairman of the Cheka, told him to take a Chekist and a militiaman and go arrest Lockhart. Lockhart was a *poseur,* a hypocrite, and a "bit of a coward," Peters said, but still a diplomat, so Malkov should be "polite and courteous" while acting "with decision." Malkov pulled on his navy pea coat, tucked his Colt in his belt, and took his two men to Lockhart's address, a handsome six-story stuccoed apartment building with white-trimmed windows.

The building was dark and they had to use lighters as they climbed the stairs to the fifth floor. Malkov knocked hard at Lockhart's door. A woman opened the door. Malkov thought it was Lockhart's secretary. But it could have been the maid, or Moura Benckendorff, Bruce's latest girlfriend. Whoever it was, she kept the chain on. Malkov said he asked politely if he could speak with Lockhart. She said no. Then Hicks came to the door. He admitted Malkov and his two men, but refused to wake Lockhart. Malkov brushed past Hicks, went to the bedroom, and woke Lockhart up.

Bruce greeted his old acquaintance in a friendly though surprised manner, Malkov said. He showed Lockhart a warrant and told him he was under arrest. The apartment was searched while Lockhart and Hicks dressed. Malkov seized some papers and weapons, then transported the two subjects to the Lubyanka. Malkov later wrote that nothing was ripped open and no guns were drawn.[5]

Peters's office in the Lubyanka was just off Broadway, a main corridor where the decapitated head of a terrorist was kept preserved in a jar of alcohol for passersby to see.[6] The office was a long dark room lit only by a desk lamp. When Lockhart went in he saw a revolver on the desk. Jacob sat in the darkness behind the desk with only his hands in the lamplight.

❖

Peters was a short, stocky, thirty-two-year-old Latvian peasant who dressed stylishly in European suits and sometimes wore his hair long in a Bohemian style. As a young man in Latvia, Peters had belonged to a Bolshevik wing of the Social Democrats and served a year and a half in a tsarist prison. He fled to London in 1909 and settled in London's East End. He got a job as a rag picker and rented an apartment at 48 Turner Street, Whitechapel, from an anarchist at three shillings a week. He joined a local anarchists' club, learned English, and married an Englishwoman with whom he had a child. Then he got involved in one of the saddest cases in British police history: the Houndsditch Murders.

In December 1910 a group of anarchists from imperial Russia (which included Latvia at the time) rented a house at No. 11 Exchange Buildings in Cutler Street, London. Cutler was accessible by Houndsditch, a road so named because it used to be a dumping ground for debris including the carcasses of "dead dogges." The Exchange Buildings in Cutler Street formed a cul-de-sac of sooty brick structures in what's now Devonshire Square. The house at No. 11 backed up to the rear wall of a jewelry shop at 119 Houndsditch owned by H.S. Harris, a goldsmith and silversmith. On the 16th of that month a gang of at least ten anarchists inside No. 11 went to work with hammers and drills to break through the brick wall into the jewelry shop.

It was late Friday and the neighborhood was quiet for the Jewish Sabbath. That allowed a neighbor to hear the burglars' noises. He reported them to the police, and five City of London officers went to investigate. It was near midnight. They knocked on the door of No. 11, identified themselves, and asked to be let in. A voice inside told them to go away. They said they were investigating a burglary. No burglars in here, the voice replied. The coppers went in anyway.

They were armed only with whistles and truncheons. They didn't see the gunman in the darkness until he opened fire from the top of the staircase. The officers had entered in single file and were shot down one by one. One of the burglars was also shot by the gunman, apparently accidentally.

The shooting continued out in the street. Three of the police had been killed and the other two wounded. Three men and a woman walked quickly from the scene. The wounded man was helped by the others. Within minutes the entire neighborhood was swarming with police. Suspects were rounded up and taken to Old Jewry police station for questioning.

On Christmas Eve, Jacob Peters was arrested and charged with murder. It was later reduced to harboring and assisting a murderer (George Goldstein, the man accused of killing Sergeant Charles Tucker). Peters went on trial with seven other anarchists. A key witness, Isaac Levy, a tobacconist, had seen the fleeing burglars. But only one streetlight had been burning in the block, so Levy couldn't identify any faces. He was also distracted by the sight of the pistols the burglars pointed at him. Peters was acquitted May 3, 1911, because of "unsatisfactory evidence."[7]

Peters abandoned his English wife and child after the trial and went to Russia. When the Bolsheviks took power, Peters was hired as Dzerzhinsky's chief assistant in the Cheka. His job was to co-sign Iron Felix's execution orders and see that the killings were carried out efficiently. Beyond that, his primary function was to run the shop while the boss was out. A journalist described Jacob as a confidant, polite man.[8] But in the early hours of August 31, 1918, his charm was not evident.

❖

"His lips were tightly compressed, and as I entered the room his eyes fixed me with a steely stare," Lockhart said of meeting Peters that night. "He looked grim and formidable."

Peters asked Lockhart if he knew Fanny Kaplan. Bruce stood on diplomatic immunity and refused to answer. He said Peters had no right to question him. Peters asked where Reilly was. Lockhart again declined to answer.

Peters brought out a piece of paper. It was the pass that had been given to a Latvian who was supposed to have gone to Archangel to talk to the Allied commander. Peters asked Lockhart if the signature on the note was his. Bruce still refused to talk. Peters stared at him long and hard. He warned him it would be better to tell the truth. Lockhart still didn't respond. Peters sent him back to the cell he shared with Hicks.

It was then that the gravity of Lockhart's situation hit him. That pass, with his name on it, would be admissible evidence in a revolutionary tribunal. Had the Latvians been arrested and the pass taken from one of them? Had they been tortured? How much had they said? The absence of information was terrifying.

Lockhart had a notebook in his pocket that listed the payments he had made to the Latvians. He had to get rid of it. He asked to go to the toilet.

Two guards went with him. But they wouldn't let him close the door. They stood and watched as he conducted his business. Then he tore out the pages of his notebook, used them as toilet paper, and flushed the evidence away.

At six that morning a woman was brought into Lockhart's cell. He said she looked tired and stressed, with rings under her eyes. "Her face was colorless. Her features, strongly Jewish, were unattractive."

She went to the window and stared out. No words were exchanged. After a while the sentries came and took her away.

Lockhart figured she was the woman who had shot Lenin and that the Cheka was listening for anything she and Bruce might talk about. But neither said a word. At nine o'clock the next morning Lockhart and Hicks were released. Georgy Chicherin, commissar for foreign affairs, had called Peters to protest their arrests.[9] But Peters kept Moura and Lockhart's maid locked up. Kaplan was held, too.

Malkov was glad to see Lockhart go. He said he was tired of Bruce's whining about the food.

❖

Like Lockhart, George Hill had tried to help the Soviets for a while. He had organized an intelligence service against Germans on the Russian fronts and assisted Trotsky in planning for a new Red air force. That was done with London's blessing on the theory that British aid might get Russia back in the war.

But Hill led a double life. He wore his British uniform during the day as an adviser to the Soviets while slipping out at night in mufti to direct operations against them. After the shooting of Lenin he had to go underground for good. But he was able to operate a secret courier service for Allied agents and to continue issuing weapons to peasants for action against the Soviets. He also derailed Red troop and supply trains. When Trotsky figured out he had been double-crossed, he signed an arrest warrant for Hill.

In his new secret life Hill burned his English clothes, dyed his hair, and changed to Russian workman's overalls. He could no longer drive the Pathfinder he had used as a military adviser, so he walked.[10] He kept eight apartments in Moscow as safe houses and slept in a different one every night. Papers hidden inside his jackets made a crackling noise when he moved, so he started typing messages to his agents on pieces of linen and sewing them into the coat linings. He kept a bottle of gasoline handy so he could burn his typewriter in case of a raid.

"I was constantly haunted by the fear of being caught, and always before my mind I had a vivid picture of the spies I had seen executed in Macedonia," he recalled. "I maintain that however stout-hearted a spy may be, if he has any imagination at all, the idea of capital retribution does get on his nerves and at times affects his work. That is why in time of war I would always urge death as the penalty for espionage."[11]

Reilly had left for Petrograd to meet with Cromie, so Hill sent a courier to warn them of the Cheka raids being conducted in Moscow. But the courier got arrested as he boarded his train. Hill then sent a courier, Vi, to find Reilly's courier/girlfriend, Elizaveta Otten, in Moscow and tell her that he was taking over for Sidney.

The Cheka was already there when Vi arrived. Berzin had found this address written on the back of Reilly's calling card at that apartment in Petrograd a week earlier and had turned it over to Peters and Dzerzhinsky. Vi's cover story was that she was delivering a blouse to Elizaveta. Like Lockhart, Elizaveta lived near the tony Arbat quarter. But when Vi rang the bell of the apartment, the door was opened and she looked down into the muzzle of a pistol.

"Come in," the Chekist said. "Whom do you want?"

"I have come to deliver a blouse," Vi replied. "Is the lady in, and will she please pay for it?"

Vi and Elizaveta were questioned intently by three Chekists in the apartment. Some of the time, pistols were held to their heads. But the two women pretended not to know one another, and Vi's story held up. After several hours, she was released. Elizaveta was arrested.

But when Vi opened the door to leave, she found another woman out in the corridor. Some people were with her. She appeared to be under arrest.[12]

The apprehension of this woman was about to break another guy-wire holding up the increasingly shaky structure of the Lenin Plot.

31

NO MERCY FOR ENEMIES

The mystery woman outside Elizaveta Otten's door had been picked up in an "ambush" surveillance operation the Cheka set up in a nearby street to watch for anybody suspicious approaching Otten's building. Pavel Malkov said a woman "scout" (apparently a volunteer neighborhood watcher helping the Cheka) spotted a tall woman in her early thirties walk up the street that night with a milk can in her hand. That was kind of odd.

The scout, whom Malkov described as a stern, upstanding, dedicated young Bolshevik wearing a tailored semi-military suit, collared the woman and took her upstairs to Malkov. He in turn delivered her to Peters.[1]

"Her beautiful face was framed in thick, light-brown hair which peeped with an unruly elegance from beneath a modish hat," Malkov wrote of the arrested girl. "She was dressed with an elegant modesty in well-tailored, tasteful clothes which displayed her slim figure to advantage. She carried a light summer coat over her left arm, and her right hand gripped a milk can . . ."

The scout handed Peters a packet of papers she had found on the woman. The packet was sealed and carried no address. Peters shook the scout's hand, commended her tailored semi-military diligence, and dismissed her. Malkov sat on the corner of the desk watching as Peters opened the packet.

The Cheka record of the case said the packet contained a document titled "Report No. 12," written by an agent returning from a trip to Tula, Oryol, Kursk, Voronezh, Gryazi, and Kozlov between the 18th and the 30th of August. The report described the mood of the inhabitants, the food situation, travel difficulties, factory production schedules, and the condition of the local economies. The report said residents saw Red Army troops as "thieves and brigands" and that sometimes local soviets ignored orders from Moscow.

"The general impression created by everything seen and heard is one of fatigue and passivity on the part of the middle class and an agonizing wait for salvation, regardless from whom or from where, if only to live in peace without fear or oppression," the report continued. The location and strength of German and Austrian military forces on the Russian fronts and in Finland and Ukraine were also analyzed.[2]

Those were stolen Red Army military secrets. Another big break for the Cheka had just walked into the room.

"A strange man handed it to me," the arrested woman claimed, coolly and confidently. "But I've absolutely no idea what's in it."

She said she went out this morning to buy milk. She held up the milk can. "You see?"

She claimed she was walking along in the dark when that strange man stopped her. He told her he had to take a packet to a certain apartment in the house she was passing.

"He said he was in a great hurry and would I be so kind as to deliver it for him. He was very convincing and gave the impression of being a decent, refined man."

Peters said nothing. Along with his winning PR man's smile, he could also turn on an adamantine cop's stare. When the woman started to describe this strange man further, he cut her off.

"You're lying . . . It's a pack of lies, all of it . . . Have you any relatives? Any family?"

Yes, she did. The mystery woman turned out to be Maria Friede, sister of Colonel Alexander Friede, head of Red Army communications in Moscow, the most valuable anti-Communist mole that Kalamatiano and Reilly had at military headquarters.

After intense interrogation, Maria identified relatives of hers who worked for the Allies. Chekists, some bicycle soldiers, and a police commissar were sent to question Alexander Friede, who lived at 12 Durasovsky Alley, Apartment 12.

The Cheka report says that when the agents entered the apartment, Elizaveta Sergeevna Friede (apparently Alexander's wife) ran to the bathroom and threw out some papers. The raiders recovered them. The documents reported that a factory in Sestroretsk, on the Gulf of Finland, was being moved to Petrograd in anticipation of a possible German advance.

"If a German offensive against Petrograd does arise, no one expects serious resistance on the part of the Soviet forces," the report said, "first because there are no forces there and, second, because everyone in Petrograd is convinced that the Northern Commune (of soviets) is not only operating in full contact with the Germans, but in close alliance with them."

The intelligent population of the region was "passive" toward German occupation, the report continued. Peasants were said to have a "negative" attitude toward Soviet power. The harvest was expected to be poor and some districts had no food other than herring. All available Red Army forces had been moved north to meet the anticipated Wilson invasion.

Friede's report was discovered along with other papers and 50,000 rubles concealed in the cover of a shaving kit hidden behind a mirror. The Friede apartment was "one of the most significant centers for the plot involving the counter-revolutionary organization of the Anglo-French imperialists [Lenin plotters]," the Cheka account concluded. Colonel Friede was arrested and admitted what he had been doing. He also admitted issuing Kalamatiano identity papers in the name of Sergei Serpukhovsky. An order to arrest the American agent was issued. In a report he later made to Poole, Kalamatiano said Colonel Friede's brother, mother, and another sister were arrested, too, on the basis on Maria's confession.[3]

The Cheka used posters and newspaper stories to break the news that they had broken up a spectacular Allied plot against Lenin. They called it the Lockhart Conspiracy. Although Bruce had been only one piece of a broken tea cup, the name had a nice ring to it, and it stuck.

❖

Cheka raids continued on the afternoon of Black Saturday, August 31. The Cheka's next major Allied target was Commander Francis Cromie, the British naval saboteur in Petrograd who had first interviewed the Latvian Shmidkhen and referred him to Lockhart.

Like Lockhart and Hill, Cromie had also been on good terms with Trotsky, for a while. Cromie had met with Lev Davidovitch to offer Allied help against Germany and had saved large supplies of Russian precious metals from areas threatened by the Germans. But Cromie eventually saw there was no future in trying to deal with the uncooperative Lenin government. He got deeply involved in espionage and sabotage operations against the Soviets and urged London to intervene militarily in Russia.

Cromie's biographer Roy Bainton described the commander as a married man with a daughter, and a charming and witty conversationalist much in demand at parties, where he wore his dress uniform with medals. Cromie's chummy manner made him an easy touch for people with plots to pitch. So it was no surprise that after he recruited Shmidkhen and Berzin back in June, he was approached by another two men with a coup on their minds.

They said their names were Steckelmann and Sabir. They showed a letter of introduction supposedly written by Lockhart. Steckelmann said he had 60,000 anti-Soviet troops in Finland ready to invade Russia. They could link up with Allied forces from Archangel and march on Petrograd and Moscow. Cromie liked that idea. He also suggested they blow up the Ochta railway connecting the Nicholas Station to the Finland Station in Petrograd.

Cromie arranged a meeting between Steckelmann and some representatives of anti-Soviet groups in Petrograd. But Steckelmann didn't show up. The next time Cromie heard from him was on Black Saturday. Steckelmann called the British embassy on the Palace Quay in Petrograd and told naval agent H.T. Hall that he was ready to move with his troops. Hall set up a meeting with Cromie at four that afternoon.

When Steckelmann and Sabir got to the embassy, Cromie and Hall showed them into a private room on an upper floor for talks. Meanwhile, Sidney Reilly went to the apartment of British agent Ernest Boyce. Reilly revealed his scheme for a Latvian uprising in Moscow. Boyce thought it was risky; Lenin had been shot the day before, and the Cheka was conducting a bloodbath.

But maybe now *was* the time to move, before the rest of the Allied agents got arrested. The conversation went back and forth until Boyce finally agreed that Reilly's Latvian plot could be merged into the Steckelmann-Sabir plan. Boyce said he would go and fetch Cromie for further talks.

At the embassy, Cromie heard a car pull into the backyard. He got up to look out the window. At the same time, someone tried to open the door of the room. Hall unlocked it and found a stranger standing in the corridor holding a pistol on him. Hall slammed the door. Then Cromie drew his own pistol and pulled the door open again. He told the man to clear out. He complied.

The man in the hallway belonged to the raiding party of Chekists and soldiers who had just barged into the embassy in violation of international diplomatic law. The thirty or so people in the building scrambled to get out. It was so dark in there that matches had to be used in some areas for light, so accounts vary on what happened next. But Bainton wrote that Cromie ran down the stairs to the ground floor, pursued by several Russians. Shooting broke out both upstairs and down, and Cromie fell dead on the bottom step.

Later, when his body was prepared for burial, two bullet entry wounds were found in the back of his head.

Reilly thought the raiders were looking for him. The government version published in *Pravda* said they were searching for Savinkov. They were probably looking for both.

A book written by Lockhart's son portrayed Cromie as descending the stairs, heroically blazing away with a pistol in each hand, killing three soldiers before being shot down himself. A British TV mini-series about Reilly made the same claim.[4] But Cromie's biographer quoted the government as saying one Russian was killed and two wounded, and that the soldier's death occurred in a downstairs room. So, as terrible as the incident was, it's unclear exactly who shot whom.[5] The Soviets spent the rest of the day arresting all the English and French they could find.

❖

Sunday, September 1: Chekists raided a French high school in Moscow where the saboteur Henri de Verthamon maintained a cover job as a teacher. In his bedroom they discovered eighteen pounds of pyroxilin, an explosive similar to guncotton, along with detonators, a codebook, and 28,000 rubles, all hidden in cabinets and under the bed.[6] But Henri escaped and went into hiding in the Swedish embassy. Most of the foreign diplomats took refuge in the Norwegian embassy. Norway and Sweden were neutral nations, and the Soviets did not raid their buildings. But they surrounded them on orders to arrest any French or English going in or out.

Tuesday, September 3: Lockhart went back to the Lubyanka to find out why Moura had not been released. Bruce protested that there was no plot against the Soviets. Even if there were, he said, Moura knew nothing about it.

"Entering my office, he was very embarrassed, then reported that he was with the Baroness Benckendorff in intimate relations and asked her to be released," Peters recalled in a supplementary Cheka report published in 1924. Peters listened quietly and assured Bruce that he would take it all into consideration.

"Baroness" Benckendorff (Moura) was another agent working against the Allied plotters. She was born in Ukraine, daughter of a rich landowner and Russian Senate official. She attended finishing school in England and married an Estonian, Ivan Alexandrovich Benckendorff. He called himself a "count," though he did not belong to the line of Benckendorffs who were real counts. Ivan Benckendorff took Moura with him when he went to Berlin as Russian embassy secretary. She might have met Lockhart in England before the war.

After the revolution, Ivan, Moura, and their two children rented an apartment in Petrograd, where her parents lived. When Ivan went back to Estonia for a while, he was clubbed to death by peasant revolutionaries, and the Benckendorff home was burned. A few years later, Moura married another Estonian, Nikolai Budberg, whose family had been in the tsarist military and government bureaucracy for years. From Nikolai she picked up the title of "baroness" to add to her earlier handles as "countess" and "princess."[7]

But after the revolution of February 1917 and the Bolshevik coup that October, Russia had millions of residents who hung onto titles of one kind or another, valid or otherwise, from various palaces of the empire—minor royalty, deposed royalty, faded royalty, royalty in exile. Titles, though, didn't do them much good in a time of bread lines, soup kitchens, and expropriated property. Moura was thrown out of her Petrograd flat by a Bolshevik housing committee. She managed to keep some clothes but was otherwise broke. She moved in with a former family cook and began dropping by the British embassy. She renewed her acquaintance with Lockhart, became his lover, and moved into the apartment he shared with Hicks. Moura was twenty-six years old in 1918. Her biographer Nina Berberova described her as a plump woman with a pleasant face, dark hair and eyes, and a clever smile.

Lockhart described her as a "Russian of the Russians." He said she had a "lofty disregard for all the pettiness of life and a courage which was proof against all cowardice. Her vitality, due perhaps to an iron constitution, was immense and invigorated everyone with whom she came in contact. Where she loved, that was her world, and her philosophy of life made her mistress of all the consequences."[8]

Peters held two things against Moura. First, she lived with Lockhart. She went with him everywhere as his "interpreter." That necessitated their sharing information. Moura also knew some of the important Allied spies that Bruce worked with, including George Hill and the late Francis Cromie. That was the first thing that led Peters to believe she was an Allied agent.

Second, Peters thought Moura had been a German agent during the war. In that 1924 report he said he based his opinion on the confession of a prisoner held by the Cheka and on documents found on another subject of interest, a "Prince P." It was enough for Peters to hold her for the time being.[9]

Peters's accusation was later backed up by the French Sûreté. Their investigators concluded that Moura had indeed been spying for both the Soviets and the Germans, and that those activities continued after the end of the Russian Civil War in the early 1920s.

One Sûreté report described her as "*une agente secrete redoutable* (a formidable secret agent)" and "*membre de la Tcheka de Petrograd* (member of the Cheka in Petrograd)."[10] Another report said "*la baronne Budberg parait être une très dangereuse espionne au service des Soviets* (Baroness Budberg seems to be a very dangerous spy in the service of the Soviets)."[11] Supporting this was the fact that after the war she made four trips to the USSR in three years.[12] Yet another document said "*cette femme parait être un agent double des Soviets et des Allemandes* (this woman seems to be a double agent of the Soviets and the Germans)."[13] That last report adds that Moura's second husband, Baron Budberg, was an "*ancien agent secret* (former secret agent)" for the tsar.

If Moura was indeed spying for the Germans and Soviets while warming Lockhart's bed, why would she do that? Lockhart's son Robin thought it was because she was a political opportunist, and not the first to change sides. Indeed, Sidney Reilly, also an opportunist, might have worked for the Okhrana himself at one time, not out of loyalty to the Romanovs, but to serve his own ends.

"Stalin himself had worked for the Tsar's secret police," Robin Lockhart wrote.[14] "There can be little doubt that the Baroness was playing both sides against the middle and had adopted a self-assumed role of double agent."[15] Actually a triple agent, if you consider her involvement with Lockhart, to whom she undoubtedly was supplying information.

But back to Lockhart in Peters's office. With a glint of pleasure in his eye, Jacob thanked Bruce for coming in. Lockhart had saved him some time.

Why was that?

It was because Peters had a warrant for his arrest.

❖

As the Red Terror intensified, DeWitt Clinton Poole fired off a letter of protest to the commissar for foreign affairs, Georgy Chicherin, a distant relative of Aleksandr Pushkin's. Chicherin was a scholar and musician who early on had cast off his cape and cane to put on the cap of a revolutionary. He used his wealth to support labor movements in Germany, France, and England before the war, and was arrested in London during the Bolshevik coup. He had supported the SRs in the 1905 revolution but then joined the Bolshevik Party.[16] He was freed in January 1918 in a swap for British Ambassador George Buchanan.

Bruce Lockhart said Chicherin liked to wear a "hideous" yellow-brown English tweed suit. "With his sandy-colored beard and hair and his sandy-colored suit he looked like one of those grotesque figures made by children on the seashore," Bruce wrote. "Only his eyes, small and red-rimmed like a ferret's, gave any sign of life."[17]

American military spy Marguerite Harrison said that before she met Chicherin, two of his relatives had described him as a "devil" and a "lunatic." When Harrison was picked up for entering Russia illegally (the first time) she was summoned to Chicherin's office for a chat. It was on the top floor of the Hotel Metropol, which served as the Soviet foreign commissariat. Chicherin lived in another wing of the hotel. He worked from 10 P.M. until nine the next morning. She was shown in at 2 A.M.

"It was a large, gloomy apartment with one green-shaded light over a table buried under an untidy mess of documents and papers," she wrote later. "Behind it sat Tchitcherin [sic], pencil in hand, revising a typewritten document. He looked up as I came in and I found myself face to face with a tall, thin, delicate-looking man of about forty-eight, with sandy hair thin around the temples, a small pointed beard and mustache, and a peculiar pallor, accentuated by the green lamplight. Around his neck was a woolen muffler which almost obscured his chin." His pale blue-green eyes showed the strain of overwork, she said, and he kept interlacing his long fingers as they talked. They were the fingers of "a patrician or an artist."

Chicherin's manner was correct but disconcerting, Marguerite added. "It was neither friendly nor unfriendly, merely mildly curious and rather scornful. He was examining me as he would a rather unusual bug he had happened to find on his desk."

Harrison wrote that Chicherin had once been a tsarist diplomat. He told her he used to be a Social Democrat, and was exiled for ten years after the 1905 revolution, and like Trotsky, he didn't go over to the Bolsheviks until 1918. Both Harrison and Chicherin came from wealthy backgrounds and they talked on a mutually agreeable social level. Chicherin saw Marxism as mainly a "political theory" and kept an "invisible wall of class" between himself and the proletariat, she said. He was a man of cynical wit and fine sarcasm, she added. And none of that "comrade" malarkey for him. He was "Monsieur Chicherin."

Chicherin scolded Harrison for sneaking into Russia illegally. She apologized, saying she was just doing her job as a correspondent to report on Russia's war with Poland. Besides, she had come in with a Red Army unit from Poland. They had sort of adopted her, and escorted her to Moscow. Chicherin let her go, this time.[18]

DeWitt Poole wrote in his memoirs that Chicherin had entered a sanitarium twice to try to cure his homosexuality. It didn't work. Poole said Georgy Vasilyevich went in a "homo" and came out a Bolshevik.[19] Despite the impracticality surrounding that treatment, Chicherin was a pragmatic man, a realist, a faithful servant to his government, whatever that government happened to be. A man for all seasons.

❖

Poole's message to Chicherin was an official protest against the ramped-up Red Terror. DeWitt also tried to appeal to their friendship. Poole was irritated, though, because he saw Chicherin as a weak man who never did anything without checking with Lenin first. He called him Lenin's Charlie McCarthy.[20]

"It is impossible for me to believe that you approve of the mad career into which the Bolshevik government has now plunged," Poole wrote to Chicherin. "Your cause totters on the verge of complete moral bankruptcy. There is only one possible means of redemption . . . You must stop at once the barbarous oppression of your own people."

Poole also sent Washington a note: "I cannot doubt that the American people will in the end proceed against a tyrannical and persistently lawless government in central Russia no less vigorously than they are now proceeding against a government of the same character in Germany."[21] It sounded like a call to war against the Soviets.

Poole did not receive a response from Charlie McCarthy. Poole got so frustrated he contacted Herbert Hauschild, German consul general in Moscow, through a mutual Swedish friend. Poole knew Hauschild was a "forceful and respected" man who had influence with the Soviets.

"I sent word to Hauschild that the problem was broadly a human problem, that if he would protest to Chicherin, and any other contacts he might have, in the name not only of Germany but of everybody, that we on our side would do the same. We felt so strongly about this that we actually moved toward a common front with our enemy."[22]

Allen Wardwell, commander of the American Red Cross in Russia after the departure of Raymond Robins, also contacted Chicherin about the Terror. Chicherin sent back a testy reply confirming that 500 hostages had been executed in Petrograd alone. Chicherin said those shootings were "insignificant in comparison with the horrors which these enemies [of the Reds] tried to prepare for us and in comparison with the immeasurable horrors of the whole system [of capitalism] with which we are at present at grips in a life-and-death struggle."[23]

Then Chicherin sent an answer to Poole:

"The note energetically protested against the invasion of our territory without cause and without a declaration of war; against the destruction of the property of the toiling masses of Russia, against the seizure and pillage of our cities and villages, and the execution of the local workers who were faithful to the Soviet power," Chicherin recalled two years later. "We did not declare war, the note further stated, but we would reply to these actions by appropriate measures of defense and by resorting to the necessary preventive measures . . ."[24]

Around this time, Hauschild was approached by a man claiming to be a Latvian officer working for the Soviets in Moscow. This Latvian said he could place himself and his soldiers at the disposal of the Germans if they guaranteed amnesty and repatriation to Latvia. Hauschild contacted Berlin. They weren't as gullible as the Allies. To paraphrase Virgil, they told Hauschild to beware Latvians bearing gifts. He kept his gates barred.[25]

❖

Tuesday, September 3, was also the day when Fanny Kaplan's time ran out. Kremlin premises did not include a prison per se, so Pavel Malkov kept her locked in a big room with a barred window in the semi-basement of the Grand Kremlin Palace. Latvian guards watched her at all times. Varlam Alexandrovich Avanesov, secretary of the All-Russian Central Executive Committee, summoned Malkov to the Lubyanka. Kaplan had not asked for a trial or for clemency. She was to be shot immediately. Malkov was ordered to do it.

Remembering it later, Malkov described his conflicting feelings about the assignment. On one hand, there was his revolutionary devotion.

"Yes, Red Terror has to be more than empty words, idle threats," he said. "There should be no mercy for enemies of the revolution."

On the other hand, killing a woman bothered him. It was no easy thing, he said. "It was a heavy, very heavy responsibility."

But in the end he decided that he had never been called on to carry out a "more just sentence than this."

Malkov parked a car inside a closed gate at the end of a long narrow Kremlin courtyard between tall buildings. He stationed two Latvian troops to guard the gate while he went to get Kaplan. At the same time, he told some other soldiers to bring trucks out of their garages in the buildings and start the engines to make noise.

A twenty-five-year-old writer, Efim Pridvorov, the "proletarian poet," lived upstairs in one of the buildings overlooking the courtyard. He heard the noise of the trucks and went downstairs to take a look. Pridvorov wrote under the pen name of Demyan Bedny (Damian the Poor) and turned out verse in "factory couplets" based on workers' slogans. Lenin didn't think Bedny's poems were very good—he used imagery like "evil creeps" and "quivering moons"—but at least they were useful for propaganda.

Bedny ran up to Malkov when he saw the commandant approach with Kaplan. Bedny saw what was about to happen. Malkov said the boy stopped, bit his lip, and stepped back. But he refused to leave. That irritated Malkov. He proceeded, though, with his assignment.

"To the car," he ordered Fanny.

She shrugged and started toward the car. As she did, Malkov shot her in the back of the head. She dropped dead on the bricks. It was four o'clock on a cool and sunny afternoon.

The body was burned in a barrel of gasoline in the Kremlin. Bedny had wanted to watch Kaplan's execution for "revolutionary inspiration" but he fainted at the smell of burning flesh.

Asked later if he would ever again raise his revolver to the head of a woman, Malkov said his hand would not shake, just as it did not shake that day in the Kremlin.

Lenin had not requested leniency for Kaplan. "A charming tale existed that he had asked that Kaplan's life be spared and that she was seen in a camp on Solovki Island or Kolyma [prisons] in 1932 or even 1938," Malkov recalled. "But these were nothing more than stories."[26]

Bedny wrote a poem titled "Crow" that might have drawn some "revolutionary inspiration" from the execution of Fanny Kaplan:

> *In the midst of a sleeping vague dream of the capital,*
> *Severity is full.*
> *The Kremlin loopholes are standing,*
> *Stand, thoughtful, thinking*
> *About the past, terrible and great.*[27]

32

CAUGHT IN A TRAP

X enophon Kalamatiano and DeWitt Poole were the only American spies the Cheka had identified, and arrest warrants were issued for them. Poole burned his code books as he turned the U.S. consulate over to neutral Norway. The Norwegian flag was raised and Poole confined himself to the safety of the building. He and other Westerners in Moscow were making plans to flee the country but it would take time to get everybody together, issue passports, and arrange for transportation to the Finnish frontier. Around thirty Americans worked for the consulate in official roles, with another sixty or so doing other jobs. There were also American businessmen with families living in Moscow.

American consulate employees in Petrograd, too, were making plans to get out of Russia. Another State Department "information service" was run up there by a Russian, Lieutenant Michael Peretz, formerly of the tsarist army. Peretz was chief assistant to Vice Consul Robert Whitney Imbrie, another State Department spy, and volunteered to stay behind and continue gathering intelligence for the United States. For this task he was given 100,000 rubles.[1]

The Soviets had refused to issue Kalamatiano's wife and stepson Russian passports that would allow them to leave the country, so Kal got them U.S. passports placing them under American protection. But they were still in danger from Chekists and Red Guards who might decide to arrest them just because they were Westerners. In Samara, Kal put his family on the Trans-Siberian railway and sent them through Czech-occupied territory to Allied-held Vladivostok. It was a journey that Katherine later described as dangerous and frightening.

The judicious thing would have been for Kal to leave Russia with his family. But he had offered to stay behind, and he was a man of his word. He got on another train for the three-day trip back to Moscow, accompanied by a Czech named Pshenichka. George W. Williams, American consul in Samara, was sending Pshenichka to Moscow, apparently to confer with DeWitt Poole on Czech Legion military strategy against the Soviets.

Kalamatiano and Pshenichka arrived in the capital on Wednesday, September 18, 1918. The city was still struggling with starvation and the Soviet government had broadcast an SOS for farmers to rush corn to the capital. The farmers ignored the appeal. The cholera epidemic raged on, and Red Guards were hauling the corpses to lime pits outside the city. The streets were patrolled by soldiers. Machine guns were set up at major intersections. Anyone without papers risked arrest. There was a saying: Every Russian has sat, is sitting, or will sit, in prison.

But in the midst of all this summer's troubles, a strange thing happened to lift the spirits of the people. Some called it a miracle.

It involved a big red cloth the Soviets had hung to hide a plaster ikon of St. Nicholas the Miracle Worker above the Kremlin's Nikolsky Tower gate. The ikon was a fresco dating back to the 15th century. The tower had been damaged by gunfire during the Bolshevik coup but the plaster saint emerged only slightly wounded. Its stubborn survival became a symbol of resistance against the Bolsheviks. The government responded by hiding it under the red shroud. Then the shroud fell into shreds.

Had someone torn it down? Had wind ripped it apart? No, witnesses said, the cloth simply came apart. Destroyed by the hand of God, they said. Word spread. Thousands of pilgrims flocked to Red Square to witness this divine intervention. All was not lost, they felt. The Russian people would be saved from the Reds.[2] They didn't know it would take seventy-one years.

Kalamatiano walked from the train station to his apartment through a desolate, ugly heat. When he reached his building, at 8 Tolstovskiy Alley, he stopped a safe distance away. A guard was posted outside. Kal learned from neighbors that his place had been raided by the Cheka on the day of Lockhart's second arrest. Pshenichka, too, had been arrested; apparently he had arrived at the apartment before Kalamatiano, and was caught in a trap. Chekists had also raided the Moscow YMCA and arrested Paul Anderson, the local secretary. Now they were looking for Kalamatiano under his real name and under his alias as Serpukhovsky.

"This is of interest because my stay in Moscow under an assumed name was known only at the consulate, and then only to a few people," Kal wrote in his report to State. Specifically, he named Alexander Friede and Sidney Reilly as knowing about his Serpukhovsky cover. That led to speculation that Reilly was a double agent working for the Cheka. But there is little evidence of that other than the fact that Reilly carried that Cheka ID issued to him by the secretly anti-Communist judge Vyacheslav Orlovsky. Reilly used the ID to pass through Cheka lines and collect intelligence. Further, Robin Lockhart saw no "credence" to the theory that Reilly had been working with Dzerzhinsky against the Lenin plotters.[3]

The next thing Kalamatiano did on the day he returned to Moscow was to go to Alexander Friede's residence. It, too, was under surveillance. Kal found out that the Cheka had arrested the colonel and his sister Maria. Kalamatiano moved on. He had reports and letters from Samara to give Poole.

"I decided to take no more chances," he reported later.[4] He went directly to the U.S. consulate.

The Soviets had cut off the consulate's electricity and water. But the Allied internees secretly got water through a line connected to the church next door. That allowed them to take all the showers and make all the coffee they wanted. And their cook was allowed to go out for food.

Eight French and British officials were holed up with Poole. They included French Consul General Fernand Grenard and military attaché General Jean Lavergne. Grenard and Lavergne tried to leave at one point but were grabbed at the gate. Poole rushed out to intervene. He told the guards this property was sacred ground. They backed down but Grenard and Lavergne had to stay inside the compound.

The Allied prisoners played soccer out in the yard as a way of blowing their captors a raspberry salute. Despite Poole's earlier fear of being arrested, he was in fact allowed to come and go from the building, apparently because Chicherin knew him. The guards didn't bother Poole as long as he didn't look like he was making a run for it. But he was getting nervous. The Norwegians gave him a message relayed from Washington. The State Department didn't want Poole to end up as a hostage. He was told to get out.

"Department has approved your remaining at Moscow but now desires you to proceed immediately Stockholm, Archangel or Omsk, whichever you can arrange, and report from there," the wire said. "Any Americans remaining should accompany you if possible."[5]

That was fine with Poole. He had no hopes of conducting any further business with the Soviets.

But before they left, the Italian consul general went to see Jacob Peters at the Lubyanka and inquired about prisoners the Cheka was holding. He said that during their conversation, Peters signed seventy-two death warrants without reading them and that the firing squads were shooting outside in the courtyard. The consul general then went to a revolutionary tribunal and demanded that four Italian citizens be released. They were, but others on the list were shot before he left the building.[6]

When Kal got to the consulate that afternoon he was wearing his usual suit, hat, and spats, with his gentleman's cane in his hand. As always, that was dangerous. It branded him a member of the hated bourgeoisie and a target for headhunters. But Kal, perhaps naïvely, still felt he could move around freely by posing as an American businessman.

He walked back and forth in the street, studying the Chekists and troops stationed around the consulate. The captain of the guard at the front gate was a girl about twenty years old. In his memoirs, Poole described her as intelligent, good-looking, and charming, though tough and stern. After a while, the coast looked clear. Kal decided to slip in. He strolled through a consulate gate into the courtyard. A guard appeared and stopped him.

Kal was thirty-six years old, a physically fit former athlete who had broken track records in college. He probably could have outrun the guard. But he decided to take a different tack.

"I thought that I could bluff my way through, declaring that I was an American going to the consulate for my passport . . ."

It didn't work. He was surrounded and arrested. A car was called. He was whisked off to the Lubyanka, leaving behind a cloud of exhaust smoke and a grinding of gears.

❖

Kalamatiano was a big catch for the Cheka. Dzerzhinsky turned the case over to his assistant, Jacob Peters. Peters in turn brought in two rising talents to help in the interrogation, Lev Mikhailovich Karakhan and Viktor Eduardovich Kingisepp.

Karakhan was a twenty-nine-year-old protégé of Chicherin's, a former Social Democrat before going over to the Bolsheviks. He was a member of the Bolsheviks' Petrograd Revolutionary Military Council in October 1917 and then secretary of the Soviet delegation to the Brest-Litovsk talks. Lev Mikhailovich was an ambitious employee who wanted to move up to the coveted commissariat for foreign affairs, a ministry whose power and independence rivaled that of the Cheka. Karakhan was the one who had called Lockhart to report Reilly's flamboyant appearance at the Kremlin when Sidney first got to town.

Kingisepp was a thirty-four-year-old Estonian and former journalist for *Pravda* and an Estonian workers' newspaper, *Kiir* (the Ray). He had been a revolutionary since the age of seventeen, first in Tallin, then in St. Petersburg. He helped organize the Red Guards in Estonia and then went to work for the Cheka. Since then, he had been assigned to work two choice investigations—the attempted coup by Left SRs in July, and now the so-called Lockhart Conspiracy. Like Karakhan, Viktor Eduardovich was a focused up-and-comer.[7]

Chekists had caught four more of Kalamatiano's Russian agents in a stake-out on Colonel Friede's house. A fifth was arrested after a receipt bearing his name was found on Kal. A sixth was picked up after Chekists found a blackmail letter from him in Kalamatiano's rooms. But three of Kal's agents in Moscow and eight in Ukraine were safe.[8]

No doubt about it, the Cheka had broken up a major Western spy ring. Kalamatiano's interrogators tried to get him to admit that a plot against the Soviet government was discussed at that August 25th meeting in the American consulate. As evidence of that, Peters revealed René Marchand's written exposé of the meeting. Kal replied that he had "never seen Marchand" and was in "no way" connected with the consulate.

"I took the following stand," Kalamatiano reported to State. "My presence at the meeting, my identity and my connection with Friede and the others were established quite definitely, this I very quickly discovered, so I considered it useless and even harmful to deny something which they could prove."

Kal told the Cheka he knew nothing of any special meeting called for any particular purpose. Yes, he was at the consulate that August day, but claimed he'd heard nothing of any plots against the Soviets. He admitted he had met Reilly and de Verthamon at the consulate and knew they were going to stay behind in Moscow after the diplomats left. He also admitted they had exchanged addresses. But he insisted he didn't know what their business was.

Then Kalamatiano's cane acquired a voice of its own.

Historian Alexander Orlov, a twenty-three-year-old Red Army officer at the time, recalled that while this talk was going on, Kingisepp noticed that Kal was holding on to his cane. He wouldn't let it go. Kingisepp went over and took the cane away from him and began to examine it.

"Kalamatiano turned pale and lost his composure," Orlov wrote. "The investigator soon discovered that the cane contained an inner tube and he extracted it. In it were hidden a secret cipher, spy reports, a coded list of thirty-two spies, and money receipts from some of them. Kalamatiano no longer resisted and gave candid testimony about himself and his network."[9]

But what exactly was that "candid testimony?" Orlov implies that Kal confessed. But confessed to what? Kal never admitted he was a spy. Nor did he ever use the word "intelligence."

"I stated that I had been in Russia for many years representing business houses and that this could easily be proved," Kal reported to State. "That in view of the present situation it had been impossible to do actual business but that I had remained, believing that eventually business would be resumed. That for the same purpose I had some time previously organized a small force of men whose business it was to travel and report on such conditions as could immediately affect business."[10]

On its face, possession of a code or cipher meant nothing sinister. Many businessmen sent reports that way because it saved money in telegraph fees. And those thirty-two "spies" could have simply been business observers that Kal kept on the payroll. And he had receipts for money he paid them. So what?

Peters didn't believe Kalamatiano's claims of innocence, especially after he admitted he had issued business "bulletins" to the American consulate and to de Verthamon and Reilly. But Kal still refuted all of Marchand's accusations.

Kalamatiano had committed two serious breaches of security. He attempted to stroll openly into the consulate when he could have sent someone in to talk with Poole and obtain instructions. And Kal carried his code books and the coded names of his agents in his cane. He was in hot water that he himself had drawn.

The interrogations ran about ten days. Kalamatiano was taken out of his cell two or three times a night for grilling. Peters was the heavy and roughed him up. Kingisepp came on as the logician, offering measured arguments as to how hopeless Kal's case was. Karakhan was the smoothie, with offers of immunity if Kal's testimony was "satisfactory."

Kalamatiano demanded to be confronted with Marchand. They told him that was undesirable, or impossible, something like that. On one of his trips to the interrogation room, Kal ran into two American consuls. They had also been arrested.

Finally it became clear to Peters, Kingisepp, and Karakhan that their prize catch had nothing more to say. Kalamatiano was formally charged with being an agent of the U.S. government and with taking part in the Allied plot against Lenin. Then he was transferred to Butyrka prison.

Butyrka was a rambling four-story pile of mildewed bricks in the Tverskoy district in central Moscow, close to police headquarters and the Kremlin. Tverskoy was a pleasant green neighborhood of homes, churches, and theatres. Its wide streets were home to lime and chestnut trees alive with squirrels and pigeons in warm weather, and the main thoroughfare, Tverskaya Street, was lined with impressive mansions and hotels. For more than a hundred years Tverskaya had been the southern terminus of the royal highway from Moscow to Petrograd, the "Main Street of Russia."

But in the midst of this beautiful and serene neighborhood sat the local blight, Butyrka. It was one of the most infamous prisons in Russia, the government's main warehouse for political prisoners. It was hot in summer, cold in winter, and infested with vermin. Among its attractions were vertical cages where inmates were forced to stand for days. The place was so ominous-looking that an apartment building was later built around it to shield it from public view. Butyrka was built five years before the American Revolution and was supposed to be inescapable, though Harry Houdini got out of one of their cages in twenty-eight minutes flat.[11]

❖

Here was the bottom line for the Soviets: The Cheka had that note for a Latvian courier, signed by Lockhart. They had Reilly's business card with Otten's address on the back. They had confessions from Colonel Friede and his sister Maria implicating Kalamatiano. They had Marchand's letter. They had Kal's codebook and a list of names the Cheka claimed were Kal's agents. And they had his admission that he had given bulletins to the U.S. consulate.

But what direct and irrefutable physical evidence did they have against him? His codes and ciphers could obviously have been intended for business purposes, as he claimed. And in open court, with foreign correspondents present, defense attorneys might argue that the Friedes had been coerced into confessing. Considering the Cheka's reputation, some of the judges might agree.

And what about Marchand? What kind of witness was he, a hack for *Le Petit Parisien*, a French scandal sheet? Marchand was in league with the Cheka, and that was useful to the Reds. But to the outside world, Marchand was a traitor. Kalamatiano was not.

The Soviets could believe their evidence all they wanted. But what would world opinion say? Specifically, what would *Washington* say? Lenin desperately needed U.S. aid to fight the coming famine. He did not need another diplomatic disaster like his massacre of the royal family. At the same time, Dzerzhinsky and Peters wanted their pound of flesh.

To shoot Kalamatiano or not, that was the question.

33

THE STING

Jacob Peters considered the Americans the "worst compromised" in the Lenin Plot, and if DeWitt Poole could be captured, that would cement the Cheka's case against the Yanks.[1] Poole knew he had to get out fast. He sent a message to Chicherin's assistant, Karakhan, asking for a pass to leave Russia. He promised to return the favor someday.

Karakhan responded quickly with travel papers. Evidently the Soviet foreign commissariat didn't want complications like American diplomats getting shot by the Cheka. Better to help Poole get out of the country as quietly as possible.

Poole packed a bag and gave it to the consulate cook. The guards were accustomed to seeing her come and go with parcels, and when she walked out with Poole's bag that morning they didn't stop her. Later, around ten o'clock, Poole strolled out the gate. Because he was on friendly terms with the girl in command of the guard, he was not accosted.

Poole walked up the sidewalk, trying not to panic, and got into a waiting car, probably placed at his disposal by the Norwegians. Then he was whisked away. Where was he going, to see his friend at the foreign ministry? No, to catch a train. Step on it.

Poole got to the station without trouble and was reunited with his suitcase. But the trains were running with Soviet efficiency and he had to sit and keep his head down until ten o'clock that night. Apparently the guard commander at the consulate hadn't raised an alarm yet about his absence. Or maybe she had, and Karakhan was running interference for Poole. At any rate, DeWitt boarded the Petrograd train safely. A few days later he reached the Finnish border, accompanied by a Norwegian consul and a Norwegian diplomatic courier.

Poole knew one of the Russian guards at the frontier. DeWitt had previously bribed him with $1,000 to let some Americans through. After a long wait, Poole was allowed to walk across the little bridge into German-held Finland. But when he got to the train station on the other side he found the tracks ahead had been torn up as a precaution against a Russian invasion. He had to keep walking, in a cold rain, for six miles, to reach his next train.

Poole hadn't been able to sleep much in Moscow while the consulate was under siege, so when he got to Christiania (now Oslo), Norway, he treated himself to a good meal and a comfy hotel room. Then one day Poole was stopped on the street by a Norwegian courier who had crossed the border behind him.

The courier said that ten minutes after Poole escaped Russia, the Soviet border station received a wire from the Cheka ordering his arrest.[2]

❖

Sidney Reilly got out of Russia using a passport in the name of Georg Bergmann, a fictitious merchant in Riga. It was one of the boots (forgeries) the British embassy kept on hand for smuggling people out. George Hill gave it to him. Hill got out, too, but lost fourteen of his agents in the process.

In Moscow, one of Reilly's women agents had booked him a train compartment for Petrograd. When he got to the station it was raining hard and the platform was crowded. A fight broke out between a soldier and an old lady over some problem with her papers. A railroad official joined the fray. Sidney took advantage of the confusion and slipped onto the train just in time.

When Reilly got to his compartment he found a young man there wearing glasses and a cutaway coat. He jumped up from his seat and bowed to Sidney.

"Guten Abend," he said.

Reilly's faithful Moscow agent had got him a berth in the German embassy's car. Was that a little dose of humor on her part? Oh well, Sidney was fluent in German and he was carrying a passport in a German name. He decided to blend in.

His roommate was a wounded veteran who had been observing Russian economic conditions for the German government. Now he was going home. Sidney was going to be sleeping with the enemy that night, or at least in the same compartment.

But Reilly was one of those people who could get along with anybody when he wanted to. Perhaps *use* people is a better word. He and the German opened their food parcels and proceeded to enjoy a picnic. Then after supper the German began to write a report about Russia. Sidney said he helped him by supplying information (or disinformation) about the Russian situation.

Reilly almost got arrested that night. The train stopped at Tver, northwest of Moscow, and Red Guards boarded the train.

"Pokazat svoi dokumenti," a commissar told Sidney. Show your documents.

Documents? Reilly had no documents except a phony passport. It might have fooled the conductor, but dealing with a commissar was a different matter. Sidney decided to take the bull by the horns. He jumped up angrily.

"What documents?" he demanded in German. "We are members of the German embassy."

That got the commissar's attention. *"Prosti minyat,"* he blurted out. Pardon me. He touched his cap and quickly withdrew.

Reilly stayed with friends in Petrograd long enough to grow a beard as a disguise. Then he paid 60,000 rubles to a Netherlander to sneak him out of the country. This man owned a ship that was tied up on the quay and was about to return home. But there was a problem. The skipper had been doing business with the Soviet government and was entertaining a commissar aboard the ship. They had to get rid of the commissar before sailing. How to do it? Reilly was carrying a Colt revolver. Should they shoot him?

No, they got him drunk, carried him ashore, and dumped him. Farewell, comrade. The ship cast off with Sidney aboard.

Their first stop?

The German naval base at Estonia. It was enemy territory but at least Reilly was safe from the Soviets.[3]

❖

Boris Savinkov didn't leave an account of how he got out of Russia. But his Union for the Defense of Fatherland and Freedom had organizations in western Russia around the Polish border, down at Odessa, and up in Finland, so his agents in one of those areas probably got him out. Savinkov's pattern all his life had been to make a beeline for Paris whenever he got into trouble in Russia. That's what he did now.

Following old habits, Boris used an assumed name to rent a top-floor apartment with a view of the street below. One of the addresses he used was 32 rue de Lübecke, a narrow street of seven-story buildings with balconies in the Chaillot district.[4] It was a quiet middle-class quarter offering the infamous terrorist the anonymity he needed to discreetly blend into the shadows while he planned new operations against Lenin. It also allowed him access to rooftops in case he had to suddenly relocate in the middle of the night.

Savinkov contacted his old friend Reilly, who had returned to London. Being a man of wealth and taste, Sidney moved into a bachelor's flat in the Albany, a posh manse built in 1770 in the West End, east of the Burlington Arcade and the Royal Academy of Arts.[5] Lord Byron had lived there. So had Mr. Fascination Fledgeby, a moneylender in the Charles Dickens novel *Our Mutual Friend*. The London *Daily Telegraph* recently called it a "haven for incurable oddities."[6]

Reilly supplied Savinkov with money for new plots against Communist forces in Russia, Poland, Byelorussia, and Ukraine. Those donations would appear to further offset rumors that Reilly was a double agent for the Cheka.[7] But Boris needed more money than Sidney could afford, so he went to talk with Winston Churchill and Lloyd George in England and Benito Mussolini in Italy. They admired Savinkov but didn't have any war purses to offer him.

Admiral Alexander Kolchak, former chief of the imperial navy's Black Sea fleet, appointed Savinkov his representative in Paris. Kolchak had thrown away his Golden Sword of St. George, awarded for bravery under the imperial government, and resigned from the navy in 1917 after the breakdown of the military, which he blamed on Kerensky. Then the Provisional All-Russian Government at Omsk, not to be confused with the original provisional government, appointed Kolchak "supreme ruler" of the country. Aside from the Czechs, Kolchak's army was the only one in Russia still scoring significant victories against the Reds. But he needed Allied support, and Boris contacted potential donors for him.

Savinkov was heavily guarded in Paris. His social life centered on conducting an affair with Aimée Derenthal, wife of his secretary. She and her husband Alexander tipped off Boris that he was the target of a kidnap plot, and he managed to stage one of his dramatic escapes.

But how did the Derenthals find out about the plot? Did they have contacts with the Cheka? Later on, some people would suspect them of being double agents for the Soviets and responsible for Savinkov's capture.

❖

Bruce Lockhart was locked up for five days in the Lubyanka after his second arrest. He was kept in a small room where commissars interrogated prisoners while he watched. The questioning went on day and night. Lockhart slept on the floor. His meals were potatoes, weak tea, and pea soup. Jacob Peters came to see him. He brought books and news of Lenin's slow recovery. They talked about England, and Moura. Jacob showed his hands where his fingernails had been pulled out by tsarist torturers. Bruce saw Peters as a sentimental man but still a Communist fanatic.

One afternoon Lockhart and Peters stood looking out the window when a Black Maria pulled into the courtyard below. A squad of armed men jumped out. They were there to pick up some prisoners. A door was opened in the building and three former tsarist ministers were marched out and loaded into the van. They were followed by a screaming, crying priest. He was pushed and carried to the van and thrown inside. Bruce asked where they were going.

"To another world," Peters replied. They were among the thousands being killed in retaliation for the shooting of Lenin.[8]

That was when Peters told Lockhart that the Americans were the worst compromised in the Allied plot against Lenin. It was a reference, of course, to Kalamatiano and Poole. But Peters said that for "political reasons," the Soviets were not implicating the Americans as much as the French and British.[9] Those "political reasons" apparently were the Soviets' desperate need for U.S. foreign aid.

Lockhart was transferred to a clean and comfortable Kremlin apartment with sitting room, bedroom, kitchen, and bathroom. It was a big improvement, despite the fact the loo had no tub. And Lockhart's mood was not improved when he found out that the last prisoner in the apartment was one of the former ministers recently taken out to be shot. A guard informed Bruce that the Kremlin was reserved for the most unfortunate political prisoners. None ever came out alive, he reported sadly as he left.

Lockhart had company for a day and a half. It was Jan Shmidkhen, the Latvian whom Francis Cromie had sent to see Lockhart about a Moscow coup. Shmidkhen, like Kaplan, was probably put in Lockhart's cell to see what they would talk about. Bruce ignored him.

Lockhart wrote a letter asking Peters to release Moura Benckendorff. Peters did so, and sent Bruce a basket of food and some clean clothes. Then Jacob showed up to announce that Lockhart was being released in a swap for Maxim Litvinov. He was Moscow's unofficial and unaccredited representative in Britain, currently conducting diplomatic affairs from a London jail cell, though British officials ignored him. Jacob was smiling and holding hands with Moura.

What did that mean?

Some have said that Moura was the love of Bruce's life. Maybe. But like Reilly, Lockhart was a man who fell into love with different women on a regular basis. Moura, though, represented the Old Russia that Bruce had loved since his first day in the country. He thought *he* had gotten *her* out of prison, but it might have been the other way around. Moura had a reputation as a libertine. She might have peddled her charms to lonely Jacob Peters in order to get Lockhart out of stir.

Which poses the ultimate question: Exactly how much could Bruce really trust Moura?

That subject came up after a friend of Lockhart's in Moscow passed along a tip to Bruce from a third party who said the Soviets had obtained a copy of the British codes that Lockhart kept locked in his apartment.

A visitor could not easily have stolen them. Lockhart and Hicks were always there when a guest arrived. And their trusted maid would have intercepted an intruder. That left Moura as a suspect.

The "baroness" was a member of the hated nobility struggling to survive under the new and dangerous Communist reality. A good way of doing that would have been to play ball with the Cheka. She later told an *Izvestia* correspondent that Peters indeed tried to turn her, but she claimed he failed.

"Moura said Peters was like Count Dracula," the reporter wrote. "He was very rough with her and threatened to have her shot within twenty-four hours unless she told him everything she knew about Lockhart." Moura said she replied: "All I can talk about is Lockhart's sexual prowess. I don't know anything else."[10]

But after the Russian Civil War burned out, Moura's ties to the Soviets became public knowledge, and would continue over the years. Aside from the Sûreté reports, there's confirmation from former KGB Colonel Igor Prelin. He said Moura was a friend of Stalin's and likely was Genrikh Yagoda's lover. Yagoda was a deputy chairman of OGPU, a successor to the Cheka, and supervisor of many executions during the Stalinist purges.[11]

Moura was Yagoda's "private agent" with privileges to come and go from the USSR at will, Prelin said. In Britain today she is remembered as Moura

Budberg and the great-great-aunt of Nick Clegg, former deputy prime minister, 2010–2015.[12]

❖

Maxim Litvinov, the other half of Lockhart's swap deal, was born Meyer Wal-
lach, a Polish merchant's son. The British had arrested him for distributing
Red propaganda in London. A U.S. military intelligence report said he was
swapping Red rubles for pounds sterling and shipping the English notes to
Russia, after skimming a percentage off the top for himself.[13] That was the
sort of profiteering that could have got him shot by the Cheka. He would
later serve as Soviet ambassador to the United States, 1941–1943, and push for
a strong alliance between the Soviet Union and the Western powers against
Nazi Germany.

Lockhart left Moscow on October 3, 1918. He and forty or fifty other
Westerners, including General Lavergne, were put on a special train and sent
north to Novy Bieloostrov, a Russian village on the Finnish border. They were
escorted by Latvian troops assigned by the Cheka. But Litvinov had not yet
arrived at Bergen, Norway, for the exchange, so they had to wait three days
before crossing the frontier.

To pass the time, they played games of pitch and toss on the station platform. Then after a game was played and as they were picking up their coins,
word came that Litvinov had crossed into Norway. At the same time, they
were told that Austria was suing for peace and the Germans' Hindenburg
Line had collapsed.

They raised a cheer. The war was almost over.

❖

Henri de Verthamon did not leave with Poole or Lockhart. A revolutionary
tribunal declared "Monsieur Henri" an enemy of the working class and
sentenced him to be shot if captured. He disguised himself as a Russian
peasant and walked nearly 500 miles from Moscow to the Finnish border.
He evaded capture by sleeping in the daytime and hiking at night. He
reached Paris on October 27, 1918.

Charles Faux-Pas Bidet was not so lucky. Bidet was arrested on September 1
in the Russian town of Vyborg, one of the crossing points to Finland. He was

returned to Moscow and was treated to a chat with Dzerzhinsky at Cheka headquarters. They were joined by Trotsky. Lev Davidovitch sarcastically complained that things were "not very friendly" these days between France and Russia.

"It is the march of events," Bidet replied.

Dzerzhinsky did not have Bidet shot. At Trotsky's suggestion, Bidet was locked up as a hostage. Thus, two years after Bidet saved Lev Davidovitch's life in Paris, the favor was returned. Bidet was shuffled from prison to prison, interrogated, and finally put on a boat with 1,500 other nearly starved prisoners and traded for Russians held by the West.

❖

The political arm of the Allies' Lenin Plot had been chopped off by the Cheka, leaving only military options now. But as so often happens in the world of espionage, the Moscow plot was more than what it appeared to be. From information willingly supplied by his interrogators and from details Jacob Peters let slip, Xenophon Kalamatiano found out that he and the other plotters had been fooled by a mirage. No, a parallax view.

The script read this way: In the early summer of 1918, Lenin deduced that the Allies were plotting a coup against him. According to Alexander Orlov, Lenin suggested to Dzerzhinsky that the Cheka catch the conspirators "red-handed" and expose them to the world.[14] Kalamatiano later agreed that the approach by the Latvians had looked "very much like a piece of 'provocation.'"

The Allies were set up in a Cheka sting operation. Berzin and other Latvian officers acted as agents provocateurs to draw the Western spies into exposing their coup conspiracy. That made the affair a "Lenin plot" in more ways than one. The Russians could rightly claim it as one of history's most spectacular counterintelligence victories. The Western agents were understandably stunned, angry, and bitter.

The Lenin Plot turned out to be a colossal embarrassment for the United States and the Allies. They had plotted a coup against a former ally, Russia. Two of the chief plotters, Reilly and Savinkov, had intended to murder Lenin, Trotsky, and everybody else in the Soviet government they could get their hands on.

Since America and the Allies had never declared war on Russia, the Lenin Plot would seem to place them squarely in the business of international terrorism.

❖

But how directly involved were American diplomats and spies in the *military* side of the Lenin Plot, specifically Wilson's upcoming invasion at Archangel? What do official documents show?

First, State Department records quote DeWitt Poole in Moscow as telling Ambassador Francis in June 1918 that he was sending U.S. consuls to areas of Russia where Allied troops were expected. Those consuls would make preparations "in advance of military movements." [15] In July, Poole reported that Kalamatiano's spies were collecting "important military information" which could be used "very advantageously." Then in August, Poole said America should concentrate on military support for the Czechs.

"The Czechs must not only be promptly supported from the rear, but a junction effected in the north without further delay," Poole said in a wire to Lansing a week later. "At the same time, the [Czechs'] now much exposed Samara flank must be protected and the way prepared for a junction with the British from Baku supported by Dutov, Alekseev, and other active elements in the intermediary region as pointed out in previous telegrams." [16]

The day after that, Ambassador Francis, then in Archangel, said that as soon as American troops landed in North Russia he wanted them to invade the interior down to Sukona, Vologda, Petrograd, and Moscow. [17]

In September 1918, after the Cheka began reprisals for the shooting of Lenin, Poole said it was America's duty to "shield the numberless innocents" who were suffering under the Red Terror. [18] He urged Washington to "proceed" against the "treacherous and persistently lawless government" of Soviet Russia. [19]

❖

Dzerzhinsky had taken only about three months to break up the Lenin Plot. It had cost the Allies untold millions of dollars, francs, pounds, and rubles. The Cheka's sting, combined with the shootings of Uritsky and Lenin, resulted in thousands of arrests and murders by the Soviets.

In addition to the Allied agents' naïve trust of Jan Shmidkhen and Eduard Berzin, and the discovery of that card with Reilly's Moscow address on it, the Western plotters had made disastrous mistakes in the latter weeks of the Lenin Plot:

—René Marchand crashed the secret spy conference in Poole's office and reported to the Cheka. Reilly had suspected him immediately. So did de Verthamon. Why didn't they at least ask Marchand to wait in another room during the meeting?

—Kalamatiano tried to openly stroll into the American consulate while it was surrounded by Soviet guards. It would have been safer for him to leave Russia while he could. His supreme miscalculation led to the roll-up of most of his agents.

—Poole actually admitted to Chicherin that the United States was running an "information service" in Russia, supposedly because Soviet newspapers were unreliable. Poole wasn't clear what possessed him to offer that revelation. Chicherin must have known what Poole was talking about because he was terrified of the Cheka and was "nearly frightened . . . out of his chair" by Poole's admission.[20]

—Lockhart was burned by that travel pass he signed for a Latvian courier, and by one of the interesting women he was always picking up. There's no way of telling how much information Moura got from Bruce and passed on to the Reds and the Germans. How many Allied lives did she put in jeopardy? One might say that Lockhart should have known better than to trust her. But love, they say, is blind.

Error was piled on error. Was it stupidity on the part of the plotters? Arrogance? Or simply sloppiness? Whatever it was, the smartest guys in the room were outfoxed by a dumpy little man in a cheap brown suit.

With the roll-up of the Lenin Plot, the Allies were down. But they weren't out, not yet. They still had President Wilson's invasion coming up at Archangel. Washington, Paris, Rome, and London were hoping the invaders could link up with Kolchak's army from the east and the Czech Legion in the interior, and march on Moscow and Petrograd for a decisive blow against Lenin and the Soviet government.

PART III
SNOW TRENCHES

34

WHERE IS THE FRONT?

The Allies invaded Archangel for the second time on Wednesday morning, September 4, 1918, beneath hard rain and a cold north wind. A Russian mystic (and there were a few of those) might have said the storm was an omen.

The men of Detroit's Own docked at ten o'clock at Bakaritza, the "Brooklyn of Archangel," on the left bank of the Dvina River. The city of Archangel (*Arkhangelsk*) was on the right bank of the Dvina where it flowed into the White Sea. It was the largest town in Russia's far north, a neat little community of wide streets and sidewalks, parks, shops, churches, an onion-domed cathedral, and a streetcar system. Workers' homes were built from logs; merchants lived in brick and stone houses. White stuccoed walls and red roofs downtown lent the town a uniformity of mood characteristic of old Russian towns.

Archangel traced its history back to 1584, when a fortified monastery was built there and dedicated to Saint Michael the Archangel. (He wasn't really a saint but the leader of all angels, the protector of soldiers and police, and the guardian of Israel.) The town thrived as Russia's main northern port, with miles of wharves and warehouses on both sides of the river, until the much larger St. Petersburg was built in the early 1700s. Archangel then went into decline. It was resurrected by the opening of the railroad in 1898, linking it to Vologda and St. Petersburg, with connections to Moscow and the rest of Russia.

During this war, more than 600 ships, including American vessels, had visited Archangel each year during the six months the harbor was ice free. The town's main street, Troitsky Prospekt, a broad thoroughfare of mansions, churches, state buildings, and a statue of Peter the Great, followed the curve of the river for three miles. American affairs at Archangel had been handled for years as a sideline by a local Danish businessman. When he was exposed as a possible German agent in 1917 he was replaced by a fulltime U.S. consul, Felix Cole, an experienced businessman in Russia.

The swollen wartime population of Archangel included Cossacks and former imperial officers who paraded through the streets in their dress uniforms and medals. Food and jobs were scarce. Lenin rubles were almost worthless. Bales of them were stacked up and used as kindling.

Archangel lay just below the Arctic Circle, and autumn had come early this year. Storms stripped trees of their bright orange and yellow foliage and left a soggy carpet of leaves on the muddy ground. Several hundred American soldiers were still sick with flu when they got off their ships, and the British put thirty of them in the local Russian Red Cross Hospital. With its dirt floors, it was not a very sanitary place. The rest of the sick men were dumped into an old Russian barracks and had to bunk on pine boards without mattresses. With a shortage of blankets, the sick men slept in their cold wet clothes.

"Death stalked gauntly through, and many a man died with his boots on in bed," three U.S. officers wrote in their history of the expedition. [1]

The World War of 1914–1918 was the first time that American and British troops had fought on the same side in large numbers. Aside from the expected differences in tactics and policy, most of the front-line troops from both nations seem to have gotten along fairly well on the western front. But that was before a "special relationship" existed between the United States and Britain. Each side watched the other with suspicion and distrust.

Officially, Yanks shared a common language with Brits, though large swaths of North America also spoke French and Spanish, and still do. Americans admired British writers such as Charles Dickens and Arthur Conan Doyle, and Shakespeare's plays were regularly staged. "America," the unofficial U.S. national anthem in 1918, used the melody from "God Save the King." But British influence was felt mainly on the East Coast, home of England's original colonies. Other nationalities such as the French, Spanish, Swedes, Norwegians, Irish, Germans, and Russians had settled most of North America.

America's relationship with France was different. Americans admired the French for their food, wine, artwork, science, fashion, architecture, and, of course, Napoléon. Most of all, Americans sympathized with the French passion for republican democracy. France was America's oldest ally. That partnership went back to 1775, when France began to assist the American colonies in their rebellion against the English crown. The American Revolution was followed by the French Revolution. Those two events rattled thrones throughout Europe. They were inspirations for Russian revolutionaries as far back as the early 1800s, under Alexander I.

In Russia, all the Allies were supposed to be united against the Red Army. But there was another battle going on, between British officers on one side, and American and French officers and enlisted men on the other. That animosity threatened the expedition from day one.

One of the first examples was that refusal of the British to admit dough-boys to the clean, warm English army hospital. In the British view, a cold and dilapidated old Russian barracks was good enough for the Yanks. But outraged American doctors demanded their own hospital. The British blocked them, claiming no medical supplies or personnel were available. Letters to London asking for supplies got lost in red tape.

Finally, the American Red Cross in Archangel stepped in and supplied the necessary equipment, and a building was found. Some doughboys were trained to run the new hospital, and Russian nurses were hired. Red Cross workers and doughboys climbed on the roof of the building, raised the American flag, then dared the British to do anything about it.

❖

On September 6, two days after the expeditionary force landed, the British ordered the 1st Battalion of the U.S. 339th Infantry onto boats and sent them south, up the Dvina, to establish a front deep in the interior. At the same time, the 3rd Battalion was loaded into box cars and sent down the Vologda rail line to relieve a French force. It was late afternoon and still raining when they left Archangel. The men rode on the train all night and slept on the floor of the boxcars. Next morning they arrived at the village of Obozerskaya, a hundred miles south of Archangel. Obozerskaya had to be secured in order to set up an Allied supply depot on the railroad.

The village was nearly deserted. The peasants had fled into the woods to escape the Reds, and took their horses and cows with them. But once the Yanks arrived to reinforce the *poilus,* villagers filtered back in. The peasants traded fresh vegetables to the soldiers for tobacco and cans of bully beef, and used their carts to haul supplies for the troops.

But the rain got heavier. The village flooded. Some French soldiers built fires to dry out but a British officer ordered them doused. Nevertheless, a bridge was repaired and a landing field was built. An armored train with naval guns was brought up. Obozerskaya was transformed in a few days into a major forward base.

"We are fighting an offensive war," a British colonel told the doughboys.

That ran counter to President Wilson's orders that no Americans should go into combat in Russia. But the British were not the only ones who ignored Wilson's instructions. Ambassador Francis had moved the American embassy with its staff of 200 to Archangel in late July and had asked for an invasion of Petrograd and Moscow. Now after the U.S. landing in September he sent a wire to Lansing to repeat his appeal.

"My conclusion is that the only way to end this disgrace to civilization [Bolshevism] is for the Allies immediately to take Petrograd and Moscow by sending sufficient troops therefor [*sic*] to Murman and Archangel without delay; 50,000 would serve but 100,000 would be ample."[2]

❖

The rural villages the men found in Archangel province were generally friendly but humble places. If a rail line ran through, the station was just a platform that stretched out beneath a scorched tin roof, guarded by a delegation of peasants sitting on barrels chewing sunflower seeds. The village itself was usually a cluster of log cabins, trashy yards, and rotting planks for sidewalks. The main street was unpaved, and patrolled by geese, dogs, and sometimes a tinker with a load of pots and pans on his shoulder. The dominant institutions were the copperdomed Orthodox church and the *traktir*, predictably a smoky dive that offered moonshine vodka, consumptive whores, and knife fights.

Two platoons of M Company of the 339th were ordered out on patrol near one of those villages. They immediately got into a battle with a heavy force of Reds, which the Brits called "Bolos" (Bolsheviks). Then L and I companies got into it. They fired until they ran out of ammunition, and charged the Reds with bayonets. The Bolos outnumbered them, but broke and ran. A bomber crash-landed into a field. An American major ran out to greet the pilot.

"Don't fire!" he shouted. "We are Americans."

The plane in fact was a Red Army bomber. The pilot answered with a few rounds from his machine gun and ran for the woods.

Thereafter, the major's greeting became famous in Archangel.

❖

British General Robert Gordon-Finlayson popped up at Obozerskaya and ordered a bigger attack against the Reds. An American officer protested that the men weren't ready. They didn't have good maps, their Cossack scouts were not reliable, and nobody knew exactly where the Reds were. That was sort of necessary for an attack—to know where the enemy was. But, by Jove, Finlayson wanted his battle. He sent out a Franco-American force to engage the Bolos, who were waiting, out there, somewhere.

The force stumbled through the woods in a cold rain. It got dark. The Americans got separated from the French. They all got bogged down in a swamp, completely lost. The French, though, managed to reach a bridge held by the enemy. After a heated battle they drove the Bolos back. The Americans heard the gunfire and ran to reinforce them. The Reds counterattacked but the combined Allied force sent them packing.

A British colonel named Sutherland, not knowing the bridge had been secured, ordered an artillery barrage laid directly on it. An observer reported that when Sutherland was informed that he was shelling Allied soldiers, he called for another bottle of whisky and didn't correct the range until later. Sutherland then ordered the Americans to abandon the bridge. The American commander at the bridge, a Major Nichols, refused.

Finlayson's bumbling attack and Sutherland's neglect of duty cost the lives of four Americans, with fourteen more wounded and five missing. The French lost eight. That would be the familiar pattern for the invasion—attack and counterattack, attack and counterattack again, with nothing to show for it but another stalemate and more people dead, wounded, or lost.

American troops dispatched to Russia were fresh recruits, healthy, well-trained, and enthusiastic. Many of their British commanders were arrogant, incompetent, and drunken. The majority of the Brits were classified as Category B2 or B3, mental and physical rejects who weren't considered up to snuff for duty in France. They were called "crocks" or the "hernia brigade." Naturally they would have preferred duty at a comfortable base in England. Russia was the last place they wanted to be. They tried to relieve their bitterness with vindictiveness aimed at the Americans and French, and with the 40,000 cases of Scotch whisky the British War Office had sent over with them.[3]

❖

Several American officers who served in the heat of battle wrote books describing their experiences in Archangel. One of them was Harry J. Costello, quarterback of the 1918 Camp Custer football team. He wasn't very tall but had broad shoulders, and could turn on a menacing gridiron face when he wasn't flashing his big Irish smile.

Costello came out of the Dublin Hill section of Meriden, Connecticut, north of New Haven. He was a team standout in high school and was coached by the legendary Glenn "Pop" Warner at Georgetown. Then he played with Jim Thorpe for the Canton Bulldogs, one of the founding teams of the National Football League. Costello was teaching math and coaching football at the University of Detroit when he was drafted into the army on August 15, 1917. After officer training camp at Fort Merritt, New York, he was assigned to the 339th at Camp Custer.[4]

Yes, the American army was sent to Russia to guard Allied supplies at Archangel and to keep the Germans from moving into the area, Lieutenant Costello wrote in his book.[5] At least, that was the official story the U.S. government issued to the press. But as soon as the doughboys landed in Archangel, Costello said, they were informed by their British officers that they were there to restore the Eastern Front and invade deep into Russia to assist the Czech Legion and Admiral Kolchak's army in defeating the Soviets. That, of course, was what the Lenin plotters in Moscow had in mind all along.

"We'll just rush up there and re-establish the great Russian army, reorganize the vast forces of the tsar," a British officer told Costello and the men in his machine gun company. And "beware the mosquitoes," he added.[6]

❖

America contributed the largest number of combat troops to the Archangel campaign—143 officers and 4,344 enlisted men from Camp Custer.[7] Britain sent 2,420 marines and infantry, with 600 officers. But most English officers were crocks who pulled garrison duty and never fired a shot. Another 2,000 "batmen" came over with them as valets.[8] They didn't see any action, either. They shined the officers' shoes, served them drinks, and laid out their uniforms for them.

France contributed 1,700 men and officers—a machine gun company, a battalion of the 21st Colonial Infantry, part of a regiment of regulars, and a unit of the French Foreign Legion.[9] Ottawa sent 500 men from the 67th and 68th batteries of the 16th Brigade of the Canadian Field Artillery, the "Saskatchewan Swains (country boys)."[10] Scottish, Polish, Italian, Estonian, Serbian, Lithuanian, Czech, and Chinese contingents were also present. Australia did not officially get involved, but at least 200 Aussies volunteered.

Despite the multinational flavor of the invasion force, "It was mostly an American fight," Costello said.[11]

The Allies were augmented by Cossacks and local volunteers, called "Archangel Russians," who were faithful to the Allied cause. But many of the local Russians joined up just to get hot food and new clothes, and then deserted. It was a continuing problem.

The British command established seven fronts or "columns" in Archangel province, a vast swampy area of timberland that reminded many doughboys of upper Michigan. During the White Nights of summer when the sun didn't completely set, the land was hot, humid, rainy, and plagued by insects. Trails through the woods were hard to use in warm weather because they were muddy. They were more useful in winter, when frozen. Most long-distance travel was done in boats on the rivers until the water froze. Then they became convenient ice highways for sleds.

The fronts, or columns, were:

—The Onega front, on the river of that name southwest of Archangel near the White Sea. A couple of hundred Americans and Archangel Russians were stationed at the village of Onega, backed up by two field guns.

—The Pinega front, at the village of Pinega on the Pinega River, a tributary of the Dvina east of Archangel. About 400 Yanks and 300 Russians were there. Pinega and Onega were the smallest fronts in the war.

—The railroad front, running south from Archangel. If the railroad column could be extended down to Vologda, troops and heavy supplies such as tanks and artillery could press south toward Petrograd and Moscow. The railroad front was manned mostly by three companies of French troops reinforced by American and Archangel Russian riflemen, Cossacks, and Canadian gunners. Their base at Obozerskaya was a little more than a third of the way to Vologda.

—The Seletskoe-Kodish front, close to Obozerskaya and the railroad. This front had two wings, left and right, manned by a French machine gun section, some U.S. riflemen, half a platoon of British marines, and two British field guns. Seletskoe-Kodish was important because it was on the old Imperial Highway that ran down to Petrograd and was used for moving troops and supplies. It was the scene of continuous hard fighting.

—The Bereznik front, at a major town on the Dvina, 170 miles upriver from Archangel. Bereznik is just below the point where the Vaga joins the Dvina. It didn't see much action but it was a major Allied supply base, and three American companies were stationed there to defend it.

—The Dvina front, the biggest river column. It was mostly a British show, with four companies of Royal Scots, 100 Russian riflemen, two British field guns, and an assortment of small naval vessels. Most of the major naval battles took place on the Dvina. The Allies wanted to take the town of Kotlas at the head of the river. It was the base for Red operations on the Dvina. If the Allies could take Kotlas they would have a rail line down to Vyatka, then Vologda, Petrograd, and Moscow.

—The Vaga front, the smaller river column. The Vaga River was a narrow tributary that flowed into the Dvina. The Vaga column consisted of a few hundred Yanks in blockhouses assisted by several hundred Archangel Russians, and British gunships.

All the different armies had their own lower-ranking officers but overall command was held by British colonels and generals. Once in a while an Italian officer came over from Murmansk for a look-see, and from time to time a Japanese officer was spotted. Red Army spies were everywhere. Dressed like Russian peasants, they were just about invisible.

The flu continued to stalk the troops. Another sixty died the first week of the invasion. At Bereznik the British would not allow sixteen sick Americans aboard their hospital boat. They were exiled to an outhouse where three of them died without receiving medical attention.[12] United States Lieutenant Edward Saari picked up twenty-one sick Scots. Their British officers had refused to look after them.[13]

Combat issue for each doughboy was one blanket, half a shelter tent, an extra pair of socks, a mess kit, and 120 rounds of ammunition to go with his hated Russian rifle. American soldiers were issued British uniforms but no helmets, gas masks, or replacement shoes. The only army food the frontline troops got was the British "iron ration" of bully beef, hardtack, and tea. Bully beef was salty and greasy like today's Spam. Many of the men couldn't eat it. British hardtack (crackers) also came in cans. Harry Costello called them "worm castles." The Yanks hated English tea and cigarettes. They smoked the tea in their pipes when their tobacco ran out.

There was no bread, butter, sugar, milk, or fruit juice. The only medications available were aspirin and "No. 9" pills (laxatives). Soldiers continued to barter with villagers for fresh food. Any kind of Allied currency was accepted. Artillery was towed by horses. They had to be fed, too.

❖

A trip from Archangel upriver to the supply base at Bereznik required a three-day boat ride. From Bereznik it took several days more to deliver supplies and relief troops up the two rivers. Those travel times give an idea of how vast an area the Allies were trying to capture. The river forts were not the big sturdy concrete kind found on the western front in France. They were rough blockhouses built of logs with moss stuffed into the cracks for insulation. Barbed wire was installed around the perimeter, but it could not stop an enemy attack. The wire simply slowed the attackers until machine gunners could take them out.

The river forts were strung out over long distances like Pony Express stations in the Old West. Between them were miles of dense forests and swamps occupied by wolves and enemy troops. The forts were built on bluffs so the gunners could fire down on enemy boats. Each fort, however, was manned by only a few hundred men and was occasionally overrun by the enemy. Then the enemy was overrun by a counterattack.

On the railroad front, the men lived in boxcars. The men sped up and down the line in armored trains to engage the enemy in the woods beside the tracks. The Red Army fought back with their own trains. The two sides loaded their trains with big naval guns and had daily artillery duels. Those fights not only killed troops but also tore up sections of the track and knocked out bridges. After a while, each side backed off, repaired the tracks and bridges, then went at it again.

But whether the fighting was on the railroad or the rivers or out in the woods, the pattern was the same: win ground, lose it, then win it again. On and on it went, day after day, week after week. With their outdated maps, Allied military headquarters at Paris couldn't keep up with what was going on in Russia. At one point they sent a wire to Archangel:

"Exactly where is the Pinega front?"[14]

35

SANITY ARRIVES

W here are the bloody Bolsheviks and which is the way to Kotlas?" a British commander demanded as his monitor, a small riverboat carrying big guns, sailed up the Dvina from Bereznik. Somebody pointed the way to Kotlas. When the commander got there he opened up on Soviet positions around the town. But apparently he didn't hit anything strategic. The Bolos lobbed a big shell onto the monitor, killing several sailors and knocking the boat out of commission.

The most accurate Allied gunners were Canadians. They were always in demand. The most coveted gun was the French 75-millimeter field cannon. The 75 had almost no recoil and an experienced crew could fire it thirty times a minute. It was the most efficient field piece ever developed and was copied by the American and German armies.

One evening in September 1918 a Franco-American patrol outside Kodish happened upon a Red armored train parked in the woods. They couldn't attack because of rain and darkness, but the target was a proverbial sitting duck. They slept in the woods that night under wet blankets. They got up before dawn but dared not build a fire, so they had no hot coffee or breakfast. The platoons spread out in a wide line for an attack while it was still dark.

At daybreak a bugler blew "Charge!" A mass of blue (French) and khaki (American) uniforms ran wildly out of the woods yelling and shooting. That woke the Soviets up. They panicked. They thought they were under attack by a huge army. They fired their artillery and machine guns wildly into the woods. But that was where the attackers *had* been. The Bolos backed their train out and fled. The tactic had been a big risk for the Allies but it paid off with hundreds of Red casualties.

"Marvelous luck," a U.S. officer recalled. "We monkeyed with a buzz saw and suffered only slight casualties, one American killed and four wounded. Two French wounded."[1]

Up on the Dvina, the Bolos took Seltso, a river town surrounded on three sides by marshes.[2] The swamps were so deep the Yanks had to go in without artillery support. The Reds opened up with machine guns and pom-poms, small rapid-fire cannons firing clips of one-pound shells. The fighting went into the next day. Finally, heavier artillery arrived to back up the Americans. They shelled the town and burned it down. The Reds ran for the woods. Eight Americans were killed and eight wounded. Heavier casualties were recorded at Seletskoe.

The Yanks took Shenkursk on the Vaga without firing a shot. The Reds had heard gunboats coming and abandoned the town, a large summer resort built on high bluffs with sturdy brick schools, homes, churches, and businesses. From Shenkursk, doughboys and loyalist Russian troops probed farther up the Vaga. If they could open the river to its source, they could reach Vologda faster than the Allied naval force that was trying to navigate a longer route on the Dvina.

Canadian troops in Russia had come from four years on the western front and showed the Americans how to loot the bodies of enemy dead. First they took their money and other valuables, then their knives, fur hats, and boots. Lieutenant John Cudahy, of Company B of the 339th, said the Canadians were "ghoulish" but not individually debased or vicious.

"They were undeliberate, unpremeditated murderers who had learned well the nice lessons of war and looked upon killing as the climax of a day's adventure, a welcomed break in the tedium of the dull military routine."[3]

The Yanks picked up the looting habit, Cudahy said, because their shoes were rotting and falling apart. Soft Russian felt boots, *valenki*, kept feet warm in coldest temperatures and were popular with troops on both sides, but weren't waterproof like leather. Big fur coats were also taken from the dead. They weren't regulation army issue but everybody wore them.

As the first snows fell in the autumn of 1918, American troops began to burn Russian villages in the name of "friendly intervention," Cudahy said. The doughboys had no heart for the job, he added, but the villages could not be left to the Reds. Costello called this kind of warfare "caveman stuff."[4]

❖

October 1918: Artic winds howled, bringing a deep numbing freeze. The British did not send up winter clothing to the troops at the fronts. And food was running out. Costello said hundreds of tons of canned Argentine beef had been shipped to Russia but they were being consumed by crocks in Archangel. And when some meat and American cigarettes did find their way to the fronts, he added, they were sometimes stolen by British officers.[5] The British also stopped shipping medical supplies to the troops. The American Red Cross filled in by dispatching their own expeditions to the fronts.

The snows turned heavy. The midnight sun receded and daylight grew dimmer. The rivers froze and supplies had to be sent by sleds, a slow and difficult process. Frontline troops were stuck in their little forts, surrounded by larger enemy forces. Most of the winter fighting would consist of Reds attacking the forts.

The main Red Army force was the Sixth Independent Army, commanded by Alexander Alexandrovich Samoilo, a forty-nine-year-old Russian nobleman from tsarist days, known for his tactical skills. Before the war, he spied for the imperial army in Austria-Hungary, Germany, and England. During the war, he attained the rank of major general. After the Bolshevik coup he volunteered to work for the Reds and became a military negotiator at Brest-Litovsk.[6] He was also smart politically, as evidenced later by his survival of Stalin's purges.

General Samoilo had around 14,000 men in his command, including Finns, Chinese, and Germans. He used local Red partisan ski troops for reconnaissance, led by Osip Palkin. One of Samoilo's key field commanders was Ieronim Petrovich Uborevich, a twenty-two-year-old Lithuanian who had also served in the tsarist army during the war.[7] Uborevich would later be murdered in 1937 during Stalin's purge of accused Trotskyites in the army.

The Reds, too, suffered from a lack of warm clothing. They were also short on rifles, ammunition, and food. They had little training, which translated into a much higher casualty rate than that of the Allies. Some Red regiments refused to fight. Desertions were rife.[8]

November 1918: The temperature dropped to 20 below freezing (°F). Flu spread through the villages but no doctors were sent to care for U.S. soldiers on the Kodish front. On other fronts, American doctors ran out of iodine and bandages while the British kept medical supplies in Archangel for their hospital. Wounds were sutured with sewing needles and thread. Sometimes an amputation was done with a pocket knife.

One doctor, Major John C. Hall of Centralia, Illinois, stationed at Shenkursk, was ordered by General Finlayson to leave his post and take over as senior medical officer for the Vaga column. That meant he would have to turn his wounded American patients over to the British. He refused. A British colonel threatened to have him shot.

"I immediately told him I was ready to take any punishment they might administer," Hall wrote later, "and sooner or later the news would travel back to the U.S.A. and the general public would awaken to the outrageous treatment given the American soldiers by the hands of the British."

Hall was recalled to Archangel for duty at the American Red Cross hospital. The incident was hushed up.[9]

December 1918: The long Arctic night settled in. The sun barely climbed above the horizon, hung there for a couple of hours, then winked out again. The British had taken away the Americans' air-cooled machine guns and replaced them with water-cooled Vickers guns. The Yanks could not figure out why they had done that, since the Vickers froze up in freezing temperatures. One soldier came up with the idea of filling the cooling tanks with the local moonshine vodka as antifreeze. That worked until Russians drank it.

The outposts were solidly locked in by ice. Their barbed wire was buried beneath several feet of snow. With no supplies and no relief, the front-line troops felt abandoned and forgotten. Some of the Yanks went native. They put on peasant clothes. They lit candles, burned incense, and prayed before Russian ikons. Red Army soldiers stood up at night and made speeches to them from across no man's land. Lieutenant Costello said some of them spoke English with accents from New York's Lower East Side. They usually piped down after somebody took a shot at them.[10]

"Link by link the ties that had bound us to the rest of the world were slipping and breaking," Costello wrote. "The only friends we have are the North Star and the Aurora Borealis."[11]

❖

Problems at the front were compounded by conflicts in the rear. American and French soldiers who went back to Archangel on leave found British officers dining on hot roast beef with gravy, fresh vegetables, toast with butter and jam, and sugar and cream for their tea. They rowed through receptions, banquets, dances, toboggan races, and sleigh rides on a sea of scotch. Cases of empty whisky bottles sat out on sidewalks. Broken bottles littered alleys.

Lieutenant Cudahy wrote that British crocks promenaded down the Troitsky "whipping the air with their walking sticks and looking very stern and commanding as they answered many salutes in a bored, absent-minded way." John Cudahy came from a wealthy Milwaukee meat-packing family. He graduated from Harvard in 1910 and went to law school at Wisconsin. John was accustomed to a comfortable life and would someday inherit the Cudahy fortune. But he was not a spoiled young man. He was appalled at the "jolly" and "amusing" time the British crocks had in Archangel while combat soldiers, "sick men and broken men, men faint from lack of nutrition, and men sickened in soul, were doing sentry duty through the numbing cold nights . . ."[12]

American soldiers who went to the British supply depot in Archangel were either ignored or faced endless arguments and red tape. When one of their French comrades appeared, the crocks pretended they couldn't understand the language, even with an interpreter.

In fairness, it should be noted that things weren't any better at U.S. headquarters. American officers in their warm offices apparently didn't want to be bothered by inconvenient problems from *out there* somewhere. Their attitude seemed to be that this was a British show, let the "limeys" sort it out.[13] Costello complained that U.S. supply officers were not very good, but that the British supply officers brought over by General Poole were "incompetents" and a "disgrace to England."[14] DeWitt Poole was witness to abuse and neglect by all the commanders, and reported them to Washington.

Poole had been sent back to Russia after escaping the country ten minutes ahead of the Cheka. His new assignment was chargé d'affaires for the floating U.S. embassy, which had washed up on the shores of Archangel.[15] He took over the duties of Ambassador Francis, who had left for England to have prostate surgery. Poole became America's top diplomat in Russia, a heady job for a young man who had been with the State Department only seven years.

Poole's closest associates in Archangel were French Ambassador Noulens, who still dreamed of conquering Russia and collecting that 13 billion francs his country lost when Lenin took over, and the Italian ambassador, Pietro Paolo Tomasi Della Torretta. Poole described him as a pleasant man who dressed elegantly and flowed through the motions of diplomacy with impressive flourishes. The Marchese Della Torretta was privy to many of the intrigues of the Lenin Plot and could have contributed in some way. Instead, it was said, he would have preferred to go to sleep and not wake up until it was all over.[16]

❖

The American army commander in Archangel was Colonel George Evans Stewart, a forty-six-year-old training officer from Camp Custer. He was an Australian whose family had emigrated to the United States. Stewart joined the army in 1896 and fought in the Philippine-American War. He was a second lieutenant in the infantry when he waded into a river under enemy fire and rescued a wounded enlisted man. For that, Congress awarded him the Medal of Honor. He served on the western front in France but was sent to Archangel as commander of the Polar Bears, apparently because of his prior duty in another cold outpost, Alaska.

With his combat experience, Stewart should have played a major role in the Archangel campaign. But the overall commander, Major General Frederick Poole, did not tolerate any American or French challenge to his authority, and didn't include Stewart in his inner circle of officers. General Poole shuffled Stewart off to a warm office in the local institute of technology and gave him nothing to do. That must have been humiliating to a war hero like Stewart. DeWitt Poole said Stewart spent his remaining days in Russia sitting in the lunchroom drinking coffee with his staff, gazing out the window as the days passed and their talents went ignored. Descriptions of Stewart suggest he didn't wish to rock the boat.

General Poole was a short man who stood erect and issued orders in a crisp, direct manner. No bull at the bar there. He had fought as a gunner in the Tirah Campaign in India, then in the Second Boer War in South Africa, the Anglo-Somali War, and on the western front in France. He had shown bravery in battle and won the Distinguished Service Order. But Poole didn't like the Americans and the French. He told them they had to drink tea instead of coffee. He refused to go to the fronts to encourage them, to see how they were doing or what they needed. He sent the inept General Finlayson to do that. Finlayson was not well received. Some of the American and French officers refused to salute him.

General Poole had retired after twenty-five years in the army, then got activated again when war broke out. He was forty-five years old that year. In 1918 perhaps he didn't want to leave his roses, his dogs, his horses, and his wife, and get shipped off to what he saw as a ridiculous little sideshow like Archangel. Poole was very much a part of the English class system, and that was probably his greatest tragedy. The class system ruled the British army.

Officers were gentlemen who'd been born on the right side of the tracks. They had cruised through the best universities and belonged to the best clubs. Not many Cockney pipefitters from the East End in those ranks.

Such a system was frowned upon in the American and French armies. Some officers like Harry Costello came from the same working-class background as the enlisted men who served under them. John Cudahy, by contrast, was lace curtain middle-class, but he knew that troops responded best to a commander who spoke their language and understood their daily lives. General Poole seemed incapable of that. Perhaps he felt old and tired. Perhaps he simply didn't care.

But dirt cannot be hidden under the rug forever. President Wilson was enraged at reports of General Poole's arrogance. Secretary of State Lansing fired off a telegram to U.S. Ambassador Walter Hines Page in London, threatening to withdraw American troops from Poole's command. He asked that Page relay that to the British government.[17]

Page passed Lansing's complaint to Foreign Secretary Balfour. He replied that he "shared the views" of Washington and had already taken "vigorous steps to mend matters."[18] Thirteen days later, Wilson, Lansing, and General Peyton C. March, U.S. army chief of staff, stated flatly that no more American troops would be sent to Russia.[19]

Wilson further insisted that all U.S. offensive operations cease, except for guarding the port of Archangel and the surrounding area as originally planned. He also banned U.S. forces from moving into the interior and linking up with the Czech Legion.[20] But General Poole had already sent thousands of American and French troops south. As long as he was in command, he would fight his war the way he bloody well wanted to.

London did not agree. Within days of Balfour's reply to Page, British Field Marshal Henry Hughes Wilson, chief of the imperial general staff, called into his office a young infantry brigade commander from the western front. This was Lieutenant Colonel William Edmund Ironside, a graduate of the Royal Military Academy and recipient of a Distinguished Service Order award.[21] Sir Henry told Ironside that he was being sent to Archangel as the general staff's representative in Archangel. It was an inspector's job, not a field command.

"The worst had happened," Ironside wrote in his history of the Russian campaign. "But the protest I had been preparing, should I be reverted to Staff duty, died on my lips and was never delivered."[22]

❖

Ironside was a Scot, 6 foot 4 and as wide as the River Clyde. Naturally, his nickname was Tiny. His father was an army doctor who died and left his widow a small military pension. Living on the Continent was cheaper than in Britain, so Ironside's mother had spent considerable time in Europe, allowing her son to learn several languages. In the Second Boer War he disguised himself as a wagon driver and went undercover to spy on the Germans in South West Africa. He was captured and escaped unharmed from that mission, but was later wounded three times.

Ironside was thirty-eight years old when he arrived in Archangel the first week of October 1918. He was under Poole's command so he immediately reported to the general's warm mansion on the Troitsky Prospekt. Poole greeted Ironside cordially. He laughingly said he couldn't imagine why a staff officer had been sent out; everything was in good order here, you know. They sat down before the fire, and Poole gave Ironside a lecture on what Allied strategy should be in Archangel. The Bolos had no army and no officers, Poole said. Now was the time to finish them off.

Then Poole surprised Ironside by announcing that he was going back to England on a short leave. Ironside would cover for him while he was gone. That was all Poole said. Two weeks later, Ironside saw him off on the HMS *Attentive*. Poole never came back.

The War Office in London promoted Ironside to the brevet rank of briga-dier general and told him he was now running the show in Archangel. Tiny was already on the job. He wrapped himself in furs and rode out to all the fronts to see the men. He talked to them not just as their commander but also as a comrade. He saw to it that food, ammunition, and medical supplies were sent up promptly. The troops were rotated so they could all get a rest. The men responded to him immediately. Hope and sanity had arrived.

Ironside returned discipline to the British officers. Slackers and drunkards were no longer tolerated. If they had nothing to do, he found assignments for them. When a British officer refused to confer with a French officer because their interpreter was an enlisted man, Ironside relieved him of his command. Some of the crocks were sent to the front lines.

Ironside admired the American army for saving the western front in France. But here in Russia he was shocked that the doughboys were raw recruits. And they had a style completely alien to him. A British soldier would march briskly into an office, stamp to attention, offer a magnificent salute, and shout "Sir!" An American would just sort of *appear*. Sometimes that was a bit startling. Ironside would turn around, and there he was. And when the soldier received an order, he would hold out his hand and say, "General, I'm with you."

Ironside prided himself in being an unconventional sort, but he never could figure out what that meant. Did the Yank agree with the order? Or had he merely heard it?

"They had a lot to learn," he said, "but like all troops of good heart they shook down to their difficult task."[23]

Ironside had trouble with Colonel Stewart, though. He apparently saw in Stewart some useful qualities that General Poole had missed, or ignored. Ironside asked Stewart to go out in the field and take command of the railway column. Stewart refused. He said he had instructions not to engage in combat and he was not going to leave Archangel. Ironside pressed him. Stewart was adamant. He had his orders from President Wilson. Ambassador Francis backed Stewart. He thought Stewart simply had his hands full.

"Stewart, while not shirking responsibility, dislikes leaving Archangel and I prefer he remain here, as he commands three battalions, and Archangel is [the American] base of operations," the ambassador wrote to Lansing.[24] Still, it was disappointing, Ironside said.[25]

Meanwhile, as the war was being fought in the north, key players in the Lenin Plot's political wing went on trial in Moscow.

36

TO THE WALL

It was the first of what would later be called "Moscow show trials" of enemies of the Soviet state. The Lenin plotters were tried in the Mitrofanov Hall in the Imperial Senate building in the Kremlin. At one time it had been an elegant chamber. But now the plush furniture was piled in the corners, and wooden benches had been moved in for the judges and spectators. The crystal chandelier still hung from the ceiling as big as a glacier but the red carpet had been torn out so the hundreds of onlookers could spit sunflower seeds and drop their cigarette butts to the floor.

Streams of workers and soldiers moved in and out without any respect for courtroom decorum. Angry voices argued in the hallway outside. Some women came in disguised as Russian Red Cross nurses so they wouldn't be arrested as members of the bourgeoisie. It was Monday, November 25, 1918, a dark, iron-cold day in old Moscow.

Xenophon Kalamatiano was the only major Western plotter hauled into court. Bruce Lockhart, Sidney Reilly, French Consul General Fernand Grenard, and saboteur Henri de Verthamon were being tried in absentia. DeWitt Clinton Poole had not been charged but an arrest warrant was out for him.

Jacob Peters observed the trial for the Cheka. The foreign commissariat was represented by the richly dressed Lev Karakhan, Chicherin's aide who helped Poole escape, and by Adolf Abramovich Yoffe, the current Soviet representative to Germany. Yoffe came from a wealthy Crimean family and had been in charge of the Russian delegation to the Brest-Litovsk talks. Yoffe had not wanted Lenin to sign the treaty. He told a German at Brest that countries should get along through "love."

"Mr. Yoffe was dressed like a real diplomat," one of Kalamatiano's lawyers, Sergey Kobyakov, later wrote. "He wore a splendid fur coat of gray beaver, lacquered shoes, and blue gloves." Karakhan and other Soviet representatives were also "elegantly and warmly dressed," he added. "What a contrast to the accused and the counsel for the defense."[1]

Kalamatiano, Colonel Alexander Friede, his sister Maria, and the rest of the accused sat with their lawyers in the muddy and chilly room, watched by a motley crew of Red Guards wearing an assortment of mismatched uniforms, boots, and caps.

Intelligence operations in the Lenin Plot had been exposed by the Cheka. This trial showed that. But neither the Soviets nor the Allies could yet tie off the case and relegate it to a file cabinet somewhere. A political scandal never truly ended until it hit rock bottom. That was a long way off.

❖

The proceedings in this room were called a revolutionary tribunal. It was covered by Soviet reporters and foreign correspondents. Kalamatiano had been charged on November 20, 1918, with being a U.S. agent organizing a spy network and taking part in the Lenin Plot, referred to by the court as the Lockhart Plot. The rest of the defendants were charged with spying. If found guilty, they could all be shot.

Seven judges heard the case. A Latvian named M. Karklin presided. The prosecutor was Nikolai Vasilyevich Krylenko, chairman of the Supreme Revolutionary Tribunal. Krylenko was son of a former tsarist tax collector in Smolensk and had commanded the Bolshevik army before Trotsky took over and renamed it the Red Army. Kobyakov said Krylenko wore a contemptuous expression. Marguerite Harrison said he had bad teeth and never smiled, but was a brilliant speaker.[2]

Krylenko had a reputation as a focused, hard-driving, merciless prosecutor. Kal's lawyer, Kobyakov, saw Krylenko as a "super Pharisee," a self-righteous man with pretensions to sanctity. Kobyakov said that when the tribunal earlier sentenced Admiral Aleksey Mikhailovich Schastny to be executed for trying to set up a "dictatorship" of the Baltic Fleet, separate from the Soviets, Karklin shouted "To be shot in twenty-four hours!" and Krylenko nodded in satisfaction.

The Bolsheviks had abolished the death penalty after their October 1917 coup, but it was reinstated by decrees of February, June, and September 1918, specifically permitting executions by the Cheka. Still, the defense lawyers rushed over to Krylenko to protest Schastny's sentence. Krylenko wanted to know why the lawyers were upset. The admiral had not been sentenced to death, he said.

"Schastny is to be shot—and that is not the same thing."

Bruce Lockhart called Krylenko an "epileptic degenerate."[3]

Aside from Kobyakov, Kal had two other lawyers, Nikolai Konstantinovich Muraviev and Alexander Semenovich Tager, retained for him by the Norwegian legation, though it's not clear who paid them. A Miss Steinberg was hired to make copies of documents.

Kalamatiano in his report to State identified some of the others standing trial with him: a Captain Chevalinski; a man named Ishewski, who had tried to blackmail Kal; Pshenichka, the Czech who came to Moscow with Kal on the train from Samara; de Verthamon's landlady, a Madame Morans; former military judge Major General Z. Zagriazhsky; Olga Dmitrievna Starzhevskaya, another one of Reilly's girl Fridays; and others identified only as Potemkin, Ivanoff, Solius, and a Colonel Golitsin.[4] Kobyakov remembered a British subject called Hoyt, two more Czechs, and "a number" of Russians, including Major General P. Politkovsky from Kalamatiano's network, and Reilly's girlfriend Elizaveta Otten. Because of the many defendants, they were tried in separate groups.

Elena (Helen) Razmirovich, Krylenko's wife, chaired the tribunal's investigatory committee and had conducted a preliminary examination of the Lenin plotters.[5] One correspondent described her as a prim-looking woman wearing wire-rimmed glasses, with her tunic buttoned up to her chin. She stood up to deliver her findings to the court.

Comrade Razmirovich was brief. To the surprise of her husband and the rest of the prosecution team, she told the judges that Kalamatiano was indeed a Russian-American businessman and that he had been collecting information. But there was no proof he was a spy. Then she sat down.

❖

Krylenko was undaunted by his wife's report. He had three key witnesses: Jacob Peters of the Cheka, Latvian Colonel Eduard Berzin, and the journalist René Marchand. Peters testified first. He confirmed that Berzin had been an agent provocateur for the Cheka and set into play the sting operation against the Lenin plotters.

Berzin took the stand next. He said that Reilly offered him 10 million rubles to start a mutiny among the Latvian troops. Then Allied troops were supposed to march in from Archangel and hang Lenin, he said.

Berzin also claimed he had met with Lockhart only once. Reilly and Grenard were there, he added. Berzin confirmed that he found Reilly's card in Sidney's Petrograd safe house, with Elizaveta Otten's address written on the back.

Kalamatiano contended that Berzin's employment by the Cheka disqualified him as an independent witness and that his testimony could not be relied on. Kal told the tribunal the same thing he had told the Cheka, that he was not a spy. He claimed he had been collecting commercial information for Poole and U.S. commercial attaché Chapin Huntington and that the military information he gathered concerned the Germans in Ukraine.[6] All plotting was done by Reilly and Berzin, Kal later claimed in his report to State, which he wrote for the official U.S. record, without mentioning American spying.

"About this plotting there was no more actual proof than the Marchand letter and Berzin's own statement," Kal wrote.

And what *about* Marchand? Where was he?

Kal again demanded that he be confronted with his accuser. He was told that Marchand "could not be found." This, Kal noted, was despite the fact he was currently writing articles for Moscow newspapers.

Further testimony by people who knew Reilly brought out absolutely nothing, Kal said in his report, except to confirm their acquaintance with Sidney. As far as a plot was concerned, the witnesses were about as useful to the prosecution as the three wise monkeys: see nothing, hear nothing, say nothing. De Verthamon's landlady Madame Morans took the same line. So did the Czech, Pshenichka.

But Alexander Friede made an unfortunate admission. He told the tribunal that he knew DeWitt Poole. Since Poole was America's spymaster in Russia, Friede's statement could be interpreted several ways, none of them good for him. But Kalamatiano was still upbeat.

"I can state with satisfaction that nothing was proved either in regard to any conspiracy of myself or others with the consulate of the United States," he reported to Washington.

The speeches for the defense lasted two days. When they were over, Krylenko took a hard line in his summing-up. The "accuser for the people"

(Krylenko's official title) warned the judges of Kalamatiano's "cleverness" in covering the "tracks" of the Lenin plotters.

"It is unimportant whether or not these people are guilty of the charges made against them," Kobyakov quoted Krylenko as saying. "The important thing is that they will never cross the borderline that divides them from us. Therefore, they must be destroyed!"

The judges retired to another room to decide the case. The defense lawyers stood in groups talking about possible verdicts. Peters went up to them.

"What is the use of your excitement?" Kobyakov recalled him saying. "It is superfluous. This isn't the way to handle such matters."

Kobyakov asked what that meant.

"Bring a machine gun, that's all," Peters said. "The result will be the same."

❖

The judges stayed out a long time. The lawyers and the relatives of the defendants sat in the cold, stinking chamber and waited. Finally, the judges filed back in and took their seats again on the benches behind the red-draped table. The room fell silent.

Kalamatiano and Alexander Friede were found guilty as charged and sentenced to be shot within twenty-four hours. Lockhart, Reilly, and de Verthamon were also declared guilty and would be shot if they ever returned to Russia or if England became a socialist state. Some in the audience clapped. Others remained silent.

Maria Friede, Major General Zagriazhsky, Colonel Golitsin, Potemkin, and several others were sentenced to five years in labor camps. The three Czechs were sent to a concentration camp until the end of the Russian Civil War. Madame Morans, Elizaveta Otten, Major General Politkovsky, and Hoyt were acquitted.

Kalamatiano estimated that by the time of his trial, eighty Allied agents, most of them Russian, had been arrested. One of the Americans was Roger Culver Tredwell, a consul at Petrograd.[7] He had grown up in Brooklyn, New York, and was a Yale graduate. Tredwell had worked for the State Department in Washington a year before getting his first posting, as vice consul at Yokahama, in 1910.[8] He was consul at Turin before being sent to Russia in 1918, when he was thirty-three years old.

Tredwell was first arrested in March of that year at Tashkent, Russian Turkestan, but was quickly released, with apologies. He was arrested again in October. When Cheka agents asked him what he was doing down there he said he was on an agricultural mission to check out cotton production in the area. That aroused Cheka suspicions because cotton was used in making nitrocellulose (guncotton) for smokeless gunpowder. They suspected him of spying, which was probably an accurate assessment of the situation.

The Soviets placed Roger under house arrest until February 1919, then sent him to a Moscow prison, condemned to the death sentence. But the Soviets had no intention of executing him. They wanted to swap him for two American socialists—Eugene V. Debs, jailed in Illinois for strike activity, and Tom Mooney, convicted of murder in the 1916 Preparedness Day bombing that killed ten people in San Francisco.[9] They also wanted Russian railway expert George Lomonosov returned from America.

Washington said no to those demands, except for the return of Lomonosov.[10] Tredwell was freed a few weeks after his imprisonment in Moscow. The Soviets said an "error" had been made in his arrest. The State Department figured Lenin had intervened in his case.[11]

Kalamatiano seemed bitter that Reilly's girlfriends and other people connected with Sidney were released. That prompted Kal to do some checking. He found, somewhat belatedly, that Reilly had an "unfavorable" reputation. He criticized Reilly for "criminal carelessness" in leaving an address that led to arrests.

Maybe Lockhart and Cromie had concealed Reilly's background because sometimes hasty trust was the order of the day in wartime. At any rate, Reilly seemed to be a *débrouillard*, a good man in a tight fix, as long as he was on your side.

❖

Krylenko was furious at the verdicts. Instead of twenty death sentences, he had only two. Colonel Friede was taken out that night to be executed in Petrovsky Park but was shot on the Kremlin Bridge instead. Kobyakov wondered if the Cheka's car had run out of gas. Krylenko's anger was compounded when Kalamatiano was not shot but taken back to prison.

Kalamatiano praised Friede as a "gallant gentleman" who "did what he considered his duty to his country." Friede was shot because of his slip in admitting he knew Poole, Kal said. He admired the way Friede took some of the blame himself. He compared that to the conduct of the former military judge Zagriazhsky, who, "with the idea of saving himself, almost told everything he knew, and more, too."

For Krylenko, one execution simply would not do. "The bloody hand of the general prosecutor wanted more blood," Kobyakov wrote. He, too, called Krylenko a "degenerate."

Krylenko turned his rage on the French. De Verthamon and Grenard had escaped from Russia, so Krylenko got the Soviet attorney general to slap a treason charge on all members of the French mission still in the country. They were accused of contacting the Murman Railway Council with a plan to help Allied forces occupy the area around Murmansk.[12]

But the trial was never held. French Prime Minister Georges Clemenceau (the Tiger) quickly intervened. After the Armistice, France had emerged as the most formidable military force in Europe and "Clemenceau's powerful voice demanded the safe return of the entire mission," Kobyakov said. "The Bolsheviki were frightened and allowed the mission to return home." The Tiger's approach toward the Soviets would later be employed by the United States.

Next, Krylenko had seven Russians dragged into court and charged with high treason. "The guilt of these seven Russians consisted in the fact that they had been acquainted with members of the French mission," Kobyakov said.

The tribunal listened to statements from the seven but did not let their attorneys argue their case. The judges abruptly ended the trial and ordered all seven shot that night.

Others accused of having connections to the Allied plotters were executed en masse in a prison outside Petrograd. They included 148 other men and twenty-eight women. They were shot by Russian and Chinese machine gunners in the prison courtyard. It was early morning, with a temperature of 17 below. One of the men was so sick he couldn't stand up. He was shot sitting in a wheelbarrow.[13]

But why was Kalamatiano not shot immediately, as the court had ordered?

He guessed, correctly, that a struggle was being fought behind the scenes between the Cheka, which wanted blood, and the diplomatic corps, which wanted American foreign aid. That meant Dzerzhinsky and Peters versus Chicherin.[14] Russia was suffering from drought, epidemics, and starvation, and facing a famine of biblical proportions. It was no time to risk losing a U.S. bailout. The Allies figured that Lenin had sided with Chicherin and decided to hold Kalamatiano and other Americans in Moscow as hostages for American foreign aid. Kal received a stay of execution, but it could be lifted at any time.

Washington had no idea how many Americans were locked up in Russian prisons. They did know that a Red Cross captain and two newsreel photographers were held in Moscow, along with John M. Flick of the *Evening Star* in Washington, Albert Boni representing the *New York Sun*, Mrs. Harrison Cotton of the *Associated Press*, and Mrs. Marguerite Harrison from the *Baltimore Sun*.

Flick had been arrested on suspicion of espionage. He was kept in solitary for six weeks, then put to work chopping wood for the kitchen. The worst thing about Butyrka, he said, aside from the food, was the "monotonous conversation" of the twenty-five other men in his cell. "I sat on my bench in the corner as if I were going to remain there for the rest of my life," he said. [15]

At least a dozen other arrested Americans were allowed to roam freely in Moscow but not allowed to leave the capital. They included an engineer, a former International Harvester executive, the wife of the U.S. consul at Cardiff, a clerk at the Moscow consulate, two YMCA secretaries, and a couple of American socialists. [16] In addition, at least fifty American POWs from Archangel were reported to be in Moscow. Since they didn't have Russian passports, they couldn't leave the capital

❖

Kalamatiano was sent back to solitary confinement and guards were posted outside his door. He was not allowed to receive any messages from the outside, which meant he didn't know if his wife and stepson had made it to Vladivostok. And he had no idea what his government was doing to free him. Wilson had not stood up to the Soviets the way Clemenceau had. For the moment, the State Department had simply sent a telegram of protest:

"This government views with grave apprehension the threatened execution of Kalamatiano and must reply that if Kalamatiano is executed for reasons stated and investigation shows execution unlawful, this government will insist that persons responsible for the execution shall be adequately punished for his execution." [17]

Démarches like that were standard operating procedure in the world of diplomacy. But exactly how could Washington "punish" Kalamatiano's executioners? Mount a coup to depose Lenin? They'd already tried that. Defeat Russia militarily? They were working on that now, without much success.

President Wilson was in Paris focused on the treaties formally ending the war and on creating a League of Nations, his pet project. Russia was a matter he left to Lansing and Edward House, the president's chief foreign affairs adviser. But they didn't always keep Wilson up to speed.

It was during this period that Kalamatiano was taken out to be shot. Guards pulled him from his cell and stood him up before a firing squad. The riflemen aimed at him. He was given a final chance to sign a confession. He refused. The order to fire was given. The firing pins snapped on empty chambers.

The Cheka's desperate attempt to break him failed. But next time, the rifles might not be empty.

"Will my turn come on the morrow?" Kal wondered.[18]

They took him out again. Again he was told to confess. Again he ignored them. Again the rifles merely clicked.

After that, the nightly interrogations and mock executions stopped. The Cheka had thousands of other enemies of the people to process. Kal's value would come as a hostage.

The nights were numbing cold but all Kal had was a blanket. He slept on a shelf with no mattress. The food was the same as before: kasha, watery soup, and thin tea. With no newspapers or books to read, he tried to pick up news by eavesdropping on his guards. He communicated with other prisoners by tapping on the walls in code. Other than that, he had nothing to do but stare at four walls while waiting, and waiting, and waiting.

William Christian Bullitt Jr., an assistant to Lansing and a country club socialist, visited Kalamatiano in prison and reported he was "well" and being "treated well." Bullitt said Moscow offered to release Kal in exchange for Professor Lomonosov. He was the former assistant director general of railways for the Duma who had been sent to the United States in 1917 by the provisional government.[19] The Soviets had fired Lomonosov because he was not a Bolshevik. But now they needed his skills in Russia, so all was forgiven, but a visa technicality was holding up his return.[20] There might have been more to it than that, though. The U.S. government was detaining Russians and Americans who either had ties to the Soviet government or simply supported it.

American peace negotiators at Paris didn't put much stock in Bullitt's glowing report of Kalamatiano's condition. A Norwegian consul had earlier visited Kal on death row and found that he didn't know of U.S. efforts to free him.

"His mental state is desperate and he is in great danger of going mad," the consul said. [21]

Another U.S. note was sent to Moscow. It said that the detention of Kalamatiano and Tredwell was "a matter which will not be dropped or forgotten." [22]

But other than that, nothing was done.

37

RISKY MISSION

The United States had no intention of stopping spy operations in Russia after the defeat of the Lenin Plot in Moscow and the conviction of Xenophon Kalamatiano. Military intelligence records in Washington show that Mrs. Marguerite Harrison was sent to Moscow as a U.S. army spy well after Kalamatiano was put on death row. That made her another important figure in America's midnight war against Soviet Russia. But Harrison's mission, like other U.S. operations in Moscow, was doomed, and she landed in prison with Kalamatiano, facing execution with her countryman.

Marguerite Elton Baker Harrison was probably America's first woman spy in Soviet Russia who wasn't a State Department agent. She came from a wealthy old Southern (and Yankee) family in Baltimore.[1] The Bakers owned a major transatlantic shipping company and had delivered relief supplies to Russia during the 1881–1892 famine that killed half a million. Marguerite grew up on both sides of the Atlantic and learned French, German, Italian, and Spanish at an early age.

She attended a Maryland private school and grew up a world of fox hunts, mint juleps, and cotillion balls. Her mother wanted her to wed a titled English diplomat but Marguerite turned around and married Thomas Harrison, the "most handsome boy in Baltimore." He died fourteen years later, leaving her a widow with a young son.

In her autobiography, Marguerite Harrison described herself as attractive but not beautiful. Languages were her only real talent in life, she wrote. That, and her independent spirit. She never joined any political groups.

"The woman suffrage movement left me cold," she said. She believed women should vote but was "not prepared to lift a finger" to help the movement. She felt that Congress would take care of the voting issue, sooner or later.

Restlessness was another one of Harrison's traits. She got caught up in the patriotic spirit after America entered the war in 1917 and looked around for something to satisfy the tapping of her foot. A family friend got her an interview at the *Baltimore Sun*. As soon as she walked in the city room, she fell in love with the place. Reporters were talking on phones and banging out stories, editors yelled for copy, and the air was heavy with the "exhilarating" smells of paper, ink, and tobacco smoke.

It was a good time for women to enter journalism. Millions of men had been called up in the draft, and women were recruited to take their places in newsrooms. Harrison went to work as an assistant society editor, then a music, drama, and movie critic. She was paid $30 a week ($646 today).

But writing wasn't enough for her. She craved adventure. In August 1918 a family member arranged a meeting between Harrison and U.S. Brigadier General Marlborough Churchill. They met in a Baltimore hotel lobby.

The war was almost over and Harrison offered to go to Germany as a news correspondent and take a look around for the army. She had traveled through Germany as a child and was fluent in the language. Churchill said fine. He felt it was America's "manifest destiny to play a leading role in world affairs." She "heartily agreed."

Churchill wanted to set up a permanent army intelligence operation in Germany, and after this interview he wrote in Marguerite's file that she seemed a "very competent person" for a spy's job. Following a background check, she was hired on September 30, 1918. As a spy she drew an army captain's pay, $38 a week, just $8 more than the *Sun* paid her. She was thirty-nine years old.[2]

Her first stop was France. The *Sun* gave her cans of motion picture film to take over. That was her cover, showing movies to homesick doughboys. She also carried *Sun* press credentials. She left her son Tommy with their faithful cook Rebecca.

It wasn't unusual for American women to go over as war correspondents. Peggy Hull of the *El Paso Morning Times* was already in Europe. So was Mary Boyle O'Reilly for the Newspaper Enterprise Association; Alice Rohe from United Press; Mary Roberts Rinehart and Corra Mae Harris of the *Saturday Evening Post*; Bessie Beatty for the *San Francisco Bulletin*; Marie Hecht from the *Chicago Daily News*; Rheta Childe Dorr of the *New York Evening Mail*;

Mrs. Harrison Cotton for the *Associated Press*; and Inez Milholland, Margaret Fuller, and Madeline Z. Doty for the *New York Tribune*. Mary Roberts Rinehart later became a novelist; Marie Hecht was married to Ben Hecht, who became the highest paid screenwriter in Hollywood.

After the Armistice was signed in November 1918, Churchill sent Harrison to occupied Germany. She got there in early 1919. She stayed up late at night writing reports in her room at the Hotel Adlon and left the sealed documents at the front desk for her control officer, a Colonel Bouvier of the U.S. Military Intelligence Division, to pick up later in the day. Harrison supplied information on various subjects, including Robert Minor, an American radical journalist in Europe who was an associate of Lenin, Trotsky, Tom Mooney, and anarchist Emma Goldman.

After the Treaty of Versailles was signed on June 28, 1919, the first of five treaties to end the war, Harrison returned to Baltimore as arts critic for the *Sun*, got bored once more, and went to see General Churchill again. This time, Harrison wanted to go to Russia. She now considered herself a socialist and wanted to take a look at the Soviet system.

Churchill was agreeable. He was frustrated with President Wilson's indecision regarding Russia and thought a mission to Moscow by Harrison would provide a "great service" to Washington by securing information that might lead to "some definite policy toward the Bolsheviks." But Marguerite had never been in Russia and didn't speak the language. Churchill did warn her it would be a risky mission.

❖

Harrison entered Russia by walking across no man's land outside Borisov, Poland, on a snowy day. She carried press cards but upon reaching Moscow she was arrested by a small, dark, nervous-looking man with a briefcase, named Rosenberg, from the Commissariat of Foreign Affairs. He allowed her to stay in Moscow, but said the stories she filed would have to be censored by the commissariat and the Cheka, now called the GPU, the State Political Directorate.

For a while, Marguerite's work as a correspondent progressed smoothly. Then she was arrested by the GPU and all her valuables were taken, including 1.5 million Red rubles. She was locked up in the Lubyanka and interrogated by Solomon Grigorevich Mogilevski, a GPU official who dealt with important cases of espionage and counterrevolution. She described him as a courteous man with a dark face like a "black puma."

"We are fully aware of the nature of your mission to Russia," Mogilevski told her. He accused her of spying for America in Germany and Russia. A later U.S. army report quoted unidentified Soviet officials as claiming they had a "word for word" transcript of a conversation Harrison had conducted earlier in Washington with a Colonel Grant and a Colonel Eichelberger.[3] That suggested the Soviets had an agent inside army intelligence, or at least a Communist fellow traveler.

Over tea and cigarettes, Mogilevski pitched a deal. If Harrison would supply information on foreign visitors, she would not be shot as a spy. She could continue work as a correspondent while collaborating with the GPU. Marguerite thought it over. She had a lot of new information to send to MID. She needed to get on with that.

"I accept your proposition," she said. She was released the next day.

Harrison wrote in her autobiography that she gave Mogilevski only "partial or misleading" information while gathering new product for the MID. As she fed Mogilevski "harmless gossip" she charmed him with news of an (imaginary) socialist revolution brewing in America. He wasn't a bad sort, she decided—just a government hack. She kept up her supply of chickenfeed to Mogilevski while secretly sending intelligence reports to U.S. military attachés in Riga and Berlin by couriers and news correspondents.

Mogilevski finally realized Harrison had double-crossed him. He warned her to get with the program. She didn't. She was also accused of soliciting information from American writer Louise Bryant, a Soviet employee, who apparently turned Marguerite in. Harrison was arrested again and thrown into Novinsky Prison for Women, outside Moscow. Then they locked her up in the Butyrka with Kalamatiano. Marguerite got sick in her cell and almost died. Another prisoner sneaked in medicine for her.

Harrison was later denounced by a Bostonian, Grover Shoholm, who claimed that Marguerite became an "agent" of the Soviet secret service while in Moscow and that she "betrayed her accomplices to the Soviet government."[4]

Shoholm was a conscientious objector who had refused to fight in the war and was sentenced to a work farm. After the war he went to Moscow and worked for the Soviet foreign office correcting wireless telegrams. Harrison had earlier told General Churchill that she was interested in studying the

Soviet system, but Shoholm offered no evidence of any collusion on her part with the secret police.

In a letter to Samuel Harper, Kalamatiano wrote that Harrison "went to Russia with a purpose—get a story—she had no scruples about it, did anything to ingratiate herself, sat on a platform with communists, traveled in Trotski's [sic] train and I think would have done about anything else . . . she showed remarkable ability, and if I had her purpose I don't know but what I would have done the same."[5]

❖

While Harrison, Kalamatiano, and other Americans sat in Moscow prisons, the Red Army continued to fight the Allies and other anti-Soviet armies across Russia. Lenin and his cabinet, Sovnarkom (the Council of People's Commissars), realized they were in dire straits. A breakthrough on any of those fronts could topple the Soviet government in a matter of weeks, even days.

That military threat, and Russia's desperate need for American aid, led Lenin to decide it was time to negotiate peace with the Allies. But negotiations would quickly get complicated, leading to more frustrating delays in the release of Kalamatiano, Harrison, and other Americans.

38

A POISONED APPLE

F ighting between the Allies and the Central Powers was supposed to have stopped with the signing of the Armistice of Compiègne in France on November 11, 1918. But that agreement mainly covered combat operations on the western front. Fighting continued in Russia, Siberia, Poland, and the Baltic. The World War would not be over officially until the Paris Peace Conference convened on January 18, 1919, to negotiate the various treaties between the belligerents, assign reparations, and try to settle border disputes. Even then, it would be January 1920 before all the nations ratified the treaties, and the Allies would continue fighting the Reds until that year. Nevertheless, Lenin in 1918 wanted a quick peace with the West.

After Litvinov was swapped for Lockhart, he was appointed Soviet plenipotentiary (a diplomat who could act with the full authority of his government behind him) and in December 1918 he wrote to the American, French, Italian, and British ministers in Sweden, officially proposing peace talks.

But the idea of peace negotiations quickly got bogged down. First, every political force that claimed to be the legitimate Russian government insisted on taking part in the peace conference. That included the Provisional Government of Autonomous Siberia at Omsk, represented by S.D. Sazonov. Former provisional government Prime Minister George E. Lvov also wanted in, along with various socialist groups such as the SRs. They were all determined to wrest power away from the Soviets.

The main Allied representatives at Paris, called the Big Four (America, France, Italy, and Britain), gave their decision after meeting six days before the peace conference convened. Wilson and Lansing were there, along with French Foreign Minister Stéphen Jean-Marie Pinchon, Italian Prime Minister Vittorio Emanuele Orlando, British Secretary of State for Foreign Affairs James Arthur Balfour, and British PM Lloyd George. They announced that it was not up to them to decide who the legitimate government of Russia should be. Therefore, the Soviets would not be represented at the Paris peace talks.[1] The French, in fact, wanted to continue supplying money and arms to armies fighting the Reds.[2]

But Moscow was desperate. Litvinov said his government was "prepared to compromise on all points," including offering amnesty to political enemies.[3] Ambassador Francis answered that Lenin was a "fanatic" and that Communists had never represented the Russian people. Lansing jumped in to warn that if the Soviets continued to dominate Russia, then Germany would "exploit" the country, recoup her war losses, and again become a "menace to civilization."[4]

As a compromise, the "Associated Powers" invited Siberia and small European nations that had formerly belonged to the old Russian empire to attend a special conference at the Turkish island of Prinkipo to plan the future of Russia. The term Associated Powers referred to all twenty-eight nations fighting the Central Powers, but led militarily and politically by the Big Four. Prinkipo, in effect, would be a new constituent assembly for Russia.

The Soviets, though, were not invited to Prinkipo. It was another slap in the face to Lenin. He wanted to grab those little countries and create a Soviet empire (which in time would include the Warsaw Pact nations of Eastern Europe). At the same time, the Big Four urged all anti-Soviet armies in Russia to stop fighting until the Paris Peace Conference was concluded. The Associated Powers also pledged not to send any more troops to Russia.[5]

❖

Chicherin, commissar for foreign affairs, stepped up to the plate next. Stung by the Prinkipo snub, he accused the Western press of telling "lies" about Russia. He claimed that some recent military victories by the Red Army had resulted in a "general relaxation of tension in the interior." Moscow now offered to pay her foreign debts, plus interest, through exports of raw materials. Chicherin said Russia would offer mining and timber concessions to the Allies and would not "exclude" discussing independence for those former countries of the old Russian empire.[6] All that, if only the Soviets would be invited to the Prinkipo talks.

DeWitt Poole was not impressed. He said Chicherin had offered "not one word of condemnation" for the Bolsheviks, whom Poole saw as the main enemy of the true Russian Revolution of 1917. Poole further denounced the "utter wickedness" and "cynicism and cruelty" of the Soviet government.[7]

Winston Churchill, British minister of munitions, suggested the Soviets could be invited to Prinkipo if they first stopped fighting on all fronts. But the Reds continued combat operations throughout Russia, and so weren't invited. Then Churchill suggested the Associated Powers send a new military force to protect Finland, Estonia, Livonia, Poland, and Rumania against annexation by Russia. The United States killed that idea.[8]

Finally, Soviet Russia was invited to Prinkipo. Hearing that, the smaller countries boycotted the talks in protest. The Prinkipo project ended stillborn.

The Soviets were furious at being excluded from peace talks. The Big Four had no sympathy for them. They felt that Lenin and Trotsky had stabbed the Allies in the back when they pulled out of the war and signed a separate peace with the enemy. In Allied eyes the Bolsheviks were traitors and had to be defeated. Thus was born the Cold War of the 20th century.

In the 1920s and '30s the Cold War would be a time of Soviet spying, theft of military secrets, and union agitation in the Western nations. There would be a brief pause in animosity when the Western powers joined the USSR in a common front against Germany in 1933, but Russia was not considered a true ally. Moscow stole atomic bomb plans from the Allies during the war, along with the secrets of radar, the proximity fuse, and other military weapons. So that wartime alliance was more a case of strange bedfellows. After World War II, the Cold War continued with more decades of spying, hostile annexations, surrogate hot wars, and threats of nuclear annihilation.

The Bolshevik withdrawal from World War I, the Lenin Plot, and the Allied invasions of Russia, along with the Western refusal to talk peace with the Soviets, meant a state of undeclared war between East and West had been carved in ice since the Bolshevik coup of October 1917.

❖

America's last attempt to deal with the Soviets came with the dispatch of William Bullitt on a special mission to Russia. That was the trip that had included Bullitt's visit to Kalamatiano in prison. Bullitt was twenty-seven years old, son of Philadelphia socialites, and a Yale graduate. He was a self-proclaimed radical socialist and an assistant to Lansing at the Paris peace talks. Officially, he went to Russia just to gather "information." But he carried instructions from Lansing, which made him a back channel for talks with the Soviets.

Bullitt's mission was arranged by Edward House. Wilson was busy creating a League of Nations and apparently was left out of the loop. Bullitt entered Russia on March 9, 1919. His first stop was Petrograd, to talk with Chicherin and Litvinov. A preview of things to come was Bullitt's opinion that "reports of frightful conditions here ridiculously exaggerated."[9] Bullitt met with Lenin in Moscow and reported that Comrade Chairman, along with Chicherin and Litvinov, were all "full of a sense of Russia's need for peace and therefore disposed to be most conciliatory." He was certain the Soviets desired to be "reasonable."

That was when Chicherin proposed peace talks between Russia and the Western powers. Russia would agree to elections in Finland and other countries of the old Russian empire, he said, so they could decide their own forms of government. Prisoners of war would be exchanged and a general amnesty offered to opponents of the Soviet government. Chicherin further wanted the Allied blockade of Russia lifted and trade with the West normalized. Those ideas didn't sound so bad, except for the last part, which Winston Churchill didn't like. Churchill was a veteran of the western front and wanted to keep Russia encircled and contained in a cordon sanitaire.

After that, Chicherin's proposal got increasingly sticky. The Soviets demanded "unhindered transit" and "free entry" into Finland and other former countries of the old empire. They also demanded "use of all ports" in those countries and "full security" for Russians entering them. Further, Chicherin wanted America and the Allies to stop aiding anti-Soviet armies. And last but not least, those former countries of the empire should help pay Russia's foreign debts.[10]

In a follow-up report, Bullitt claimed that the Soviet government was "firmly established" and the Communist Party was "strong politically and morally." He said there was order in Petrograd and Moscow, with no riots, uprisings, or prostitution, and almost no robberies. He felt as safe as he would have in Paris. The Red Army was growing, high-spirited and well-equipped, he added.

"They carry themselves like free men . . . very like Americans," he reported. Lenin was "straight-forward" and "broad-minded."

The Soviet government was the "only constructive force in Russia today," Bullitt continued. The Communists could be destroyed "only by producing anarchy . . . Then we shall finally have to intervene over the dead bodies and dead hopes of the simple Russian people." The Soviet system, he said in conclusion, offered a "better way for the common good."[11]

In nine days, Bullitt had been converted to Soviet Communism. In a popular saying of the time, he had become a "Red over easy."

The Big Four were not fooled. Lenin had tried to be clever. He had offered the Allies a sweet ripe apple. It tasted like peace, amnesty, elections, independence, and freedom for all. But then the poison oozed out. The Soviets wanted free access to the countries of the old tsarist empire. They wanted to use the railroads and ports of those nations. And they wanted to be protected while they did it. It was an invitation to an invasion or a Soviet coup.

Lloyd George and Clemenceau said no to Chicherin's proposals. Wilson was in ill health, and his relations with House had soured, so he didn't address the issue directly. The deadline for replying to Chicherin passed and the matter was dropped. Bullitt resigned in protest.[12]

Later in the year, when he was feeling better, Wilson explained his aversion to Soviet rule. In a Kansas City speech, he said Russia was run by thirty-four men (apparently a reference to Sovnarkom). The Soviets were a minority in Russia, yet they held a monopoly of power because they did not allow free and open elections. And now they were spreading their ideology to other countries.

It was "the poison of disorder, the poison of revolt, the poison of chaos," Wilson said.

The president said he did not believe in minority rule. As long as Russia was run by a minority that was more cruel than the tsar had been, he could find no effective way to help the Soviets.[13]

That finally closed the door on America's diplomatic relations with Lenin and Soviet Russia, such as they were, until 1933, when President Roosevelt sent Bullitt back to Russia, as U.S. ambassador.[14] But after three years, Bullitt became hostile toward the Soviets and turned anti-Communist.

After both world wars the Soviets had an advantage in spying against the West because the Allied nations were free and open societies. Somebody talking with a Slavic accent and wearing a Russian suit was accepted as part of the scenery. The Communist Party was allowed to operate openly in Western nations despite the fact it was a hotbed of Soviet spying.

The USSR, by contrast, was a closed society. A visitor from the West was placed under surveillance immediately he got off the plane. His hotel room was bugged. So were the offices of Western news agencies. One Christmas Eve some American reporters sat around their shabby little Moscow bureau talking about where they could go for dinner, and after a while the phone rang and an anonymous Russian voice gave them the name of a good place to eat, then hung up.

But back to 1919. While diplomacy between Moscow and the West failed, the Allied war against the Red Army continued in North Russia, long after the Armistice was signed.

39

FIGHTING FOR WHAT?

The Winter War in Russia, as some called it, was an eerie experience for the Allied commander in chief, General Edmund Ironside. He was accustomed to the lights and noises of the western front in France, but on still nights in Russia he found the silence in the forests "almost absolute." When traveling, he heard only the drumming of his pony's hooves on the ice and the grinding of his sled's runners as they rocked and skidded up the frozen trails. When the driver stopped to rub the pony's frozen nose for a few minutes, Ironside would get out to stretch his legs. It was then that he got the feeling that somebody was stalking him. He would draw his pistol and wheel around. But there was nothing out there. The black stillness was broken only by the crack of a frozen limb breaking.

"It was all very weird and at first I felt very alone," he wrote in his account of the expedition, "but I soon got used to it."[1]

The expedition had been star-crossed from the beginning. Aside from the destructive animosity between British officers and American and French troops, there were desertions and mutinies. One of the first came on October 1, 1918, when an American platoon attacked the village of Wazientia and the Cossack squad attached to them took off and ran.

Then on October 16 two sections of a French company on the railroad front heard rumors of an armistice in France and refused to go up to the front line. "*La guerre est finie*," they said. The war is over. That left an American company alone to repulse a massive Red attack. Ninety of the mutineers were arrested. The French battalion commander, a Major Alabernarde, shamed the rest of his men into going back to the line to assist their "much admired American comrades."[2]

A third warning came on December 11. French and British commanders had been raising Russian regiments from Archangel volunteers, and Ambassador Francis planned to spend $1.3 million in forming an American-Slavic Legion but was turned down by Wilson.[3] Ironside's Slavo-British Allied Legion (SBAL) had 1,500 men in barracks. Some of them mutinied. They didn't kill their officers or cause property damage but refused to turn out for an inspection. An officer sent in machine guns and Stokes mortars to restore discipline. Two mortar shells were fired and one hit the roof of the barracks. After that, the mutineers ran out and surrendered. Thirteen ringleaders were arrested, court-martialed, and sentenced to be shot. Ironside found out they had been prisoners of war in Germany and had picked up Bolshevik propaganda. He commuted their sentences and sent them across the lines to the Soviet side.[4]

But despite those setbacks, the Allies did not shrink from heavy combat. The Reds took advantage of a temporary thaw on the Dvina and attacked Finlayson's headquarters with 6-inch guns and a wild infantry charge. Canadian gunners and American and Scot riflemen moved up to help English troops repulse the attack. Twenty-eight Allies were killed and seventy wounded. They counted 350 enemy dead.

After the Armistice, though, Western troops began to ask why they were still in Russia. Lieutenant John Cudahy cited a British military proclamation that stated they were there to defeat Bolshevism, "which was entirely in the hands of the Germans." The proclamation also accused "a few men, mostly Jews," of bringing the country to "such a state that order is non-existent."[5] That wasn't good enough for Cudahy. As far as he was concerned, this war against Russia had not been sanctioned by the American people.

As Allied losses mounted, Ironside ordered his forces to stop offensive action. He told the men to dig in and hold their positions while he recruited more SBAL Russians. That force was supposed to train during the winter and take over the war in the spring of 1919. But Russians were not naturally volunteers, Ironside found out. The Archangel provisional government had to start a draft. Eventually, a standing force of 22,000 Russians would be raised.

Time pressed heavily on Ironside. Under his command, most of the enlisted men from the various nations seemed to get along well, when things were going well. But the doughboys and French were still united in their hatred of British officers below Ironside. And the feeling was mutual. That was affecting the conduct of the war. After a Royal Air Force plane bombed the Allied front at Obozerskaya, killing one American and wounding another, an incensed mob of Yanks marched on RAF headquarters. The British fliers took up rifles and barricaded themselves inside. Finally an American officer got the doughboys back to their dugouts and transferred them to another front. The pilot, a Canadian, was exonerated. But later a Yank went crazy, confronted a British officer, told him to say his prayers, and shot him.[6]

Maria Botchkareva arrived in Archangel after completing her tour of America and England. She wore American boots, a khaki Russian uniform, and bandoliers looped across her tunic. Her adjutant and translator Lieutenant Filippov was still with her. She reported to Ironside and tearfully repeated the plea she had given President Wilson. Ironside wasn't impressed.

"She presented a pathetic figure, with greying untidy hair, and looking much older than she really was," Ironside wrote. "Her broad ugly face, mottled complexion and squat figure showed clearly her Eastern parentage."

Ironside sent her to see one of the Russian commanders, a former imperial general named Marousheffsky. While Marousheffsky admired Botchkareva's previous service, he had no use for a *baba* in his command. Military duties were not "appropriate" for a woman, he said. They would be a "disgraceful stain" on the North Russian population. He ordered her to take off her uniform. Then he ordered Filippov to register for service in Archangel.[7]

American officers later found Botchkareva still in her uniform, but apparently she didn't fight in any battles in Archangel. She went east and joined Kolchak's army. She was reported shot by the Reds in 1920.

❖

The Polar Bears' last major battle in Russia was at Shenkursk. It was also the scene of America's final defeat in Russia. Shenkursk was the second largest town in Archangel *oblast* (province), a middle-class trading town of 4,000 souls who stood only a generation removed from peasant poverty. Shenkursk was prosperous and sophisticated, Lieutenant Cudahy said, peopled by "Russians of literature, cultivated and mannerly in appearance, soft-spoken in approach, and accustomed to the niceties, the softer things in life." Shenkursk had given sanctuary to Russians escaping from the Reds to the south, and they welcomed the Allies to their town.[8]

An American forward outpost was set up at the tiny village of Ust Padenga, a few miles up the Vaga River from Shenkursk in the direction of a Red naval base. Peasants in the area reported that a huge enemy army was massing in the woods for an attack on Shenkursk. A second large Red Army force had been seen to the north, marching overland toward Shenkursk from the Dvina.

Shenkursk and Ust Padenga, along with Kotlas on the railroad front, marked America's deepest advances into the Russian interior. But the Yanks were still 230 miles from Vologda, where they could theoretically link up with the Czechs and with Kolchak's army. The Red commander, Samoilo, had drawn a line in the snow. He and war minister Trotsky intended for Shenkursk to be America's Waterloo.

The fight began after local British commanders ordered the Americans to go out and "stir up the enemy" above Shenkursk. That violated General Ironside's orders to cease offensive action. Nevertheless, two patrols of Americans and SBAL Russians went out "seeking contact." They were ambushed and only one man came back.[9] Red deserters and POWs confirmed that Samoilo's Sixth Army was moving on Shenkursk. The Allies saw a state of siege coming. Cudahy got a haunted feeling as he waited in the frozen dark.

A "blighting influence, a devastating nether presence, filled the air like the spell of an evil spirit," he wrote. The atmosphere was "closely akin to that heavy stifling calm that in the summertime hangs over all before the wind swoops down and the first big pelting raindrops fall from blackened thunder clouds, the advance guard of the drenching storm . . ."

At dawn on January 19, 1919, that pelting sound was the slam of enemy artillery rounds hitting the U.S. forward outpost at Ust Padenga. Commander Samoilo had surrounded Ust Padenga and Shenkursk with 3,100 Red infantry, a 6-inch gun, and several 4-inch howitzers.[10] Enemy soldiers wearing white smocks rose up from the snowy ravines and charged the Ust Padenga blockhouses. The Americans defended their position with machine guns and field artillery until the Reds shelled the surrounding village with incendiary shells and burned it to the ground. With fire closing in on their outpost, the defenders retreated to Shenkursk. Half the company was killed. Cudahy said the corpses on the snow looked like raisins on rice pudding.[11]

Shenkursk was defended by two companies of Americans and the 38th Canadian Field Artillery, together only a few hundred men.[12] They were backed up by a detachment of Cossacks and 1,200 SBAL Russians. Aside from light arms, the defenders had four field pieces and three trench mortars. Some SBAL Russians were sent out to engage the Reds. They came running back in a panic. After a few shots, two of their companies had deserted.

Shenkursk was surrounded. The river was frozen. Rescue boats couldn't get in. The defenders faced annihilation.

❖

Four days later, at 3:10 P.M. on the dark cold afternoon of January 22, river command headquarters at Bereznik ordered the Allies to evacuate Shenkursk. Then the phone went dead. How were the troops supposed to get out? The Reds occupied all the major roads.

Then somebody remembered a seldom-used winter trail that led north toward Bereznik. At midnight, the exodus began. Lieutenant Costello said the British commander wanted to leave the wounded behind. He was ignored and the wounded were put in sleds for evacuation.[13] A three-month supply of food, ammunition, and medical supplies was left for the townspeople, and each evacuee took only what he could carry in his pockets and backpack. The Cossacks led the way, followed by the artillery caissons and the foot soldiers. Hundreds of civilians brought up the rear.

They marched all night. Shackleton boots were slippery and useless. Many of the men threw them away and walked in their socks. Footing on the trail was treacherous. Men fell from exhaustion and didn't want to get up. Their buddies had to violently shake them to rouse them. As an anemic dawn broke through the trees they heard the roar of cannon behind them. The Reds didn't know about the evacuation. They were still shelling Shenkursk.

The evacuees trudged on, all day. They arrived at the village of Shegovari at five o'clock in the afternoon. An Allied garrison was stationed there and they rested for a few hours. They had walked forty-four miles, mostly in the dark, with only a couple of hours of light. Many of the men had frostbitten feet. Some would later have to undergo amputations.

That night they saw rockets in the sky all around them. The Reds were in pursuit. They were closing in. The Allied column responded with artillery fire and set out marching again. At eleven o'clock that night they saw bright flames behind them. Shegovari was burning. At midnight the evacuees stopped at Vistavka, fourteen miles away.

They dug snow trenches around Vistavka. They weren't as good as earthen trenches but the ground was frozen and the ice offered at least a measure of protection against small arms fire. The Allied defenders set up their artillery and settled down to defend the village. Soon the Reds arrived. But the Allies received reinforcements from Kitsa and stood up to attack after attack. Finally they were forced to flee on March 9. They marched ten miles to Kitsa. The river was starting to thaw and they held on there until they were rescued.

With the loss of Shenkursk, it was all over for the Western troops on the Vaga. At the same time, the British navy had failed to take the Reds' main base at Kotlas on the Dvina. All troops were ordered back to Archangel. There they set up a defense perimeter around the city and waited for the first big thaw so ships could come in and take them home.

The Soviets with their overwhelming numbers could have finished off the Western troops during the retreat from Shenkursk. But the United States had millions of fresh and well-equipped troops in Europe. Cudahy said the Reds feared that a massacre of Yanks in Russia would bring on a massive American invasion of Russia.[14] Lenin and Trotsky simply wanted to drive the Americans and their allies out of the country.

DeWitt Poole was distraught. On the night of the Shenkursk disaster he wired the dire news to Washington:

"We are more and more put on the defensive, subjected to more and more frequent attacks and bombardment, suffering many casualties. We have no reserves. Our men are often called upon to remain on duty for long periods without relief."[15] The next day Poole blamed the Shenkursk disaster on the "intoxicated condition of a British colonel."[16]

"What are we fighting for?" Lieutenant Costello asked.[17]

❖

After the fall of Shenkursk, the mutinies continued. In late January 1919, British soldiers on the Kodish front refused to "carry on" unless certain questions regarding this Russian war were answered by none other than Lloyd George himself. Lieutenant Cudahy said those men had come from four years of combat in France and saw themselves as "the hapless forfeit in a confused international melee without wit or reason." They demanded to be sent home. Ironside responded by reading them the riot act with "an eye like Mars to threaten and command." The men returned to the line and Ironside took no further action.[18]

Another British mutiny came on February 26. A battalion refused to fight any longer. The local commander couldn't do anything with them so he called in some armed American, SBAL, and British soldiers. Two sergeants who appeared to be the ringleaders were arrested and court-martialed for mutiny and sentenced to death. But Ironside had been secretly ordered by King George not to carry out any executions after the armistice. He commuted their sentences to life imprisonment and sent them back to England.[19]

A few days later, the French mutinied again. A battalion on leave in Archangel refused to go back to the railroad front. They were lying on their bunks and did not even stand up when Ironside walked in. *"Assez de cette guerre contre les bolshevists,"* a corporal said. Enough of this war against the Bolsheviks. Ironside had them arrested by French marines from the *Guédon* and sent home for trial.[20]

Americans caught the mutiny bug at Toulgas in February 1919. They threatened to walk out unless they were promised an early ticket home. Cudahy said the men came from factory jobs where strikes were legitimate expressions of collective discontent. But this was the army. Refusal to follow orders in a war zone was a serious offense. Ironside explained that to them and they returned to duty.[21]

DeWitt Poole continued to report the incidents to Washington. President Wilson again showed his impatience with the war. "It would be fatal to be led further into the Russian chaos," he told the peace negotiators at Paris.[22]

London agreed. The War Office on March 4 informed the Supreme War Council of the "dangerous situation" in Archangel. Allied soldiers were "tired, dispirited, homesick and inclined to mutiny," a report said. A British relief force was raised to help get the Allied troops out of Russia before autumn.[23]

A more serious American mutiny occurred at Archangel on March 30. Company I of the 339th at Smolny Barracks was ordered to load their equipment onto sleds for deployment to the railroad front. They refused. Captain Horatio G. Winslow was summoned.

The men complained about Russian troops drilling in the safety of Archangel while they had to go to the front. Winslow asked one man specifically if he was ready to turn out. He said no, unless the others were. Winslow arrested another soldier whose tone turned insubordinate. Then he called Colonel Stewart.

The men were assembled at the YMCA hut. When Stewart arrived he read them the article of war that pronounced death as the penalty for mutiny.

A long silence followed.

Stewart asked for questions. One soldier spoke up.

"Sir, what are we here for, and what are the intentions of the U.S. government?"

Stewart replied that he could not answer that question. But he said the expedition was in danger of extinction. The lives of everyone depended on successful resistance.

Another silence fell on the room. The men warned Stewart that a general mutiny would come soon unless U.S. troops were sent home.

Stewart then applied a military disciplinary tactic based on what Cudahy called the "antithesis of mob psychology." Stewart lined up the men. He said that any man who wished to refuse duty should take three steps forward. Great heroes "quail at this test," Cudahy wrote, "for it is one thing to rebel in company or in the secret counsels of one's inner conscience; quite another to stand out stark alone . . ."

No one stepped forward. The men grumbled a while, then loaded their sleds and went to the front.[24] An inspector general investigated, classified the incident as an "alleged mutiny," and said that after the men were returned to the front their service was "satisfactory." He suggested the matter be dropped.

But Secretary of War Baker had to explain the incident to a Michigan congressman who'd heard about it. Newspapers got hold of the story and went all the way up with it. The War Department tried damage control by hinting publically that "Bolshevik propaganda" was involved. The bad press continued, though. An editorial cartoon in Detroit showed a doughboy going round and round fighting hopelessly with a Russian bear. Another publication reminded its readers that Napoléon's army had been defeated by the Russian winter. Did that sound familiar?

The Archangel mutiny showed that Colonel Stewart could apply himself as a commanding officer when he wanted to. But the indoor general was replaced on April 17, 1919, by a genuine outdoor commander, Brigadier General Wilds Preston Richardson of the 61st Infantry, fresh in from twenty years as an army explorer and engineer in cold climates. Richardson was a Texan and a West Point man. He was fifty-seven years old when he stepped off a big icebreaker at Archangel with a welcome load of engineers and supplies. The arrival of an American general was a major affront to the British, signaling that the United States was no longer subservient to a foreign command.

Washington then tried to avert further doughboy discontent in Archangel by having Richardson read the troops a message from General Pershing. "Inform all our troops that all America responds with the praise of the splendid record the American expeditionary forces have made," Pershing said. He sent the men greetings from their "comrades" in France and promised to get the doughboys out "at the earliest possible moment." Meanwhile, he urged the troops to come home with "unblemished reputations."[25]

General Richardson bore a resemblance to Bull Moose Teddy Roosevelt at a younger age. Richardson had been head of the Alaska Roads Commission and built the highway from Valdez to Fairbanks. Now he put his men in Russia to work laying a highway back to Archangel. It occupied their minds while they waited to be evacuated. He proved to be a popular commander and was awarded the Distinguished Service Medal for his work in Russia. Later, an army fort and a naval warship would be named for him.

❖

The Americans celebrated Memorial Day (May 30) with a ceremony at the military cemetery in Archangel. Ambassador Francis had bought the land for the graveyard before leaving the country. Russian and Allied troops marched with the doughboys to the site.

"The graves before us are tangible evidence of the deep and sympathetic concern of the older democracies," DeWitt Poole told the troops. "These men have given their lives to help Russia . . . They have given their lives to the progress of civilization and their memory shall be cherished as long as civilization lasts." The service ended with a military salute and a bugler playing "Taps."

"Honor be to the fallen," remarked the *Northern Morning*, a Russian daily in Archangel, "blessings and eternal rest to those protectors of humanity who gave their lives away for the achievement of justice and right."[26]

❖

The next major project facing the Western troops was getting out of Russia. A British relief force of 8,000 arrived in Archangel on June 10, 1919, led by two generals. Once they were in place, U.S. forces left on June 27 aboard the USS *Des Moines*, leaving behind a few civilians to assist the French and British in wrapping up matters. A total of 563 doughboys were dead or missing. Some of the Brits considered the Yanks quitters. They called them "Detroit's Own Welfare Association."[27]

Ironside still held out hope that he could raise an SBAL force large enough and competent enough to secure Archangel Province. Archangel could then be the base for future Allied operations against the Soviets. But Kolchak's army was in retreat and the Czech Legion was on its way to signing an armistice with the Reds and going home. The Red Army was becoming larger and more professional, and the Allies were running out of surrogates to fight them. Then still more mutinies broke out.

The most serious involved the so-called Dyer's Battalion at Troitsa on July 7. This was a fighting detachment made up of Bolshevik POWs who were supposed to be loyal to the Allies. But Ralph Albertson, an American YMCA secretary, said the men harbored long-simmering resentments toward the way the British had treated them. Those hatreds finally erupted one night and they murdered five British officers and eight Russian officers, then deserted. The British in turn captured a "considerable" number of them and executed them.

Shortly thereafter, the British suspected a new mutiny was brewing in a Russian company on the railroad front. Albertson said the British disarmed them and decimated the ranks (shot every tenth man). In another Russian company under suspicion, fifteen of the eighty men in the unit were executed.[28]

Andrew Soutar, a *Times* correspondent traveling with Ironside in Archangel, said the last straw came when the Russian regiment in the Onega district mutinied and handed over the entire Onega front to the Reds. Further unrest was found in nearly all other SBAL units, and they had to be stabilized with British troops.

"It was clear that we had failed to create a reliable Russian army and that our hopes of leaving the Russian Government at Archangel in a strong position were unlikely to be realized," Soutar wrote.[29]

❖

DeWitt Poole and Ralph Albertson of the YMCA left Archangel on September 7, 1919. They were the last Americans to go. After striking a "disengaging blow" to keep the Reds at bay, the final shipload of Western troops sailed on October 12, 1919. Archangel Russians then held the city for four months before finally surrendering to the Reds. Soutar said 48,975 Allied troops and civilians had served in both Murmansk and Archangel. Add to that 22,000 Russian recruits. A total of 41 British officers and 286 men were dead.[30]

Ironside in his memoirs said the withdrawal went smoothly. Albertson said it got nasty toward the end. The British shot more Russians suspected of Bolshevik sympathies, Albertson wrote, and Archangel Russians responded by beating two British officers to death in the streets. As the last ships pulled out from Archangel, great fires broke out in the lumber yards on the river. Albertson called it a "sinister emblem of the ruin and hatred" that the invasion left behind.[31]

Ironside was a professional soldier. He had been taught to stand and fight, and he did not easily brook defeat. The general claimed victory in the Archangel campaign but admitted it had been a "hasty improvisation conceived without much previous consideration . . . almost in desperation."[32]

"We had waged war upon Russia," Cudahy wrote, "an unprovoked intensive, inglorious little armed conflict which had ended in disaster and disgrace." It would "blight forever the good name of America when soldiers gather to tell of the Great War." No peace was made with Russia, as no state of war had been recognized, he added. That left it with the status of a "freebooters' excursion."[33]

In his diary, Ironside expressed regret for British mismanagement of their concentration camp for Red POWs on Mudyug Island. He said it was a "scandalous camp" that had disease, food shortages, and supervision problems. "I am responsible," he wrote.[34]

Upon returning to America, John Cudahy was angry for an additional reason. He said that Americans who fought on in Archangel long after the Armistice was signed in France were simply shooed off to civilian life without recognition of their service. The "whole embarrassing matter was expunged from the war record," he said.[35]

40

FAMINE AND FREEDOM

The defeat of America and the Western Allies in Archangel did not bring freedom for Xenophon Kalamatiano. But two months after his conviction, his death sentence was commuted to life imprisonment. Later it was reduced to twenty years, then five. The Soviets made various proposals for exchanging him, but nothing came of them. Aside from Butyrka, he also served time in two prison camps, including Andronovsky. He began receiving food parcels from the U.S. legation at Warsaw, from the Red Cross, and from Quaker workers in Russia. He gave the Red Cross a list of things he "badly needed," including shirts, socks, underwear, pajamas, a suit, a cap, a pair of boots, soap, tooth powder and brush, cigarettes, razor blades, and "food of all kinds."[1] He hoped his wife and stepson had been able to get out of Russia, but messages from the outside were still not allowed.

A note, however, managed to reach him in June 1921. Kal received a food parcel with his name written on an envelope that served as the address label on the box. When he opened the envelope he found a letter. Prison guards had either overlooked it, or simply allowed it through. It was from L.J. Cochrane, an officer with the U.S. legation in Warsaw and a Sigma Alpha Epsilon fraternity brother from New York.

"I am located at Warsaw and found by reading a daily from the [SAE] convention that you and I were connected in the bonds of Minerva," Cochrane wrote. "Before that for nearly a year and a half I had known of your case in our files and have naturally wished to do all that I could to help but now I am at your service more than ever. You may rest assured that no stone is being left unturned in the United States."

That was news heaven-sent. But then Kal discovered another delight. In addition to the usual items in the food package, Cochrane had packed cans of sardines and boxes of crackers. Kal decided to celebrate. He had been on

good behavior and the prison officials had made him a trusty, allowing him
to roam around the building. So he rounded up some of his friends and neighbors in the cell block and they sat down to a candlelit banquet of sardines
and crackers. It wasn't John Daley's Woodlawn Diner in Chicago, but it beat
kasha and Lenin loaves.

Kalamatiano, being an educated man fluent in Russian, worked as a prison
clerk. One of his unpleasant duties was to obtain an advance list of prisoners
to be executed the next day. Then on the morning of the scheduled killings
he was given a second list of names. Those lists were his guide to rounding
up the prisoners to be shot. But sometimes the lists didn't match. What was a
humble clerk to do? He wasn't supposed to call prisoners if their names weren't
on the second list. So he didn't call them. That way, he saved many lives. He
would have been in big trouble if he'd been caught.

Meanwhile, though Kal didn't know it, the State Department was dragging its feet in giving his wife Katherine his accrued salary. "How can she
draw his salary?" a consular bureau clerk in Washington demanded to know.

Katherine had the smart, fashionable look of one of magazine illustrator
Charles Dana's Gibson Girls, a "New Woman" of the new century. She was
also very determined. She left Pasadena, where she and her son had been
staying with Kal's mother, and went to Washington to plead her case. Her
husband was a faithful government employee, she told the department, and she
was in dire need of his salary. She declared that she would stay in Washington
until the matter was settled.

State stonewalled her. They argued that Kalamatiano's salary could be
paid only to him and only if he signed a receipt for it. Claude Nankivel, one
of Kal's former business partners, wrote a letter on his behalf. The department
replied with one of their NFA (no further action) decisions.

Finally, somebody decided to show some sympathy for the woman's plight.
If paying Kal's "salary" to his wife was against the rules, why couldn't they
pay her from the department's "emergency" fund and settle up later?

DeWitt Poole and President Wilson okayed paying Katherine $1,200 from
Kal's 1920 salary. While they were at it, the department deducted a bill for
$378.98 to cover the cost of food and supplies purchased for Kal in prison. [2]

Katherine didn't stop there. She began campaigning for her husband's
release. His health was "badly broken," she told reporters in San Francisco,
"and he is wondering if his country has forgotten him. He placed duty above
personal safety, above his family, above everything else, for America. Now

America owes it to herself as well as to him to do her utmost for this, her servant in his dark hour."

Better relations between America and Russia had been her husband's dream, she said. "And I am taking this opportunity now to ask the State Department and all who are interested in foreign relations and the welfare of Americans abroad to do whatever may seem wise to bring about the liberation of my husband."

She added that her own health was "badly shattered" after her long harrowing journey out of Russia. Part of that time she had traveled disguised as a Red Cross nurse, but always faced exposure and arrest.[3]

News of Katherine's campaign was picked up by SAE national headquarters. They sent out more than 20,000 letters to SAEs all over America. They in turn wrote letters to their congressmen and senators urging that Kal be freed. The American Legion joined in. So did the new president, Warren Gamaliel Harding, a Republican.

Harding's interest in Kal's case was probably influenced by the success the French had recently had with the Soviets. Lenin had promised to release all remaining French prisoners in Russia, then reneged and tried to bury the issue in useless negotiations. Tiger Clemenceau finally told Comrade Chairman that the French Black Sea Fleet would bombard Russian coastal cities unless the prisoners were freed. Just one high-explosive shell could turn a building into rubble and set fires to burn down an entire block. A prolonged attack could raze nine southern ports, including Odessa. Russia had no warships capable of stopping that. Lenin quickly released all French prisoners.[4]

After that, "drastic action" against Russia was suggested by Vice Admiral Albert Parker Niblack, commander of U.S. naval forces in Europe. Niblack announced he was ready to take twenty warships into the Black Sea, including an armored cruiser and twelve destroyers. He wanted to make "a visible display of the earnestness" of the U.S. government in securing the release of all American prisoners.[5]

❖

While sabers rattled, Lenin continued to allow a few Westerners access to Kalamatiano and several other Americans held in Moscow. This had been going on, now and then, since 1919 in an attempt to smooth out relations with the United States as Russia's need for U.S. foreign aid grew drastic. The Soviets hand-picked politically reliable visitors. One of them was New York businessman Washington B. Vanderlip. He went to Moscow to seek a sixty-year concession for fisheries and for oil and coal exploration in Kamchatka and other Siberian areas.[6] The deal was going to be worth $3 billion ($44 billion today) to Vanderlip, so after he visited Kalamatiano in prison, his report was upbeat in favor of his new Soviet friends Lenin, Litvinov, and Chicherin.

Vanderlip wrote that he found Kal in an open cell on the third floor of the Butyrka, sitting on a well-blanketed bed. Two tables in the cell were stacked with books. The guards carried no weapons and joined in recreation with the prisoners, Vanderlip claimed.

"The kitchen was immaculate," Vanderlip said. He enjoyed a "savory meat stew" and a "superior quality" of bread. Kalamatiano was "well-dressed and in good health." However, a photo of their meeting shows Kal standing beside Vanderlip, glaring at the camera.

Vanderlip claimed he got twenty-three Americans released on parole, though Kal was not one of them. The parolees were given hotel rooms and theatre tickets, Vanderlip said.[7] But his Siberian deal with Lenin fell through. Vanderlip failed to get support from either the U.S. government or financial investors. He became known as the Khan of Kamchatka.

Lenin's jailhouse public relations schemes were finally blown publicly by a controversy set off by Louise Bryant, widow of American writer John Reed, who had recently died of typhus in Russia. Bryant had worked for a frivolous society magazine, the *Spectator*, after graduating from the University of Oregon and constantly changed her birth date to appear younger. She married a Portland dentist who led a conventional life except for the times when he threw ether-sniffing parties. Bryant harbored radical thoughts and ran off to New York with Reed in 1915. She pursued a writer's life in Greenwich Village and wrote for the *Masses*, a radical magazine, where she poured life's injustices into a beaker labeled socialism. She was a feminist who opposed any legislation to protect women, since she thought such laws would only emphasize gender differences.[8]

Bryant married Reed, also from Portland, who had covered the Mexican civil war in 1914 for *Metropolitan Magazine*. Bryant assumed the role of revolutionary, laborite, and free-love advocate. The couple went to Russia in 1917 to cover the revolution, Bryant for *Metropolitan Magazine* and Reed for the *New York Call*. She was around thirty-two years old.

Reed had been a cheerleader at Harvard and he applied his rah-rah talents to the Bolsheviks. He was hired as a propagandist for the Soviets, and Bryant shook her own pom-poms as his faithful fellow traveler (with a Soviet courier's pass). Reed and Bryant wrote from the Bolshevik point of view. That resulted in their disseminating disinformation, as would be seen in their testimonies before the U.S. Congress and by Bryant's account of her visit to American prisoners in Moscow in 1921.

Bryant wore cowboy boots and a Russian fur hat on her prison tour. She denied she was there in "any political capacity," but only as a journalist. Nevertheless, she was accompanied by two steadfast Communists—Santeri Nuorteva, an aide to Chicherin, and Henry Alsburg, a writer for the *Daily Herald*, a tiny socialist daily in London (now the *Sun*). Bryant later wrote a letter to the editor of an American newspaper and described the prison as a "beautiful place" with a "lovely old garden." She claimed the prisoners were receiving generous supplies of canned beef, bacon, beans, butter, and sugar in addition to their regular rations. She said the prisoners were so well fed that they had nothing to do but lie around all day.

"I got the impression I was in a rest home and not in a prison at all," she wrote.

One of the inmates, American Red Cross Captain Emmett Kilpatrick, asked Louise about a friend held in another prison. Bryant replied that the man had "done wrong" and would be "punished." Other American prisoners, she said, were "getting what they deserved."

When Kilpatrick complained about the forced labor in the prison, Bryant replied that the inmates "ought to be glad to get the exercise." Her claims appeared in an interview with *Izvestia*, the official Soviet government newspaper, and in the English language propaganda sheet *Russian Press Review*, before being picked up by the wire services and published in U.S. papers.[9]

After the recent American war against Russia and the continued imprisonment of U.S. citizens in Moscow, Soviet propaganda was not very popular in the States. Nor was Louise Bryant. Despite his indictment in America for treason, John Reed had been a popular guy with a laid-back sense of humor. Even his political enemies told funny stories about him. *Did you hear what Jack Reed did the other day?*[10] But Louise lacked Jack's social skills, as evidenced by her arrogance while testifying later before Congress. She seemed to have a talent for making people dislike her, and her haughtiness set off a media firestorm, especially after Kilpatrick got out of Russia and challenged her in a rebuttal he wrote from Paris.

Kilpatrick accused Bryant of "startling misinformation." Instead of feasting in prison, the prisoners had been starving, he said. The food was "very bad" and "entirely insufficient in quantity." If the prisoners were lying around, it was because they were so weak they can barely stand, he said. After he talked with Bryant, Kilpatrick said he was put back in underground solitary confinement. He did not blame her "entirely" for that, but readers caught his drift.[11]

That ended Bryant's journalism career. She wrote two books but then worked the lecture circuit giving pro-Communist speeches at American colleges. She liked to appear on stage in an expensive cape with a revolutionary red lining. Despite her elitist attitude she insisted she had been "with the proletariat" all her life. She married William Bullitt in 1924. He divorced her in 1930, telling the court that she was a drunkard and a lesbian. He got custody of their daughter. Bryant died in 1936.

❖

Finally President Harding, like Clemenceau, decided that he'd had enough of the Soviets. The new secretary of state, Charles Evans Hughes, sent Moscow a formal demand for the release of American prisoners. Nothing came of it. They were finally freed by another Republican, a future president by the name of Herbert Clark Hoover. He was a Quaker from Oregon and had entered the first class of the new Stanford University. He graduated as an engineer and married his Stanford sweetheart, Lou Henry, whom he had met, over rocks, in the geology club.

For a few years after graduation, Hoover worked around the world as a mining engineer. He and his wife achieved a measure of fame after they helped 120,000 U.S. citizens return to America from Europe when war broke out in 1914. President Wilson named Hoover head of the U.S. Food Administration during the war. Then after the peace treaty was signed, Hoover managed the American Relief Administration in Europe. He was given almost dictatorial powers to run railroads, docks, and telegraph systems as he delivered millions of tons of relief supplies to war refugees.

Fridtjof Nansen, a Norwegian explorer who was also involved in relief work for European refugees, had warned Wilson in 1919 that "hundreds of thousands of Russians were dying monthly from sheer starvation and disease" and that a Western relief operation should be organized on humanitarian, not political, grounds.[12] In Paris, the Big Four agreed that supplies could be found, but the main problem would be transportation and distribution inside Russia. Until all fighting in Russia ended, a relief operation would be "futile" and "impossible to consider."[13]

But by summer 1921, those hundreds of thousands dying had become millions. One estimate put it at 27 million from starvation alone, including some 9 million children.[14] Photographs show butchers selling human arms and legs for food. As before, Lenin and his government seemed incapable of dealing with it.

In Moscow, Patriarch Tikhon of the Russian Orthodox Church and a fervent anti-Soviet, sent an appeal to the Archbishop of Canterbury in England and to the Archbishop of New York, advising them of the famine. "Great part of her population doomed to hunger death," he said. Aid needed immediately. "The people are dying, the future is dying."

Maxim Gorky, a Russian writer and independent Marxist who had been exiled by Lenin for opposing the Soviet dictatorship, sent his own appeal: "Gloomy days have come for the country of Tolstoy, Dostoyevsky, Mendeleyev, Pavlov, Mussorgsky, Glinka and other world-prized men," he wrote. Russia's misfortune offered a "splendid opportunity to demonstrate vitality for humanitarianism," he added.[15]

Ten days later, Hoover replied to Gorky, saying certain conditions would have to be met before U.S. aid could be sent: All Americans had to be freed. American relief workers had to have complete freedom to do their jobs. Distribution would be on a non-political basis. The relief workers would need free transportation, storage, and offices.

Lenin stalled. He was convinced the aid workers would be spies. Hoover then ignored Lenin and sent Walter L. Brown to represent the ARA in talks with Litvinov. They met at the Latvian Foreign Department in Riga, and after tedious negotiations struck a deal on August 20, 1921. The agreement had twenty-seven sections, all dictated by Brown. Litvinov signed it, and a hundred American prisoners were on their way home.

"The number was a surprise, as our government knew the names of less than twenty," Hoover wrote later. "We served the first meals from imported food in Kazan on September 21—just one month later."[16]

But Hoover soon found that a much wider relief operation was needed. He knew Lenin had been using tsarist gold to subsidize revolution in foreign countries. Hoover wanted a big chunk of that gold for the relief. Lenin refused.

But when Hoover threatened to abandon the program, Lenin backed down and gave up $18 million in gold. The U.S. Congress then appropriated $20 million from the U.S. Grain Corporation and $8 million in army surplus medical supplies. Public contributions brought the total to $78 million (over $1 trillion today). The Communist Party of the United States of America raised a million, ostensibly for Russian relief, but actually spent the money on propaganda, Hoover said.[17]

The British, too, were concerned about the situation in Russia, though assistance to the Soviets was a controversial subject.

"Government are fully alive to the terrible state of the famine-stricken areas of Russia, and in spite of the heavy burdens resting on the shoulders of this country owing to the recent war and the consequent trade disturbance, they have already made substantial contributions of material and stores to assist in alleviating the suffering," Lloyd George told Parliament. "They hope to give further assistance in the same direction. But the best—in fact, the only—hope for Russia lies in the prospect of bringing that country into closer community with the rest of Europe."

The prime minister was challenged by former Royal Navy Lieutenant Commander Joseph Montague Kenworthy, a Liberal MP from Central Hull who had been hostile toward Lloyd George for some time. He wanted to know if Britain intended to exact her "pound of flesh" before helping Russia.

And Lord Curzon, representing Battersea South, asked if the prime minster would "give an assurance that before helping the starving people of Russia he will extend the same assistance to the starving population of Cornwall?"

Lloyd George replied that "very considerable sums of money" had already been spent on the unemployed in Britain.[18]

Another nation working with Hoover also found itself tasting a bit of controversy. Captain Thomas C. Gregory, the ARA's representative to Hungary, accused Hoover of having conspired with the French, Italians, and British in 1919 to oust Béla Kun, dictator of the Hungarian Communist Party and Red Army leader in that country. Marshal Foch reportedly suggested a force of 250,000 could do the job. But such a plot, factual or not, had not been necessary. Moscow didn't have the money to support Kun's tiny Hungarian Soviet Republic, which covered less than a quarter of the country. Kun's régime collapsed and he fled Hungary.[19]

Hoover's relief workers issued fifty pounds of corn per month to each person in Russia, along with bread (real bread) and cans of milk and stew.

Children got extra meals. The cost was one dollar per person per month. The ARA also issued wheat seeds to farmers. That helped end the famine, since many starving Russian farmers had eaten their seeds. But the 200 American relief officers in Russia stayed into 1923 to be sure the Soviets didn't steal food from the children.

Lev Kamenev, chairman of the Moscow Soviet, sent Hoover an elaborate scroll of thanks, saying the USSR would "never forget the aid rendered to them by the American people . . ."[20] Hoover's successful management of post-war American aid to Europe, including Russia, made his reputation as a major U.S. political and humanitarian figure.

But Lenin was determined to have the last word. After the ARA completed its mission and the Americans went home, many Russians who had worked in the relief operation were arrested and thrown in prison. Hoover said they were never heard from again.

❖

Xenophon Kalamatiano lost all sensation of forward motion while he was in prison. He didn't ride in a car, horse cab, trolley, bicycle, or train for three years. "Even the sight of a dog walking across the prison courtyard made me nervous," he told a reporter.[21] He didn't know if he could handle the train trip from Moscow to the border. But when he was finally released he had no trouble getting aboard the special car the Soviets provided him.

The Americans were freed in groups of six. Kal was released a few days before the Riga agreement was signed, and his little delegation arrived at the Estonian frontier the morning of August 10, 1921. Border guards smiled and opened the barbed-wire gate and waved the Russian train through. A reporter who boarded the train at the frontier described Kal as "cool and calm" while the five other evacuees looked nervous and hungry. One man said he'd had only two baths in a year. Kal needled his Soviet guards about how haggard they looked compared with the healthy and well-dressed Estonians. The fruits of Communism, he told them.[22]

The group was transported to the Estonian capital, Tallin, a bright clean city on the Gulf of Finland. The Red Cross deloused them and gave them new clothes, and they checked into a good hotel for baths, dinner, and wine. They also shaved off their beards. They sent cablegrams to their families and rested for a few days before leaving for Latvia. In Riga, Kal was debriefed by

U.S. Commissioner Evan Young, another SAE. Kal filed a lengthy report to Washington and headed home.

Xenophon was grateful for what his fraternity had done for him. He visited SAE national leader William Levere in his Evanston, Illinois, office and saw the big file of correspondence appealing for his freedom. He described the surprise letter he'd received in prison from the SAE brother in Warsaw.

"I think that as we grow older we feel more deeply how dear to us are the associations of younger college days," Kal wrote in the December 1921 issue of the SAE *Record*. "But I think very few have had this fact brought home to them as forcibly as I have had . . . at a time when all seemed to have deserted me."[23]

A FINAL WORD

I t must have seemed like a good idea at the time: Overthrow Lenin and the Soviet government on humanitarian, military, and economic grounds and install a benevolent dictator in Moscow until a democratic government could be elected. But it failed. It failed because it was a tragedy in the classical sense—flawed from the very beginning. And those tragic flaws brought on the Lenin Plot's own destruction. After it was over, not much had changed in Russia except that a lot of people were dead and a lot of money had been wasted. Lenin was still in power and Soviet methods would only get more extreme in the decades to come.

The main flaw on the political side of the Lenin Plot appears to have been slipshod security on the part of the conspirators. Agents were not properly vetted. Some seemed to have been accepted solely because they were fast talkers. That laid the plot open to infiltration by the Cheka.

But even if the Allied coup in Moscow had succeeded, how long could the Western powers have held Russia? The country might have risen up in a new revolution, against the Western occupiers. Russia is a big place. Nailing down power there would have required an Allied force as big as the one on the western front in France.

The military phase of the Lenin Plot carried its own fatal flaws. The first of those was the inadequate size of the invasion army. The Allies might have been able to take Petrograd and Moscow with a couple of hundred thousand troops, as Ambassador Francis suggested, but not with the puny forces they landed at Archangel and Murmansk. The invasion force at Siberia was larger, but still inadequate for a major offensive.

A second flaw was animosity between French and American troops and their British commanders. The inevitable result was a compromise in battlefield cooperation. In his analysis of the Archangel campaign, U.S. Army historian Peter Sittenauer wrote that the Western invaders lost the "tempo" of the war as early as October 1918. (He defined "tempo" as the "speed and rhythm of military operations.") Sittenauer said forces should never operate under foreign command. They should remain "homogeneous," with their own officers.[1] Blackjack Pershing had found that out on the western front. It's a mystery why President Wilson didn't learn it from Pershing.

A third flaw was underestimating the Red Army. Too many British officers were convinced that Trotsky's ragtag force was hopelessly incompetent, no matter how large it got. The most damaging flaw, though, was undoubtedly the tactic of sending inadequate Allied forces too far into hostile territory without adequate supplies and reserves. And when General Ironside ordered the Allied columns to stop advancing and dig in until a new Russian army could be raised, his orders were ignored by some of his own field commanders. The result was the defeat at Shenkursk. After that, the invaders were driven to the sea.

There was also the folly of trying to defeat Russians in a Russian winter in the first place. Russians were accustomed to fighting in a deep freeze. They knew how to acclimate themselves and turn the weather against their enemies. Napoléon had learned that. Why didn't America and the Allies profit from the lessons of history?

After all the bodies were counted, the Russians saw the Lenin Plot as proof that the West was out to destroy the Soviet state. Russia was a former ally in the war. She had never invaded America, France, Italy, or Britain. Russia had not plotted to assassinate Wilson, Clemenceau, Victor Emmanuel, or George V. While the Lenin Plot was forgotten or covered up in America for many years, it was studied and analyzed in the Russian spy school. Succeeding generations of Soviet bosses have used it to justify stealing thousands of Western military secrets.[2]

But what became of the major players in the Lenin Plot? A look at the lives of some of them shows that not all their stories ended well.

❖

President Wilson, one of the original architects of the Lenin Plot, helped establish a League of Nations (predecessor to today's United Nations) after the war. But the Republican-held U.S. Senate rejected the idea, citing Article 10 of the Treaty of Versailles, which they claimed would have ceded American war powers to the Council of the League of Nations.[3] Wilson took his case to the American people on a train tour but suffered a series of strokes in September 1919. He was taken back to the White House, incapacitated. His wife Edith took over the day-to-day duties of the White House. That led some to say that she in effect was America's first woman president. Wilson died in bed in 1924. He is the only president buried in Washington.

Secretary of State Robert Lansing, Wilson's partner in early planning of the Lenin Plot, directed foreign policy and conducted cabinet meetings for five months while Wilson lay in his sickbed. That prompted the president to request his resignation in 1920. Lansing opened a law practice in Washington and died in 1928.

Edward House, Wilson's executive agent who assisted in trying to set up the 1917 plot against Lenin, worked with the president in formulating the League of Nations covenant. But they clashed on whether to compromise on certain ideas. Then Edith Wilson saw a newspaper story suggesting that House was pumping up his own reputation in Paris at the president's expense. The first lady confronted House and he fled the room. After that, relations between House and Wilson cooled.[4] House returned to New York and spent his last years defending his legacy, and Wilson's. He died in 1938.

DeWitt Clinton Poole, America's spymaster in Russia, headed the State Department's Russian affairs division during the Harding administration and supported a continued lockout of the Soviet Union. But he backed President Roosevelt's recognition of the USSR in 1933 on the grounds of recruiting "a potential friend in the rear of a potential enemy [Germany]."[5] He returned to espionage work in World War II as head of the Foreign Nationalities Branch of the Office of Strategic Services (father of the CIA). He collected intelligence regarding foreign immigrants in the United States and later ran a CIA front that operated Radio Free Europe. He retired in 1952 and died that year.

Ambassador David Francis, who assisted the Lenin Plot spies and vigorously supported the invasion of Russia, spoke out in favor of the League of Nations after the war. He felt the league could establish a protectorate over Russia until free elections could be held, but that didn't happen. Francis retired to St. Louis and sold his newspaper, the *St. Louis Republic*, to the *Globe-Democrat*. He considered running for the U.S. Senate in 1920 but was not nominated. He died in 1927 after an illness.

Charles R. Crane, one of Wilson's main agents of influence in Russia, was appointed in 1919 to a commission advising the president on post-war Middle

Eastern policy. Crane was an Arabist who warned that the establishment of a
Jewish state in the Middle East would commit the United States to use of
force in the region. In 1931, Crane helped finance the discovery of oil in Saudi
Arabia and the acquisition of petroleum concessions there. He died in 1939.

Samuel N. Harper, who worked as both a volunteer and a paid U.S. operative in Russia, went on to become a translator for the State Department. He
visited the Soviet Union several times in the twenties and thirties, and was
criticized for accepting some of the "confessions" made by Old Bolsheviks
in Stalin's purge trials. He also defended Stalin's treaties with Hitler. Harper
spent the rest of his life lecturing and teaching. After suffering nervous col-
lapses from work, he died of a stroke in 1943.

William Chapin Huntington, an aide to the Lenin plotters through his
post as a commercial attaché in Russia, worked at the American embassy in
Paris after the war, then became an industrial consultant. In 1933 he published
a book about Russians who had fled the country after the Bolshevik coup,
including Cossacks who survived in Paris by washing dishes and driving
taxis.[6] He was a member of the Washington Literary Society and died of a
stroke in 1958.

Red Cross Colonel Raymond Robins, a valuable source of intelligence
for the Lenin plotters, settled in 1924 on his Florida plantation. In 1932 he
toured the country to support Prohibition, suffered an attack of amnesia, and
went missing for three months before being found in North Carolina under
another name. He became a consultant to both Democrats and Republicans,
and in 1933 visited Russia for FDR. In 1935 he fell and broke his back and
was paralyzed from the waist down. Robins died of a heart ailment in 1954.
He willed his plantation to the government as a wildlife sanctuary.

Army spy Marguerite Harrison was released from prison in Moscow
when the other Americans were freed. She wrote in her autobiography that
after confinement, traffic noises sounded deafening and confusing, and she
had trouble crossing streets. She returned to Baltimore, wrote her book, then
left for the Far East as a magazine correspondent. She was arrested in Chita,
which was supposed to be in the Far Eastern Republic, an independent state,
but which had been annexed by Soviet Russia.

Harrison was returned to Moscow and locked up in the Butyrka again.
An old indictment was brought forward and she was threatened with execution while Mogilevski offered her $250 a month in gold to do some spy work.

"No," she said.

She languished in prison, getting weaker by the day, while she awaited execution. Then an ARA official appeared. He had learned of her arrest at Chita, but the GPU claimed no knowledge of her. The ARA put pressure on the GPU and they gave her up "with a rather bad grace," Harrison wrote.

Marguerite and a Floridian, Merian C. Cooper, a founder of the Kosciusko Squadron in the war, got together and made a travel documentary, *Grass,* about the nomadic Bakhtiari in Persia. Harrison then resumed her own nomadic lifestyle as a correspondent in the Middle East and the Balkans, sometimes accompanied by her son. Marguerite never remarried. She died in 1967.[7]

❖

Henri de Verthamon, one of Kalamatiano's closest French spy associates, returned to country life at his family's ancestral home, the Château de Taupignac, south of the commune (village) of Breuillet in the Ile-de-France region. Photos show a large farm with ponds, ducks, and fields, dating back to the 16th century. Henri served as mayor of Breuillet, 1943–1945. In 1960 he wrote a letter to the French navy's chief of staff, complaining that he had not been named a Commander of the French Legion of Honor. He died in a traffic accident in 1963.

Charles Faux-Pas Bidet returned to his wife and daughter in their apartment at 37 rue du Renard in Paris after he was swapped by the Russians in 1919. Bidet went back to counterintelligence work in France and in 1928 he arrested two Soviet agents known as the Phantomas.[8] He retired at age fifty-two with a pension. In 1940, German occupiers of Paris arrested French CI agents who were working against the Nazis. They exiled Bidet to Vichy France, a de facto client state of Germany. He died there in 1940, separated from his family.[9]

French Ambassador Joseph Noulens returned to France and became minister of agriculture and food supply for Clemenceau, 1919–1920. He supervised post-war prices and transportation of food, and adopted Herbert Hoover's idea of requiring food packages be labeled so shoppers would know what they were buying. Noulens intervened as a peacemaker when fights broke out at big markets between merchants and their customers. He was a senator from Gers, 1920–1924, and active in the Society of French Interests in Russia, a group opposed to recognizing the Soviet Union until they paid their old tsarist debts. Noulens died in 1944 at Sorbets, in southwest France.[10]

Joseph-Fernand Grenard, consul general in Moscow, was named a Knight of the Legion of Honor in 1919, and an Officer in 1924. He was assigned as chargé de mission to Poland in 1919, then ambassador to Yugoslavia in 1927. He never lost interest in Asia or Russia. He wrote *La Révolution Russe* (Paris: Librarie Armand Colon, 1933), along with books on Baber of the Moguls and Genghis Khan. He died in 1942.

❖

Bruce Lockhart, the British agent who paid Allied money to the Latvians for the 1918 coup attempt in Moscow, wrote several books after the war. *British Agent*, his account of his Russian adventures, was made into a movie of the same name in 1934. During World War II he coordinated British propaganda against the Axis powers, and afterward became an editor at the London *Evening Standard*. Sir Robert died in 1970 after a long struggle with alcoholism.

Moura Budberg, Lockhart's Moscow girlfriend and "interpreter," identified by the French as an agent for the Soviets and the Germans, became a friend of Stalin's after the war and was given privileges not available to enemies of the state. She resumed her affair with Bruce in Paris in the thirties. Their favorite meeting places were out-of-the-way Russian cafés. She was called "Elena Moura" in the movie *British Agent.* Her biographer and friend, Nina Berberova, said Moura belonged to a Russian generation that had been destroyed, and as a result she learned to live for the moment, for life itself, and in her later days led a lazy pointless existence.[11] Moura became a British citizen and died in 1974.

Boris Savinkov, one of the Allied conspirators who intended to murder Lenin, not just kidnap him, was persuaded to return to Russia in 1924. He was told the government was in bad shape after Lenin's death and needed his assistance. Savinkov crossed the border accompanied by Alexander and Aimée Derenthal, and was arrested. One of Savinkov's biographers who knew Boris in Paris after the Lenin Plot, suspected the Derenthals were paid by the Soviets to set him up. Aimée was "beautiful and false to the depths of a lying heart," he wrote.[12]

Savinkov made a deal with Dzerzhinsky to confess to his crimes against the Soviets and in return would be rehabilitated and given a useful job. But the court sentenced him to ten years. After that, he died in a plunge from a prison window in 1925. "He was killed by his jailors!" Aimee screamed upon hearing of his death. Winston Churchill called Savinkov a "hero" and a "martyr."[13]

Sidney Reilly, another Allied plotter who planned to assassinate Lenin, was lured back to Russia in 1925. He thought he was returning to join the Trust, an anti-Soviet resistance group. It was actually another sting organized by the Soviets, and he was arrested. Reilly grew accustomed to being taken for an evening drive after his interrogations, but one night when he and his two guards got out of the car for a walk in the woods, they shot him. He was posthumously awarded the British Military Cross for his spy work in Russia.

George Hill, Reilly's sidekick, was sent to the Middle East on a mission after fleeing Russia, and was decorated for his service. But "Jolly George" was broke, and he and his wife had to live in a trailer home in Sussex. Churchill rescued him from poverty by hiring him as an explosives instructor for an outfit later absorbed by the Special Operations Executive (SOE). One of Hill's students was British spy Kim Philby, a double agent for the Soviets.

In 1941 the SOE sent Hill back to Russia, this time to work with the NKVD, a successor to the Cheka, in propaganda and sabotage projects against the Nazis in Europe. George was given a suite in the Hotel National overlooking the Kremlin. He acquired a Russian lover and spent 1,500 pounds a month pursuing a playboy's life. Some people in England thought he had been turned by the Soviets. But it might have been more a case of manipulation and neutralization by the NKVD. In October 1944 an SOE officer complained that "none of the work he [Hill] has done has advantaged SOE in any substantial way."

Hill was recalled to London in 1945 and retired as an SOE brigadier. In 1947 he became a director of Apollinarius, a British-owned German mineral water company. He was awarded one of West Germany's highest decorations in 1957, ostensibly for helping the country recover economically from the war. But a former colleague suspected that George had been a triple agent during the war, working for the British while selling secrets to the Soviets and the Germans, and that the medal was Deutschland's way of saying thanks.[14] Hill died in 1968.

❖

Pavel Malkov, the Kremlin commandant who arrested Lockhart and rounded up agents working for Reilly and Kalamatiano, served in the Red Army, 1920–1922, then went on to economic managerial work. He retired in 1954 and wrote two books. He said the amount of money that Lockhart and Reilly paid to Eduard Berzin was 1.2 million rubles and that it was given to the Latvian soldiers whom the Allies were trying to recruit for the Lenin Plot. Malkov was awarded the Order of Lenin and died in 1965.

Eduard Berzin, the Latvian army officer who set the Lenin Plot sting into play for the Cheka, was rewarded in 1931 with a job as first manager of Dalstroy (the Far North Construction Trust in Siberia). Berzin ran eighty forced-labor Gulag camps near the Arctic Circle for gold mining. He lived in a comfortable house and drove a Rolls-Royce formerly owned by Dzerzhinsky. Berzin was a world traveler. On a trip to the United States he bought a Gramophone for playing his Italian opera records. In 1938 he was executed in Stalin's purge of Old Bolsheviks.[15]

Nikolai Krylenko, the prosecutor at the trial of the Lenin plotters, was appointed Soviet commissar for justice in 1931 and ran Stalin's purges. Krylenko was a chess buff and had often played Lenin. He later became secretary of the Soviet Chess Federation, organized popular chess tournaments, and was awarded the Order of Lenin. But Stalin, looking for any excuse to liquidate Old Bolsheviks who opposed his power, ordered him arrested in 1937. The charge was "wrecking" the development of chess in Russia. He was tortured and confessed but repudiated the confession in court. His 1938 trial lasted twenty minutes. Krylenko was declared an enemy of the state and shot.[16] His sister Elena fled to America.

"I suppose chess playing is now considered wrecking the government," she said.[17]

Felix Dzerzhinsky, who with Lenin masterminded the sting to capture the Allied spies in the latter weeks of their Moscow coup plot, was appointed head of Stalin's first Five-Year Plan, in 1924. But he became paranoid and feared contact with people. He also had heart trouble, possibly angina pectoris. By 1926 he could no longer work. In July of that year somebody tried to poison him. The attempt failed when Felix forced the cook to eat the meal. The cook, as expected, did not live to enjoy dessert.

When Dzerzhinsky addressed the All-Russian Communist Party the next day he bitterly denounced a number of people. Some party members thought he was a lunatic and arranged for him to be liquidated. He saved them the trouble by dying in his sleep.[18] He could have been poisoned by Stalin. He could have committed suicide. He could have died of heart failure.[19] His statue in front of the Lubyanka was removed after the fall of Communism in 1991 but a bust of Iron Felix was quietly returned to Moscow police headquarters in 2005 by president Vladimir Putin, a former KGB officer.

Jacob Peters, who interrogated Kalamatiano, Maria Friede, and other members of Kal's network, worked for Soviet intelligence in Turkestan in the twenties and became chief of the Eastern Division of OPGU. His English wife arrived in Moscow and found Peters had married again without divorcing her. She got a job as a maid while their daughter May studied ballet and worked as a telephone operator in the new British embassy. In the late thirties Soviet agents kidnapped May on the street and sent her to a concentration camp. She was last heard from in 1955.[20]

Stalin ordered Peters shot in 1938, along with hundreds of other agents who had worked for Dzerzhinsky. They were murdered by the men who replaced them. Then the executioners themselves were murdered. The Soviet government rehabilitated Peters in 1956.

Lenin, the originator of the sting to break up the Allied plot against him, began to crack in 1920 under the strain of his duties. Lenin suffered a series of strokes while organizing a purge of party members. He got headaches, he became confused, he could not solve simple math problems. Lenin's leg became paralyzed and he could not write legibly. He had foreboding thoughts, and flew into rages, but was unrepentant about things he had done in the past. He remembered that an old peasant told him once that when his time came, he would go out with a stroke.

The Central Committee didn't know exactly what to do about Lenin. They put him on leave and the Politburo isolated him from political work. He was relegated to retirement in a wheelchair at Gorki, his country retreat. Lenin asked his wife and Stalin to poison him if his condition became hopeless. Before he died, Lenin wrote a "Testament" to a future Communist Party Congress, recommending Stalin be removed as secretary-general of the party. At the same time, Lenin was a little easier in his opinion of Trotsky. Stalin got hold of the documents and took measures to neutralize Trotsky's standing.

Lenin's death in 1924 was due to several causes, primarily atherosclerosis. One of the doctors who conducted the autopsy said Lenin's arteries were so calcified that when tapped with a scalpel they made a sound like metal hitting rock.

Russian cities, streets, and factories were named after Lenin, though in recent years Russia has undertaken a de-Sovietization and the name of Leningrad was changed back to St. Petersburg. Lenin's body was embalmed and placed in a stone sarcophagus in a Red Square tomb that's open to public viewing. A team of sixty scientists and technicians are assigned to keep his remains from deteriorating. The crew at this "Lenin Lab" change his fluids every year—a cocktail of glycerol, formaldehyde, potassium acetate, alcohol, hydrogen peroxide, acetic acid, and acetic sodium. It takes them six weeks each time. Still, Lenin's body has decomposed a bit. His nose and face have been remolded with plastic patches, his eyelashes replaced, his skin fat treated with chemicals. Under his clothes the body wears a rubber suit to keep embalming fluid wet on the skin.[21]

Hundreds of millions of rubles have been spent to keep "Lenin's Lantern" burning. And new techniques are being examined all the time. One of them is plastination, injecting the body with polymers to turn Ilych into a plastic sculpture. That would make the man, like his ideas, permanently mummified.

❖

On the military side of the Lenin Plot, Edmund Ironside, who probably saved the Allies in Archangel from annihilation, was promoted to major general and began to advocate the idea of mechanized warfare through coordinated attacks by tanks, armored cars, and planes. The British army's "old men" didn't like that; they were still using horse cavalry. When World War II came, he was assigned as chief of the imperial general staff. That didn't work out, and he was reassigned as commander of home forces. But the army didn't like his Archangel spread-out-and-dig-in strategy for the defense of Britain. Neither did Churchill, who became PM in 1940. Ironside was again relieved of command, promoted to field marshal, given a peerage, and sent home in 1941. The idea of mechanized warfare was picked up by Germany, resulting in what the Wehrmacht called *blitzkrieg*.

George Evans Stewart was promoted to full colonel following the Archangel campaign. He went back to training duty at Camp Custer in 1919 and, as a Medal of Honor winner, made some appearances at army events.[22] He retired in 1931 and moved with his wife to Texas. He died in 1946.

John Cudahy, a U.S. officer who wrote a searing account of the Archangel campaign, suffered health problems after the war but recovered after a long visit to the Canadian Rockies. In the thirties he served as FDR's ambassador to Poland and Belgium, and minister to Ireland and Luxemburg. He interviewed Hitler in 1941 and set off a controversy when he wrote that America should not interfere with *der Führer*'s aims in Europe.[23] Cudahy wrote six books, including an account of exploring Baja California with rifle and camera. He was an experienced equestrian but was killed in 1943 when thrown by his favorite horse.

Harry Costello, another officer who severely criticized the Russian invasion, became a sportswriter for the *Detroit News* and the *Washington Times*. He died in 1968. At one point Harry worked in New Orleans as a PR man for Louisiana State University football, hired by U.S. Senator Huey P. Long, the "Kingfish" of the Bayou State. Costello said he first met Long after a night out in Washington. Harry got in a taxi and told the driver to take him to the Mayflower Hotel. But Costello passed out before he could give his room number. The driver, though, thought he recognized the man on the back seat. He took him to the hotel, got a key from the desk clerk, and deposited him on one of the beds in the room. When Harry woke up the next morning he looked over to the other bed. The man sleeping there looked like Harry's twin.

"Holy cow," Harry said. It was the Kingfish.

❖

Xenophon Kalamatiano was not welcomed with open arms in Washington. The Lenin Plot had been a colossal embarrassment for the U.S. government, and the State Department wanted to forget it ever happened. Kal encountered DeWitt Poole in Washington and apologized for getting captured. But Kal was seen as a dinosaur and was turned down for further assignments. He was kept on the federal payroll until November 20, 1921, then released.

Kalamatiano took a job teaching languages at his alma mater, Culver Academy, and settled there with wife Katherine and stepson Vladimir. A Culver photo shows him in a captain's uniform, looking thin and cold. Kal wrote a book about his experiences in Russia but couldn't find a publisher. He suffered from what's now called post-traumatic stress disorder. His violent rages sent Katherine fleeing to the homes of other faculty members but apparently he didn't injure her.

Kal's health seems to have been weakened by his years in Soviet prisons. On a hunting trip in 1923 he suffered frostbite in one of his feet and infection of a blister. He was hospitalized in suburban Chicago and several toes were amputated. Kal rallied, but then his condition deteriorated. That was before the era of antibiotics, and he died on November 9, 1923, of subacute septic endocarditis, a bacterial infection that went to his heart. He was forty-one years old.

Katherine stayed on in Culver and opened a beauty shop. It failed and she moved to Chicago, where she died of an illness in 1927. Vladimir graduated from Culver, briefly attended college, then vanished for several years. He showed up in 1937 as a laborer for the Union Pacific Railroad and died in a hospital for epileptics in 1946. Kal's daughter Vera, by his first wife, lived to the age of ninety-three.[24]

Kal's mother Vera moved to New Mexico in 1918 and opened a school, Duchess Castle, to teach pottery making to Pueblo Indians. She returned to California in 1930, worked as a writer, and died in Pasadena in 1942.[25]

Kalamatiano's stepfather, C.P. de Blumenthal, escaped from Russia in 1923 with his son Michael and went to Culver to join Kal. They arrived the day after Kal died. C.P. took Kal's teaching job and was soon joined by his new wife and their two daughters. C.P. left Culver after six years and went on the road again. He wandered across America and died in Maryland in 1939, one of the victims of the Great Depression.[26]

Kal's flaw, if that's what it was, likely was his youthful overconfidence. While he was in Samara, Poole warned him that their networks in Moscow were being rolled up by the Cheka. He could have fled to the safety of Vladivostok. Instead, he decided to stay on the job.

It was a brave decision, though a risky one. After that, his life went downhill: arrest, imprisonment, torture, loss of federal employment, mental and physical breakdowns, and early death. As his wife noted, Kal had placed duty above personal safety, above his family, above everything else, for his adopted country.

But Washington never publicly acknowledged his service. They debriefed him, paid him off, and sent him on his way.

SELECTED BIBLIOGRAPHY

A Chronicler (John Cudahy). *Archangel: The American War Against Russia*. Chicago: McClurg, 1924.

Albertson, Ralph. *Fighting Without a War: An Account of Military Intervention in North Russia*. New York: Harcourt, Brace and Howe, 1920.

Alekseno, Dmitry M. *High-Impact Terrorism: Terrorist Proceedings of a Russian-American Workshop*. Washington, DC: National Academy Press, 2002.

American Field Service. *History of the American Field Service in France*. Boston: Houghton Mifflin, 1920.

Anonymous (Clinton Wallace Gilbert). *The Mirrors of Washington*. New York: Putnam's, 1921.

Ash, Lucy. "'Death Island': Britain's 'Concentration Camp' in Russia." *BBC News Magazine*, 2017. www.bbc.com.

Bainton, Roy. *Honoured by Strangers: The Life of Captain Francis Cromie CB DSO RN 1882–1918*. Shrewsbury: Airlife, 2002.

Beatty, Bessie. *The Red Heart of Russia*. New York: Century, 1918.

Bennett, Van S. *Diaries of Van S. Bennett*. Madison: Wisconsin Historical Society Archives, www.content.wisconsinhistory.org.

Berberova, Nina. *Moura: The Dangerous Life of the Baroness Budberg*. Translated by Marian Schwartz and Richard D. Sylvester. New York: New York Review of Books, 1988.

———. *Zheleznaia Zhenshchina*. Moskva: Knizhnaia Palata, 1991.

Blackwell, Alice Stone, ed. *The Little Grandmother of the Russian Revolution: Reminiscences and Letters of Catherine Breshkovsky*. London: T. Fisher Unwin, 1918.

Botchkareva, Maria, and Isaac Don Levine. *Yashka*. New York: Frederick A. Stokes, 1918.

Bowler, Letitia. "An Englishwoman's Experiences in Bolshevik Prisons." *Blackwood's Magazine*, 1921.

British Parliament. Army. *The Evacuation of North Russia, 1919*. London: H.M. Stationery Office, 1920.

———. Lindley, F.O. "Report on the Work of the British Mission to North Russia, June 1918 to 31st March 1919." *British documents on foreign affairs—reports and papers from the Foreign Office confidential print, Part II, from the First to the Second World War, Series A, the Soviet Union, 1917–1939*. Kenneth Bourne and D. Cameron Watt, eds. Frederick, MD: University Publications of America, 1984.

———. *Russia No. 1 (1919). A Collection of Reports on Bolshevism in Russia*. London: H.M. Stationery Office, 1919.

Brook-Shepherd, Gordon. *Iron Maze: The Western Secret Services and the Bolsheviks*. London: Macmillan, 1998.

Brusilov, General Aleksiei Aleksieevich. *A Soldier's Notebook, 1914–1919*. Westport, CT: Greenwood Press, 1971.

Buchanan, Sir George. *My Mission to Russia and Other Diplomatic Memories, Volume II*. London: Cassell, 1923.

Budberg, Moura. Intelligence reports on Moura Budberg. Vincennes, France: Service Historique de la Defense, 2015.

Burke, Edmund, John Wright, John Knox, and John Entick, eds. *The Times History of the War*. London: The Times, 1920.

Calder, Robert Lorin. *W. Somerset Maugham and the Quest for Freedom*. New York: Doubleday, 1973.

Cambon, Paul. *Correspondence 1870–1924, Volume 3*. Paris: Éditions Bernard Grasset, 1946.

Carley, Michael Jabara. *Revolution and Intervention: The French Government and the Russian Civil War*. Montréal: McGill-Queen's University Press, 1983.

Chew, Allen F. "Fighting the Russians in Winter: Three case studies." *Leavenworth Papers*. Fort Leavenworth, KS: Combat Studies Institute, 1981. www.armyupress.army.mil.

Chicherin, Georgi. *Georgi Chicherin Archive, 1872–1936*. USSR History Archive. www.marxists.org.

Churchill, Winston. *Great Contemporaries*. London: T. Butterworth, 1937.

Clark, Faye. *As You Were: Fort Custer*. Galesburg, MI: Kal-Gal Printing, 1985.

Cliff, Tony. *Lenin, Volume 3: Revolution Besieged*. London: Pluto Press, 1978.

Cook, Andrew. *On His Majesty's Secret Service/Sidney Reilly; Codename ST1*. Charleston, SC: Tempus, 2002.

Costello, Harry J. *Why Did We Go to Russia?* Detroit: Harry J. Costello, 1920.

———. Service record. Lansing: State Archives of Michigan. www.michigan.gov.

Crane, Charles Richard. *Memoirs of Charles R. Crane* [1934]. New York: Columbia University. www.archive.org.

"Crude oil prices." *Literary Digest*, 1920.

Deacon, Richard. *The British Connection: Russia's Manipulation of British Individuals and Institutions*. London: Hamish Hamilton, 1979.

Dearborn, Mary. "Reviving Louise Bryant." Portland: Oregon Cultural Heritage Commission. www.ochcomm.org.

"Department of State and Counterintelligence." National Counterintelligence Center. Washington: Federation of American Scientists. www.fas.org.

Doty, Madeleine Z. "Revolutionary Justice." *Atlantic Monthly*, 1918.

Edith Wilson. National First Ladies' Library. www.firstladies.org.

Elwood, R.C. *Inessa Armand: Revolutionary and Feminist*. Cambridge University Press, 1992.

Engels, Friedrich. *Anti-Dühring: Herr Dühring's Revolution in Science*. Moscow: Progress Publishers, 1947.

Fine, Sidney. "Frank Murphy in World War I." Ann Arbor: University of Michigan. www.libumich.edu.

Finnegan, John Patrick, and Roma Danysh. *Army Lineage Series: Military Intelligence*. Washington: Center of Military History, 1998. www.history.army.mil.

Fischer, Louis. *The Life of Lenin*. New York: Harper & Row, 1964.

Foglesong, David S. *America's Secret War Against Bolshevism: U.S. Intervention in the Russian Civil War, 1917–1920*. Chapel Hill: University of North Carolina Press, 1995.

Francis, David Rowland. *Russia from the American embassy: April, 1916–November, 1918*. New York: Scribner's, 1921.

———. Letters of David R. Francis. St. Louis: Missouri Historical Society Archives.

Galkina, Yuliya Mikhailovna. "The question of French involvement in the Lockhart affair: Who is Henri Vertamon?" Ekaterinburg, Russia: Ural Federal University, 2018. www.academia.edu.

Golinkov, D.L., and S.N. Semanov. "Yaroslavl Revolt of 1918." *Great Soviet Encyclopedia*. New York: Macmillan, 1979.

Goncharov, V.A., and A.I. Kokurin. *October guardsmen: The role of the indigenous peoples of the Baltic countries in establishing and strengthening the Bolshevik system*. Moscow: Indrik, 2009.

Gregory, Thomas C. "Russian Famine: Mr. Hoover's Sinister Role in Hungary." *World's Work*. New York: Doubleday, Page, 1921.

Hahn, Jeffrey W., ed. *Regional Russia in Transition: Studies from Yaroslavl*. Washington: Woodrow Wilson Center Press, 2001.

Harding, Stan. *The Underworld of State*. London: George Allen & Unwin, 1925.

Harper, C.P.V., and Ronald Thompson, eds. *The Russia I Believe In: The Memoirs of Samuel N. Harper, 1902–1941*. University of Chicago Press, 1945.

Harper, Samuel N. Letters of Samuel N. Harper. University of Chicago.

Harrison, Leland. Biography of Leland Harrison. Cambridge, MA: Harvard University, www.library.harvard.edu.

Harrison, Marguerite E. *Marooned in Moscow: The Story of an American Woman Imprisoned in Russia*. New York: George H. Doran, 1921.

———. *There's Always Tomorrow: The Story of a Checkered Life*. New York: Farrar & Rinehart, 1935.

———. Margaret [*sic*] Harrison file, U.S. Army Military Intelligence Branch. Washington: National Archives and Records Administration.

Hartman, Robert B.D. "I Spy?" *Alumni Message Center*. Culver, IN: Culver Academies, 1991.

———. "Saga de Blumenthal." Culver Academies, 1991.

Haynes, John Earl, Harvey Klehr, and Alexander Vassiliev. *Spies: The Rise and Fall of the KGB in America*. New Haven: Yale University Press, 2009.

Hendrick, Burton J. *The Life and Letters of Walter H. Page*. Garden City: Doubleday, 1923.

Hilger, Gustav, and Alfred G. Meyer. *The Incompatible Allies: A Memoir-History of German-Soviet Relations, 1918–1941*. New York: Macmillan, 1953.

Hill, George Alexander. *Go Spy the Land*. London: Biteback Publishing, 2014.

Hoover, Herbert. *The Memoirs of Herbert Hoover*. London: Hollis and Carter, 1952–1953.

Hoppe, Jon. "The Russian Intervention of 1918–1919." Annapolis: U.S. Naval Institute. www.navalhistory.org.

Horne, Charles F., and Walter F. Austin, eds. *The Great Events of the Great War, Volume V*. New York: National Alumni, 1920.

Hsu, Jeremy. "Lenin's Body Improves with Age." *Scientific American*. New York: Springer Nature, 2015.

Huntington, W. Chapin. *The Homesick Million: Russia-Out-of-Russia*. Boston: Stratford, 1933.

Ingram, Alton Earl. "The Root Mission to Russia, 1917." Baton Rouge: Louisiana State University, 1970. www.digitalcommons.lsu.edu.

Ironside, William Edmund, Baron. *Archangel, 1918–1919*. London: Constable, 1953.

Jansen, Marc. *A Show Trial Under Lenin: The Trial of Socialist Revolutionaries, 1922*. The Hague: Martinus Nijhoff, 1982.

Jaxa-Ronikier, Bogdan. *The Red Executioner Dzierjinski*. London: Denis Archer, 1935.

Jeffreys-Jones, Rhodri. "W. Somerset Maugham: Anglo-American Agent in Revolutionary Russia." *American Quarterly*. Baltimore: Johns Hopkins, 1976.

Kalamatiano, Xenophon DeBlumenthal. Federal personnel record. St. Louis: National Personnel Records Center.

———. *1902 Cap and Gown*. University of Chicago. www.babel.hathitrust.org.

———. Letters to Samuel N. Harper. University of Chicago Library.

———. Student transcript. University of Chicago registrar's office.

———. Intelligence file. U.S. Army Military Intelligence Branch. Washington: National Archives and Records Administration.

———. Reports from Russia to U.S. Department of State. College Park, MD: National Archives and Records Administration.

Karttunen, Klaus. "Joseph-Fernand Grenard." *Persons of Indian Studies*. www.whowaswho-indology.info.

Kavtaradze, A. "The June Offensive of the Russian Army in 1917." *Military-History*, 1967. The Russian Army in the Great War project. www.grwar.ru.

Kennan, George F. *Soviet-American Relations, 1917–1920, Volume II, The Decision to Intervene*. New York: Antheneum, 1967.

Kerensky, Alexander. *Russia and History's Turning Point*. New York: Duell, Sloan and Pearce, 1965.

———. *The Catastrophe: Kerensky's Own Story of the Russian Revolution*. New York: D. Appleton, 1927.

Kerzhentsev, Platon. *Life of Lenin*. New York: International Publishers, 1939. www.archive.org.

Kesaris, Paul, ed. *Confidential U.S. Diplomatic Post Records, Part I, Russia 1914–1918*. Frederick, MD: University Publications of America, 1982.

Khodnev, Alexander. "A Benchmark History of Yaroslavl in the Twentieth Century." *Regional Russia in Transition: Studies from Yaroslavl*. Washington: Woodrow Wilson Center Press, 2001.

Khromov, Sejriyon, ed. *Felix Dzerzhinsky: a biography*. Moscow: Progress Publisher, 1988.

Knox, Major General Sir Alfred. *With the Russian Army, 1914–1917: Being chiefly extracts from the diary of a military attaché*. London: Hutchinson, 1921.

Lansing, Robert. *War Memoirs of Robert Lansing, Secretary of State*. New York: Bobbs-Merrill, 1935.

———. Official papers. *Papers Relating to the Foreign Relations of the United States, 1918, 1919, 1920, 1921, Russia*. www.history.state.gov.

LaVO, Carl. "Olympian Effort to Save the Olympia." *Naval History Magazine*. Annapolis: United States Naval Institute, 2016. www.usni.org.

Lenin, V.I. *Collected Works*. Moscow: Progress Publishers, 1972. Marxists Internet Archive. www.marxists.org.

Levere, William C. *The History of the Sigma Alpha Epsilon Fraternity.* Nashville: Benson Printing, 1911.

———. *The History of Sigma Alpha Epsilon in the World War.* Menasha, WI: George Banta, 1928.

Levin, Dov H. "Partisan electoral interventions by the great powers: Introducing the PEIG Dataset." *Conflict Management and Peace Science,* 2016. www.journals.sagepub.com.

Levine, Isaac Don. *Eyewitness to History: Memoirs and Reflections of a Foreign Correspondent for Half a Century.* New York: Hawthorn, 1973.

Link, Arthur S., ed. *The Papers of Woodrow Wilson.* Princeton University Press, 1966.

Litvin, Alter L., ed. *The Case of Fanny Kaplan, or Who Shot Lenin?* Kazan, Russia: 1995, 2003.

Lockhart, Robert Hamilton Bruce. *Memoirs of a British Agent: being an account of the author's early life in many lands and of his official mission to Moscow in 1918.* New York: G.P. Putnam's Sons, 1933.

———. *The Diaries of Sir Robert Bruce Lockhart, 1915–1938.* London: Macmillan, 1973.

Lockhart, Robin Bruce. *Reilly: Ace of Spies.* New York: Dorset Press, 1986, 1987.

Lomonosoff, George V. *Memoirs of the Russian Revolution.* Translated by D.H. Dubrowsky and Robert T. Williams. New York: Rand School of Social Science, 1919.

Ludendorff, Erich. *My War Memories: 1914–1918.* London: Hutchinson, 1923.

Madelin, Phillipe. *Dans le secret des services: La France malade de ses espions?* Paris: Éditions Denoël, 2007.

Madison, Wisconsin, City Directory 1902. Madison: G.R. Angell, 1902. Madison: University of Wisconsin Library.

Malkov, Pavel. *Reminiscences of a Kremlin Commandant.* Translated by V. Dutt. Moscow: Progress Publishers, 1959.

March, Peyton C. *The Nation at War.* Garden City: Doubleday, Doran, 1932.

Marchand, René. "Why I Support Bolshevism." Translated by Eden and Cedar Paul. London: British Socialist Party, 1919.

Marcu, Valeriu. *Lenin.* Translated by E.E. Dickes. New York: Macmillan, 1928.

Maugham, W. Somerset. *Ashenden: or, The British Agent.* New York: Grosset & Dunlap, 1928.

———. *A Writer's Notebook.* New York: Penguin Books, 1984.

Mehney, Paul D. "The Custer Division." *Michigan History.* Lansing: Historical Society of Michigan, 2001.

Melgunov, Sergei Petrovich. *Red Terror in Russia.* Westport, CT: Hyperion Press, 1975.

Moore, Joel R., Harry H. Mead, and Lewis E. Jarns. *History of the American Expedition Fighting the Bolsheviki.* Detroit: Polar Bear Publishing, 1920.

Morgan, Ted. *Maugham: a biography.* New York: Simon & Schuster, 1981.

Neu, Charles E. *Colonel House: A Biography of Woodrow Wilson's Silent Partner.* Oxford University Press, 2014.

Nickles, David Paull. *Under the Wire: How the Telegraph Changed Diplomacy.* Cambridge, MA: Harvard University Press, 2003.

Nicolaievsky, Boris. *Aseff: the Russian Judas.* London: Hurst & Blackett, 1934.

Noulens, Joseph. *Mon ambassade en Russie soviétique (1917–1919).* Paris: Plon, 1933.

"Oil and Gas Developments." *Standard Daily Trade Service.* New York: Standard Statistics Company, 1920.

Orlov, Alexander. *The March of Time: Reminiscences.* London: St Ermin's Press, 2004.

O'Sullivan, Dónal. *Dealing with the Devil: Anglo-Soviet Intelligence Cooperation During the Second World War.* New York: Peter Lang, 2010.

O'Toole, G.J.A. *Honorable Treachery: A History of U.S. Intelligence, Espionage, and Covert Action from the American Revolution to the CIA.* New York: Atlantic Monthly, 1991.

Palmer, Frederick. *Newton D. Baker: America at War.* New York: Kraus, 1969.

Parkinson, Russell J. *Foreign Command of U.S. Forces.* Washington: U.S. Department of Defense. www.dtic.mil.

Pershing, General John J. *My Experiences in the First World War.* New York: Da Capo, 1995.

Peters, Jacob, and Viktor Eduardovich Kingisepp. "The Lockhart Case: Report by Comrade Peters on the Lockhart Case." *Cheka Archives: a Collection of Documents [1918].* Edited by V. Vinogradov, A. Litvin, and V. Hristoforov. Translated by John Puckett. Moscow: Kuchkovo Pole, 2007. www.skoblin.blogspot.com.

Phillips, William. *Ventures in Diplomacy.* London: John Murray, 1955.

Pipes, Richard. *The Russian Revolution.* New York: Knopf, 1990.

Poole, DeWitt Clinton (Jr.). Letters to David R. Francis. St. Louis: Missouri Historical Society Archives.

———. *1902 Tychoberahn.* Madison High School. Madison: Wisconsin Historical Society.

———. *1907 Badger.* University of Wisconsin-Madison. www.library.wisc.edu.

———. *1910 Cherry Tree.* George Washington University. www.archive.com.

———. "Reminiscences of DeWitt Clinton Poole." Columbia Center for Oral History, Columbia University, 1952.

———. Reports to the U.S. Department of State. *Papers Relating to the Foreign Relations of the United States, 1917, 1918, 1919, 1920, 1921, Russia.*

———. Student transcript. University of Wisconsin-Madison registrar's office.

Poole, DeWitt Clinton (Sr.). Army personnel record of D.C. Poole. Madison: Wisconsin Veterans Museum.

———. State of New York. *Documents of the Senate of the State of New York, 89th session (1864).* Albany: Legislative Printer, 1865.

———. *United States Army and Navy Journal and Gazette, 1904.* New York: Army and Navy Journal, Inc. www.catalog.hathitrust.org.

Quiner, Edwin Bentley. *Quiner Scrapbooks: Correspondence of the Wisconsin Volunteers, 1861–1865,* and *Diaries of Van S. Bennett.* Madison: Wisconsin Historical Society.

Reilly, Sidney George. Letters to Winston Churchill. Churchill Archive Center. Cambridge University, Churchill College.

Reilly, Sidney George, and Pepita Bobadilla. *Britain's Master Spy: The Adventures of Sidney Reilly.* Northvale, England: Dorset, 1985.

Robien, Louis de. *The Diary of a Diplomat in Russia, 1917–1918.* Translated by Camilla Sykes. New York: Praeger, 1970.

Rockoff, Hugh. "Until it's over, over there: the US economy in World War I." *The Economics of World War I.* Edited by Stephen Broadberry and Mark Harrison. Cambridge University Press, 2005.

Rosenthal, Herman, and Max Rosenthal. "Kishinef (Kishinev)." *Jewish Encyclopedia.* www.jewishencyclopedia.com.

"Royal Flying Corps and Royal Air Force Family History." Imperial War Museum, London. www.iwm.org.uk.

Samoilo, Alexandrovich. *Samoilo biography*. Ministry of Defense of the Russian Federation. www.encylopedia.mil.ru.

Saul, Norman E. *The Life and Times of Charles R. Crane, 1858–1939*. Lanham, MD: Lexington Books, 2013.

Savinkov, Boris. Letters to Winston Churchill. Churchill Archive Centre. Cambridge University, Churchill College.

——. *Memoirs of a Terrorist*. Translated by Joseph Shaplen. New York: Albert & Charles Boni, 1931.

——. *Pale Horse* (V. Ropshin). Translated by Z. Vengerova. Miami: Hardpress, 2015.

——. Trial of Boris Savinkov. Transcript translated by Emanuel Aronsberg. Stanford: Hoover Institution on War, Revolution and Peace.

——. *What Never Happened: A Novel of the Revolution* (Ropshin). Translated by Thomas Seltzer. New York: Alfred A. Knopf, 1917.

Scholz, Hermine. "The World War I Survey: North Russian order of battle." Carlisle Barracks, PA: U.S. Army Military History Institute.

Scott, Hugh Lenox. *Some Memories of a Soldier*. New York: Century, 1928.

Sittenauer, Peter. "Lessons in Operational Art: An Analysis of the Allied Expeditionary Forces in North Russia, 1918–1919." Leavenworth: U.S. Army School of Advanced Military Studies.

Skopinski, Nicolas. "Charles Adolphe Faux-Pas Bidet, l'ennemi de Trotski." *Ouest-France*. www.ouest-france.fr.

Snodgrass, John. "Trade and Industries of Russia." *Russia: A Handbook on Commercial and Industrial Conditions: Special Consular Reports*. Washington: Government Printing Office, 1913.

Soutar, Andrew. *With Ironside in North Russia*. London: Hutchinson, 1944.

Spence, Richard B. *Trust No One: The Secret World of Sidney Reilly*. Los Angeles: Feral House, 2002.

Srodes, James. *Allen Dulles: Master of Spies*. Washington: Regnery, 1999.

Starling, Edmund W. *Starling of the White House*. New York: Simon & Schuster, 1948.

Steinberg, Isaac. *Spiridonova: Revolutionary Terrorist*. Freeport, NY: Books for Libraries Press, 1971.

Sukanov, N.N. *The Russian Revolution 1917: Eyewitness Account, Volume II*. Translated by Joel Carmichael. New York: Harper, 1955.

Sutton, Antony C. *Wall Street and the Bolshevik Revolution*. West Hoathly, England: Clairview Books, 2001.

Taubenberger, Jeffery K., and David M. Morens. "1918 Influenza: the mother of all epidemics." *Emerging Infectious Diseases*. Atlanta: U.S. Centers for Disease Control and Prevention, 2006.

Telberg, George Gustav, Robert Wilton, and N. Sokolov. *The Last Days of the Romanovs*. New York: George H. Duran, 1920.

"The Currency of Russia under the Soviet Government." *Federal Reserve Bulletin*. Washington: Federal Reserve Board, 1922.

Transcript of the Trial of Zurka Dubof, Jacob Peters, John Rosen, and Nina Vassileva. Old Bailey Proceedings Online, 1674-1913. www.oldbaileyonline.org.

Trotsky, Leon. *The History of the Russian Revolution*. New York: Simon & Schuster, 1933.

——. *Jacob Sverdlov*. Moscow: Bureau of Party History, 1926. www.marxists.org.

———. *The Military Writings of Leon Trotsky*. New York: Pathfinder, 1971.

Ullman, Richard H. *Intervention and the War: Anglo-Soviet Relations, 1917–1921, Volume 1*. Princeton University Press, 1961.

U.S. Bureau of Commerce and Labor. *International Harvester Company*. Washington: Printing Office, 1913.

U.S. Central Intelligence Agency. *History of American Intelligence*. Langley, VA: Center for Study of Intelligence. www.cia.gov.

———. *l'Orchestre Rouge*. CIA Online Library. www.cia.gov.

U.S. Department of State. *Diplomatic Security Service: Then and Now*. Washington: Bureau of Diplomatic Security. www.state.gov.

———. *Papers Relating to the Foreign Relations of the United States, Russia*. Washington: Government Printing Office, 1918, 1919, 1920, 1921.

———. "Special Agents, Special Threats/Creating the Office of the Chief Special Agent, 1914–1933." *History of the Bureau of Diplomatic Security*. www.state.gov.

U.S. Navy. "American Ship Casualties of the World War." Washington: Naval History and Heritage Command. www.history.navy.mil.

U.S. Senate. Subcommittee of the Committee on Foreign Relations. *Russian Propaganda Hearings, Sixty-sixth Congress, second session*. Washington: Government Printing Office, 1920.

———. Subcommittee of the Committee on the Judiciary. *Bolshevik Propaganda Hearings. Sixty-fifth Congress, third session*. Washington: Government Printing Office, 1919.

Vertsinsky, E.A. "Year of the Revolution: Memoirs of an Officer of the General Staff, 1917–1918." The Russian Army in the Great War Project. www.grwar.ru.

Volkogonov, Dmitri. *Lenin: A New Biography*. Translated by Harold Shukman. New York: Free Press, 1994.

Weber, Ralph E. *United States Diplomatic Codes and Ciphers, 1775–1938*. Chicago: Precedent Publishing, 1979.

Wędziagolski, Karol. *Boris Savinkov: portrait of a terrorist*. Clifton, NJ: Kingston Press, 1988.

Wolfe, Bertram D. "Lenin and Inessa Armand." *Slavic Review*. Cambridge University Press, 1963.

York, Dorothea. *The Romance of Company "A," 339th Infantry, A.N.R.E.F.* Detroit: McIntyre Printing, 1923.

Zalyubovsky, Anatoly Petrovich. "Supply of the Russian Army in the Great War with rifles, machine guns, revolvers and cartridges." The Russian Army in the Great War Project. www.grwar.ru.

Zeman, Z.A.B., and W.B. Scharlau. *Merchant of Revolution: The Life of Alexander Israel Helphand (Parvus) 1867–1924*. Oxford University Press, 1965.

ENDNOTES

PREFACE

1   Russian Provisional Government counterintelligence agents had collected evidence of the Bolsheviks' "German Key" as far back as 1917. For additional information on the man who set up Lenin's deal with Germany, see Z.A.B. Zeman and W.B. Scharlau, *Merchant of Revolution: The Life of Alexander Israel Helphand (Parvus) 1867–1924* (Oxford University Press, 1965). Also, Dmitri Volkogonov, *Lenin: A New Biography*, trans. by Harold Shukman (New York: Free Press, 1994), 123. Berlin's payments to the Bolsheviks are listed in World War I records of the German Foreign Ministry, held by the National Archives in Washington, DC.

2   Andrew Cook, *On Her Majesty's Secret Service: Sidney Reilly, Codename ST1* (London: Tempus, 2002), 9–10, 243. Bond was undoubtedly a cocktail of many blends, as most fictional characters are.

3   The United States landed another invasion force at Vladivostok on the Pacific but President Wilson forbade those troops from moving west beyond the Urals, so they had little to do with the Lenin Plot.

4   A Chronicler (John Cudahy), *Archangel: The American War with Russia* (Chicago: A.C. McClurg, 1924), 213. Lieutenant Cudahy commanded an infantry company in Russia.

5   Joel R. Moore, Harry H. Mead, and Lewis E. Jahns, *History of the American Expedition Fighting the Bolsheviki* (Detroit: Polar Bear Publishing, 1920), 283–87. The authors all served in combat against the Red Army.

6   President Roosevelt to the President of the Soviet All-Union Central Executive Committee (Kalinin), October 10, 1933, in *Foreign Relations of the United States, Diplomatic Papers, The Soviet Union, 1933–1939*, 711.61/287a, www.history.state.gov. Hereafter referred to as *FRUS*.

7   Ronald Reagan, State of the Union address, January 25, 1984, www.presidency.ucsb.edu.

8   Dov H. Levin, "Partisan electoral interventions by the great powers: Introducing the PEIG Dataset," *Conflict Management and Peace Science*, September 19, 2016, www.journals.sagepub.com.

PART I: THE FIRST ATTEMPT

1   London: Victor Gollancz, 1929.

1: A FORGOTTEN MAN

1   Marguerite E. Harrison, *Marooned in Moscow: The Story of an American Woman Imprisoned in Russia* (New York: George H. Doran, 1921), 298.

2   Kalamatiano's description of his arrest, interrogation, trial, and imprisonment can be found
     in his report sent by the Commissioner of the United States, Riga, Cable #165, August 23,
     1921, to the Secretary of State, courtesy of Catherine Brennan, National Archives and Record
     Administration, RDT2, College Park, hereafter referred to as Kalamatiano trial report, and
     NARA; and a message that Kalamatiano smuggled out of prison to DeWitt Clinton Poole, in
     RG59 (1910–1929) 8.11.20212/7 and 811.20261/1494, Box 7460, NARA, hereafter referred to
     as Kalamatiano prison report.

          Other details of life in Russian prisons of this time come from Madeleine Z. Doty,
     "Revolutionary Justice," in the *Atlantic Monthly*, July–December 1918. Doty was a
     correspondent for the *New York Tribune*. She said prisoners feared a general massacre every
     night. Also, Letitia Bowler, "An Englishwoman's Experiences in Bolshevik Prisons," in
     Blackwood's Magazine, December 1921. Bowler, a teacher, said suicides were common. One
     prisoner drank poison while standing and talking to her. Another cut his throat with a piece of
     broken plate. See also Marguerite Harrison, *There's Always Tomorrow: The Story of a Checkered
     Life* (New York: Farrar & Rinehart, 1935), and Stan Harding, *The Underworld of State*
     (London: George Allen & Unwin, 1925).

3   A prison photo of Kalamatiano can be seen in William C. Levere's "An SAE in a Soviet
     Cell," *The History of Sigma Alpha Epsilon in the World War* (Menasha, WI: George Banis,
     1928), 240.

4   The Cheka considered establishments to be subversive if they acted against the state in some
     way, such as money laundering, hiding fugitives, or acting as a dead drop for messages. But
     Chekists often used the designation as an excuse to go in and seize whatever they wanted.

5   Harrison, *Marooned*, 249.

2: THE CHICAGO GROUP

1   X.B. Kalamatiano to Professor Samuel N. Harper, May 11, 1915, Harper letters, University of
     Chicago Library.

2   Kalamatiano to Harper, June 1, 1923, Harper letters.

3   C.P.V. Harper and Ronald Thompson, eds., *The Russia I Believe In: The Memoirs of Samuel N.
     Harper, 1902–1941* (University of Chicago Press, 1945), 1.

4   *Cap and Gown 1902*, University of Chicago yearbook, 337, 341, Hathitrust Visual Library,
     www.babel.hathitrust.org.

5   Crane was vice president of the Crane Company, one of the world's largest manufacturers
     of plumbing fixtures. They also made locomotive brakes in partnership with George
     Westinghouse. Crane made his first visit to Russia in 1887, to see some of his wife's relatives.
     He fell in love with the country—the military parades, the food, the Russian and Gypsy folk
     songs, the church choirs. Most of all, he bonded with the Slavic people. He then made several
     trips to Russia to establish the new Westinghouse Brake Company.

6   *History of American Intelligence*, Central Intelligence Agency Center for the Study of
     Intelligence, hereafter referred to as CIA CSI, www.cia.gov.

7   Dr. Harper saw Russia through Crane's eyes, and he was impressed. Harper hired Pavel
     Milyukov, a historian who had served time in a tsarist prison for his liberal political views, to
     occupy the first Slavic chair at the University of Chicago.

8   *Cap and Gown 1902*, 67.

9   Harper, *Memoirs*, 9.

10   Harper, *Memoirs*, 15.

3: AGENTS OF INFLUENCE

1   Harper, *Memoirs*, 32.

2   Valeriu Marcu, *Lenin*, trans. by E.E. Dickes (New York: Macmillan, 1928), 146–47. Marcu
     was a Romanian historian. An interview he conducted with Lenin in Zurich before the 1917
     revolution appears in Klaus Mann's *The best of modern European literature (Heart of Europe): an
     anthology of creative writing in Europe, 1920–1940* (Philadelphia: Blakiston, 1945).

3   Harper, *Memoirs*, 49–50.

4   Samuel N. Harper to Richard T. Crane, August 25, 1915, February 5, 1916, and February
     17, 1916; Joseph Tumulty to Crane, February 10, 1916; Harper to Crane, February 11, 1916;
     Crane to Harper, February 14, 1916; Tumulty to President Wilson, February 24, 1916; Harper
     letters.

5   Harper, *Memoirs*, 63.

6   Harper, *Memoirs*, 78–80.

7   Charles Richard Crane, *Memoirs of Charles R. Crane*, 232–38, Columbia University Rare Book
     and Manuscript Library, www.archive.org. Information on Crane's life and career, including
     direct quotations, is drawn from this 1934 memoir.

8   Edmund W. Starling, *Starling of the White House* (New York: Simon & Schuster, 1948), 47.

9   "Woodrow Wilson," Library of Congress, hereafter LOC, www.loc.gov.

10   Anonymous (Clinton Wallace Gilbert), *The Mirrors of Washington* (New York: Putnam's, 1921), 28.

11   Crane, *Memoirs*, 250–51.

4: GO SEE THE ELEPHANT

1   See Barnes Carr, *Operation Whisper: the capture of Soviet Spies Morris and Lona Cohen*
     (Lebanon, NH: ForeEdge, an imprint of University Press of New England, 2016).

2   Author's interviews with Richard Spence, PhD, history professor at the University of Idaho.
     Spence has written biographies of two of the Lenin Plot's key conspirators, Sidney Reilly
     and Boris Savinkov. Earlier writers have given Kalamatiano's birthplace as Vilimar, Austria,
     as listed on his Illinois death certificate. That information apparently was supplied by
     Kalamatiano's widow.

3   *Wesleyan Argus*, May 1, 1900, Illinois Wesleyan University, Bloomington, IL. In this untitled
     news article in the student newspaper, Vera alluded to her years in France as she described
     the lectures on Russia that she was giving while teaching at the university. Tate Archives and
     Special Collections, the Ames Library, Illinois Wesleyan University.

4   A SUCCESSFUL BOOK/TALENTED WOMAN WINS FAME, *Daily Pantagraph*, Bloomington, IL, July
     20, 1903. Unsigned book review reprinted from the *Chicago Record-Herald*.

5   SELLS LACE IN AID OF PEASANTS, *San Francisco Call*, February 3, 1908.

6   C.P. BLUMENTHAL IS NOW JUDGE IN RUSSIA, *Daily Pantagraph*, July 7, 1919. Reprint of an
     interview of Blumenthal conducted in Russia by C.P.R. Wright of the *Chicago Daily News*.
     Unless otherwise noted, information in this chapter on Blumenthal's background in Russia
     and America is drawn from this interview.

7   *Fortieth Annual Catalogue of Courses*, Illinois Wesleyan University, 1897.

8   C.P. BLUMENTHAL, *Daily Pantagraph*, July 7, 1919.

9   Spence interviews.

10   Robert B.D. Hartman, "Saga de Blumenthal," *From the Alumni Message Center* newsletter,
     Culver Academies, Culver, IN, June 1991. Hartman drew on de Blumenthal's personnel file for
     details of his years at Culver.

11   John Snodgrass, "Trade and Industries of Russia," in *Russia: A Handbook on Commercial and Industrial Conditions, Special Consular Reports*, vols. 59–66 (Washington: Government Printing Office, 1913), 61. Snodgrass was U.S. consul general in Moscow. He wrote this report for the U.S. Department of Commerce, Bureau of Foreign and Domestic Commerce.

12   A SUCCESSFUL BOOK, *Daily Pantagraph*, July 20, 1903. The book was titled *Folk Tales from the Russian* (Chicago: Rand, McNally, 1903). She wrote the book as Verra de Blumenthal. It was first published by Charles Carrington, Paris, 1897.

13   RUSSIANS TO LOCATE IN LOWER CALIFORNIA, *Washington* (DC) *Times*, September 6, 1905.

14   CAPTAIN DE BLUMENTHAL'S ABSENCE STARTS CONFLICTING RUMORS, *Los Angeles Herald*, September 14, 1906.

15   MADAME DE BLUMENTHAL TALKS OF HER HUSBAND, *Pasadena Daily News*, December 11, 1906.

16   Hartman, "Saga de Blumenthal."

5: XENOPHON THE TERRIBLE

1   Xenophon de Blumenthal-Kalamatiano transcript, University of Chicago registrar's office.

2   Track team statistics, *Cap and Gown, 1902* and *1903*.

3   William C. Levere, *The History of the Sigma Alpha Epsilon Fraternity* (Nashville: Benson Printing, 1911), 112–13.

4   Levere, *The History Sigma Alpha Epsilon*, 117.

5   *Racine* [WI] *City Directory, 1904* and *1906*, and conversation with Sue Kowbel-Keller, reference librarian, Racine Public Library.

6   Ray Heller, Case archivist, to author. Inflation calculations can be found at the U.S. Bureau of Labor Statistics website, www.bls.gov.

7   RUSSIAN TREATY AND THE IMPLEMENT TRADE, *Implement Age*, December 30, 1911.

8   *The International Harvester Company*, report by the U.S. Bureau of Commerce and Labor (Washington: Printing Office, 1913), 147–48.

9   Hartman, "Saga de Blumenthal."

10   NEW RUSSIAN TRADE PROJECT, *Chicago Commerce*, September 3, 1915; ORGANIZATION TO GO AFTER RUSSIAN TRADE, *Federal Trade Reporter*, September 15, 1915.

11   J.I. CASE THRESHING MACHINE, *Wall Street Journal*, December 18, 1917, www.calculator.net.

12   APOSTLE OF TRADE HERE FROM RUSSIA, *New York Times*, March 23, 1915.

13   FREE HARBOR DISTRICTS TO CAPTURE THE TRADE OF RUSSIA, *Evening Star* (Washington, DC), February 20, 1916.

14   Kalamatiano interview, *Chicago Commerce*, September 3, 1915.

6: WASHINGTON NAPPING

1   FIRST WORLD WAR CENTENARY: THE ASSASSINATION OF FRANZ FERDINAND AND HOW IT HAPPENED, *Daily Telegraph* (London), June 27, 2014.

2   A hand-held "automatic" pistol is actually semi-automatic. That is, each shot must be fired separately. A fully automatic pistol is called a machine pistol. Browning Old Model semi-automatics, also called self-loaders, were small, light, reliable, and easily concealed, making them a favorite of both detectives and terrorists.

3   John Patrick Finnegan and Roma Danysh, *Military Intelligence, Army Lineage Series* (Washington: Center of Military History, United States Army, 1998), 16–17, www.history.army.mil.

4   G.J.A. O'Toole, *Honorable Treachery: A History of U.S. Intelligence, Espionage, and Covert Action from the American Revolution to the CIA* (New York: Atlantic Monthly, 1991), 180, 214. O'Toole was a former CIA employee and historian.

5   Major General Sir Alfred Knox, *With the Russian Army, 1914–1917: Being chiefly extracts from the diary of a military attaché* (London: Hutchinson, 1921), xxi. Knox kept statistics throughout the war.

6   Maria Botchkareva, *Yashka* (New York: Frederick A. Stokes, 1918). Botchkareva dictated her book in Russian to Isaac Don Levine, who translated it into English. Quotations from Botchkareva in this and succeeding chapters are taken from this book. Levine covered the Russian Civil War for American newspapers. See his book, *Eyewitness to History: memoirs and reflections of a foreign correspondent for half a century* (New York: Hawthorn, 1973).

7   Botchkareva, Chapter VI, "I Enlist by the Grace of the Tsar."

8   Botchkareva, 84–85.

9   Knox, xxv. He quotes *Danzer's Armée Zeitung*, an Austrian weekly military affairs newspaper published in Vienna.

10   Anatoly Petrovich Zalyubovsky, "Supply of the Russian Army in the Great War with rifles, machine guns, revolvers and cartridges," The Russian Army in the Great War project archives. Online at www .grwar.ru. Hereafter referred to as RGR project. Zalyubovsky was a Russian weapons designer who was sent to the United States during the war to reorganize his country's purchase of American arms.

11   General Aleksiei Aleksieevich Brusilov, *A Soldier's Notebook, 1914–1919*, Chapter 1, "Before the War" (Westport, CT: Greenwood Press, 1971). This is a reprint from the original 1930 edition published by Macmillan in London.

7: A LAST HURRAH

1   Spence to author.

2   Botchkareva, Chapter VIII, "Wounded and Paralyzed."

3   Botchkareva, 114–15.

4   Brusilov, 245, 267–68.

5   Alexander Kerensky, *Russia and History's Turning Point* (New York: Duell, Sloan and Pearce, 1965), 147–48.

6   Major General Hugh C. Scott, U.S. chief of staff, report from Russia to the Secretary of War, July 25, 1917, 19, U.S. Department of State records, microfilm 367, roll 48, NARA.

7   Knox, 542.

8   Alexander F. Kerensky, *The Catastrophe: Kerensky's Own Story of the Russian Revolution* (New York: D. Appleton, 1927), 99.

9   Botchkareva, Chapter IX, "Eight Hours in German Hands."

10   "Timeline of the Russian Revolution (1917)," Marxists Internet Archive, www.marxists.org.

8: WHO'S IN CHARGE?

1   E.A. Vertsinsky, "Year of the Revolution: Memoirs of an Officer of the General Staff, 1917–1918," RGR project.

2   Lansing, 124–25.

3   Ralph E. Weber, *United States Diplomatic Codes and Ciphers, 1775–1938* (Chicago: Precedent Publishing, 1979), 246–48.

4   Robert Bruce Lockhart, *The Diaries of Sir Robert Bruce Lockhart, 1915–1938*, entry of Thursday, 16 September 1915 (London: Macmillan, 1973), 24–25.

5   Kerensky, *Turning Point*, 160.

6   Kerensky, *Catastrophe*, 29–30.

7   FINAL SCENE WITH THE TSAR: A MIDNIGHT INTERVIEW, *Manchester Guardian*, March 18, 1917, account given by a member of the executive committee of the Duma; GENERAL RUSSKY'S ACCOUNT OF THE CZAR'S ABDICATION, *Current History*, vol. 13 (1917), 272–74, a description by General Nicholas V. Russky, the Russian army's chief representative in abdication talks with Nicholas.

8   Kerensky, *Catastrophe*, 162–64.

9   Colonel A. Kavtaradze, "The June Offensive of the Russian Army in 1917," *Military-History*, 5:111-17, 1967, RGR project.

10   According to the service record of Petr Alexandrovich Polovtsov at the RGR project, he escaped from Russia in January 1918 while commander in chief of the Terek-Dagestan region. He was given an American passport, then disguised himself as a minister and got out aided by two British agents. He died at Monte Carlo.

9: LENIN'S GERMAN KEY

1   Testimony of Samuel N. Harper, *Bolshevik Propaganda Hearings Before a Subcommittee of the Committee on the Judiciary, United States Senate, Sixty-fifth Congress, third session, February 11, 1919, to March 10, 1919* (Washington: Government Printing Office, 1919), 94. The subcommittee chair was Senator Lee Overman of South Carolina. Hereafter referred to as Overman.

2   Marcu, 250.

3   Volkogonov, *Lenin*, 8–9.

4   Volkogonov, *Lenin*, 16.

5   Volkogonov, *Lenin*, 30.

6   A verst was equal to .6629 mile. The measurement is no longer used.

7   R.C. Elwood, *Inessa Armand: Revolutionary and feminist* (Cambridge University Press, 1992), 207.

8   Marcu, 65–66.

9   Elwood, 175. Elwood quotes Nikolay V. Valentinov, an Old Bolshevik who, along with others, chose not to reveal this information until three decades after Lenin's coup.

10   Bertram D. Wolfe, "Lenin and Inessa Armand," *Slavic Review*, vol. XXII (1963), 96–114.

11   Elwood, 249–50.

12   Lenin to Vorovsky, August 1918, as cited in Volkogonov, *Lenin*, 117.

13   Marcu, 237.

14   James Srodes, *Allen Dulles: Master of Spies* (Washington: Regnery, 1999), 80–81.

15   Marcu, 103.

10: THE YANKS ARE COMING

1   See Friedrich Engels, *Anti-Dühring: Herr Dühring's Revolution in Science* (Moscow: Progress Publishers, 1947). This a reprint of the original serialized version that appeared in *Vorwärts*, January 3, 1877–July 7, 1878.

2   Correspondence with Peter Eltsov, PhD. Eltsov was born and raised in Russia and came to the United States in the nineties. He is a professor of international relations at the National Defense University in Washington.

3   Marcu, 138.

4   The full name was the Party of the Socialist Revolutionaries. But the common initialism SR is most used.

5   Music and lyrics by Albert Piantadosi and Alfred Bryan (New York: Leo Feist, 1915). See "Songs of the Peace Movement of World War I" at the website of the Library of Congress, www.loc.gov.

6   Albert C. Anderson, editor and publisher, the *Southern Sentinel*, Ripley, MS.

7   "American Ship Casualties of the World War," Naval History and Heritage Command, at www .history.navy.mil. The tanker *Healdton* was sunk on March 21, 1917, north of the Netherlands.

8   David Paull Nickles, "Under the Wire: How the Telegraph Changed Diplomacy," CIA CSI. To view a copy of the telegram, see "The Zimmermann Telegram" on the NARA website.

9   Copyright 1917 by George M. Cohan.

10   Hugh Rockoff, "The Economics of World War I," Working Paper 10580, the National Bureau of Economic Research, Cambridge, MA, www.nber.org.

11   "Historical National Population Estimates," U.S. Census Bureau, 1918, www.census.gov.

12   Edith Wilson biography, National First Ladies' Library, www.firstladies.org.

13   Starling, Chapter Four, "Wilson—the courtship."

14   Wilson Wedding Quiet and Simple, *Oakley Herald*, Oakley, ID, December 24, 1915.

11: SEND IN THE SPIES

1   Alton Earl Ingram, "The Root Mission to Russia, 1917" (Baton Rouge: Louisiana State University Historical Dissertations and Theses, 1970), 163, 177, www.digitalcommons.lsu.edu. Monetary inflation calculations come from Morgan Friedman, www.westegg.com.

2   See Hugh Lennox Scott, *Some Memories of a Soldier* (New York: Century, 1928), 29. Scott studied Indian history and languages while he was in the West with the Seventh Cavalry, Custer's old outfit. Among his published works is an account of Custer's last stand as related to him by Chief Feather Earring, a Sioux warrior at the Battle of Little Big Horn.

3   Scott, 583.

4   Root Commission report, Scott to Secretary of War Baker, filed by wireless from the USS *Buffalo* en route from Vladivostok to Seattle, July 25, 1917, NARA.

5   Raymond Robins testimony, Overman, 780. Quotations from Robins in this and other chapters come from this testimony.

6   Sir George Buchanan, *My Mission to Russia and Other Diplomatic Memories, Vol. II* (London: Cassell, 1923), 137, www.archive.org.

7   George V. Lomonosoff, *Memoirs of the Russian Revolution*, trans. by D.H. Dubrowsky and Robert T. Williams (New York: Rand School of Social Science, 1919), 18, Hathitrust.

8   Kerensky, *Turning Point*, 60–61.

9   Ingram, 187–88.

10   Norman E. Saul, *The Life and Times of Charles R. Crane, 1858–1939* (Lanham, MD: Lexington Books, 2013), 130.

11   Kavtaradze, RGR project.

12   Soldiers Defy Their Committees, *Times* (London), July 21, 1917.

13   David R. Francis to Secretary of State, November 7 (Western calendar), 1917, Lansing Papers, Box 2, Folder 2, Seely G. Mudd Manuscript Library, Princeton University, www.webspace .princeton.edu.

14   Leon Trotsky, "The Capture of the Winter Palace," *The History of the Russian Revolution*, vol. III, chap. 45 (New York: Simon & Schuster, 1933), Marxists Internet Archive.

15   N.N. Sukanov, *The Russian Revolution 1917: Eyewitness Account, Volume II*, trans. by Joel Carmichael (New York: Harper, 1955), 642, www.archive.org. Nikolai Nikolaevich Sukanov (né Himmer) was a Socialist Revolutionary who had known Lenin and Trotsky in the old days

in Paris. He was active in the 1905 revolution, and in 1917 became a member of the executive committee of the Petrograd Soviet.

16   "Reminiscences of DeWitt Clinton Poole," 1952 unpublished typescript, Columbia Center for Oral History, Columbia University, 105.

17   Bessie Beatty, *The Red Heart of Russia* (New York: Century, 1918), 216–17. Like John Reed and Louise Bryant, Beatty wrote her stories from the Bolshevik point of view and rejected facts she didn't agree with. When she later had a women's chat show on radio in New York, *Time* magazine called her one of the "Mrs.-Know-It-Alls" on the air.

18   Sukanov, 620.

19   Russia Under the Bolshevists, *Times*, November 20, 1917.

20   Charles F. Horne and Walter F. Austin, eds., *The Great Events of the Great War, Volume V* (New York: National Alumni, 1920), 336.

21   The Fight for the Kremlin, *Times*, November 19, 1917; Russian Peace Rumours in Stockholm, *Times*, November 20, 1917.

22   Lansing statement, December 4, 1917, Lansing Papers, Princeton, Box 3, Folder 2. Lansing spelled Lenin's name the way it was pronounced in Russian, as "L'neen." The Lenine spelling was common in English at the time.

23   Starling, 47.

24   Lansing to Wilson, June 8, 1917, *The Papers of Woodrow Wilson*, ed. by Arthur S. Link, (Princeton: Princeton University Press, 1966), 42:463.

12: INDOOR MINDS

1   Ted Morgan, *Maugham: a biography* (New York: Simon & Schuster, 1981), 226.

2   W. Somerset Maugham, *Ashenden: or, The British Agent* (New York: Grosset & Dunlap, 1928).

3   W. Somerset Maugham to William Wiseman, receipt of cash, July 18, 1917, in Wiseman Papers, File 91-112, as cited in Robert Lorin Calder, *W. Somerset Maugham and the Quest for Freedom*, Appendix B (New York: Doubleday, 1973), 276.

4   Morgan, 261.

5   Rhodri Jeffreys-Jones, "W. Somerset Maugham: Anglo-American Agent in Revolutionary Russia," *American Quarterly* (Spring 1976), 28:92.

6   W. Somerset Maugham, *A Writer's Notebook* (New York: Penguin Books, 1984), 136.

7   Maugham, *Ashenden*, 294.

8   Maugham, *Notebook*, 146–47. In German, "Katzenjammer" means a hangover. The literal translation is "the wailing of cats." *Katzenjammer Kids* is a comic strip created by a German American, Rudolph Dirks, in 1897 and is still in syndication. It's the longest-running comic strip in history.

9   Susan Robbins Watson to author. Watson is manager of the American Red Cross historical archives.

10   Antony C. Sutton, *Wall Street and the Bolshevik Revolution* (West Hoathly, England: Clairview Books, 2001), Chapter V, "The American Red Cross Mission to Russia–1917," online at www .reformed-theology.org.

11   Overman, 779.

12   Overman, 775.

13   Overman, 794–95.

14   Overman, 770, 795.

15   Lockhart, *Diaries*, 33.

13: WANTED: ONE DICTATOR

1   Vancouver Barracks, National Park Service, www.nps.gov.

2   Edwin Bentley Quiner, *Quiner Scrapbooks: Correspondence of the Wisconsin Volunteers,*
     1861–1865, 9:101, Wisconsin Historical Society, www.content.wisconsinhistory.org.

3   *Diaries of Van S. Bennett,* Thursday, May 28, 1863, vol. 1, 1863–1864, in *Quiner Scrapbooks,*
     9:101.

4   *Documents of the Senate of the State of New York, 89th session (1864),* II:9 (Albany: Legislative
     Printer, 1865).

5   Romantic Career of Colonel Poole, Now Dead, in Indian Service, in War
     and in Lincoln's Private Office, *Madison* (WI) *Democrat,* December 1, 1917;
     Personnel record of D.C. Poole, Wisconsin Veterans Museum, www.wisveteransmuseum
     .pastperfectonline.com.

6   *Madison, Wisconsin, City Directory, 1902* (Madison: G.R. Angell, 1902), 356, State of
     Wisconsin Collection, www.digicoll.library.wisc.edu.

7   *Madison, Wisconsin, City Directory, 1902.*

8   *Tychoberahn 1902,* Madison High School, Dane County Historical Society via Wisconsin
     Historical Society.

9   "Historical Timelines," University of Wisconsin-Madison, www.wisc.edu.

10   DeWitt Clinton Poole Jr. transcript, registrar's office, University of Wisconsin-Madison.

11   *Badger for 1907,* University of Wisconsin, www.digital.library.wisc.edu.

12   Untitled article, *Sunday Cardinal,* February 29, 1906. The *Daily Cardinal* is one of America's
     oldest student newspapers, published independent of the University of Wisconsin.

13   *United States Army and Navy Journal and Gazette* (New York: Army and Navy Journal, Inc.),
     October 29, 1904, 42:210, www.catalog.hathitrust.org.

14   Information on GW comes from the George Washington University Library, Americana
     Collection, including the student yearbook, the *1910 Cherry Tree,* and the independent student
     newspaper, the *University Hatchet,* for 1910, www.archive.com.

15   DeWitt C. Poole, Former U.S. Consul Official, Dies, *Capital Times* (Madison, WI),
     September 4, 1952; Sunday Thoughts, *Wisconsin State Journal,* September 2, 1928; Alexius
     Bass, All Around the Town, *Capital Times,* September 10, 1952.

16   Summers to Francis, August 17, 1917, Francis Letters.

17   Consul General at Moscow (Summers) to the Secretary of State, December 6, 1917,
     763.72/8033, *FRUS, 1918, Russia, Volume II,* www.history.state.gov.

18   The consul general at Moscow (Summers) to the Secretary of State, November 8, 1917,
     861.00/934, *FRUS, 1918, Russia, Volume II.*

19   The Secretary of State to President Wilson, December 10, 1917, *FRUS, Lansing Papers,*
     1914–1920, Volume II, 861.00/807a.

20   Lansing to Wilson, December 10, 1917, 861.00/807a.

21   Lansing to Wilson, December 10, 1917, 861.00/807a. Lansing and Poole both from time to
     time spelled Kaledin phonetically, as in *Kala-deen.*

22   Draft Telegram to the Ambassador in Great Britain (Page), December 12, 1917, *FRUS, Lansing
     Papers, Volume II,* 861.00/804d. Lansing's wire was sent the next day.

14: MONEY, GUNS, CHAOS

1   Poole, "Reminiscences," 141.

2   Poole, "Reminiscences," 141.

3   Poole, "Reminiscences," 139.

4   Poole, "Reminiscences," 96, 170–71.

5   Poole to Francis, "Confidential report to the ambassador respecting the movement in the Don country for the restoration of order in Russia, the holding of a constitutional assembly, and the continuance of the war," January 28, 1918, David R. Francis Papers, Missouri Historical Society Archives, St. Louis.

6   Crane, 327.

7   Poole to Francis, "Confidential report."

8   THE TRIAL OF BORIS SAVINKOV, August 27, 1924, *Pravda*, August 30, 1924, transcript trans. by Emanuel Aronsberg, courtesy of the Hoover Institution on War, Revolution and Peace, Stanford University. Hereafter referred to as Savinkov testimony.

9   William Phillips, *Ventures in Diplomacy* (London: John Murray, 1955), 40. Phillips was Third Assistant Secretary of State at this time.

10   Poole to Department of State, January 18, 1918, Francis Letters.

11   The Special Representative (House) to the Secretary of State, December 2, 1917, 763.72/7926, *FRUS, 1918, Russia, Volume II.*

12   Phillips, 40–41.

13   The Consul at Tiflis (Smith) to the Secretary of State, November 23, 1917, 861.00/711, *FRUS, 1918, Russia, Volume II.*

14   COSSACKS' WAR WITH BOLSHEVISM, *Times*, January 29, 1918; COSSACK QUARRELS, *Times*, February 8, 1918.

15   DEATH OF GEN. KALEDIN REPORTED, *Times*, February 20, 1918; KALEDIN'S SUICIDE, *Times*, February 21, 1918.

16   COSSACKS FIGHT AGAINST BOLSHEVISTS, *Times*, February 21, 1918.

15: A REMARKABLE AMERICAN

1   Poole, "Reminiscences," 208.

2   Russian Propaganda Hearing Before a Subcommittee on Foreign Relations, United States Senate, Sixty-sixth Congress, Second Session, 1920, (Washington: GPO, 1920), 360. Hereafter referred to as Foreign Relations hearing.

3   Kalamatiano's federal service record from the Consular Bureau of the U.S. Department of State, National Personnel Records Center, NARA, St. Louis. Hereafter cited as Kalamatiano personnel file.

4   Summers to Francis, November 30, 1917, Francis Papers.

5   David R. Francis, *Russia from the American Embassy, April, 1916–November, 1918* (New York: Charles Scribner's Sons, 1921), 320–21.

6   DeWitt Poole to Ambassador David R. Francis, June 21, 1918, Francis Papers.

7   Kalamatiano to Poole, undated report, courtesy of NARA. Kalamatiano smuggled this report out of prison a few weeks after he was arrested. He probably gave it to a Norwegian consul who visited him.

8   Poole, "Reminiscences," 209.

9   George Alexander Hill, *Go Spy the Land* (London: Biteback Publishing, 2014), 231. Reprint of original Cassell edition, 1932.

10   Sidney George Reilly and Pepita Bobadilla, *Britain's Master Spy: The Adventures of Sidney Reilly* (Northvale: Dorset, 1985), 14. Reprint of original 1932 Harper Bros. edition. Reilly started this reminiscence of his adventures in Russia, and Pepita, his last wife, completed it after

his death. Some parts of the book are obviously fanciful but George Hill vouches for it "to a certain extent." See Hill, 231.

11   Robert Hamilton Bruce Lockhart, *Memoirs of a British Agent: being an account of the author's early life in many lands and of his official mission to Moscow in 1918* (New York: G.P. Putnam's Sons, 1933), 252–53. The description of Radek comes from Victor Serge, *Memoirs of a Revolutionary 1901–1941*, trans. by Peter Sedgewick (London: Oxford, 1963), 159. Radek's support of Trotsky got him shipped off to a labor camp during Stalin's purge of Old Bolsheviks. He was reportedly shot at Stalin's order in 1939.

12   Overman, 786.

13   Harrison, *There's Always Tomorrow*, 305–6.

14   V.I. Lenin, "Draft Decree on the Dissolution of the Constituent Assembly," *Collected Works*, vol. 26 (Moscow: Progress Publishers, 1972), 434–82. Published in *Izvestia* according to the original manuscript, www.marxists.org.

15   Total population, European Russia plus Siberia, was about 180,000,000. Russia, China, and India were the most populous countries in the world. Russia had the largest land mass, about one sixth of the world's area.

16   Raymond Robins put the figure of urban proletariat trained in revolutionary socialism at about nine percent of the total Russian population. Overman, 817.

17   Xenophon Kalamatiano, "The Russian Soviet Government," Report No. 1, Office of the Commissioner of the United States, Riga, to the Secretary of State, No. 1171, received Washington, September 14, 1921, NARA.

18   "European Russia," *Russia: A Journal of Russian-American Trade*, January 1918, 24.

19   Lenin, "Theses on the Constituent Assembly," *Collected Works*, 379–83. Published in *Pravda*, according to the manuscript, verified with a typewritten copy bearing Lenin's corrections, www.marxists.org.

20   RUSSIAN COUP D'ÉTAT, *Times*, January 21, 1918.

21   'RED SUNDAY' IN MOSCOW, *Times*, January 23, 1918.

22   DEATH TO ALL ENEMIES, *Times*, January 24, 1918.

23   Tony Cliff, "The Peace of Brest-Litovsk," www.marxists.org.

24   Overman, 807.

25   Transcript of President Wilson's speech in Baltimore, April 6, 1918, in *Current History*, vol. VII, part I, no. 2 (May 1918), 276.

16: A CONFEDERATE AT COURT

1   Leon Trotsky, "Work, Discipline, Order," report to the Moscow City Conference of the Russian Communist Party, March 28, 1918, in *The Military Writings of Leon Trotsky*, vol. 1, 1918 (New York: Pathfinder, 1971), via Marxists Internet Archive, www.marxists.org.

2   Trotsky, "Work, Discipline, Order."

3   Francis to Lansing, December 29, 1917, Lansing Papers, Box 2, Folder 3.

4   Horne and Austin, VI:36. Address by Lenin on February 23, 1918, stating his views of the treaty.

5   The Ambassador in Russia to the Secretary of State, February 20, 1918, 861.00/1142, *FRUS, 1918, Russia, Volume I*.

6   The U.S. consulate in Petrograd was a more modest, utilitarian-looking office building at 37 Furshtatskaya Ulitz.

7   GOVERNOR FRANCIS GIVES $200 BAIL, *Tacoma* (WA) *Times*, March 12, 1910, online at www .chroncilingamerica.loc.gov.

8   Francis, *Russia*, 3, 4, 10.

9   Lockhart, *British Agent*, 272, 279.

10   Page to State Department, March 27, 1917, in Burton J. Hendrick, *The Life and Letters of Walter H.
        Page*, Chapter XXII, "Waging Neutrality" (Garden City: Doubleday, 1923), www.lib.byu.edu.

11   Lockhart, *British Agent*, 4.

12   Overman, 564. Reed admitted to Congress that his employer was the International Bureau of
        Revolutionary Propaganda, attached to the Commissariat for Foreign Affairs.

13   William Phillips, *Ventures in Diplomacy* (London: John Murray, 1955), 38–39. Phillips was
        Third Assistant Secretary of State at the time.

14   Overman, 808.

15   Overman, 808–10. Robins said this wire was sent, in State Department cipher, just before the
        Treaty of Brest-Litovsk was ratified.

16   The Chargé in Sweden (Whitehouse) to the Secretary of State, November 13, 1918,
        861.24/105, *FRUS, 1918, Russia, Volume III*.

17: HEADHUNTERS AND MOLES

1   THE MISERIES OF RUSSIA, *Times*, July 23, 1918.

2   PETROGRAD CHOLERA EPIDEMIC, *Times*, July 30, 1918.

3   Sejriyon Khromov, ed., *Felix Dzerzhinsky: a biography* (Moscow: Progress Publishers, 1988),
        Chapter One, "Childhood and Youth," and Chapter Five, "Protecting the Revolution." Online
        at www.redstarpublishers.org.

4   Marguerite Harrison, DIRECTOR OF RED TERROR WAS A NOBLE, *New York Times*, August 1, 1926.

5   John Earl Haynes, Harvey Klehr, and Alexander Vassiliev, *Spies: The Rise and Fall of the KGB in
        America* (New Haven: Yale University Press, 2009), xxx. "The vetting process started," former
        Soviet spy Vassiliev recalled, "and I was 'clean': no Jews in either my background or my wife's."
        The name of the security service would be changed through mergers and reorganizations over
        the years to GPU, OGPU, NKVD, NKGB, MVD, MGB, MVD, KGB, FSK, and now FSB,
        the Federal Security Service.

6   Russian President Vladimir Putin was a KGB officer in the former East Germany during that period.

7   Poole, "Reminiscences," 135.

8   Poole to Francis, May 3, 1918, Francis Papers.

9   Klaus Karttunen, "Fernand Grenard," *Persons of Indian Studies*, February 13, 2017. Online at
        www.whowaswho.indology.info.

10   Paul Cambon, *Correspondence 1870–1924*, vol. 3 (Paris: Éditions Bernard Grasset, 1946), 180,
        as quoted in Michael Jabara Carley, *Revolution and Intervention: The French Government and
        the Russian Civil War* (Montréal: McGill-Queen's University Press, 1983), 23.

11   Carley, 44.

12   Galkina to author. See also Yuliya Mikhailovna Galkina, "To the question of the French
        involvement in the Lockhart affair: Who is Henri Vertamon?" in cleo No. 3, 2018, Institute of
        Humanities and Arts, Ural Federal University, 176–86, www.academia.edu.

13   Poole, "Reminiscences," 290–91.

14   Phillipe Madelin, *Dans le secret des services: La France malade de ses espions?* (Paris: Éditions
        Denoël, 2007), 19, www.rackcdn.co.

15   Nicolas Skopinski, "Charles Adolphe Faux-Pas Bidet, l'ennemi de Trotski," *Ouest-France*,
        November 6, 2017, www.ouest-france.fr.

16   Skopinski, "Charles Adolphe Faux-Pas Bidet."

17   Louis de Robien, *The Diary of a Diplomat in Russia, 1917–1918*, trans. by Camilla Sykes (New York: Praeger, 1970), 149.

18   Poole, "Reminiscences," 175.

19   Poole, "Reminiscences," 262, 265.

18: THE INVASION OF RUSSIA

1   Lockhart, *British Agent*, 76.

2   Robert Hamilton Bruce Lockhart, *The Diaries of Sir Robert Bruce Lockhart*, ed. by Kenneth Young (New York: St. Martin's, 1974), 30. The original was published in 1973 by Macmillan London.

3   Spence to author.

4   Overman, 801. Raymond Robins recounted what Lockhart had told him.

5   Buchanan, *My Mission to Russia*, 225–26; Buchanan to Foreign Office, November 27, 1917.

6   Overman, 780–81.

7   Overman, 787.

8   Buchanan, *My Mission to Russia*, 244.

9   Pavel Malkov, *Reminiscences of a Kremlin Commandant*, trans. by V. Dutt (Moscow: Progress Publishers, 1959), 269.

10   Lockhart, *British Agent*, 224.

11   Ludwig C.A.K. Martens testimony, Foreign Relations hearing, 157.

12   Crane, 283–84.

13   Malkov, *Reminiscences*, 270.

14   Malkov, *Reminiscences*, 271.

15   Lockhart, *British Agent*, 238.

16   Overman, 874.

17   Murmansk was also the main port for receiving Allied supplies during World War II. The trip was called the Murmansk Run.

18   Allen F. Chew, "Fighting the Russians in Winter: Three case studies," *Leavenworth Papers*, No. 5 (December 1981), Combat Studies Institute, Fort Leavenworth, KS, online at www .armyupress.army.mil. Dr. Chew compares the difficulties faced by Napoléon, Hitler, and the Allies in 1918–1919 while fighting winter wars against Russia.

19   Carl LaVO, "Olympian Effort to Save the Olympia," *Naval History Magazine* 30, no. 4 (August 2016), U.S. Naval Institute, www.usni.org. The *Olympia* was called the "hot rod of the Navy." It's the only surviving steel American warship from the 19th century (commissioned in 1895).

20   Jon Hoppe, "The Russian Intervention of 1918–1919," U.S. Naval Institute, www.navalhistory.org.

21   Lindley, "Report on the Work of the British Mission."

22   The Commanding Officer of the USS *Olympia* (Bierer) to the Commander, U.S. Naval Forces Operating in European Waters (Sims), "Temporary Agreement owing to Exceptional Circumstances between the representatives in Murmansk of Great Britain, United States of America, and France, and the Presidium of the Murmansk Regional Council," July 6, 1918, 861.00/11422, *FRUS, 1918, Russia, Volume II*. The State Department officially approved the agreement on October 14, well after the Murmansk and Archangel landings.

19: FIRST SHOTS FIRED

1   Polk was named under secretary of state in 1919 and then acting secretary for a while in 1920.

2   Hendrick, Chapter XXII.

3   "In the Driftway," *Nation* 107:703 (December 7, 1918), www.books.google.com.

4   *Woodrow Wilson, War Messages*, April 2, 1917, Sixty-fifth Congress, first session, Senate Document No. 5, Serial No. 7264, Washington, DC, 1917, www.lib.byu.edu.

5   Lansing to Wilson, November 20, 1915, as cited in "Department of State and Counterintelligence," National Counterintelligence Center, Federation of American Scientists, www.fas.org. Unless otherwise noted, information in this chapter on the Office of the Special Agent and the Bureau of Secret Intelligence comes from that source and from "Diplomatic Security Service: Then and Now," U.S. Department of State, Bureau of Diplomatic Security, www.state.gov. The Office of the Special Agent and the Bureau of Secret Intelligence went through many changes over the years and emerged as today's Bureau of Diplomatic Security.

6   Leland Harrison's biography courtesy of the Harvard University Archives, Pusey Library.

7   "Special Agents, Special Threats/Creating the Office of the Chief Special Agent, 1914–1933," *History of the Bureau of Diplomatic Security*, Chapter 1, U.S. State Department, www.state.gov. Information on Harrison comes from this source.

8   Robert Lansing, *War Memoirs of Robert Lansing, Secretary of State* (New York: Bobbs-Merrill, 1935), 325–26, www.babel.hathitrust.org.

9   George F. Kennan, *Soviet-American Relations, 1917–1920, Vol. II, The Decision to Intervene* (New York: Antheneum, 1967), 159.

10 In *FRUS, 1918, Russia, Volume II*: The Acting Secretary of State (Polk) to the Ambassador in Japan (Morris), January 12, 1918, 861.00/956; The Ambassador in Japan (Morris) to the Secretary of State, January 13, 1918, 861.00/948; The Japanese Chargé (Tanaka) to the Secretary of State, January 14, 1918, 861.00/951; and The Consul at Vladivostok (Caldwell) to the Secretary of State, April 5, 1918, 861.00/1429.

20: THE SAVINKOV METHOD

1   Alice Stone Blackwell, ed., *The Little Grandmother of the Russian Revolution: Reminiscences and Letters of Catherine Breshkovsky* (Boston: Little, Brown, 1917), 108.

2   Unless otherwise noted, information in this chapter on the assassination of Plehve is drawn from Boris Savinkov, *Memoirs of a Terrorist*, trans. by Joseph Shaplen (New York: Albert & Charles Boni, 1931).

3   Herman Rosenthal and Max Rosenthal, "Kishinef (Kishinev)," *Jewish Encyclopedia*. Online at www.jewishencyclopedia.com.

4   "Visions of Terror," University of California at Berkeley, www.stpetersburg.berkeley.edu, quoting Dmitry M. Alekseno, "From the Experience of the Intelligence Services of the Russian Empire in Combating Terrorists," *High-Impact Terrorism: Terrorist Proceedings of a Russian-American Workshop* (Washington: National Academy Press, 2002), 69–75. This site contains a map of the routes Savinkov and his bombers took to the murder scene.

5   Savinkov, *Memoirs*, 349.

6   V. Ropshin, *The Pale Horse*, trans. by Z. Vengerova (publisher not given, 1917). A later edition is B.V. Savinkov, *The Pale Horse* (Miami: Hardpress, 2015).

7   Ropshin (Boris Savinkov), *What Never Happened: A Novel of the Revolution*, trans. by Thomas Seltzer (New York: Alfred A. Knopf, 1917), 31. Events in the book occur following the Russian defeat by the Japanese in 1905.

8   A new edition of Bely's translated book has been published by the Indiana University Press in Bloomington, 2018.

9   In Russia, to "rehabilitate" means to be returned to legitimacy, to acceptance by the government.

10   "Kerenski and Korniloff," *Fortnightly Review,* vol. 110 (1918): 341.

11   Savinkov testimony, 7–8.

12   For more on Savinkov's life and career, see Savinkov, *Memoirs*; Karol Wędziagolski, *Boris Savinkov: portrait of a terrorist,* trans. by Margaret Patoski (Clifton: Kingston Press, 1988); Richard B. Spence, *Boris Savinkov: Renegade on the Left* (Boulder: East European Monographs, 1991); and Winston Churchill, *Great Contemporaries* (London: T. Butterworth, 1937).

21: MURDER THEM ALL

1   Paul Kesaris, ed., *Confidential U.S. Diplomatic Post Records, Part I, Russia, 1914–1918,* Reel 9 (Frederick, MD: University Publications of America, 1982), 450-54, 582-95, 620, as cited in David S. Foglesong, *America's Secret War Against Bolshevism* (Chapel Hill: University of North Carolina Press, 1995), 115–16.

2   Richard Deacon, *The British Connection: Russia's Manipulation of British Individuals and Institutions* (London: Hamish Hamilton, 1979), 28, 263. Lansing confirmed to Crosby that money for anti-Soviet forces should be given "secretly and indirectly." See Foglesong 88, 90, 92, 103.

3   Savinkov testimony, 16. Boris made a deal in advance with Dzerzhinsky to say what the Cheka chief wanted him to say in his trial. In return, Savinkov would be rehabilitated and given a job in the new Soviet state. Thus, some parts of Savinkov's testimony undoubtedly were flavored to Dzerzhinsky's taste and cannot be trusted. Other sources, though, have verified that Boris was indeed on the Allied payroll in the summer of 1918 and plotted a coup with the Western powers.

4   Savinkov testimony, 16–17.

5   Savinkov testimony, 16–17.

6   "The Currency of Russia under the Soviet Government," from the *Federal Reserve Bulletin,* October 1922, via *Economic World,* November 25, 1922, 773; Testimony of O.L. Richard, Royal Indemnity Company vs. F. Gusman and sons, New York Supreme Court, Appellate Division, First Judicial Department (1929), 108, 110, 112–113, www.books.google.com. According to testimony, the value of a 1919 ruble was 26 cents (US).

7   Savinkov testimony, 17, 19.

8   Savinkov testimony, 14.

9   Savinkov testimony, 18.

10   Alexander Orlov, *The March of Time: Reminiscences* (London: St Ermin's Press, 2004), 81–82. Orlov was a soldier in the imperial army and an early Bolshevik. He headed the NKVD's illegals directorate in the 1930s and had access to documents from the 1917 revolution, the Bolshevik coup, and the Russian Civil War. He was head of Soviet spy operations in Spain before defecting to the United States to avoid assassination during Stalin's purge of Old Bolsheviks. He lived for years in America undetected by the FBI.

11   D.L. Golinkov and S.N. Semanov, "Yaroslavl Revolt of 1918," *Great Soviet Encyclopedia* (New York: Macmillan, 1979).

12   Alexander Khodnev, "A Benchmark History of Yaroslavl in the Twentieth Century," *Regional Russia in Transition: Studies from Yaroslavl,* Jeffrey W. Hahn, ed. (Washington: Woodrow Wilson Center Press, 2001), 26.

13   Lockhart, *British Agent,* 289.

14   Savinkov testimony, 16.

15   Savinkov testimony, 42.

16   "Oil and Gas Developments," *Standard Daily Trade Service*, February 2, 1920, 233, online at
      www.books.google.com.

17   "Crude oil prices," *Literary Digest*, March 6, 1920, 44, www.archive.org. The United States
      produced 69 percent of the world's oil in 1919 and commanded the highest prices, up to
      $5.25 a barrel ($78.88 in 2019 dollars). Some foreign producers sold crude oil for 45 cents
      a barrel.

18   Foreign Office 371/3332/92708 and FO 371/3332/95780, National Archives, Kew, England.

19   Orlov, 82.

22: GENTLEMAN AND HUSTLER

1   According to the Imperial War Museum, the RFC had become the Royal Air Force the
      month before Reilly arrived in Moscow. See "Royal Flying Corps and Royal Air Force Family
      History," www.iwm.org.uk.

2   Beatty, 440.

3   Description of the four categories of food cards, *Izvestia*, August 22, 1918, trans. and reported
      by the *Times*, September 1, 1918.

4   Malkov, *Reminiscences*, 125.

5   Report on Russian food situation, *Cologne Gazette*, July 31, 1918, via the *Times*.

6   Lindley, "Report on the Work of the British Mission to North Russia," 164.

7   Report on conditions in Russia, *Il Secolo*, Milan, July 31, 1918, via the *Times*.

8   Reilly, *Britain's Master Spy*, 4–5.

9   Reilly, *Britain's Master Spy*, 6–7.

10   Reilly, *Britain's Master Spy*, 14.

11   Lockhart, *British Agent*, 273–74.

12   Lockhart, *British Agent*, 273–74.

13   Spence, *Reilly*, 6.

14   "Paris Okhrana 1885–1905," CIA CSI.

15   Spence, *Reilly*, 16.

16   Cook, *Her Majesty's Secret Service*, 127.

17   Spence, *Reilly*, xvi.

18   Nina Berberova, a Russian historian who knew Moura, said her father was Ignaty Platonovich
      Zakrevsky, though she claimed the Zakrevskaya surname. Benckendorff was the name of
      Moura's first husband. She's remembered today as Moura Budberg, after another husband. See
      Berberova's *Moura: The Dangerous Life of the Baroness Budberg*, trans. by Marian Schwartz and
      Richard D. Sylvester (New York Review of Books, 2005), 1–2, 317.

19   Lockhart, *Diaries*, 30.

20   Cable CXM 159, March 29, 1918, Reilly Papers, as cited by Cook, *Her Majesty's Secret Service*, 135.

21   Reilly, *Britain's Master Spy*, 19.

23: PARIAHS OF THE WORLD

1   Orlov, 126–31.

2   Shmidkhen's real name reportedly was Buikis. Bredis was actually named Sprogis.

3   Reilly, *Britain's Master Spy*, 26.

4   Viktor Eduardovich Kingisepp, "The Lockhart Case (1918)," September 8, 1918. This
      report contains Peters's official testimony on the case. Courtesy of Professor John Puckett in
      Budapest, who translated the report for publication.

5   Gustav Hilger and Alfred G. Meyer, *The Incompatible Allies: A Memoir-History of German-Soviet Relations, 1918–1941* (New York: Macmillan, 1953), 3–6. These pages contain an eyewitness account of the Mirbach assassination.

6   Telegrams via Exchange Telegraph Company, London, as reported in the *Times*, July 7, 1918.

7   For more information on the murder of the Romanovs, including an eyewitness account by one of the killers, see George Gustav Telberg, Robert Wilton, and N. Sokolov, *The Last Days of the Romanovs* (New York: George H. Duran, 1920). Sokolov was a Soviet prosecutor who investigated the murders. For years afterward, there were reports that Anastasia had survived, and she was the subject of a 1956 movie, *Anastasia*. But all the bodies were dug up in 1991 and 2007, identified, and given proper funerals.

8   Czar's Two Billions Seized by Bolsheviki, *Washington Times*, July 23, 1918.

9   The Ex-Emperor Nicholas II, *Times*, July 24, 1918.

10   Editorial, *Chattanooga News*, July 22, 1918.

11   Editorial, *Canton's Weekly* (Seattle), July 27, 1918. Most newspapers and government communications used the "tsar" spelling because of the "ts" sound of the first letter in the Russian word (царь).

12   Richard Pipes, The Secrets of Ekaterinburg, *Independent* (London), November 18, 1995.

13   Eltsov to author.

14   Cole to Ambassador Francis, June 1, 1918, 861.00/2299, *FRUS, 1918, Russia, Volume II*.

15   Peter Sittenauer, "Lessons in Operational Art: An Analysis of the Allied Expeditionary Forces in North Russia, 1918–1918" (Fort Leavenworth, KS: U.S. Army School of Advanced Military Studies, General Staff College, 2014), 11, www.dtic.mil. Lieutenant Colonel Sittenauer cites Annex A, Joint Note No. 31: Allied Intervention at the White Sea Ports, Supreme War Council, Versailles, June 3, 1918.

16   March to Bliss, July 22, 1918, *Wilson Papers*, 49:57. See also *FRUS, Lansing Papers, Volume II*.

17   General John J. Pershing, *My Experiences in the First World War*, vol. I (New York: Da Capo, 1995), 291. This is a retitled reprint of Pershing's original *My Experiences in the World War*, published in 1931 by Frederick A. Stokes.

18   Botchkareva, Chapter XX, "Bearing a Message from My People."

19   A British edition of *Yashka* can be read online at www.archive.org.

20   Isaac Don Levine, *Eyewitness to History: Memoirs and Reflections of a Foreign Correspondent for Half a Century* (New York: Hawthorn, 1973), 52–54.

21   Levine, Yashka, *New York Times*, February 16, 1919.

22   Jerome Landfield to Third Assistant Secretary of State Breckenridge Long, July 13, 1918, Long Papers, Box 16, Manuscript Division, LOC.

23   Wilson to Maria Leont'evna Frolkova Bochkareva, *Wilson Papers*, 48:475. In this thank-you letter the president said he was "touched and gratified" at the gift.

24   Jusserand to Wilson, June 30, 1918, *Wilson Papers*, 48:469.

25   The Secretary of State to the Allied Ambassadors, July 17, 1918, 861.00/3054b, *FRUS, 1918, Russia, Volume II*.

24: EVERYTHING ON THE DOT

1   Many French infantrymen wore beards. Whiskers were associated with virility, and *poilu* meant "hairy" or "brave."

2   "America's Wars Fact Sheet," U.S. Veterans Administration, www.va.gov.

3   Frederick Palmer, *Newton D. Baker: America at War* (New York: Kraus, 1969), 8, 309–10. This
         is a reprint of the original Dodd, Mead edition of 1931.

4   Emmett J. Scott, *Scott's Official History of the American Negro in the World War*, (Chicago:
         Homewood Press, 1919), Chapter II: The Call to the Colors, www.net.lib.byu.edu. Scott wrote
         that 2,590,527 blacks registered for the draft.

5   When Pershing retired in 1924, Congress bestowed on him the rank of general of the armies,
         informally equivalent to a six-star general, though Black Jack chose only four gold stars for
         his uniform. During World War II a rank of general of the *army* was created, a four-star
         designation. But Pershing and George Washington remain the only soldiers in U.S. history to
         have won the rank of general of the *armies*. See www.arlingtoncemetery.net.

6   Pershing, 17.

7   Baker to Bliss, July 8, 1918, cited in Palmer, 318.

8   Paul D. Mehney, "The Custer Division," *Michigan History* (May/June 2001): 37.

9   2,000 NEGRO ROOKIES ARE INCLUDED IN LAST INCREMENT TO ARRIVE, *Trench and Camp*, May
         2, 1918. This newspaper was published by the National War Work Council for the training
         camps.

10   Sidney Fine, "Frank Murphy in World War I," Michigan Historical Collections, University of
         Michigan. Courtesy of the Kimball House Museum, Battle Creek, MI.

11   Sidney Fine, "Frank Murphy."

12   Listings of local amusements can be found in the official base newspaper, the *Camp Custer
         Bulletin*.

13   Camp Custer facts courtesy of Jody Owens at Heritage Battle Creek. She also supplied
         copies of the *Camp Custer Bulletin* and reminiscences by soldiers who trained there. For more
         information on Camp Custer, visit www.heritagebattlecreek.org. Faye Clark's *As You Were:
         Fort Custer* (Galesburg, MI: Kal-Gal Printing, 1985) was also helpful.

14   Jeffery K. Taubenberger and David M. Morens, "1918 Influenza: the mother of all epidemics,"
         Emerging Infectious Diseases 12, no. 1 (2006), U.S. Centers for Disease Control and Prevention,
         www.ncbi.nlm.nih.gov.

15   Taubenberger and Morens, "1918 Influenza."

16   Mehney, "The Custer Division," 41.

17   Hermine Scholz, "The World War I Survey," North Russian order of battle, courtesy of U.S.
         Army Military History Institute, Carlisle Barracks, PA.

18   "The Field Service and the U.S. Army," in *History of the American Field Service in France*
         (Boston: Houghton Mifflin, 1920), www.net.lib.byu.edu.

19   Col. W.P. Richardson, OFFICIAL STORY OF OUR WAR WITH RUSSIA, *New York Times*, July 11, 1920.

20   Moore, et al., 15. The authors all served in combat in Archangel. Unless otherwise noted,
         information in this and succeeding chapters on the American Expeditionary Force to North
         Russia is drawn from this history.

21   Russell J. Parkinson, "Foreign Command of U.S. Forces," Defense Technical Information
         Center, U.S. Department of Defense, 2, www.dtic.mil.

22   Edmund Burke, John Wright, John Knox, and John Entick, eds., "The Russian Expeditions,"
         The Times History of the War, Volume XXI (London: The Times, 1920), 147.

23   Burke, et al., 153.

24   The Chargé in Sweden (Whitehouse) to the Secretary of State, 861.00/2480, August 12, 1918,
         FRUS, 1918, Russia, Volume II. This telegram contains Poole's reports of both August 5 and 6.

25   BOLSHEVIKS LEAVE MOSCOW, *Times*, August 13, 1918.

26   Lucy Ash, "'Death Island': Britain's 'Concentration Camp' in Russia," BBC News Magazine,
      October 19, 2017, www.bbc.com. This site includes photos of the camp and interviews with
      Archangel residents who remember it. See also Ernest Beaux, "Souvenirs d'un Parfumeur,"
      Industrie de la Parfumerie I, no. 7 (October 1946), www.boisdejasmin.com

25: SECURITY BREAKDOWNS

1   Kingisepp/Peters, "Lockhart Case."
2   Latvia did gain freedom from Russia, for a while, but only after fighting a war of independence
      with no military aid from France, America, or Britain. Latvia was conquered by the Soviets
      again in 1940. Final independence came in 1991 after the fall of the Communist government
      in Russia.
3   Kingisepp/Peters. Writing a secret message on cloth instead of paper and hiding it under the
      lining of a coat made it harder to detect if the courier were stopped.
4   Hill, 226.
5   "The Annenkov House," from the diary of Adrian Fedorovich Timofeev, at the Russian Society
      of Historians and Archivists, www.adriantimofeev.blogspot.com.
6   Kingisepp/Peters.
7   Hill, 286.
8   René Marchand, "Why I Support Bolshevism," trans. by Eden and Cedar Paul (London:
      British Socialist Party, 1919), University of Warwick, England, www.contentdm.warwick.
      ac.uk. This text of Marchand's letter recounts what he said occurred at the August 1918
      meeting of Allied spies at the U.S. consulate in Moscow, as described in this chapter.
9   Reilly, *Britain's Master Spy*, 21.
10   Kingisepp/Peters.
11   Hill, 84–85.
12   Hill, 284–87.
13   Summers to Francis, August 17, 1917, Francis Letters.
14   Poole, "Reminiscences," 121–22. The Gabrichevsky house was described as sitting next to the
      "English church" in Moscow. That's now called the Anglican church. Church historian Helen
      Watson, a Russian, told me that the Gabrichevsky house is now No. 6 Voznesenskiy Pereulok
      (Lane). In tsarist times it was called Bolshoy Chernyshevsky Pereulok. Under Soviet rule it was
      Ulitsa Stankevicha (Stankevich Street).
15   Reilly, *Britain's Master Spy*, 31. *Qui vive* means "on the alert."
16   Reilly, *Britain's Master Spy*, 31.
17   Reilly, *Britain's Master Spy*, 32. See also "Russia's Struggle With Bolshevism," *Current History*
      XI (1920): 114.
18   The Ambassador in Russia (Francis) to the Secretary of State, 861.00/277, September 23, 1918,
      FRUS, 1918, Russia, Volume II.
19   Poole to Francis, June 2, 1918, Francis Papers.

26: A TRAITOR EXPOSED

1   Jacques Bainville, How Men Become Bolsheviki, *L'Action Française*, May 20, 1920,
      reprinted in *Living Age*, July 3, 1920, 21–23.
2   Lockhart, *British Agent*, 254.
3   Sergei Petrovich Melgunov, *Red Terror in Russia* (Westport, CT: Hyperion Press, 1975), 46–49.
      The book was originally published in Berlin in 1924. I used the 2014 translation by Terri Fabre

Kuznetsoff, www.archive.org. Sergei Petrovich was a member of the Union for the Revival of Russia, an anti-Soviet group planning its own plot against Lenin.

4   Blaming capitalism for the war was a popular claim in Russia. So was blaming it on Western bankers.

5   René Marchand, French Policy in Russia, *L'Humanité*, May 26, 1920, reprinted in *Living Age*, July 3, 1920, 17–21.

6   Bainville, *Living Age*, 21–23.

7   Foreign Relations hearing, 350–384.

27: 'THEY SHOT LENIN!'

1   Vitaliy Shentalinsky, "The Terrorist Poet," *The Star* (Russia), March 2007, www.magazines. russ.ru. Shentalinsky is a Russian writer who, during perestroika, gained access to old Cheka files on literary figures. Information on Kannengiser in this chapter is drawn from his file, No. H-196, as reported by Shentalinsky. Direct quotes come from the Cheka interrogation of Kannengiser and his family members. Shentalinsky said Kannengiser's file filled eleven volumes.

2   "Halt of Comedians," www.rusartnet.com.

3   Anatoly Lucharsky, "Revolutionary Silhouettes: Moisei Solomonovich Uritsky," Marxists Internet Archive. Lucharsky was a revolutionary who served a prison term as a political prisoner under the tsarist régime.

4   Sir M. Findlay to Mr. Balfour, September 17, 1918, *Russia. No. 1 (1919), A Collection of Reports on Bolshevism in Russia*, 1–6, www.cdm21047.contentdm.oclc.org. The Netherlands' minister at Petrograd filed Findlay's report for him.

5   The Consul at Moscow (Poole) to the Secretary of State, September 15, 1918, 861.00/2789, *FRUS, 1918, Russia, Volume I.*

6   The name has also been spelled Semenov. The Foreign Delegation of the Social Revolutionary Party spelled it in English as Semionov. See the foreign delegation's article, "The Trial of the Russian Social Revolutionaries," in the *Nation*, July 5, 1922.

7   Shentalinsky, "The Terrorist Poet."

8   Malkov, *Reminiscences*, 177.

9   Sosnovsky letter to *Pravda*, January 22, 1927, as cited in Louis Fischer, *The Life of Lenin* (New York: Harper & Row, 1964), 276–77. Fischer was a journalist and Communist sympathizer who worked for the *New York Evening Post* and the *Nation* magazine in the twenties and thirties. But he turned against the Communists during the Stalin régime. This biography of Lenin won the National Book Award in 1965.

10   Imperial and Foreign News Items, *Times*, July 22, 1918.

11   Vladimir Moss, "Tolstoy, Lenin and the Volga Famine of 1892," accessible online at www .orthodoxchristianbooks.com.

12   "The Imperial Garage: The Tsar and His Cars," www.alexanderpalace.org.

13   Lenin's full speech can be found in V.I. Lenin, *Collected Works* 28:51–52.

14   Alter Litvin, ed., *The Case of Fanny Kaplan, or Who Shot Lenin?* (Kazan, Russia: 1995, 2003), viewable at www.leninism.su. This is a collection of documents released by the Russian Federation after the fall of Communism in 1991 and published by the Society for the Study of the History of Russian Special Services. The KGB archives were closed again in 1993 due to the number of documents being sold to Western researchers. Unless otherwise noted, details of the shooting of Lenin and the capture and interrogation of Fanny Kaplan in this chapter and succeeding chapters

are drawn from these documents. For a recent critical look at the Cheka documents, see K. Morozov, "Fanny Kaplan and attempt on Lenin's life on August 30, 1918," *Bulletin of the Moscow State University, Series: History and Political Science*, 2018, 3:95-114, online at www.scholar.googleusercontent.com.

28: DEATH WATCH

1   Volkogonov, 226.
2   Litvin, *Case of Fanny Kaplan*.
3   Soloviev interview conducted by Viktor Kozhemyako of *Pravda* in October 2010, online at www.leninism.su.
4   P. Kerzhentsev, *Life of Lenin* (New York: International Publishers, 1939), 227.
5   Leon Trotsky, "Jacob Sverdlov," Bureau of Party History, 1926, Trotsky Internet Archive.
6   "An Order for the Expansion of the Red Terror (1918)," www.alphahistory.com; See also Poole, "Reminiscences," 298–99.
7   Fischer, 280–81. His description of Lenin's condition and treatment comes from Dr. Rozanov's account as published in *Vospominaniya*, 2:325-46.
8   SHOTS FIRED AT LENIN/ATTEMPT BY A YOUNG GIRL, *Times*, September 2, 1918.

29: A TERRORIST'S STORY

1   Peter Potichnyi, "Pogrom," Internet Archive of Ukraine, vol. 4 (1993), online at www.encyclopediaofukraine.org; Monty Noam Penkower, "The Kishinev Pogrom of 1903: A Turning Point in Jewish History," *Modern Judaism* vol. 24, no. 3 (2004): 187–225, www.muse.jhu.edu. For additional descriptions of the 1905 pogroms, see Elias Heifetz, *The Slaughter of the Jews in the Ukraine in 1919* (New York: Thomas Seltzer, 1921), www.archive.org.
2   Soloviev interview.
3   Isaac Steinberg, *Spiridonova: Revolutionary Terrorist* (Freeport, NY: Books for Libraries Press, 1971), 92–93.
4   Scott B. Smith, "Who Shot Lenin? Fania Kaplan, the SR Underground, and the August 1918 Assassination Attempt on Lenin," *Jahrbücher für Geschichte Osteuropas* (1998), 100–119, onlne at www.jstor.org.
5   Soloviev interview.
6   Litvin, *Case of Fanny Kaplan*.
7   Savinkov, *Memoirs*, 351.

30: BLACK SATURDAY

1   Khromov, ed., *Felix Dzerzhinsky*, 61.
2   Nina Nikolaevna Berberova, *Zheleznaia Zhenshchina* (Moskva: Knizhnaia Palata, 1991), 93.
3   Hill, 226–27.
4   Lockhart, *British Agent*, 314–15.
5   Malkov, *Reminiscences*, 263–64, 266–67, 271–74.
6   Boris Nicolaievsky, *Aseff: the Russian Judas* (London: Hurst & Blackett, 1934), 199.
7   Transcript of the trial of Zurka Dubof, Jacob Peters, John Rosen, and Nina Vassileva, 25 April 1911, in *Proceedings of the Old Bailey*, www.oldbaileyonline.org. See also SHOOTING AFFAIR IN HOUNDSDITCH, *Times*, December 17, 1910; THE HOUNDSDITCH MURDERS, *Times*, December 19 and December 26, 1910; THE HOUNDSDITCH CRIME, *Times*, January 24, 1911.
8   Levine, *Eyewitness to History*, 78.

9   Lockhart, *British Agent*, 315–17.

10   Pathfinders were heavy touring cars built in Indianapolis to compete with Cadillacs and Hudsons.

11   Hill, 215.

12   Hill, 229–31.

31: NO MERCY FOR ENEMIES

1   Malkov, *Reminiscences*, 277–79.

2   Kingisepp/Peters.

3   Kalamatiano prison report.

4   The claims appear in *Reilly: Ace of Spies* (Euston Films and Thames Television, 1983) and Robin Bruce Lockhart's book, *Ace of Spies* (London: Hodder & Stoughton, 1969).

5   Roy Bainton, *Honoured by Strangers: The Life of Captain Francis Cromie CB DSO RN 1882– 1918* (Shrewsbury: Airlife, 2002), chapters 22 and 23. Bainton bases his account on eyewitness statements, but some of the reports are contradictory, so the case remains puzzling.

6   Orlov, 134.

7   Berberova, *Moura*, 132.

8   Lockhart, *British Agent*, 241.

9   Jacob Peters, "Memoirs of Cheka Work During the First Year of the Revolution," in the journal *Proletarian Revolution* (1924), 10:381, reprinted from V.A. Goncharov and A.I. Kokurin, *October guardsmen: The role of the indigenous peoples of the Baltic countries in establishing and strengthening the Bolshevik system* (Russia: Indrik, 2009).

10   Service Historique de la Defense, Documents Repatriees, Carton 608, dossier 3529, *Renseignment, S. R. Sovietique en Reval, 20 Nov. 1921*, 1. The original DB file number is 29867.

11   Service Historique de la Defense, *A.S. de la nomme BUDBERG, ex-comtesse Benckendorf signalee comme suspecte* (former Countess Benckendorff reported as suspect), *30 Sept. 1936*, 1.

12   Service Historique de la Defense, *Renseignment, A/S de la baronne BUDBERG, 4 June 1936*, 1.

13   Service Historique de la Defense, *Secret, En response a votre demande verbale* (in response to your verbal request) *du 29 Julliet 1937, 29 July 1937*, 1.

14   Robin Bruce Lockhart, *Reilly: The First Man* (New York: Penguin Books, 1987), 55–56.

15   Robin Lockhart, *Reilly*, 59.

16   Georgi Chicherin Archive, 1872–1936, USSR History Archive, www.marxists.org.

17   Lockhart, *British Agent*, 218–19.

18   Marguerite E. Harrison, Tchitcherin, Aristocrat, *New York Times*, May 14, 1922.

19   Poole, "Reminiscences," 189–90.

20   When Poole wrote this in 1952, a comedian and ventriloquist named Edgar Bergen had a popular radio show and his dummy was called Charlie McCarthy. Mae West said Charlie was all wood and a yard long.

21   The Consul at Moscow (Poole) to the Secretary of State, September 3, 1918, 861.00/2706.

22   Poole, "Reminiscences," 311.

23   Poole, "Reminiscences," 310.

24   George Chicherin, "Two Years of Foreign Policy: The Relations of the Soviet Socialist Federal Soviet Republic with Foreign Nations from November 7, 1918, to November 7, 1919," *Soviet Russia Pamphlets*, issue 3 (New York: Russian Soviet Government Bureau, 1920), 18.

25   Richard Pipes, *The Russian Revolution* (New York: Knopf, 1990).

26   This account of the execution of Kaplan comes from Pavel Malkov's *Reminiscences*, 180–81, and P. Malkov, "Zapiski Komendanta Kremlya," *Moskva* (1958) 11:123-61.

27   Demyan Bedny, "Crow," 1920, Poems of Demyan Bedny, www.web.archive.org.

32: CAUGHT IN A TRAP

1   David A. Langbart, "Five Months in Petrograd in 1918: Robert W. Imbrie and the US search for information in Russia," *Studies in Intelligence*, vol. 51, no. 4 (December 2007). Imbrie was a U.S. army captain who drove an American ambulance for the French during the war, then joined the American foreign service in 1917 and was sent to Russia. He spied for the State Department and acquired a reputation as a violent anti-Bolshevik, reportedly beating his cane on Uritsky's desk one day. After the war he was posted as vice consul at Teheran. There in 1924 he was attacked by a mob of 2,000 Muslim clerics and Persian soldiers who accused him of poisoning a well. The police rescued Imbrie and took him to a hospital for emergency treatment. Muslims then broke into the operating room and finished him off. He was forty years old. He is buried in Arlington Cemetery with a tombstone saying only that he served in the French army.

    See also Michael P. Zirinsky, "Blood, power and hypocrisy: the murder of Robert Imbrie and relations with Pahlavi Iran, 1924," *International Journal of Middle East Studies* 18 (1986): 275–92, www.scholarworks.boisestate.edu. To view official reports describing Imbrie's murder, see Michael Robert Patterson, "Robert Whitney Imbrie," Arlington Cemetery website, at www.arlingtoncemetery.net.

2   Anton Utkin, "The Kremlin Gates: Damaged Ancient Icons to Return to Red Square," www.pravoslavie.ru. According to this 2010 essay, efforts were underway to recreate copies of all the damaged Kremlin frescoes.

3   Robin Lockhart, *Reilly*, 55.

4   Kalamatiano trial report and Kalamatiano prison report.

5   The Secretary of State to the Ambassador in France (Sharp), 123 P 78/48b, September 14, 1918, *FRUS, 1918, Russia, Volume I*. Washington could no longer reach Poole directly so Sharp was instructed to forward this message "immediately by any route available."

6   The Second Secretary of Embassy in Russia (Armour), temporarily at Stockholm, to the Secretary of State, September 21, 1918, 861.00/2760, *FRUS, 1918, Russia, Volume I*. This telegram also quoted the Italian consul general as saying the Soviets were "worried" by Poole's presence and would welcome his departure.

7   "New Light on Old Spies," CIA CSI.

8   Kalamatiano prison report. This report is not dated, but the wording indicates it was before his trial started on November 25, 1918. A press report says that a member of the Norwegian consulate in Moscow mission visited Kal at Butyrka. He might have smuggled it out for him.

9   Orlov, 134. Orlov was later promoted to head of Soviet intelligence in western Europe for the NKVD, one of the successors to the Cheka. While stationed in Madrid during the Spanish Civil War he escaped Stalin's purges by fleeing with his family to Canada. He entered the United States so discreetly that he wasn't discovered by the FBI until 1953, when he ran out of money and published a book on Stalin's crimes.

10   This coincides with DeWitt Poole's later testimony before Congress, denying spying.

11   Georgy Manaev Rir, "Butyrka: Russia's oldest prison," *Russia Beyond*, www.rbth.com. The surrounding apartment building was built before the 1980 Olympics.

33: THE STING

1   Lockhart, *Diaries*, 44–45.

2   Poole, "Reminiscences," 339–40. Poole later wrote that the Finnish government permitted Allied nationals to evacuate Russia through their country unmolested.

3   Reilly, *Britain's Master Spy*, 76–77, 79–83, 87–88, 101–2.

4   Boris Savinkov to Winston Churchill, February 3, 1923, CHAR 2/126/10, Churchill Archive Centre, www.churchillarchive.com.

5   Sidney Reilly to Winston Churchill, February 5, 1923, CHAR 2/126/5-7, www.churchillarchive.com.

6   Mark Inglefield, A CLUSTER OF SALUBRIOUS SOLITUDES, *Daily Telegraph*, April 10, 2004.

7   Robin Lockhart, *Reilly*, 115. Robin Lockhart shows a copy of a letter said to have been written by Reilly to Bruce Lockhart, in which Sidney says Bolshevism contains "practical and constructive ideas for the establishment of a higher social justice" and that "by a process of evolution" it will "conquer the world." But it's not clear whether Reilly's opinions are an endorsement of Bolshevism or a warning against it.

8   Lockhart, *British Agent*, Chapter 10. Unless otherwise noted, details of Lockhart's second imprisonment and release come from this chapter.

9   Lockhart, *Diaries*, 44–45.

10   Melor G. Sturua, ALLURING TSARIST BEAUTY BARONESS BUDBERG SPIED FOR GENRIKH YAGODA, *Daily Mail*, London, April 9, 2015, www.dailymail.co.uk. See "Melor G. Sturua," State University of Management, Moscow, www.archive.org.

11   OGPU stood for the Unified State Political Directorate.

12   Andy McSmith, WAS NICK CLEGG'S GREAT AUNT A SOVIET AGENT?, *Independent*, January 2, 2015; Jonathan Calder, THE STORY OF CLEGG'S AUNT, *New Statesman*, November 19, 2007.

13   U.S. MID File 10058-530 78, October 8, 1920, RG 165, Microfilm Publication M1194, Roll 91, NARA.

14   Orlov, 124.

15   Poole to Francis, June 16, 1918, "Russia in Transition: the diplomatic papers of David R. Francis," Box 33, University of Michigan.

16   The Consul General at Moscow (Poole) to the Secretary of State, August 26, 1918, 861.00/2711, *FRUS, 1918, Russia, Volume I*.

17   The Ambassador in Russia (Francis) to the Secretary of State, August 27, 1918, 861.00/2944, *FRUS, 1918, Russia, Volume I*.

18   The Consul at Moscow (Poole) to the Secretary of State, September 3, 1918, 861.00/2707, *FRUS, 1918, Russia, Volume I*.

19   The Consul at Moscow (Poole) to the Secretary of State, September 3, 1918, 861.00/2706, *FRUS, 1918, Russia, Volume I*.

20   Poole, "Reminiscences," 209.

34: WHERE IS THE FRONT?

1   Moore, et al., 15.

2   The Ambassador in Russia (Francis) to the Secretary of State, October 10, 1918, 861.00/2932, *FRUS, 1918, Russia, Volume II*.

3   Cudahy, 76.

4   For information on Harry Costello, thanks are due to the libraries and archives at Georgetown University, the University of Detroit Mercy, and the Meriden Public Library. Costello's service record was provided by the State Archives of Michigan.

5   Harry J. Costello, *Why Did We Go to Russia?*, (Detroit: Harry J. Costello, 1920).

6   Costello, 14.

7   Russell J. Parkinson, "Foreign Command of U.S. Forces" (1993), 2, Defense Technical Information Center, February 25, 1993, www.dtic.mil.

8   Costello, 50.

9   Chew, 2.

10   A Chronicler (John Cudahy), *Archangel: The American War Against Russia* (Chicago: McClurg, 1924), 51–52.

11   Costello, 49.

12   Costello, 26.

13   Costello, 27.

14   Moore, et al., 87.

35: SANITY ARRIVES

1   Moore, et al., 27.

2   Not to be confused with the Lithuanian-Polish town of similar spelling. In Old Russia, a *seltso* was a village adjoining a nobleman's estate. See "Life in Rural Russia," *Living Age* 227 (1900): 563.

3   Cudahy, 52.

4   Costello, 32.

5   Costello, 28–29.

6   Samoilo biography, Ministry of Defense of the Russian Federation, www.encylopedia.mil.ru.

7   Chew, 5.

8   Chew, 5.

9   Moore, et al., 90.

10   Costello, 38–40.

11   Costello, 33, 35.

12   Cudahy, 77, 97.

13   Limey was a nickname pinned on the British. The term dates back to when lemon and lime juice were added to the grog (watered down rum) issued to Royal Navy sailors to prevent scurvy.

14   Costello, 116.

15   The Chargé in Russia (Poole) to the Secretary of State, December 2, 1918, 861.00/3324, *FRUS, 1918, Russia, Volume II.*

16   Poole, "Reminiscences," 350.

17   Lansing to Page, September 12, 1918, *Wilson Papers* VIII:397.

18   Lansing to Page, September 12, 1918, *Wilson Papers* VIII:397.

19   March to Bliss, September 25, 1918, *Wilson Papers* VIII:423.

20   Lansing to Jusserand, October 22, 1918, *Wilson Papers* VIII:501.

21   Field Marshal William Edmund Ironside, 1st Baron Ironside, in the Peerage, online at www.thepeerage.com.

22   William Edmund Ironside, Baron Ironside, *Archangel, 1918–1919* (London: Constable, 1953), 13.

23   Ironside, 31–32.

24   The Ambassador in Russia (Francis) to the Secretary of State, September 10, 1918, 861.00/2661, *FRUS, 1918, Russia, Volume II.*

25   Ironside, 33–34.

36: TO THE WALL

1   Sergey Kobyakov, "Red Justice," *McClure's Magazine*, April 1923. Kobyakov's account of the
     trial, including direct quotations from him, comes from this article.

2   Harrison, *Marooned*, 102.

3   Lockhart, *British Agent*, 254.

4   Kalamatiano trial report.

5   Marc Jansen, *A Show Trial Under Lenin: The Trial of Socialist Revolutionaries, 1922* (The
     Hague, Netherlands: Martinus Nijhoff, 1982), Chapter 3, "Preparations for the Trial,"
     www.link.springer.com.

6   Kalamatiano prison report.

7   HOLD AN AMERICAN UNDER DEATH THREAT, *New York Times*, February 27, 1919.

8   AMERICAN CONSUL RELEASED, *Cincinnati Enquirer*, July 17, 1910.

9   Ten people were killed in the San Francisco bombing and Mooney was sentenced to death. But
     within a year, evidence showed that some of the prosecution's witnesses had lied at the trial,
     and his sentence was commuted to life in prison. He was finally pardoned by the California
     governor in 1939, after twenty-three years behind bars. Debs was convicted of violating the
     1917 Espionage Act, then freed by President Harding in 1921. Debs ran for president five times
     as the Socialist Party candidate. He received 915,000 votes in 1920 while he was still in prison.

10   LENINE REPORTED TO HAVE ORDERED TREDWELL FREED, *New York Tribune*, April 27, 1919.

11   AMERICAN CONSUL RELEASED, *Daily Register* (Richmond, KY), May 5, 1919.

12   MOSCOW ESPIONAGE TRIAL/BRITISH AND FRENCH OFFICERS CHARGED, *Times*, February 10, 1919.

13   GRAND DUKES' EXECUTION/MASSACRE AT PETROGRAD PRISON, *Times*, February 7, 1919.

14   Kalamatiano prison report.

15   "Brooklyn newspaperman, held as spy, back from Russia," *The Fourth Estate*, September 24,
     1921, 25.

16   Lewis S. Gannett, "Americans in Russia," the *Nation*, vol. 113, no. 2928 (1921).

17   The Acting Secretary of State (Polk) to the Commission to Negotiate Peace, 861.000/3650,
     January 28, 1919, *FRUS, 1919, Russia*.

18   Levere, *World War*, 236. Levere's book contains interviews with Kalamatiano regarding his
     imprisonment in Moscow.

19   Lomonosoff, 87.

20   The Minister in Sweden (Morris) to the Acting Secretary of State, March 21, 1919,
     811.20261/29, *FRUS, 1919, Russia*.

21   The Chargé in Denmark (Grant-Smith) to the Acting Secretary of State, March 10, 1919,
     811.20261/28, *FRUS, 1919, Russia*, 178.

22   The Commission to Negotiate Peace to the Minister in Sweden (Morris), February 26, 1919,
     861.00/292b, *FRUS, 1919, Russia*.

37: RISKY MISSION

1   Harrison, *There's Always Tomorrow*. Unless otherwise noted, information on Marguerite,
     including direct quotations, comes from this autobiography.

2   Mrs. Margaret [*sic*] Harrison Personnel File 39205, Military Intelligence Branch, Executive
     Division, General Staff, RG 165, Microfilm Publication M1194, Roll 91, NARA.

3   M/A Riga to MID, No. 3385, March 6, 1923, Harrison personnel file.

4   Report on Shoholm, April 15, 1921, Harrison personnel file.

5   Kalamatiano to Harper, June 1, 1923, Harper papers.

38: A POISONED APPLE

1 Secretary's Notes of a Conversation Held in M. Pinchon's Room at the Quai d'Orsay on Sunday, January 12th (1919) at 4 p.m., Paris Peace Conference, 180/03101/2, *FRUS, 1919, Russia.*

2 The British Chargé to the Acting Secretary of State, Memorandum No. 38, January 3, 1919, 861.00/3659, *FRUS, 1919, Russia.*

3 The Chargé in Denmark (Osborne) to the Commission to Negotiate Peace, January 18, 1919, 861.00/836, *FRUS, 1919, Russia.*

4 The Ambassador in Great Britain (Davis) to the Acting Secretary of State, January 22, 1919, 861.00/3691, *FRUS, 1919, Russia.*

5 The Commission to Negotiate Peace to the Acting Secretary of State, January 27, 1919, 861.00/3724, *FRUS, 1919, Russia.*

6 The Soviet Commissar for Foreign Affairs (Chicherin) to the Principal Allied and Associate Governments, February 4, 1919, 861.00/217, *FRUS, 1919, Russia.*

7 The Chargé in Russia (Poole) to the Acting Secretary of State, February 4, 1919, 861.00/3804, *FRUS, 1919, Russia.*

8 The Commission to Negotiate Peace to the Acting Secretary of State, February 17, 1919, 763.72119/3797, *FRUS, 1919, Russia.*

9 The Consul at Helsingfors (Haynes) to the Commission to Negotiate Peace, March 11, 1919, note for Lansing and House only, 184.02202/4, *FRUS, 1919, Russia.*

10 William C. Bullitt to the Commission to Negotiate Peace, for Wilson, Lansing and House only, 184.02202/5, March 16, 1919, *FRUS, 1919, Russia.*

11 Bullitt to the Commission to Negotiate Peace, 184.02202/5.

12 "The Bullitt Mission to Soviet Russia, 1919," Office of the Historian, U.S. State Department, www.history.state.gov.

13 Acting Secretary of State to the Consul at Vladivostok (Caldwell), September 9, 1919, 861.00/5243b, *FRUS, 1919, Russia.* The same note was sent to the Commission to Negotiate Peace.

14 Roosevelt later turned on Bullitt by refusing him a military commission during World War II. Bullitt then joined the Free French Forces. He ran for mayor of Philadelphia as a Democrat in 1943 but was defeated. Bullitt died in France in 1967. At one point he had traced his family tree in France and was appalled to find that his ancestors were peasants.

39: FIGHTING FOR WHAT?

1 Ironside, 64.

2 Moore, et al., 28.

3 Wilson to Lansing, October 2, 1918, *Wilson Papers* VIII:443.

4 Ironside, 68–70.

5 Cudahy, 31–32.

6 Moore, et al., 185.

7 Ironside, 77–78.

8 Cudahy, 175–77.

9 Cudahy, 180. Cudahy wrote that aside from Russian SBAL troops, the United States did not have 6,000 men at the various fronts. They faced at least 14,000 Red Army troops.

10 Chew, 10.

11 Cudahy, 183.

12 In World War I an American army company consisted of anywhere from 200 to 260 men and was commanded by a captain with a first sergeant as his assistant.

13 Costello, 43.

14 Cudahy, 65–66.

15 The Chargé in Russia (Poole) to the Acting Secretary of State, January 23, 1919, 861.00/3713, *FRUS, 1919, Russia.*

16 The Chargé in Russia (Poole) to the Acting Secretary of State, January 24, 1919, 861.00/3719, *FRUS, 1919, Russia.*

17 Costello, 104.

18 Cudahy, 123–24.

19 Ironside, 112–13.

20 Ironside, 113–14.

21 Cudahy, 161.

22 President Wilson to the Commission to Negotiate Peace, February 19, 1919, 861.00/274, *FRUS, 1919, Russia.*

23 *Army. The Evacuation of North Russia, 1919*, parliamentary report (London: H.M. Stationary Office, 1920), 9, 23–25, www.archive.org.

24 Cudahy, 98–100.

25 *Associated Press* dispatch from Archangel, April 17, 1919, *Evening Star* (Washington).

26 Moore, et al., 293–95.

27 Moore, et al., 289.

28 Ralph Albertson, *Fighting Without a War: An Account of Military Intervention in North Russia* (New York: Harcourt, Brace and Howe, 1920), 91–92, 94–95. This eyewitness account was written by the YMCA secretary at Archangel.

29 Andrew Soutar, *With Ironside in North Russia* (London: Hutchinson, 1944), 193. Soutar was an Archangel correspondent for the *Times.*

30 Soutar, 207.

31 Albertson, 99.

32 Ironside, 192.

33 Cudahy, 211.

34 Lucy Ash. Excerpt from Ironside's diary.

35 Records of the war against Russia are now available at libraries, archives, and military institutes in the Western nations that were involved. The Russian Federation also has records, but they are closed, though historians at Russian universities have independently published studies in recent years. For a summary of the citations awarded U.S. troops, see the introduction to this book. A full list can be found in Moore, et al., 283–287.

40: FAMINE AND FREEDOM

1 U.S. Department of War file 164-334 328X, undated, NARA.

2 Kalamatiano personnel file.

3 WIFE FIGHTS TO FREE U.S. ATTACHÉ HELD THREE YEARS BY LENINE, *South Bend* (IN) *News-Times*, March 27, 1921; *Seattle Star*, April 21, 1921.

4 The Minister in Norway (Schmedeman) to the Secretary of State, April 21, 1921, 361.11/3701, *FRUS, 1921, Russia, Volume II.*

5 NO TRADE UNTIL REDS SET FREE U.S. PRISONERS, *New York Tribune*, May 18, 1921. See also Niblack's biography at www.history.navy.mil.

6   Lenin, *Collected Works*, 45:98–99.

7   Washington B. Vanderlip, "Sidelights on Soviet Moscow," *Asia* 21 (1921): 407–9.

8   Mary Dearborn, "Reviving Louise Bryant," Oregon Cultural Heritage Commission, at www.ochcomm.org.

9   PRISONER OF THE SOVIETS/LOUISE BRYANT'S VERSION OF HER VISIT TO THEM IN THEIR JAIL, *New York Times*, August 15, 1921; SOVIETS WOULD TRADE AMERICAN WAR PRISONER FOR CONVICTED COMMUNIST, *Toiler* (Cleveland, OH), April 16, 1921.

10 Reed had gone back to America after the Bolshevik coup to become leader of the Communist Labor Party. That was when he was indicted for treason. He fled to Russia again, where he died in 1920.

11 KILPATRICK REPLIES TO LOUISE BRYANT, *New York Times*, September 22, 1921.

12 Dr. Fridtjof Nansen to President Wilson, April 3, 1919, 861.5018/9, *FRUS, 1919, Russia*. Nansen was awarded the Nobel Prize for Peace in 1922 for his relief work.

13 Messrs. Wilson, Clemenceau, Lloyd George, and Orlando to Dr. Fridtjof Nansen, April 17, 1919, 861.48/15, *FRUS, 1919, Russia*.

14 Paxton Hibben, "Propaganda Against Relief," *Soviet Russia*, vols. 5–6 (1921): 112.

15 The Minister in Norway (Schmedeman) to the Secretary of State, July 15, 1921, 861.48/1501, *FRUS, 1921, Russia, Volume II*.

16 Herbert Hoover, *The Memoirs of Herbert Hoover* (London: Hollis and Carter, 1952–1953), 23.

17 Hoover, 24–25.

18 British Parliament, House of Commons, oral answers to questions, February 9, 1922, 15:33, www.hansard.parliament.uk.

19 Captain Thomas C. Gregory, "Russian Famine. Mr. Hoover's Sinister Role in Hungary," *The World's Work*, June 1921. This monthly magazine was edited by Walter Hines Page, former U.S. ambassador to the Court of St. James's during the war, and published by Doubleday, Page & Co., New York. A reprint of this article can be read on the website of the University of Warwick Library, Maitland Sare Collection, www.cdm21047.contentdm.oclc.org.

20 Hoover, 25–26.

21 SET FREE TELLS WONDERFUL STORY OF PRISON LIFE, *Bridgeport Times and Evening Farmer*, August 19, 1921.

22 AMERICAN CAPTIVES RAGGED AND HUNGRY SAFE OUT OF RUSSIA, *New York Times*, August 11, 1921.

23 Levere, *World War*, 242.

A FINAL WORD

1   Sittenauer, "Lessons in Operational Art," 43–48.

2   Author's interviews with former KGB officers.

3   U.S. State Department, "The Paris Peace Conference and the Treaty of Versailles," www.history.state.gov.

4   Charles E. Neu, *Colonel House: A Biography of Woodrow Wilson's Silent Partner* (Oxford University Press, 2014), 412, 511, CIA CSI.

5   Poole, "Russia and the United States," *New Europe*, September 1941, 249, as cited in Lorraine M. Lees and William S. Rodner, eds., *An American Diplomat in Bolshevik Russia: DeWitt Clinton Poole* (Madison: University of Wisconsin, 2014), 309n.

6   W. Chapin Huntington, *The Homesick Million: Russia-Out-of-Russia* (Boston: Stratford Company, 1933).

7   Harrison, *There's Always Tomorrow.*

8   Report on *l'Orchestre Rouge*, CIA online library, www.cia.gov.

9   Nicolas Skopinski, "Charles Adolphe Faux-Pas Bidet, l'ennemi de Trotski," *Ouest-France,* December 6, 2017, www.ouest-france.fr.

10 Joseph Noulens biographies, www.economie.gouv.fr and www.agriculture.gouv.fr. See also the *Commercial & Financial Chronicle*, vol. 109, Part 1, July–September 1919 (New York: William B. Dana, 1919), 613.

11 Berberova, *Baroness Dudberg,* 276–80, 297–99.

12 Wędziagolski, 135.

13 Wędziagolski, iv, xxv, 134–35.

14 Dónal O'Sullivan, *Dealing With the Devil: Anglo-Soviet Intelligence Cooperation During the Second World War* (New York: Peter Lang, 2010), 52–68.

15 "Kolyma: The White crematorium," gulag.eu. This site contains photos of Berzin as director of the labor camps.

16 "Nikolai Krylenko," www.chess.com.

17 Kevin Spraggett, "Spraggett on Chess," spraggettonchess.com. This chess website shows moves Krylenko made in one of his games.

18 Bogdan Jaxa-Ronikier, *The Red Executioner Dzierjinski* (London: Denis Archer, 1935), 298–309.

19 Dzerzhinsky's Death, *Times,* July 22, 1926.

20 Berberova, *Moura,* 83.

21 Jeremy Hsu, "Lenin's Body Improves with Age," *Scientific American,* April 22, 2015.

22 Governor Reviews the 69th in Camp, *New York Times,* June 24, 1921.

23 John Cudahy, Former Envoy, Killed in Fall from Horse, (Phoenix) *Arizona Republic,* September 7, 1943.

24 Spence interviews.

25 Jessica L. Levis, "The Rise of the Santa Fe Aesthetic," MA thesis, Las Vegas: New Mexico Highlands University, 2007.

26 Hartman, "I Spy?," in Culver newsletter, 1990.

ACKNOWLEDGMENTS

By the time I began researching the Lenin Plot, all the players, major and minor, had long since died and were lost from public memory. But I was lucky in that much original information had survived in diaries, interviews, official documents, memoirs, reminiscences, and photographs. Libraries, museums, archives, and certain individuals went out of their way to assist in my project.

A special debt of gratitude is owed to Professor Richard Spence at the University of Idaho. Rick and I have been researching the life of American spy Xenophon Kalamatiano for years, sharing information and opinions. He vetted my manuscript and made some excellent suggestions for improvement, as did Professor Peter Eltsov at the National Defense University.

The late Robert B.D. Hartman, historian at the Culver Academies, was my first source on Kalamatiano's life. Bob's interest in Kalamatiano was an inspiration from the very beginning. He has been succeeded by the very able Jeff Kenney, who has joined our little Kalamatiano appreciation society and shared many additional documents on Kal's life.

Finding suitable photographs for the book was a long and often frustrating process. Much valuable help was provided by Neil Braggins, Simon Bodger, Starr Hackwelder, and Susan Lennon at the Alamy photo agency; Melissa Lindberg, Georgia Joseph, and Kelly Dyson at the Library of Congress pictures division; Diana Bachman, Karen Wright, Madeleine Bradford, Robert McIntyre, and Sarah McLusky at the Bentley Library, University of Michigan; Vladimir Freydin in Moscow; Sandra Johnston, Alaska State Library; Miranda Rectenwald, Washington University; Lynn Smith, Herbert Hoover Presidential Library; and Sam Barnes with the U.S. Army.

Recognition is due to a number of other people who helped me along the trail, and I hope I haven't left anybody out. They include my literary agent, Andrew Lownie in London, who immediately dived in to provide guidance in my search for new sources for improving the manuscript. I'm also proud to be working with Claiborne Hancock, publisher of Pegasus Books, and his associates Maria Fernandez and Daniel O'Conner.

Others who provided flashlights in the dark include Jody Owens at Heritage Battle Creek, who shared rare documents on the training of the Polar Bears at Camp Custer before they were deployed to Russia; Lee Grady, Lisa Marine, and Gayle Martinson, Wisconsin Historical Society; Sue Kowbel-Keller, Racine Public Library; Jo Ann Smith, Racine County Clerk's Office; Ray Heller, Case Corporation historian; Oscar Chavez, Christine Colburn, Barbara Gilbert, and Catherine Uecker, University of Chicago Library; John J.W. Plampin, University of Chicago registrar's office; Lesley Martin, Chicago Historical Museum; Lisette Matano and Lynn Conway, Georgetown University; Richard J. McBride, Gerald Gillespie, and Jan Franco, Meriden Public Library; Patricia Higo and Christine Yancy, University of Detroit Mercy; Karen Moen, Bloomington Public Library; Christa Cleeton and Rosalba Varallo Recchia at the Seely G. Mudd Library at Princeton University; Terry Mandigo at the Flower Memorial Library, Watertown, NY; along with the Michigan Historical Society, Madison Public Library, Harvard University, Michigan's Polar Bear Association, the Hoover Institution documents division, and the very energetic Dan McLaughlin and Christine Reeder at the Pasadena Public Library.

Cate Brennan, Loretta Deaver, Michele Brown, Sharon Culley, Professor David Fogelsong, Holly Reed, Abbi Oliver, Suzanne Isaacs, Kate Mollan, and Cara Moore at the National Archives and Records Administration helped immensely in my search for rare documents. So did Tiffany H. Cabrera, U.S. State Department; Dennis Northcott, Missouri Historical Society; Sue Lies and Tyler Stokesbary, Sigma Alpha Epsilon; Gregory McGee, California State University; Mark Peterson, Woodrow Wilson Presidential Library; Kimberly Springer, Columbia University; Annette Amerman, U.S. Marine Corps History Division; Dan Crumpler, U.S. Military Academy; Meg Miner, Illinois Wesleyan University; Stephen P. Hull and Sherri Strickland at the University Press of New England; Bruce Bendinger of the Czech Legion historical collection; Susan R. Watson at the American Red Cross; Paul Secord, a valued source on Kal's family; and Bryan Kasik at the University of Virginia Library.

In the UK, a tip of the hat to Natalie Adams, Churchill Archives Center; Richard Ward and Annie Pinder, British Parliament; Historic Hansard; the National Archives; the National Library of Scotland; and the University of Nottingham. In Russia, thanks to Juliya Galkina and Helen Watson for background on Allied spies and their Moscow operations center. John Puckett in Hungary was kind enough to provide translations of Cheka documents.

Additional references to sources are included in the end notes and the bibliography.

INDEX